Listening in Detail

REFIGURING AMERICAN MUSIC

A series edited by Ronald Radano and Josh Kun

Charles McGovern, contributing editor

Listening in Detail

Performances of Cuban Music

ALEXANDRA T. VAZQUEZ

DUKE UNIVERSITY PRESS | DURHAM AND LONDON | 2013

Designed by April Leidig

Typeset in Garamond Premier Pro by
Copperline Book Services, Inc.

Library of Congress Cataloging-in-Publication Data
Vazquez, Alexandra T., 1976–
Listening in detail : performances of Cuban music /
Alexandra T. Vazquez.
pages cm.—(Refiguring American music)
Includes bibliographical references and index.
ISBN 978-0-8223-5455-0 (cloth : alk. paper)
ISBN 978-0-8223-5458-1 (pbk. : alk. paper)
1. Music—Cuba—History and criticism.
2. Music—Performance—Cuba.
I. Title. II. Series: Refiguring American music.
ML207.C8V39 2013
780.97291—dc23   2013010157

Duke University Press gratefully acknowledges
the support of the Barr Ferree Foundation for
Publications, Princeton University, which provided
funds toward the publication of this book.

For Vincenzo

Contents

Illustrations

Acknowledgments

There is a lot of salt, love, and laughter behind the composition of this manuscript. I must first thank my advisor in all things, José Esteban Muñoz, who has given me tireless guidance, knowledge, company, and comfort in the difficult if pleasurable pursuit of the "something else." This book hopes to honor the imaginative spaces he has opened up for so many. Much appreciation goes to the rest of my dissertation committee Karen Shimakawa, Licia Fiol-Matta, Barbara Browning, and Tavia Nyong'o who nurtured the seedings of this project. Fred Moten, who taught me how to listen and read, has always been at the heart delta of the book. His instruction is present in every line and sound. Ana M. López, one of the model citizens of Greater Cuba, did so much to affirm rather than discipline the wayward energies of this project. Elizabeth Alexander helped me to take in and perform music's poetic thickets. Alicia Schmidt Camacho immediately heard it as part of la causa. Her fearless example emboldened me to insist on its place there. I am grateful to Steve Pitti for the gift of time. His visionary support gave these pages their own finishing school. As the manuscript grew up and out, Daphne Brooks stepped in as a guardian angel. Her encouragements of this project and its author are models for inspirational advocacy and care. Valerie Smith cleared paths for the work to find its way. Mary Pat Brady leant her thoughtful wisdom to making these pages as formidable as they could be. Raúl Fernández's musical tutelage turned and attuned me to jazz's capaciousness—his impact has been immeasurable. My thinking and writing have long been influenced by Gayle Wald's elegant mode of criticism. Josh Kun, long a compatriot in listening, has been unflinching in his support of what I was trying to do all along. The manuscript greatly benefitted from the insights of a late-shift manuscript workshop that included José

Quiroga and Farah Jasmine GUriffin. These people, shepherds all, have been examples in generosity and courage, both in scholarship and in the everyday. They have been grace notes throughout the arc of the project.

I've often thought of academics as a group of misfits who find home in school. I have had the honor and privilege of finding myself at home in several formative locations. Thanks to the many folks that made them so. Ann Lane, my undergraduate advisor at UC Santa Cruz's former Department of American Studies, modeled an intellectualism and commitment to learning that remains stunningly present in my here and now. Marta Miranda and Carolyn Pickard, my high school Spanish and English teachers at the New World School of the Arts, nurtured important critical and creative skills for many of Miami's young eccentrics. New York University's Department of Performance Studies, Ann Pellegrini, Lisa Duggan, Carolyn Dinshaw, Una Chaudhuri, Anna McCarthy, Jason King, and the Clive Davis Department of Recorded Music, all offered lessons in the larger scholarly project of grit and gumption. While on a postdoctoral fellowship for the Program in Ethnicity, Race, and Migration at Yale University, I was blessed to have been involved in vivid and generative conversation with Joseph Roach, Diana Paulin, Wai Chee Dimock, Matt Jacobson, Steve Pitti, Alicia Schmidt-Camacho, and Marc Robinson.

Princeton University has generously provided the much needed leave time in order to research and complete the manuscript. In addition to this vital structural support, Princeton houses an incredible network of ideal colleagues including Fernando Acosta-Rodriguez, Wendy Belcher, Wallace Best, Daphne Brooks, Eduardo Cadava, Bruno Caravahlo, Zahid Chaudhury, Anne Cheng, Arcadio Díaz-Quiñones, Jill Dolan, Jeff Dolven, Patricia Fernandez-Kelly, Diana Fuss, Rubén Gallo, Sophie Gee, Eddie Glaude, Bill Gleason, Josh Guild, Dirk Hartog, Tera Hunter, Claudia Johnson, Joshua Kotin, German Labrador Mendez, Meredith Martin, Douglass Massey, Pedro Meira Monteiro, Deborah Nord, Gabriela Nouzeilles, Jeff Nunokawa, Chika Okeke-Agulu, Imani Perry, Rachel Price, Sarah Rivett, Gayle Salamon, Starry Schor, Vance Smith, Susan Stewart, Marta Tienda, Cornel West, Michael Wood, and Tamsen Wolff. We would all be lost without the administrative artistry of Marcia Rosh, Pat Guglielmi, Nancy Shillingford, Karen Mink, Jennifer Loessy, April Peters, Dionne Worthy, and Rosalia Rivera.

My dear friend Shane Vogel is something of this book's midwife as he not only spent countless hours reading every line, but also many after hours helping me to generate them. I thank him for the too much he contributed to this project and for the shape he continues to give it and me. Only a wonderfully excessive pop song could begin to reach the respect and appreciation I have of Christine Bacareza Balance. She has been a most cherished conspirator and collaborator in the arts of laughter and survival. Ricardo Montez once said that doing interdisciplinary work might not be an applied effort, but a "way of being after a while." I aspire to his radiant way. I am grateful to Danielle Goldman, a scholar who dances as beautifully as she writes about it, for holding us all to a more thoughtful standard. She has been living alongside and supporting this project from its first awkward strains. The vitality of Hypatia Vourloumis's rembetika aesthetics, in friendship and scholarship, has been a sustaining soundtrack. Jorge Ignacio Cortiñas's experimentations with words and worlds have long offered me the best models for writing while living. It has been such a privilege to get to know Karen Shimakawa, a fount of prescient perspective, intellectual verve, and singular wit. Thanks to the luminous force that is Alina Troyano for helping Cubanía laugh through its tears. Ela Troyano's astute eyes and ears train us all to look and listen a little closer. Patty Ahn's sisterly company has been pure joy. Peter Hudson—always up for island talk—has been an unfailing ocean respite. I'm looking forward to a lifetime of conversations with Jacqueline Loss and Leo. Karen Tongson has pushed my thinking (and singing) to its limits. She helps us all to take seriously those scrappy details of where we're from. Tim Lawrence's encouragement and enthusiasm have been most electrifying backbeats. Kandice Chuh's awe-inspiring gift of knowing what to say and when to say it has been essential to the completion of this book. Jennifer Terry is a model of the good life; the balance she strikes between brilliance, sanity, and compassion is superhuman. And thanks to German Labrador Mendez for the restorative lunches in the undercommons.

There are many fellow travelers who have had a hand in shaping this book to whom I owe boundless gratitude. I am humbled by their kindheartedness, humor, and strong sense of fellowship: Joshua Chambers Letson, Scott Herring, Antonio Viego, Amitava Kumar, Cathy Davidson, Reginald Jackson, Gus Stadler, Salamishah Tillet, Brent Hayes Edwards, Jeanne Vaccaro, Lan

Duong, Sandra Ruiz, Ana Dopico, Albert Laguna, Roy Perez, Hiram Perez, Deb Vargas, Greg Londe, Lindsay Reckson, Sonya Postmentier, Ifeona Fulani, Jasbir Puar, Jill Lane, John Andrews, Laura Harris, Ricardo Ortiz, Ada Ferrer, James E. Mahon, Jennifer Doyle, Adrienne Brown, Nao Bustamante, Marga Gomez, Oscar Garza, and Juana Maria Rodriguez. I'm so lucky to have worked with many students whose presence in my seminars offered bold reminders: approaches must always be flexible and there is an important ethics in not knowing what will come next. Conversations with Sandy Placido, Priscilla Leiva, Mariel Novas, Leo Mena, Destiny Ortega, Jenesis Fonseca-Ledezma, Cara Liuzzi, Mayra Macias, Lydia Arias, and Eddie Genao have been particularly fruitful.

There are many whom I would like to toast in the larger buena gente galaxy in New York and beyond. Their support and company has kept me human and humane. Natalie Gold, my oldest and dearest friend, has been a source of noble strength and joyful diversion. I thank her for offering me companionship without explanation or obligation. Liz Kapplow and Maggie Baisch Hollinsgworth remind me of where I'm from and where I'm going. Our assemblies have been occasions for much needed merrymaking. The effects of Armando Suárez Cobián on this book have been profound. I can say with deep seriousness that it was written in two eras: before Armando and after Armando. Alongside Armando, in walked Claudia Suarez Tellagorry and Rufina Cobián Batista, two fierce women who have made the most admirable improvisatory moves. Earl McGrath and Joan Didion generously schooled me in the traditions of everynightlife. Jim Stoeri has been a model in the arts of living creatively; I hope that he can sense how much of him is in this book. Grazie to Alba and Francesco Clemente for their late-night tombolas. There are so many ways that I had to write this book for Georgina Ruiz. We are all grateful to her for having given us the gift of Alex. Ignacio "Nachito" Pla and Jennifer Ok are a fount of heartwarming camaraderie. There are so many that I need to recognize for the abundant love and support they have shown to me and my family: Chang Rae and Michelle Lee, Emilio Perez, John and Jasie Britton, Bartolomeo Migone and Julie Pierce, the honorable Alan and Susan Gold, Michael Warner, Mariano Franzese, Sarita Choudhury, Adriano Abbate, Gino Piscopo, Lauren Brooks, Sandro Manzo and Fiama Arditi, Cindy and Jonathan Hardin, Joanna Dunlap,

Valentina Centrangolo, Gino Zambardino, Luca Fadda, Giorga Zedda, Sarah and David Olivier, Ferdinando Mazzarella, Marina Torregrossa, Jorge "El Topo" Miralles, Caroline Kaplan, Mauricio Rubenstein, Aníbal Cicardi, Amy Harrison, Franklin Diaz, David and Maggie Schmitt, Gary Gabisan, Ricardo Bracho, Rosa Lamela, Maricruz Moreno, and Natalia "Smooth" Farba.

The music of this project has led me to dream-like encounters with many artists, poets, and critics who have long contoured the ways I think about things. I am so grateful to them for taking me to new heights of camaraderie and doing much to expand the respect I have for the choices artists make. Each conversation with them introduced me to a new universe. As the chapter about her reveals, Graciela Pérez forever altered my involvement with music. Michelle "Miké" Charroppin forever altered my involvement with musicians. Miké's spirit of openness and innovation made this manuscript's heart pick up a beat. I am still learning much from the positive and creative dignity of Yosvany Terry. Mil gracias to the following for conversational details and detailed encounters that changed everything: Juanito Marquez, Carlos Averhoff, Eladio "Don Pancho" Terry, Luis Fresquet, Coco Fusco, Ned Sublette, Ricky Gonzalez, Roberto "Mamey" Evangelisti, Bae Young Whan, Reina María Rodríguez, Radamés Giro, Wendy Guerra, Ernan López-Nussa, and Yudelkis Lafuente.

And now to the book's architects; to those who not only provided the nuts and bolts that gave this thing wings, but who also gave me indispensable support and guiding attention. My editor Ken Wissoker's belief in me and my work has been a perpetual lift of the spirits and constant force of renewal as I move through the profession. Thanks to his creative vision about what books can and should be, he has shown us how we can do innovative things with words. And of course, this book would never have become an actual object without the patient and adept editorial assistance of Jade Brooks. As the book inched closer to publication, I was incredibly fortunate to call on the help of an impressive crew of upcoming scholars. The book was greatly enriched by the research assistance of Patty Ahn, Sandy Placido, and Van Truong. After working across several nations, languages, and some thorny diplomatic issues, Alex Pittman deserves special applause for arranging the book's permissions. Marilyn Bliss brought her skills as a composer to the book's index. This effervescent crew enabled me to steal some time as I negotiated professional demands with the joyful challenges of early mother-hood. I cannot thank them enough for that gift. There are so many talented archivists who have enabled this book to follow incredible pathways. Thanks to Sylvia Wang at the Schubert Archives in NY, Fernando Acosta-Rodriguez at Princeton University, Lynn Abbott at the Hogan Jazz Archive at Tulane University, the staff of Florida International University's Cristóbal Díaz-Ayala Cuban and Latin American Popular Music Collection, and the staff and administration of the Cuban Heritage Collection at the University of Miami. I would also like to express much appreciation to others who helped to provide the extraordinary images and other ephemera in the book, often from their personal archives. Thanks to John Child, Petra Richterova, Ales-sandra Gavin-Mueller and Dolores Calviño. I am especially grateful for the pioneering research and assistance of Ingrid Kummels. Deepest thanks to Yong Soon Min and Byoung Ok Koh for their beautiful work and for their help in facilitating the crucial inclusion of Bae Young Whan's image. And finally, to Miriam Lee and Suejin Park of the Bartleby Bickle & Meursault Gallery in Seoul for putting me in direct contact with Bae Young Whan.

I am incredibly lucky to have been involved in several institutions and in-stitutional initiatives that have shown me the world. The Woodrow Wilson Foundation Career Enhancement Fellowship is justifiably legendary for its unprecedented support of junior scholars. In addition to the vital financial support offered by the foundation, the retreat and mentoring program en-livened my project in thrilling and unforeseen ways. The postdoctoral fel-lowship awarded by the Program in Ethnicity, Race, and Migration for the Whitney and Betty Macmillan Center for International and Area Studies at Yale University, gave me two years of significant scholarly development and invaluable time for writing. The Barr Ferree Foundation Publication Fund through the Department of Art and Archaeology at Princeton University, provided a much-needed subvention for the book's publication. A faculty research grant from the Program in Latin American Studies at Princeton al-lowed me to take a crucial research trip to Miami. Two junior faculty grants awarded by the Department of English at Princeton University were instru-mental in allowing me to conduct essential research over two summers. I would also like to thank Diana Taylor and the Hemispheric Institute for

Performance and Politics for sponsoring my attendance at the conferences held in the Ciudad de Monterrey, Mexico and Lima, Peru. The last chapter of the book could not have been completed without an invitation to the UC California Studies Consortium Project's "California Dreaming: Production and Aesthetics in Asian-American Art" hosted at UC Irvine in June of 2010. This symposium was put together by Christine Bacareza Balance and Lucy Mae San Pablo Burns and was a stunning example of collaborative scholarship. Many thanks to Eric Weisbard and Ann Powers for facilitating the annual Experience Music Project (EMP) conferences. I can say without a trace of exaggeration that EMP has been one of my greatest sources of inspiration in the pursuit of other ways to make, listen to, and write about music. Much earlier portions of chapter 2 appeared as "Una Escuela Rara: Havana Meets Harlem in Montmartre" in *Women and Performance: A Journal of Feminist Theory*, 16: 1 (2006): 27–49, and a much earlier portion of chapter 5 appeared in "How Can I Refuse?" in *The Journal of Popular Music*, 23: 2 (June 2011): 200–206.

The question begs to be asked: why do we always leave family to the end? Perhaps it is because part of the wonder of familial love is that it enables us to take them for granted. Perhaps we need the time to find the words and the way. Both at once. For that wonder and patience: Grazie a Muzzi Loffredo, Ruggero Guarini, Eugenio Amato, Heidi Fehlmann for not only raising the person who would become my everything, but also for so easily folding me into their embrace. To past and future adventures with Serena Nembri, Giuseppe Amato, Eugenio and Filippo. Hilda "Nene" Vazquez, the Delmonte, and Medina families' love of dance and music have inspired me since I began to walk. I have been so blessed to walk alongside my sisters and their loved ones: Tory Vazquez, Richard Maxwell, Nicole Mestre, Jorge Mestre, and Terry Vazquez. Your example, vivacity, and unfaltering energy and care have given me the confidence and the determination to keep becoming my best self. To the N. G. of Cecilia and Gabriela Mestre, Dolores and Shane Maxwell: we all trust you to make it better. The companionship of Blanca Rosa Gil and Caterina has been a blissful reminder of the gentler species. To my parents Virginia, Manuel, and Maria: I am humbled by the blood, sweat, and tears you have sacrificed to raise us. You are veterans of an impossible love. And while my experience with that impossible love has only just begun—caught in the early waves of unending diaper changes and musical babble of toddlerhood—even I can begin to appreciate, *really appreciate,* what you have managed to survive for almost four decades. As I nurture two young lives, your example has had much to teach me about how it is done.

Those young lives have been an integral part of the pursuit of the "something else." To Lucia Trinidad: you are the light and fight of this book. Your rising soulful songs make it all meaningful. Manuela Bonaria—who entered our familial scene during the copy editing stage—is a sunny sound of what's to come. Vincenzo Amato has given me an abundance of life and tenderness and music. I am eager and honored to keep living and working and listening in detail alongside you. The expansive exuberance with which you bring to your steel and your garden and your daughters has been the most influential muse. Más más más te adoraré más y más.

Introduction

Piano keys are gently pressed. You listen along as the player's hands begin to wander the instrument. The invitational and intimate notes signal the not-quite beginning of a show. It is a music of preparation, not a demonstration of mastery over an instrument. The sound is open, hospitable, and warm. You are not sure what direction it will go, or where you, the listener, will end up. The notes affect your stride; add gusto to your gestures. Your timing is adjusted. For the performer who is playing, the music helps to announce: I am not quite here and neither are you. The sound settles you in, not to discipline you into a model audience, but so you can pour another drink, hang your purse on the back of a chair, nod to someone in the room, get another kiss, make sure the signal is strong. You are given some time to find a place in the event as it begins.

What I begin to describe here is a moment from a performance by the Cuban composer and musician named Ignacio Villa, also known as Bola de Nieve. The nickname "Bola de Nieve" (Snowball) was offhandedly given to him by Rita Montaner, the great musical star of stage, radio, and screen as an ironic comment on his black skin and round face.[1] His intimate salon style of performing and queer charisma made him one of the most magnetic and beloved Cuban musicians of any century. He was as known for his live, late-night shows during midcentury Cuban nightlife as for his radio appearances that aired throughout Latin America. The notes above initiate a salutation, a saludo that he delivered at the start of one of his radio programs in 1951. After we are invited into Villa's performance with those soft, porous notes, he folds his voice into the music by talking not over, or under, but alongside the piano as he plays. In an audible whisper, Villa invites us in with the following:

> Buenas noches/ tengo mucho gusto de estar con ustedes/ para presentar una serie de canciones/ a mi manera,/ y con mi piano,/ digo, aunque no es mío, es de la radio./ Así que los voy a hacer sufrir, quién sabe, un poquito,/ pero con una gran placer y con una gran gana/ y una gran estima /de ustedes que son un público latinoamericano sobre todo/ y del mundo entero/ que me van a soportar un ratico./ Así que voy a empezar para ustedes con mis canciones.

> Good evening/ I am so glad to be with you all this evening/to present a set of songs/ in my way,/ and with my piano,/ well, it's not exactly mine, it's the radio station's./ So I might make it suffer just a little bit/ but it is with great pleasure and great desire and great esteem that I'll play/ for you, who are mostly a Latin American public/ and of the entire world/ who will put up with me for a little bit./ So now I am going to start playing my songs for you.

In this talking prelude, Villa's crisp voice slips through a smile. The spoken phrases bleed into the thoughtful pauses he uses to separate them. While both the piano and voice are muffled, they burrow their way through the shoddy recording. His voice is high pitched and rubbed with gravel. A feathery wheeze pushes up the ends of his words. It soothes as much as it bewilders; a sophisticated vocal combination of the grandmotherly, the juvenescent, the amorous, and the erudite. It is the sound of the misfit and the life of the party. Villa's gift for modulating his distance from a microphone—at once far away and so close—would ensure his resurrection with every repeated play. This saludo, like his other recordings, puts him in the room.

As Villa offers this greeting alongside those indirect preparatory notes, the piano is not subjugated by the voice. Instead, it is its counterpoint: a musical line that will repeatedly press against his voice and then move away.

FIG. INTRO.1: Ignacio Villa also known as "Bola de Nieve," album cover of *Bola de Nieve con su piano*, 1957.

The piano's sounds are given room to retreat into other places so that they might, in their own way, rise and fall in scale and volume. Chords are gingerly yet decidedly played in their complete forms, until the final moment, when one is taken apart and scaled so that we hear what makes it whole. The piano underscores what he says and what he says underscores the piano. Through this introduction of both instrument and voice, Villa prepares you to hear something new, as if for the first time. And yet, you are instantaneously flooded by the memories of all those standards and lullabies you have heard from this voice and this piano—so instantly recognizable—up to this point. Your infancy and futurity mingle in the smoke-filled cabaret quality of the recording. This ambient feel was well-practiced by Villa, who in his own method of receptive control and self-protection, would insist on performing late night sets to ensure that those in attendance were there to see and hear him.

Armando Suárez Cobián, the Cuban writer born in 1957 who came of age on the island during its revolution before arriving to New York City in 1992, introduced me to this recording in 2007.[2] He played it for a group of us in the after hours at his Brooklyn apartment, a refraction of the late-night tone of the recording. In the crowded room, you could sense Villa sitting alone with his piano in a dimly lit studio. The evening was one of the many occasions when Armando would give circuitous answers to my questions about growing up on the island. I can't recall exactly what we covered that night. I remember it in flashes: the cabin of his summer camp, the teacher that once lectured with a sword in hand, the childhood photograph of him dressed up as a cowboy. Together with Villa's recording, these details offered a composite of Cuban sound put together for one evening. The remainders and reminders of that evening—alongside many other details picked up before and after it—have shaped my interactions with music and with Cuba. I present them in these pages as acknowledgments of a past and present both mine and not mine, as opportunities for different interactions with history, and as invitations to listen in detail to your own surround.

To listen in detail calls into primary question the ways that music and the musical reflect—in flashes, moments, sounds—the colonial, racial, and geographic past and present of Cuba as much as the creative traditions that impact and impart from it. As I listen in detail to Villa's performance, I call attention to this past, present, and unheard future. Acknowledgment of Villa's interpretative technique, especially as he tweaks the conventions of an introductory remark, is always worth reiterating. Listen closer to how he compresses complex receptive worlds, sentiments, and performance trajectories in this recorded detail. Listening in detail ignores those accusations of going too far, of giving too much time to a recording of seemingly little significance. Listening in detail to Villa's performance makes it impossible to put both his sound and the creative traditions he indexes here at the service of instant allegory, to signify sweeping historical truths, or as a point of departure for more legible discourses about race and nation.

Villa's detail and detailed mode makes it similarly impossible for me to leave this powerful recording behind to talk more explicitly about what this book is "really about." His work establishes a few of the methods behind its writing and creates a listening environment for its reading. Villa reveals that an introduction can provide another function than a definitive mapping of the experience to follow. It can be an intimate collection of notes that signal the not-quite beginning of a show. His not-quite-here and neither-are-you ethos permits a variety of ways into the repertoire that follows. My introduction borrows Villa's inaugural model to offer a set of flexible and inviting co-ordinates that reveal the locations—musical, scholarly, and otherwise—that have made the writing of these pages possible, rather than predetermine an experience with them. It is not merely Villa's play with the formal conven-tion of an introduction that I hope to approximate here. His saludo is a structuring sound and feeling for *Listening in Detail*.

In the structuring sound and feeling of this recording, I hear intricate approaches to performance offered in just one minute. One approach modeled here involves Villa's framing of his own oeuvre. To say that this introduction is merely an exercise in self-deprecation coming from one of the island's most esteemed performers would be too easy. While self-deprecation might indeed be operative here, Villa's intention is always un-knowable and should be. Instead, listen closer to the way that Villa sets up his repertoire with precise care, he will "present a set of songs/in my way." He is precise in his promise to the audience though he cases its delivery in open terms. In the saludo, Villa gives himself interpretive room by having a specificity of task. By describing this task, simply and plainly as "in his way," he is upfront about what you are about to hear is his temporary ver-sion of things.

It is through this detail, this saludo, which Villa provides an entry point to what we are about to hear and what is in excess of it. And he does so in a way that incorporates a vast spectrum of publics. We must remember that as he records this, his radio audiences are not known or revealed to him. As he announces his presence (but not quite), however, you hear him take inventory of his surroundings without missing a beat. There is something reassuring in this: you get the sense that wherever or whatever you're com-ing from will do just fine. His recourse to the universal "del mundo entero" does not just toggle with the particular "un publico latinoamericano," but the universal and the particular are allowed to lap into each other.

As you begin to get a sense of its intense spatial reach—the listening worlds incorporated here—also note his diminutive approach to the recording session. My evocation of the diminutive is not intended for disparaging ends. The apologetic diminutive used to curtail pomposity, the belittling diminutive of power, the diminutive-as-miniature and all of its nineteenth-century baggage, the violent diminutive of cutting something down to size, are not what I evoke here. This preamble offers a clear instance of the diminutive imperative in Cuban Spanish. While this tendency to alter words (what Severo Sarduy poetically called the "game of verbal deformation") might have troublesome interpellative functions, diminutives—like nicknames—also shorthand objects of affection, those things that deserve our highest respect, what or whom we might love the most.[3] I hear Villa's diminutive imperative beyond the words he fragments or uses to diminish grand narratives of presence. He is going to make the piano suffer, "un poquito" (just a little bit). He asks that we put up with him for "un ratico" (just another little bit). His tenderness for the audience, instrument, repertoire, and occasion is carefully and lovingly detailed. This cultivation of an unassuming posture, one that an audience can choose to engage or reject, allows for a different way in to what you are about to hear.

Villa alters many things in this preamble. Note how he thwarts ownership over his actual instrument. That piano is "not exactly" his, and his repertoire, a set of songs he will perform "in his way." The instrument is not some mute, unfeeling object, but something that might be made to suffer a little bit, which might be to say, played in ways it was never intended. Or perhaps it is another moment in a creative trajectory that has had a necessary and historical relationship to theft. In all, the instrument will both affect and be affected by Villa. And so will his publics whom he thanks ahead of time for also putting up with him for a little bit. This does not sound like false modesty, but an acknowledgment that there is something greater than his performance in the here and now. His audience can always be other places. The piano can be played other ways. He will sing other interpretations of the songs.

Villa is not considered a foundational figure in the typically circulated canon of performance studies scholarship. He is among the countless details that disturb any attempt to make the field stable. In this saludo his precise but open task, refusal of grand claims, incorporation of different publics and voices, assumption that objects can never be mastered, and his knowledge that interpretation is infinite reveals an underground of performers and theorists that have and will continue to anticipate and alter a field that seeks to better describe and theorize the performance event. The field's institutional provenance sprung from a shared disenchantment with the limitations of traditional anthropology and theater studies and hoped to expand the methods and objects of study to diverse disciplinary locations and aesthetic forms.[4] Although its early works continued to emphasize live theatrical events and ethnographically observed phenomena, there have been many scholars that have opened up the field to critical experiments in sound, visuality, space, and text.

What Villa does here—as many other performers and critics have done elsewhere—is to trouble the anthropological underpinnings of the field that presume that objects can be known. He suggests that critics can do a different kind of work should they change their assumptions about having direct access to performers. And finally, he helps me to underscore that every performance is an introduction and an invitation. It is by way of Villa's sound, diminutive cast, and creative play in this detail that I pick up an ethos for the critique of performance; an ethos I try and sustain throughout the book. This ethos bears a set of necessary protocols: one must be able to adjust to a different sense of time, be eager to go to unexpected places, remain open to being altered, ready to frame a project in the diminutive, and prepared to assume there is always some other way.

Such protocols are also vital for the writing of and about Cuba. Recall that there is another introduction at work here: my encounter with Villa's performed detail in Suárez Cobián's makeshift salon; an occasion where I heard a few island details both pleasurable and difficult. It was an occasion that offered a temporary version of Cuba that resisted an overdetermination of its whole. Totalizing attempts to define what and who Cuba is have long inspired possessive attachments to it. When approached through its details, and not via the overbearing bombast typical of any nationalism, Cuba offers creative furrows for being and belonging. Details of past experiences form the source material that helps many of us to imagine Cuba, especially those of us who inherit our relationship to it. For children of immigrants, details from their parents' other lived locations are precarious things. They are openings that can be sought out, avoided, honored, rejected, and loved. The details are often all that is left behind from a near past. They remind us that that place is always partial, that we will never have a fullness of a past picture or sound. Details are things that we learn to live on, imagine off, and use to find other kinds of relationships to our parents' natal locations. To listen in detail is a different project than remembering. It is not archeological work done to reconstruct the past. It is to listen closely to and assemble that inherited lived matter that is both foreign and somehow familiar into something new. As Walter Benjamin once described, the imagination is "the capacity for interpolation into the smallest details."[5]

The circuitous spirit and elusive quality of details offer rich opportunities for making criticism a creative activity. It is the performances by Villa, Suárez Cobián, and many others both close and distant, and the detail opportunities they've left behind, that have informed my approach to Cuban music, the critical and creative delta that this book is about.

"Cuban music" is a most difficult and elusive sign that places *Listening in Detail* in the cavalcade of commodities that fails to deliver it as a complete and cohesive object. "Cuban music" or *la música cubana* attempts to condense a dynamic spectrum of practices into a singular entity. It is a term that is at once unwieldy and all-too-wieldy, both convenient and inconvenient. "Cuban music" struggles to contain the historical processes at stake in its formation, but it is also relied upon to fully incorporate and shorthand them.[6] When speaking of the historical processes at stake in music, what we're really talking about is people: how they came to be a part of, what they contributed to, how they made it sound, and what directions they took it. As such, *la música cubana* has not only been deployed as an allegorical parallel to national becoming, but also has been often used as an interchangeable term for Cuba itself, whether deployed from above, below, within, and without.[7] To wholly reject operating under such a sign—or to unbind it from Cuba—is a difficult and, one could argue, impossible exercise. We might not want to. Such a conflation can and has allowed a more expansive sense of Cuba by insisting upon those historically unwanted bodies and all the sonic details they bear as part of it. And while the sign "Cuban music" has also been used as a repressive tool of inclusion and exclusion, those historically unwanted bodies and their sonic details always intervene in those terms of its delivery.

Listening in Detail is an interaction with, rather than a comprehensive account of, Cuban music. It necessarily presses against and moves away from how it has been packaged, circulated, and written about because "Cuban music" often mirrors how Cuba operates in the greater imaginary. By veering from the dominant narratives used to examine both Cuba and its music, I open up pathways to other sites and sounds that intervene in their discursive surfaces. I gesture to how the location of Cuban music is impossible to pinpoint, but it is nonetheless locatable. The definitive who of Cuban music is impossible to contain, but one can spend some time with a few people who have made contributions to it. As Guillermo Cabrera Infante once wrote, "La música, como el espíritu, sopla donde quiere" [Music, like the spirit, blows where it wants to].[8]

I follow Cuban music's unpredictable currents and accompaniments rather than uphold, validate, or reject it as a sign, or to sanction what it signifies. By doing so, I heed the established traditions behind much of Cuban music to trouble a cohesive sense of Cuba and Cubanness, even as it is relied upon to determine both. This book is decidedly indefinitive and not intended to be encyclopedic or reliable as a touristic guide. The critical instruments traditionally used to examine Cuban music (not exactly mine) might be made to suffer a little bit. There is no survey of epochs, verification of genre's firsts, musical transcription, or excavation of what has been falsely described as lost. Music—if solely defined as "songs" and/or "praxis"—might be said to make a minor appearance here. But music—if understood as what is also in excess of "songs" and/or "praxis"—can, in fact, be heard from every object that preoccupies these pages.

To borrow Villa's phrasing, I am going to present a set of songs in my way. By which I partly mean to consider how music presents itself to analysis. I keep an ear out for what is incorporated by but also interrupts a musical event: those detailed disruptions might slip by undetected but they have an undeniable impact on the whole. A grunt that keeps the song in time, an aside during a performance, filmic flashes and other intangible but felt minutiae, all uniquely animate the work in these pages. I also stretch the limits of what is typically enclosed by "music" to include other ephemera whose audibility might at first be difficult to discern.[9] For example, the sound made by texts, oral histories, and other forms of documentation, be they written, filmed, and danced. Through careful attention to those details nestled in alternative locations and histories, *Listening in Detail* offers a different set of scenarios through which Cuban music might be experienced.

I once again lean on the instructive words of Bola de Nieve: to those readers willing to put up with me for just a little bit, I will start playing my songs for you. For the remainder of this introduction—my saludo—I move through some concerns that animate the book and the critical modes that arise by way of them. By outlining a set of historical, aesthetic, and disciplinary precedents, an outlining that also allows for their later undoing, I encourage the reader to find their own place in the book as it begins.

THE GUIDING OF CUBAN MUSIC

While the narration of Cuban music—particularly in guide form—has taken place over several centuries, it is hard not to notice its proliferation in albums and texts since the mid-1990s.[10] Sequestered "World Music" sections in chain bookstores and (now defunct) record stores, seemed to suddenly overflow with commodities that promised authentic entry points into the music. The *Buena Vista Social Club*, being the most famous and fatigued example, took up considerable room but was far from alone in reinserting a particular version of Cuba in the global consumer cultural market.[11] It found counterparts in other artifacts circulated by mostly North American and European record labels. Taken together, their packaging collectively pined for the island's colonial past in addition to its cold war present and did much to renew fantasies of Cuba as a place outside of modernity and ready for excavation.[12] In the liner notes of *Buena Vista Social Club*, producer Ry Cooder writes, "The players and singers of the 'son de Cuba' have nurtured this very refined and deeply funky music in an atmosphere sealed off from the fall out of a hyperorganised and noisy world." Denying Cuba's active place in the here-and-now and the right of its own order, such sealing off dangerously participates in a tripartite set of presumptions. The idea of Cuba's isolation finds precedent in other written impressions of the island at the turn of the nineteenth century, and especially, the conquistadores who overtook it in the fifteenth century.[13] Both made it discursively ripe for conquest. Such sealing off falsely promotes the idea that Cuban musical influence has stayed within its geographical borders. And of the third assumption, it must be asked: when has Cuba ever been quiet?

Old cars, cigars, elderly black men sitting on old cars and smoking cigars, mulatas in miniskirts—usually but not always soaked in sepia—are common visual themes found on these albums and books. A handbook such as Philip Sweeney's *The Rough Guide to Cuban Music* is indicative of the many guides published in the *Buena Vista* aftermath as travel to the island by European and Canadian tourists became not only commonplace, but also made the island a tropicalized notch on many a traveler's bucket list. These trips were taken with a fevered urgency "before Castro died" and "before it changed" and "before Miami could take over." Like the faux-yellowed photographs used to capture the Cuban communistic paradise, such urgency helped to craft Cuba as a fixed, immobile, and nonchanging object. There is always a temporal abbreviation that guarantees quick, if not painless, consumption of Cuban music in these objects. They depend upon Cuba *as* time standing still—but its contents must nevertheless keep a syncopated beat.

To deny Cuba a history and futurity—a denial profoundly enacted in the consumption and circulation of its musical objects—is to participate in the fantasy that Cuba can be known fully and known quickly. These albums and guides are often made to replicate a traveler's journey and/or a journey through history organized by genre. With these taxonomies in place, quickly abbreviated discussions on the racial origins of the musics are perpetually repeated with little nuance or research. These kinds of objects that emerge in the 1990s and onward are far from novelties in the larger circulated ideas about Cuba and its music. They all hope to answer the market demand that the world has long made of Cuba: be accessible and available. This demand continues in spite, and it could be argued because of, the half-century embargo of Cuba by the United States and the untold psychic and material damage it has caused. In addition to being the go-to ideological instrument for both nations, the embargo continues to elevate Cuba's forbidden appeal to tourists.[14] It must be admitted that such albums and guides—no matter how fraught or provocative or thoughtful—is how many come to hear contemporary Cuba, particularly as recordings of Cuban musicians both past and present have been difficult to come by.

I confess having long been seduced by the fight against the guiding of Cuban music as outlined in the above. Such seduction was cut short, many years ago, when a wise teacher asked me: "But what do the musicians actually *sound* like?"[15] In other words, to not listen to what the performers are doing—regardless of how they were packaged and traded on and off the island—would be to enact another kind of violence upon them. Throughout *Listening in Detail*, the kinds of critiques I make in the above are always on the mind, but I insist on an ethical and intellectual obligation to the question: what do the musicians *sound* like? To reduce my discussion of the music and the musicians to those argumentative frames, however critically, would promote a kind of listening that easily collaborates with the sealing off of the island from the fundamental place it has in music specifically, and creativity more generally.

How then to approach and write under the sign of Cuban music with all its difficult, uncontained, and uncontainable history? There are many kinds of precedents. More than a few authors have remarked on the impossibility of analyzing the totality of Cuban music even as their work operates under the sign of it. In the rest of this section, I turn to two other saludos—introductions from textual guides—that reveal and revel in the difficulties of writing about Cuban music. They offer alternative models to the guides above, particularly in their shared refusal to become definitive monoliths. The first example in 1939 is by the Cuban composer and musicologist Emilio Grenet who illustrates some of the failures that can occur in a project on music based on genre. However, his inviting failures do not only help me to gesture to more of the methodological complexities behind such an effort, they also inspire movement into other modes of investigation. The second in 1983 is by Natalio Galán, another Cuban composer and musicologist who does much to approximate Villa's approach to repertoire in critical form.[16]

DISTRIBUCIÓN GRATUITA. "Free distribution" reads a hand-pressed stamp on an original library copy of Emilio Grenet's *Popular Cuban Music: 80 Revised and Corrected Compositions*. Grenet's opus was written, published, and disseminated in English and Spanish versions in 1939—eight years after a shark attack left the author with one leg and arm less. In an odd twist on state-sanctioned commissions, the Cuban government's Department of Agriculture had enlisted Grenet to write this instructive study of popular Cuban music. He was the likely figure for the job. Not only did Grenet come from one of Cuba's most notorious musical families, but he also lived a double occupational life as both music critic and composer.[17] His dexterousness inevitably facilitated the diptych form of the text. The first section is comprised of a scholarly essay that attempts to describe (and textually contain) the development of Cuban music in a series of titled sections. As supplement to these pedagogical missives, Grenet includes a set of eighty musical scores that he transcribed, fake book style, from a selected group of significant Cuban composers.

The text was provided free of charge to libraries and universities, in the secretary of agriculture's words, for the "diffusion of our [Cuban] culture."[18] More a pamphlet in character if not actual form, the text's entry onto the international stage betrays a set of vexed national quandaries. Given its commissary conditions, the book links music and sugar as the island's vital commodities for export. Like sugar, the music within must seek out and lay claim to markets beyond its domestic shores. This export could potentially plant the seeds for the subsequent import of foreign capital. In this sense, Grenet's instructive book superficially masquerades as a lure for Cuban musical tourism—with all the attendant tropical, erotic, and exotic objects that might be heard and consumed there—for North American and Peninsular Spanish publics.[19] The book attempts to control, however, the visitation rights extended to outsiders. The little Spanish señorita dancing a rhumba with requisite sombrero that had determined and captivated Cuban music's increasingly internationalized audience had exhausted Grenet. In order to set certain records straight, he insists upon a few insights, whether you were to visit the island physically or experience it from afar. For Grenet, part of this erudition recognizes "the pathos of the soul which gave it origin."[20]

Popular Cuban Music renders the wondrous mess that is its object of study as something that can be known through the organization of its multifarious data. Grenet resorts to categories to make rational the irrational, to bring transparency to the opaque, and to erect order from the disorder.[21] For example, in the large section titled "Genres of Cuban Music," Grenet attempts to construct a reliable taxonomy by charting genres as separate sections with racialized headings: "Genres Bordering on the Spanish," "Genres of Equitable Black and White Influence," and "Genres Bordering on the African."[22] Genre always constructs its own hierarchical order.[23] The Indigenous/African/Spaniard triad, commonly (and chronologically) deployed as such to explain Cuba, makes the histories—and the many details that haunt them—of genocide, slavery, and European colonization to be quickly checked off without careful consideration of their residual aftermaths.[24] At the same time that Grenet wields his corrective text, he paradoxically provides the instruments that allow for Cuba's problematic consumption. Grenet's taxonomy, which figure genre and race in tandem, reproduces a user-friendly version of Cuba and its music is made palpable for the international sphere. Nevertheless, to deny the paradoxical slant to Grenet's text—as an object that hopes to capture, but can't, what Cuban music is—would be to deny those forces that have guided and misguided any project about Cuba since its conquest.

There is thus an instructive failure about this book in spite of its ambitious aim in scope. It would be a grave error to presume that Grenet was somehow unconscious of its failures. His awareness is particularly revealing through the use of the word "bordering" when trying to categorize race according to genre (and vice verse). "Bordering" does much to disrupt the sanitized rhetoric of inheritance regarding the nation's ancestry and cultures. The beginnings and endings of one group of people bleed over and onto one another. It would be of further disservice to Grenet to consider his word choice as yet another variant term interchangeable for mestizaje. His coinage more likely signals the concept's ambivalences and multiple meanings, for "bordering" reads more as tentative shorthand and less like an overarching theory.[25] Instead, Grenet conjures a disjunctive, overlapping, and somewhat elusive musical space. His usage admits the infringements and permissions, the negotiations and restrictions, the possibilities and closures that occur on these musical borders.

As Grenet and musicians from all eras have taught us, no matter how much you try and ossify genre, it will always offer tools for its own undoing. I am interested in how Grenet writes *about* genre rather than how he defines it. Note how he peremptorily unraveled his own system by the use of the word "bordering" to soften his rigid categoricals. And then there is the following detail that conspires to leave behind a powerful cultural manifesto for the contemporary Americas of past and present. The quote is featured on the first page of his text under "Subject of the Work":

> It should be made known—and this we repeat is the underlying purpose of this work—that what is now presented to the jaded European taste, avid for new stimuli as something new, capable of providing new thrills, is not something which has been improvised as a tourist attraction, but a spiritual achievement of a people that has struggled during four centuries to find a medium of expression. (ix)

His evocation of four centuries is not only a clue to his (and the music's) conditions of production, but also those factors placed upon Cuban musical commodities in the global market. Written in 1939, this passage demonstrates that the reception and circulation of Cuban popular music has long been fraught with discourses of discovery. The author calls out the current and predicts the future proliferation of Cuban music and musicians that are packaged as "new" undiscovered material, yet who are also described as "stuck in time." Grenet's brief manifesto here suggests that the "spiritual achievement" of Cuban music is not a finite one. Rather, it resonates the always already unfinished project of self-definition. Grenet's presentation and analysis of musical genres, that for which the text is commonly cited and taken to task for, informs my book insofar that it recognizes, but ultimately rejects a genre-centered program.[26] From Grenet, I take the writing about four centuries of "spiritual achievement," as a necessary responsibility that must be taken up by many. I am also made aware that to do so sometimes requires writing a manifesto.

I now turn to another introduction that self-consciously reveals how a lifetime of painstaking research and schooling in the particulars of Cuban music are always, when put to page, generative rather than definitive. Natalio Galán was a Cuban writer and composer whose career spanned the rough bookends of the twentieth century. He was born in Camaguey in 1917 and died in New Orleans in 1985. His lived itinerary—including substantial stopovers in New York, Paris, and Puerto Rico—is familiar to many of the performers and critics in *Listening in Detail*. Galán's great book, *Cuba y sus sones*, remains tragically untranslated and almost unilaterally overlooked by critics on the island and off. This kind of erasure would be familiar to Galán, as he was also the primary (and like most assistants, ghosted) researcher for Alejo Carpentier's widely circulated *La música en Cuba*, originally published in 1946 (its English translation was published in 2001). If Carpentier's text, as Timothy Brennan rightly argues is, "among the most plagiarized masterpieces of the New World canon," Galán's research in the fields (musical and agricultural) suffers from a double erasure.[27]

Cuba y sus sones spans the fifteenth through twentieth centuries and is less a survey of Cuban music and more a lively impression of the historical and contradictory forces that mold music over time. Like the mazes that gird his native city built to confuse invaders in the seventeenth century, Galán leads readers through a bewildering set of narratives, locations, gossip, and musical transcriptions both technical and imaginative, to impress a beautiful and meticulously researched composite of the island and the populations that comprise it.

This text, in vibe and verve, bustles with the play and seriousness felt on a dance floor. It is no wonder, for Galán was also reportedly an incredible dancer. His moves were once described by Guillermo Cabrera Infante as somewhere between the comic rumba dancer Alberto Garrido and the more serious Julio Richards. As he points out, "Esta habilidad natural (mezcla de sentido de ritmo, coordinación de movimientos y gusto por la música) ha guiado también su libro."[28] [His natural ability (the mix of his sense of rhythm, coordination of movements, and musical taste) has also guided his book.] The text shamelessly corrupts the binaries that often govern discussions of popular culture: the high and low, classical and popular, the serious and nonserious.

Galán was familiar with it all and his interpretational skills as a composer and dancer are brought to the page with rousing energy. The book is an inspiring and hilarious and melancholic *experience with* rather than a detached ethnographic *account of* Cuban music.

Take the first line of *Cuba y sus sones:*

En este libro se analizan leyendas históricomusicales que confundían los perfiles del sentido común. La música popular en la isla de Cuba no escapa a esos delirios mágicos. Va a encontrar pasajes de erudición inevitable, pues es necesario entrar en lo técnico de la música para saber de qué materiales está hecho el sueño, pero habrá otros compensando el análisis erudito.[29]

[This book analyzes historiomusical legends that confuse common sense. The popular music of Cuba does not escape this delirious magic. The reader will encounter inevitable erudite passages, for it is necessary to enter into the technicalities of music to understand what materials dreams are made of, but there are other things that compensate for the erudite analysis.]

From the outset of his book, and in the most simple and straightforward of terms, Galán has the nonsensical, magical, and illegible accompany the scholarly register. This is a writer who not only knew, and knew intimately, the histories of genres and their transgression, but also how combinations of notes and rhythms work together. Throughout his text, Galán offers technical notations. Some are more straightforward such as the charting of examples on musical clefs. Although I do not include technical transcriptions—a convention of many books about music—there are many moments where the scholarly and the magical sit side-by-side. As Galán reveals, popular Cuban music does not only allow but insists upon it. For Galán, even his technical transcriptions are given wide berth for graphic play as when he draws a sun shape shooting rays of light to illustrate genres and their provenance.

Listening in Detail takes interpretive license when trying to give readers a sense of what things sound like. I use description, musician's accounts, theoretical passages, and felt impressions to read performances closer rather than offer technical or graphic representations of notes and beats. As much as such analysis might or might not help to clarify what the music is technically doing, it reiterates there are things that remain vitally elusive to the critic and criticism. Galán's erudition and the space he gives to the difficult tangibles of history offers a well-established precedent when operating under the sign of Cuban music. Like Villa and Grenet, Galán is a protoperformance studies theorist whose work I do not plunder for data about history and genre. I look to Galán's work as another in a long line of attempts to write about Cuban music specifically, and performance more generally. I position Galán's work as an alternative preamble to the writings about both, a positioning that takes into account the following stunner from his introduction:

> Cuando el lector haya terminado este libro se preguntará: <<Bueno, ¿y qué?>>, sin poder alcanzar fronteras definiendo la aspiración del qué es la música cubana.[30]

> When the reader will have finished this book, they will ask: Ok, so what? They will be unable to catch up with the frontiers that define the aspiration of what Cuban music is.

In addition to underscoring the impossibility of defining Cuban music, and after a half century of research and experience and after 350-plus erudite and magical pages, Galán generously allows his labors and love be subjected to the disciplining question: Bueno, ¿y qué? With self-effacing humor, Galán does not want or care for his work to be available as a useful commodity, or as a single-use point of proof. He insists that it is one version, one writer's selection of stories and songs, that will forever be altered and alterable by the sounds it documents. Such is the humility—the certainty that one's work will be forever open to revision and debate—required by Cuban music.

Villa offers an ethos for performance, Suárez Cobián makes music an interaction with a fragmented past, Grenet reveals the forces that resist the genre-based project, and Galán suggests a mix of magic and erudition when writing about music. How can one proceed? There are, as these critics have already made clear, many options available for experimentation.

IT'S ALL IN THE DETAILS

In this book, this version, this selection of stories and songs, I put considerable energy on the detail as a way to play with and disturb dominant narratives about Cuban music. Details puncture the notion that Cuban music can be known. The desire to know a culture, particularly a culture that might emerge from a former colony, wants satisfaction through a singular text, art exhibit, tour package, and compilation album. It hopes for and needs experts to transmit a smooth and easily consumable surface. It believes in genres and treats their corruption with intransigence.[31] The mixing of genres, however, is often met with a similar enthusiasm and dread usually shared around miscegenation. As I've already mentioned, there is no shortage of objects in circulation that seek to deliver the foregoing.[32] But part of the enormous pleasure and pain of a lifetime of listening to Cuban music is its powerful ability to leave you naïve at every turn, to remind you that you know nothing.[33]

I understand details as those fugitive and essential living components that contribute, in very specific ways, to an event and its aftermath. Details might be interruptions that catch your ear, musical tics that stubbornly refuse to go away. They are things you might first dismiss as idiosyncrasies. They are specific choices made by musicians and performers and come in an infinite number of forms: saludos, refusals, lyrics, arrangements, sounds, grunts, gestures, bends in voice. There is no way to know the intention, to get under or to demystify those choices, but they can be engaged as creative work. For performers, details are oftentimes a formal necessity, what Vijay Iyer calls "minute laborious acts that make up musical activity."[34] They might keep a song in time, offer instruction to musicians and dancers, mark tradition, and turn a researcher in another direction.

Listening in detail is not merely a receptive exercise, but also a transformative one that enables performative relationships to music and writing. For example, "Mambo King" Dámaso Pérez Prado, the subject of chapter 3, described his vocal grunt as a musical cue. Throughout the chapter, the grunts are also taken up as methodological cues. As his grunts reveal, details have the ability to jolt the most steadfast arguments. They demand for more revision in that same confident instant you've finally made some sense of them. I am still listening and rethinking the clang clang of bells and the corneta china that boldly take over the final two minutes of the Cuban pianist Alfredo Rodríguez's epic "Para Francia flores y para Cuba también."[35] This detail, you will discover, also takes over the final pages of chapter 1. Rodríguez is one of the musicians I discuss that reminds that details are about patience too: you have to go through a few things to deserve that comparsa finale.

Without reproducing the satisfaction that motivates some projects of recovery—the false belief the work is done when something or someone is made visible or audible—I also mean details as those bits of history that get skipped over or left unattended. Details, are for many of us, wonderfully disruptive fissures that crack many a foundational premise behind all sorts of narratives. Feminist genealogical practices thrive in these fissures. Details, in the form of under-theorized musicians, are not deployed in this book to flesh out spotty timelines that require their erasure, but to reveal how their noise anticipates and disturbs those timelines. Not unrelated, these performers also gesture toward the fact of collaborative artistic contact between different populations. Throughout the chapters, you will find many glimmers of these collaborations. For now, imagine Ella Fitzgerald work with Machito in their unhesitant version of "One o'Clock Leap" recorded one night on Symphony Sid's radio show.[36]

There are different relationships to time that details demand. They have a unique ability to hold you up, like when you find out that the Maria Teresa Vera—one of the foundational figures in popular Cuban music—used to make nightly visits to the childhood home of Graciela Pérez. Graciela, the musician who drives chapter 2, would listen to Vera sing as she pretended to sleep in an adjacent room.[37] I hope that I have immediately given you pause. You have to just lay in moments like these. The time that details require should not be confused with a kind of micromanagement. They instead require a willing surrender to long-term schooling. One has to allow details to have a life of their own, to let them do their work. You have to put the headphones aside, step away from the computer, get down, let them bury themselves in your imagination. Delays, made possible by details, urge you to go back, listen a little harder, and continue to train yourself in whatever way possible—so that you can come back to the page with more care.

To proceed with an inclination for details bears its own kind of documentary practices. You can only play a set of songs or details in your way because, once again, you simply cannot know and do everything. You can only make an offering, a small, heartfelt contribution that might be taken up and altered some other time. Many of the musicians and critics that have made *Listening in Detail* possible have skewed circuits of reproduction and heteronormative notions of legacy by way of what they've left behind. To sing is not necessarily to ossify oneself in the record, but to lay down your voice in the hopes of being revisited and revised at some point. To publish is not necessarily to have the last word on a matter, but to leave oneself open to debate and contention. To hope that, at the very least, you might offer some kind of instruction that can be taken up, ignored, or a little bit of both.

One of the principal interventions I'm extending in *Listening in Detail* is that Cuban music, as sound and performance, makes a singular through line or univocal scholarly mode impossible. To argue for/in/under Cuban music in singular terms prohibits the pulsing and uncontained effects on all that makes contact with it. Its details offer powerful and necessarily disorienting portals into histories that resist cohesive narrative structures. I challenge the usage of details as things to be excavated and made epistemologically useful to instead allow for their retreat back into whatever productive bunker they've been hiding. They effect in flashes and refuse analytical capture. The fugitivity of details allows us to honor their effects in the here-and-now and to imagine how they will perform in some future assembly.

My understanding of details as events that instantly reveal and honor what can't be said—as well as agents that also withhold what can—corresponds to what Fred Moten has argued as the necessity of secrets, of

> the need for the fugitive, the immigrant and the new (and newly constrained) citizen to hold something in reserve, to keep a secret. The history of Afro-diasporic art, especially music, is, it seems to me, the history of keeping this secret even in the midst of its intensely public and highly commodified dissemination. These secrets are relayed and miscommunicated, misheard and overheard, often all at once, in words and in the bending of words, in whispers and screams, in broken sentences, in the names of people you'll never know.[38]

I hear the reveal and misreveal of sonic details made by musicians and their instruments, by courageous scholars' critical disruptions, by artists' material experimentations, and by those everyday nondisclosures of friends and family as a persistent struggle against the demand of being a singular, transparent, commodifiable, or in any way fixed object for display and consumption. This withholding is of historical necessity and has guaranteed the survival of ancient and newly created knowledges in Cuban music.

Details, like these secrets, are the creative obstacles that can turn a critic away from any futile attempt to make them cohere and toward another kind of work. Instead of ossifying them into evidence for a totalizing argument, details can affect listening, writing, and reading practices in ways not immediately apparent or thought possible. In chapter 4, for example, I examine cinematic details from two musical documentaries made by Rogelio París and Sara Gómez in the decade after the Cuban Revolution of 1959. Although it has been more than four decades since they were produced, and about a decade since I first saw them, they still influence how I interact with the Cuba of the past and present. The details of these films are dynamic living agents that offer a chance to catch one's breath and then to lose it all over again. Their internal crosscurrents prevent them from becoming stationary source material that I use to force an argument or static ideological position.

In addition to the performers and writers I've already mentioned, my theory of listening in detail—and specifically to the Cuban musical detail— is also under the influence of the great experimental Cuban American playwright María Irene Fornés. Consider first that Fornés has forever been assaulted for a supposed lack of Cubanness in her work. In her plays, you will be hard pressed to find much along the lines of predictably tropical and otherwise minoritarian signifiers, be they accents, easily comprehensible characters, or uncomplicated plot lines. Like many of the inscrutable performers and theorists I discuss throughout this book, Fornés forms part of a solid tradition of challenging readers' desired right of entry to her work and interior life.

Like Cuba and like performance, Fornés has long refused those burdens of representation that would have her explain in exacting terms what Cuba, performance, or Cubanness is. Her work does not provide access into facile questions around identity as they are bound up with culture, geography, gender, race, and belonging. But as much as she refuses to offer direct signals that might or might not indicate her Cubanness, she does not keep it under erasure. The question that Fornés has persistently challenged us with is, what can Cubanness sound like? How does Cubanness articulate itself by way of the secret both exposed and guarded? There is a moment in Fornés's oeuvre that helps to engage these questions, specifically around how the Cuban musical detail can expand and retract, and clarify and confuse what Cubanness can mean, especially in the relationship between listening and writing.

In her essay, "I Write These Messages That Come" Fornés made known part of her creative process behind the writing of what would become her celebrated, *Fefu and Her Friends*. Fornés writes that during the play's composition, she listened to Olga Guillot, the Cuban Queen of Bolero, on perpetual replay. She later remarked of the process, "my neighbors must have thought I was out of my mind. There was one record, *Añorando el Caribe*, particularly seemed to make my juices run. I just left it on the turntable and let it go on and on. The play had nothing to do with Olga Guillot . . . But her voice kept me oiled."[39] Fornés reveals how writing with, about, and alongside music is to permit its many details to enter the work. These details cannot be subjugated to discursive control, nor are their effects transparent in the final draft. Her voice kept her oiled, which is to say, made things run, contoured her writing, kept her imagination active. If you'd like to keep up with the metaphor, you might also say that La Guillot kept her fine-tuned, jacked-up, lubricated. And yet, I would not like to put Guillot at the service of having turned Fornés into a productive worker, for if there is *any* voice that can throw a wrench into capitalist productivity, it is Guillot's. It is a voice that's always too much, excessive, queer, deep, one that is unashamed to devote work and time to heartbreak, unrequited love, and revenge fantasies on behalf of those done wrong. Whether writing on perfumed stationary or a laptop, modeling the inquietude that is the form and content of Guillot's work is familiar to many. Hers is an all-out voice that moves the pen or keyboard stroke in approximate mimicry with those fluid arm gestures for which she is so dearly known. The voice is a testimony and an instruction: one can learn how to creatively interpret hard feelings while fully taking a stage with confident grace.

Imagine the many details operative in the anecdote above. There is Olga Guillot, a performer who impressed incredible influence on generations of Cuban singers and audiences from the 1940s and onward. While Guillot has one of the more fervent fan bases typical of most diva publics, she is still not given the critical attention she deserves. She is a significant detail in the history of Cuban music who has yet to experience a sustained due. There is the detail of the album, *Añorando el Caribe*, which contains a trove of details to get lost in, from the heavy subtle vibrato that augments her interpretation of the standard "En el tronco de un árbol," to the indignant diaphramatic

FIG. INTRO.2: Olga Guillot, album cover of *Añorando el Caribe,* 1964.

pressure she uses to push the notes out on "Obsesión." Who knows which details struck Fornés from this detailed selection of Guillot's voluminous recorded archive. What we do know: Guillot affected Fornés in ways beyond her comprehension but she is nevertheless recognized as a profound imprint on her work. Fornés cites Guillot as a contributor to her imagination. The secrets, the whispers and screams, the names that we don't and can't know that Guillot left behind on this album are an intricate, if immeasurable part of one of the experimental masterpieces of the American theater.

I take this moment in Fornés to propose listening in detail as a method that is not invested in possession or clarification. This method lets the music go on and on, though you might not be aware or in control of how it moves you. It maintains that the influence of details is often as inscrutable as the details themselves. Here Fornés shows how the revelation of details can conspire to make outside onlookers view your work with curiosity, suspicion, or generous attention. In the top spot of its definition list, the *Oxford English Dictionary* cites *method* as, "a procedure for attaining an object." The goal of method as such is to catch or overtake an object for some purpose. To the less empirically inclined in the academy, questions around method (always in the singular) are posed out of curiosity, and quite often, as a means to assault. Being unable to answer questions about method is to admit a kind of madness. Our neighbors often think that we're out of our minds. Fornés, always a profile in courage, nevertheless resists making the impressions clear: the play had "nothing to do" with Guillot and yet she acknowledges that her sound generated material effects on the writing. The proof of this sound effect is not made clear on the surface of the work, but we can nevertheless be certain that Guillot is an active part of the writer's soil, the generative material that gave it life.

To write alongside and at the same time about music requires much rehearsal.[40] It is a perpetual preparation, with the hope, long hours, and exhaustion that goes down in the process. This work is not always evident in the actual performance, but is far from undetectable. Alejo Carpentier, for one, once referred to his *La música en Cuba* as that which "trained [him] . . . to write the later novels."[41] This practice has motivated the writing of *Listening in Detail* and can be thought of as a guide for its reading. I rely on an assumption that there are many details heard on repeated play that have kept this thing oiled, even if they are not easily detectable in the text itself. As much as this practice has governed the writing of this book, it has also moved the reading and hearing of others. Rethinking the terms of Cuban music's influence in ways that cannot be proven in an epistemologically friendly package is another of the book's brazen aims. To imagine what folks were listening to, or how certain sounds took hold of them in their words and music, asks for flexibility with how we understand evidence. It has been difficult, if not impossible, to legibly fix some of the figures found in these pages to the scenes of Cuban music, both live and recorded. Their contact with it might have been fleeting, their involvement immeasurable. In a collection of papers at the Beinecke Library, I once stumbled on a slip of paper.

In his characteristic cursive, Langston Hughes wrote in pencil, "The syncopated tittering and stuttering of Cuban orchestras."[42] This kind of fleeting, though material detail, allows for tacit acknowledgment of the sonic residuals in Hughes's writing of the meantime and in the beat thereafter.

"Her voice kept me oiled" is a tremendous gift of a detail for many reasons. Beyond what it offers for thoughtful writing, Fornés extends a poetic way to trick certain oppositions that (still) get held up particularly between writing and music. Her axiom shakes a few things up, especially the false binary maintained between theater and music.[43] Music—often disregarded as the dead recorded counterpoint to the live object of theater—goes undertheorized as an intricate part of the event. Or it is denied an active, living place because it is often not made available in the live. As Fornés makes clear, music happens, music appears, music makes certain things possible in ways that are much trickier, say, than the placement of songs in the narrative arc of a play or novel or essay or history. It effects in ways that beg to differ from what Patrice Pavis calls, "incidental music."[44]

By way of the Guillotian detail, Fornés keeps the straits muddy between recording and liveness, a false opposition that would have the former presume the absence of the latter. Fornés troubles ideas around presence and absence in relation to the writing alongside, if not about recorded music. Her essay asks us to imagine the resurface of *Añorando el Caribe* and of Guillot herself in every staging or reading of *Fefu and Her Friends*, and, it could be argued, of Fornés's larger oeuvre. As she wrote, for example, consider how Guillot was present, even if her presence was by way of the recorded object. The repeated flipping of her record echoes the charged practices that have long modulated the hearing of Cuban musicians, even if the constraints have changed over time. Cuban musicians have long had to have their recorded selves occupy particular spaces or cross certain borders because their bodies are not allowed to. Such flipping reminds the listener that though they might be able to control these musicians' frequency, performers still reach out from the speakers to alter their experience in unexpected ways.

To the theory of listening in detail, Fornés also offers a way to consider the effects of Cuban musicians and musicality to a more nuanced understanding of writing, of performance, and of the practices of American experimentalism.[45] Like the resistant tones in the guiding of Cuban music, the secrets maintained by Afro-diasporic art, and music's refusal to participate in oppositions between liveness and recording, Fornés reiterates how the strategic power of details resist intelligible understandings of Cubanness and aesthetics.

To listen in detail is to enliven Cuban music's relationship to aesthetics, rather than solely to the ethnographic, which has been its primary relational and consumptive mode. Such a prevalent relationship to the ethnographic is likely to do with Cuba's colonial status of past and present, its difficult racial landscape, and the uncontained excesses of its geographical boundaries. The ethnographic use of the detail, which might be summed up as the discovery of undiscovered material for the purpose of taxonomy, sets up the detail as an observable part of a natural order. The assumption that musical practices—even (and especially) if they require extensive detective work—are always observable or audible phenomena that can be tracked, leaves out a universe of necessarily submerged details that tirelessly work to upend structures of power. To listen to the details of Cuban music as an aesthetic category, in other words, does not ignore their immediate relationship to struggle and experimentation with freedom.

Listening in detail is a mode of engaging things that are bigger than ourselves. It offers alternative approaches to the too-muchness of events. Of course, working with details and the detailed mode has haunted centuries of scholarship. Details have long been used as access points into texts and deployed, often heavy-handedly, as proof of the false order of modernity.[46] This modal usage, often marked as an extension from Hegel, right through the male trajectory of structural and poststructural thinking and into New Historicism's investment in the anecdote, has reviled and revered, rejected and depended upon the detail to show, in one way or another, that things are not what they appear to be. The rehearsal of such an itinerary could, quite rightly, occupy volumes (and has).[47] In place of such an encyclopedic account, I turn instead to Naomi Schor's entry, *Reading in Detail*, partly to acknowledge the detail's trajectory and to keep our urgent attention on how the detail's contemporary cache often refuses and denies its historical instrumentalization as gendered and sexual difference. In her words, "The detail does not occupy a conceptual space beyond the laws of sexual difference: the detail is gendered and doubly gendered as feminine."[48]

While many thinkers have taken up the detail, minute, partial, and fragmentary to interrupt the ideal in aesthetic and historical discourses, Schor's work is a powerful reminder of the alignment made between the detail and the feminine, effeminate and ornamental. Because of the extensive history of such alignment in philosophical thought, scholars cannot erase how the detail—whether in the form of gendered object, scholar, or artist—was long devalued as an insignificant, excessive, and inconvenient particularity for an idealized whole. Although she warns of getting lost in detail, Schor's work makes possible a way of thinking with detail beyond the economies of representation, for example, as the "particular" litmus of the "general."[49] She recognizes the detail as idiosyncrasy in its many guises—whether coded as ornamental, effeminate, and decadent—to alter the terms of reading, and as I would add, of listening.

Through Schor's linking of the detail as an aesthetic category to the feminine, *Reading in Detail* has done crucially important work for critical theory. I argue that her prescient and provocative work also offers useful points of critique at the intersection of music, race, and postcolonial studies. In the study and writing about music, the detail's alignment with the feminine has often enabled its fetishistic deployment. From traditional musicology to popular music studies, the musical detail is often made an object of exploration, a burden of exception, a display of prowess and proof of savvy connoisseurship. Traditional musicology's canonical refusal to consider the gendering of the detail—or gender *as* detail—is especially pronounced when put to the service of penetration, as a "way into" the music's secret.[50] There is a masculinist tendency in popular music criticism that authorizes the transformation of obscure musical details into source material that needs little to no sustained analysis. This tendency often turns into a game of one-upmanship that puts players in a race to put their tag of ownership on rare details as they come across them. These details are made into idiosyncratic anomalies for collection rather than thoughtful reflection. Schor's work helps me to remind musical scholarship of the historical uses of the detail while also giving me a few tools to reconfigure it.

I pay a brief but thoughtful homage to Schor's way of being and writing with objects to honor the reparative attention that details demand and deserve, and to reside in musical criticism as an analytical register that is conversant with a field such as literary studies, rather than derivative from it. I do not translate Schor's work into a musical register, for example, by making music adapt to the protocols of literary studies and their established reading practices. Some writings about music and performance are often made and read as executions of literary style. Such work makes music and performance the objects of writing rather than objects that produce writing. Together with Fornés, I turn to Schor's mode of reading as a mode of writing while listening; a mode of writing while listening that does not only attend to the detail as feminine, but as also and always raced and migratory. I take Schor quite seriously when she writes, "to retell the story from the perspective of the detail is inevitably to tell *another* story."[51] The details in these pages offer their own unique versions of how time has passed us by.

What might it mean to think of listening in detail as something that can't be helped? For some, getting lost in details is inconvenient, time consuming, and a general aberration. For others, getting lost in details is not a choice. To borrow Schor's words, my work with detail is partly "an effort to legitimate my own instinctive critical practice."[52] Details attend to us even as we attend to them. The comfort that details provide is, to some degree, due to their ability to embody familial and familiar substances, whether constructed from memory or made anew. There is often an instant recognition that calls your attention to a musical detail: you *can't help* but recognize a loved one, a time and place, or the sound of an experience. For similar reasons, details also carry what can feel like unbearable reminders of past violences. They keep alive history's painful parts.

To detail is also a verb, as in to lend "attention to particulars."[53] Some of those particulars need to be laid to rest, others need to be resurrected. Some need to be resurrected so that they can be laid to rest. The Hmong writer Mai Der Vang once found a tattered jacket in an unopened suitcase in her mom's closet. She discovered it was what her mom wore when having to flee her village in Laos. Vang later revealed, "You might find these relics in a suitcase and that's how these stories happen . . . Parents don't sit down and say 'Let me tell you.' "[54] Details can be portals offered and withheld by many a sage elder during the study of difficult histories. They are things that make you proceed poco a poco. In chapter 5, I proceed carefully into detailed portals left behind by immediate and adoptive family members. Although the details I examine live in Cuban America, I find their transformative potential when listening to them alongside details left behind by other immigrant populations divided by the cold wars. These details, I discover, offer compelling companionship for one another.

Although music—especially music that derives from ancient traditions from multiple continents—always resists periodization, the historical setting of this book focuses mainly on the twentieth and twenty-first centuries. It concentrates on performances enacted during the decades of Cuban history and its involvement with the United States after gaining independence from Spain in 1898, concludes with the present, and extends into a hopeful future. Alongside these flexible temporal coordinates, *Listening in Detail* depends upon a material and imaginary extension of Cuban geography in the spirit of what Ana M. López boldly termed "Greater Cuba." López extends the phrase "Greater Cuba" to incorporate the island's long tradition of exile—and the locations impacted by it—as not external to, but intricate part of Cuban nationhood. Although López initially offered the term to discuss exiled filmmakers following the 1959 revolution, she also incorporates those waves of migration during times of political upheaval, from the aftermath of Cuba's independence from Spain to the contemporary moment, into the larger Cuban imaginary. As López writes, "This significant part of the 'nation' is deeply woven into the history of 'Cuba' that exceeds national boundaries. At the margins of the nation as such, this community functions both as mirror (sharing traditions, codes, symbols and discursive strategies) and as supplement."[55] This book acknowledges and lives in the varied international locations of Greater Cuba such as Paris and Mexico City, but concentrates principally on the actual and affective geographies in the United States.

To illustrate some of the ways I am interested in the entanglement between Cuba and the United States, I offer a song and sonic detail as an entry into this book's historical context. "Un besito por teléfono" (A kiss by telephone) is a convivial cha-cha-cha with just the right elasticity for a horn section, much percussion and even some romantic cordiality.[56] Recorded by the exalted Orquesta Riverside in 1953, it is a sound for when love feels good and light; when giving (and getting) a kiss by telephone is enough to make you cross the length of the dance floor without missing a beat. Halfway through the song Pedro Justiz, the great pianist also known as "Peruchín," moves in from the percussive background to play the chorus from the standard "Jeepers Creepers." Peruchín plays it straight and then gently versions it for a few good measures before moving back into the larger orchestra. The citation sounds like a suspended figure floating above the number. "Jeepers Creepers" was a collaborative songwriting effort between Harry Warren and Johnny Mercer for the 1938 film *Going Places*. Although the song has been recorded many times over, the standard was made wildly popular by Louis Armstrong's original performance of it.[57]

Peruchín's sampling of the standard and/as Louis Armstrong—the ease with which he moves them in and out of the main texture of the song—is the kind of musical action that alters the usual trappings of the question: what do the United States and Cuba have to do with each other? The query has preoccupied many over the centuries in part due to its geographical obviousness. Permit me to repeat the melancholic repertory. On a map, even a svelte thumb can cover up the blue distance between Cuba and the United States. Currents—if they're not against you—can float you across the Florida Straits in the matter of days. By plane, transit time can be shorter than a subway ride between the Bronx and Brooklyn.[58] There have been centuries of less-than-diplomatic snarling as a result of such proximity. One can imagine how the policy implications of one impacted the other by simply taking into account this geographical intimacy.

Cuba was an early experimental site for US imperialistic pursuits off the mainland, particularly after it seized its independence from Spain in 1898. The island's struggles for independence and self-determination have been greatly impacted by its anomalous status: at once an "ever faithful isle" and a cauldron of colonial disobedience. Given that this perplexing ruckus has taken place a mere ninety miles from the US mainland, it is no wonder that Cuba has long captivated and disturbed its neighbors to the north. As Louis Pérez Jr. keenly argues,

Cuba seized hold of the North American imagination early in the nineteenth century. What made awareness of Cuba particularly significant were the ways that it acted on the formation of the American consciousness of nationhood. The destiny of the nation seemed inextricably bound to the fate of the island. It was impossible to imagine the former without attention to the latter.[59]

A comprehensive history of Cuba's grip on the American imagination (and vice verse) requires epic structure and effort. Thankfully, these energies have already been taken up elsewhere.[60] Take, as some examples, the gulf-wide plantation machine—made possible by what Kamau Brathwaite called the "slave trade winds"—and its accompanying industries, material and musical. Global port traffic between New Orleans and Havana linked up the two nations before either could claim independence. In the antebellum era, elite Cuban planters had long harbored annexationist fantasies of hitching their enterprises up with the US south.[61] There were also insurrectionist fantasies shared between the fields. As long as the island remained a Spanish possession, the United States performed relative neutrality toward Cuba. While Cuban independence fighters waged almost more than a decade of armed struggle against colonial Spanish (two organized struggles from 1868–1878 and 1879–1880), the United States could be described as a lying-in-wait.[62] It was the final Cuban Independence War (1895–1898) that galvanized US militaristic intervention. It was also, incidentally, a mission that would unite a fractured United States after the civil war.[63]

Captivated by casualties of war, atrocities inflicted by the Spanish, and the overall depletion of resources, the United States watched as Cuba limped along in battle. After months of public and legislative debate, President McKinley would execute what would become a model for US imperial benevolence. He sent the USS *Maine* to protect American lives or interests that might be in danger. A month after the ship arrived in January of 1898, the USS *Maine* exploded and almost three hundred servicemen perished. To this day, there is a debate as to the perpetrators of the incident. Regardless, it gave the United States a reason to hijack the conflict that was the Cuban Independence War, what would thenceforth be called the "Spanish American War."[64] Pérez underscores the magnitude of the event, manifest destiny as a matter of logic for an international presence was confirmed in 1898, in which Americans understood as a victory achieved—unaided—with such complete success. The empire that followed was providential, proof that Americans had been called upon to discharge their duty to mankind.[65]

The expulsion of Spain from the island also made way for a series of occupations thanks to the disturbing flexibility of the Platt Amendment. The amendment was used to generate codependant economic treaties, the facilitation of coups, formal and informal blockading, and of course, the tough spot of Guantanamo.[66]

The Platt Amendment was part of what propelled a post-independence Cuba from one colonizer to the other. Cuban energies were so adamantly focused on casting Spain adrift that resources that might be used to monitor the US accumulation of national industries, land, and capital fell under the radar of all those but the Cuban social and political elite. Cuba's consequential development into a monocultural society dependent on sugar was greatly determined by reciprocity treaties favorably tilted toward US interests.[67] Political parties and candidates who furthered the agenda of an encroaching US takeover maintained a stronghold on the island. Severe political repression, poverty, and land mismanagement were some of the effects of these neocolonial policies.

As US companies (including the Hershey Corporation and the United Fruit Company) amassed ownership over the republic's sugar industry, accompanying ideologies were also imported and instituted down south.[68] The racial ideologies of the United States combined with Cuba's own to tragically disregard the expectations and political rights of many Cubans of color in the new republic. Many of these attitudes took their cue from Jim Crow America and were institutionally implemented during Cuba's reconstruction. As Aline Helg illustrates, one of the most psychically damaging examples was the disbanding of the Liberation Army, a multiracial group of soldiers (called mambises) that had secured Cuban independence. The army, headed predominantly by Cubans of color (gente de color), had been an unprecedented body of cross-racial affiliation and solidarity during the war. Subsequent national militias were then segregated by race. In the political realm, literacy requirements decreed in the new voting laws barred the participation of many mambises and other Afro-Cubans.

For many Cubans of color, the idea of upward mobility in the new republic became what Nuyorican poet Willie Perdomo usefully termed elsewhere "a sold-out dream."[69] The US-owned companies who entered to benevolently save Cuba's tattered state installed better educated, middle-to-upper class white Cubans—many of whom already had established contacts with the United States—in primary wage-earning positions.[70] Cubans' of color increasing frustration and activism was met with brute force and the repression of participatory outlets, including the outlawing of political parties based on race, performances of "illicit" musics such as the highly percussive guaguancó, and lucumí religious practices.[71] Post-independence also saw the importation of more than three hundred thousand Spanish laborers to "whiten" the island from its increasingly darker (and possibly insurgent) demographics, reaching its height in the 1930s. This push to import betrays a resonant fear not yet overcome from the Haitian Revolution of 1789.

What do the United States and Cuba have to do with each other? This question has long been entertained by academic disciplines and its attendant scholarship. The intertwining mentioned in the foregoing does much to reveal, but also to conceal other kinds of involvements. Contrary to the seemingly sudden appearance of transnational rubrics in scholarship, this route of inquiry is a well-trod path. There are so many who, in one way or another, have left behind a deep paper trail. We might start with what the land made possible before they became nations, say by itinerant Ciboney populations or the scribed sixteenth-century wanderings of Cabeza de Vaca. Countless love letters were sent by ship across the short sea. Beyond these unpublished findings, the role of one nation in the imaginary of the other has been substantive in published works in a multitude of genres. As early as 1859, Martin Delany used Cuba as the site and substance of insurgency in his serial *Blake: Or the Huts of America*. There's Cuba in the American gothic: read about an interracial mulata romance gone wrong by way of Mary Peabody Mann's 1887 *Juanita: A Romance of Real Life in Cuba Fifty Years Ago*. Cirilio Villaverde's *Cecilia Valdés or El Angel Hill*, one of the most important Cuban novels of the nineteenth century, was written and published from New York City due to the author's exile for anticolonial activities. There was transnational circulation of *Minerva: Revista quincenal dedicada a la mujer de color* (*Minerva: The Biweekly Magazine for the Woman of Color*) in the 1880s.[72] Before the nineteenth century would take its final bow, José Martí launched manifestos for Cuban independence from Spain *and* significant treatises on Emerson and Coney Island from an apartment on the west side of New York City.

Part of the great challenge of this project is to reflect upon these involvements without resorting either to the corrective impulse or to a call for inclusion. To make a corrective suggests a finite process—the seeking out of a curative that could somehow make the racial and geographical logics of empire fully comprehensible. Some of the details in which I tread signal the mingling of populations—specifically, between Cubans and African Americans—that have always been in collaboration, musically and otherwise, in the underground of empire. To make legible these muddy, often undocumented, and hidden connections in a way that might read easily as evidence of "transnational contact" would place them at the service of a finite corrective. Consider the time when Los Muñequitos de Matanzas, Cuba's vanguard rumba collective, performed the song to the orisha Obatalá and seamlessly transitioned to a tap-dance number in New York City in 2011. The song combined a call to invocation with the melodic resistance of a chain gang. Such inventive combination, in addition to the gold sequined fedoras and vests they wore, did much to disturb desires for the folkloric that have long been harbored by US audiences. The ritual-to-tap transition does much to thwart the narratives of Cuba being sealed off and separated from the other side of the gulf. And because of the half-century long embargo enacted to separate populations from one another, this sustained conversation between these cultural forms do not lend itself to clear, evidentiary models.

Listening in Detail is a contribution to the groundwork of scholarship on the Afro-diaspora that understands blackness as an expansive experience that traverses the boundaries of the United States. It is particularly attuned to the work of Hortense Spillers and Fred Moten that evokes blackness as not only as a thing, but also a doing; blackness conjures people and a flexible set of mobile practices. For this reason, this book disturbs the situational binary that can overdetermine work in black studies. Its locational details, and the theories I use to examine them, troubles that false divide that separates domestic US-based experiences from the diaspora. The US.-based experience is often employed as the control part of the experiment in comparative work with other national racial paradigms. Although "diaspora" is an expansive, important, and ambiguous descriptive, it tends to create centers and margins, especially, though not exclusively, around language. Anglophone and Francophone nations have been made central to the diaspora of black studies as Hispanophone nations remain in the margins. Nations such as Cuba, Puerto Rico, and the Philippines, however, can't be relegated to a distinct or comparative "diasporic" experience because they were, and in the case of Puerto Rico, still are part of US empire. This book lives in theories of blackness that allow for experiences and cultural practices of African Americanness as they necessarily intersect with those of the Afro-diaspora. It does not force Cuba into a canon of African American studies, or reify it as part of the Afro-Latino/a project, which can limit blackness to skin color and issues of representation. Details in Cuban music, as I suggest throughout this book, break down the domestic/diaspora tendency in black studies at the level of sound, personhood, geography, and scholarship. They, together with the scholars I've mentioned in the above, unhinge blackness from notions of property or possession.

Interrelational precedents between the nations and populations and scholars are impossible to reduce here. There are too many details to set down in this and any text. I offer these incomplete fragments in the spirit of Junot Díaz's footnotes on contemporary history of the Dominican Republic that guide his *The Brief and Wonderful Life of Oscar Wao*. Works that involve things Caribbean are usually required to offer these kinds of orienting backbeats to set up their stakes for outsiders. I also include these precursory fragments to insist on how the book's performers and critics, across the media, cannot be cut off from the prehistory of the Cuban Revolution of 1959. The US embargo against Cuba, waged in 1961, has done much to produce what Ned Sublette has called a "communications blackout" between the United States and Cuba. This blackout has fostered a tendency in scholarship and the everyday to use the year 1959 to violently partition contemporary Cuban history in half. This partition is not only ideological, but also material. For nations that are still embroiled in the cold wars, walls and the other literalizations of dividing lines are built into the nation and national psyche. Such demarcations have done much to impact but not prevent the mobility of its people and their music across the divides. *Listening in Detail* works with these cracks of light from the start of chapter 1 until the performers featured in the fifth and final chapter blow it wide open.

The example of "Un besito del teléfono," that I described in the above foreshadows, to borrow Lisa Brock's useful phrase, the "unrecognized linkages" that grab a hold of this book.[73] I've also offered other conditions of entanglement as facilitated through policy, economy, literature, transnational migration, and multiple forms of correspondence. As much as the question is asked—what do Cuba and the United States have to do with each other?—it has also gone persistently unasked, especially when it intersects with that other spectral question: what do race and empire have to do with each other? It is at this interstice that much work has been done to both confront and avoid the question. And it is at this interstice that much of *Listening in Detail* is situated. Throughout its pages, I'll offer my own meditations on how music offers other ways of approaching these twinned questions that might augment the important work of literary historians, musicologists, and the larger sociological project. This is not an invective against these knowledge productions, but rather, an acknowledgment that said productions can leave behind productive silences that, paradoxically, do much to amplify muted objects of study. Nor is this acknowledgment about any desire on my part to capture what they ostensibly missed. I'd simply like to transmit what critical alternatives music offers.

Such transmissions might not sound or feel like the usual scholarly work on race, nation, empire, and gender. Music has forever offered other ways of writing under these rubrics.[74] Music has been used as structure, storyteller, subterfuge, camouflage, backbeat, and way of being. Consider how W. E. B. Du Bois would use music to arrange his work on and about the color line or how Lydia Cabrera's stunning work on lucumi songs and rituals do more to reveal what official history does not. Consider how Yolanda Broyles-González's arrangement of Lydia Mendoza's autobiography navigates the intersection of gender, ethnicity, and nation. Although I teach (and never tire of teaching) *With his pistol in his hand*, I am always struck by how Américo Paredes made his study on the musics of the US-Mexico border not only a documentation of oral traditions, but also an inscription of those bloody violences enacted on the border on the greater American memory. Listen to how Paredes peppers his text with a demonstration of the scholarly chops likely necessary to do the work he really wanted to do, say via his citations of his research on Scottish balladry. Talk of his "conditions of labor" can't begin to adequately acknowledge the deft moves he made and left behind for the rest of us to pick up and make our own.[75] That he did so, while making his way through the midcentury academy, shows the kind of camouflage and commitment required by those of us who might work on areas, archives, and populations unfamiliar to certain academic disciplines and institutions.

DIRECTIVES FOR WRITING AND READING

Listening in Detail hopes to offer an *experience with* rather than *account of* Cuban music. Each chapter is a performative explication of the practice of listening in detail rather than belabored exemplar of it. Because I am not interested in wielding "listening in detail" as a fixed theoretical formula, the reader should know in advance that I rearticulate it in my writerly practices. I reiterate that "listening in detail" is a practice, not a heavy anchor that I use to ground this book. For example, in this introduction—my saludo—I began with a detail and detailed listening of a performance and performer. Bola de Nieve opened up an alternative milieu for the writings on Cuban music, moved me into histories blatant and submerged, required a meditation on the relationship between writing and listening, offered a sense of what it feels like to do this kind of work in the contemporary US academy— all while helping to set up an environment for theories on the detail as a mode of engagement with the sonic. This directional flow of ideas, a flow that moves from performer and performance to analysis, shapes each chapter.

Details are, after all, supple directives. It is through the illegible but palpable, familiar and foreign, nowhere but locatable substances of and in performer's directives that have long guided and carried away my prose. Recall those early directives that made listening directly impact you everyday. For example, those commands that enhanced nascent and current delinquencies: a voice that shaped your adolescent rage, a guitar that made you skip class. Recall a vocal grain that made you want to get older. A chord that inspired kindness. A beat that made you shut up and dance.

I conclude with a directive offered by a song that inspired the book's writing and will hopefully offer one for its reading: the Orquesta Ritmo Oriental's 1975 "Yo bailo de todo," which translates roughly to "I dance to all of it." I surface this song for serious reasons. Filling the page with their sound is the best, most get-down way I can introduce a practice I humbly hope to approximate in not just my work and teaching life, but I should also say, my everyday. I engage this song in the work less by talking about what it musically is, and more about what it does. While being able to say more about the formal structure of "Yo bailo de todo" and its relationship to genre is interesting work, it is not what I do. Besides, Kevin Moore has already entered into the formal thickets of the song in superb and jaw-dropping detail.[76] Following in the school of Christopher Small, I'm after what it does.[77]

The song is one of the most driving and difficult charanga-style songs put to practice.[78] It pulls together instruments introduced through migration and conquest into a baroque whirlwind of percussion, strings, assertive vocals, and an irreverent flute. They are arranged in ways that affirm that everything is in fact possible. Its tangled tempos are such that only the deftest of dancers could anticipate and follow they ways they switch up in the song. The charanga style is relentless dance music. It is a repetitive grind, an unforgiving and unforgetting whirl of sound that refuses to stop. The charanga's universe of different drums, violins, and the flute carry ghosts of pasts and present. The song—and the greater tidal charanga effect—alters every and any scholarly landscape discussed throughout this book. Such is a convention and contribution of the islands' creative and critical practices. As Glissant wrote,

> The Caribbean, the Other America. Banging away incessantly at the main ideas will perhaps lead to exposing the space they occupy in us. Repetition of these ideas does not clarify their expression; on the contrary, it perhaps leads to obscurity. We need those stubborn shadows where repetition leads to perpetual concealment, which is our form of resistance.[79]

The musicians of the Orquesta Ritmo Oriental, with their dexterity and craft with repetition and their unhalting rhythmic drive, summon the stubborn shadows of history but also give them room to retreat.

The details of and in this song come together to offer a vital directive for the writing and reading of this book: an openness for interdisciplinary work and an instruction to have a good time while doing it. The song offers a mantra the book borrows to proudly proclaim scholarly flexibility to work between the fields. The rock and roll fantasy: to answer the question, "What is your field?" or "What fields does your book occupy?" with: "I dance to all of it." I invite the reader to do the same. The song's musical complexity, with its difficult rhythms, the incredible ways all the instruments—and the histories they shorthand—are compressed in this brief life of recording, reveals a willingness to take in past, present, and future at once. The virtuosity in this song—and the histories that made such virtuosity possible—would of course require several lifetimes to approximate. That is not to say, however, that we can't try.

It is musicians' detailed directives that organize the chapters of this book. Chapter 1, "Performing Anthology: The Mystical Qualities of Alfredo Rodríguez's *Cuba Linda*," takes the extraordinary album *Cuba Linda* (1996) by the Cuban pianist Alfredo Rodríguez to construct an alternative acoustic map of Cuban music. I hear the album's details as portals into the late nineteenth-century New Orleans to contemporary Paris, and work with them to defamiliarize the historical and discursive protocols used to explain Cuban music. The album's genealogical threads can be traced into jazz and early twentieth century touring theatrical reviews. Together with these performative precursors, I also contextualize *Cuba Linda* alongside the African American literary anthology as envisioned by James Weldon Johnson. By bridging studies of performance with the literary, I argue that *Cuba Linda* offers innovative sonic work that reveals the limits and potential that studies of genre, live revues, and literary anthologies often fail to do. The album is an object, like so many Cuban musical objects, whose compact vastness allows for many creative responses to the forces of history and the people who were impacted by them.

The second chapter, "Una Escuela Rara: The Graciela School," analyzes the work of Graciela Pérez, best known as the vocalist for the New York based band Machito and His Afro-Cubans, a founding group for what comes to be known as "cubop" or Latin jazz in the mid-1940s. Pérez's oeuvre, however, spans from the early 1930s to 2004, travels through several continents and genres. Although mindful listening to her recorded music moved the writing of the chapter, I also focus on a set of details from a series of oral histories Pérez recorded with the Smithsonian Museum in 1998, and others conducted by myself between 2005–2008. Through careful attention to her interviews, I argue Graciela left behind a set of instructions for close and attentive listening practices. Such instructions do not only reveal how musicians are constantly theorizing their own practices, but in Graciela's case, demand and encourage scholarly improvisation when writing about them.

Chapter 3, "Itinerant Outbursts: The Grunt of Dámaso Pérez Prado," takes up a notable detail from the mambo craze of the early 1950s: the vocal grunt of Dámaso Pérez Prado. The Cuban Pérez Prado was the agreed upon "King of Mambo," a title in what is often held up as a Cuban genre, though it paradoxically found its early audiences in Mexico City in the mid-1940s. Using the diverse manifestations of Prado's characteristic vocal grunt as a lens, the chapter grapples with how sound can be written at the same time that it asks if and how improvisation can be represented. By analyzing the grunt alongside other performative traditions of outburst, the chapter necessarily moves through locations too often left off the radar of Cuban musical history, including archival ones. I dissent from the limited view that typically positions New York City as Cuban music's only home in North America. Instead, the chapter follows mambo and Prado's grunt through the Jim Crow south, Mexico, and California. The chapter also considers Prado's movement through literature, including Jack Kerouac's travel narrative *On the Road* and the coming of age novel by the Cuban American author Achy Obejas titled *Memory Mambo*.

Chapter 4, "Visual Arrangements, Sonic Impressions: The Cuban Musical Documentaries of Rogelio París and Sara Gómez" examines two film documentaries on Cuban music made in the years following the Cuban Revolution (1963 and 1967). The films partly offer rare glimpses of the disappearing traces of the formal US presence on the island, including its official musical channels, jazz clubs, and tourist cabarets. The chapter is most interested in how the films import the sonic details of centuries of musical experimentation into the visual register. I focus on a few details from París's *Nosotros, la música* (1963) and Gómez's *Y . . . tenemos sabor* (1975) to reveal the creative responses to the hardening post-revolutionary cold war climate. Beyond those temporal restraints, I look to the directors' configuration of music as an opening into the past antecedents of their vibrant and precarious present.

The fifth and final chapter, "Cold War Kids In Concert," examines recordings by Alex Ruiz, Los Van Van, and X Alfonso, and other ephemera of separation that lives in my personal archives to reflect on the different kinds of protocols necessary when listening from a distance, and the sentimental attachments that arise by way this receptive mode. Blockades depend upon fissures: their escape routes quite literally sustain those populations most directly affected by them. I argue that music has long been a vital part of the contraband necessities for living between the United States and Cuba. The challenges of being a critic caught in these watery crossroads demand a few urgent questions: If you can't make an object available because it is illegal, or to do so would be against the law, how must you still talk about it? What are the creative and careful ways that you can engage it? Describe it? Reference it? Through the playful category I call "cold war kids," the chapter considers—and borrows—alternative channels of belonging arranged by a few other children of the cold war from Viet Nam and Korea in and outside of the United States. These undertheorized affiliations reveal how critical and artistic works can't be explained by way of the assured protocols of comparative study. My writing and interaction with the less transparent details of affiliation between these populations are part of the chapter's hopeful intervention into comparative ethnic studies. What I offer in this last chapter is a conclusion for the book and an opening for another.

I enthusiastically share Galán's embrace of possible responses to *Listening in Detail* anywhere in the neighborhood of: Bueno, ¿y qué? To which I might respond by describing the book as not an answer, but a set of heartfelt and hard-felt efforts; as not a display of experthood, but a willingness to be taken away by details. To listen in detail is a practice that is in excess of my own capacity. Adorno writes, "Music reaches the absolute immediately, but in the same instant it darkens, as when a strong light blinds the eye, which can no longer see things that are quite visible."[80] It is my hope that the book's movement through a series of musical flashes can instantaneously reveal and obscure a few meditations about Cuba of past, present, and future, in and beyond its geographical borders.

Chapter One

Performing Anthology

The Mystical Qualities of Alfredo Rodríguez's *Cuba Linda*

I. A JAZZ RECOURSE

As he made a right-hand turn onto Malcolm X Boulevard one humid Harlem afternoon, I asked the saxophonist and chekeré player Yosvany Terry about his experience sessioning on *Cuba Linda*, an album that came to life after an exhaustive itinerary. Under the tender direction of the late Cuban-born, Paris-based pianist Alfredo Rodríguez, the album was recorded in 1996 between Santiago de Cuba and Havana, mixed and mastered in London, manufactured in Canada, and published by Rykodisc, the independent label whose Salem, Massachusetts, offices are now closed. I'll soon return to Rodríguez and the many locations compressed into *Cuba Linda*. But first, some preliminaries. Terry, one of Cuba's brilliant young musical emissaries who for more than a decade has found home in Harlem, responded this way:

> To me, the experience was . . . you know when you see the old footage of Miles recording with Gil Evans, it was just one big studio? Everybody at the same time, one microphone. And that was the concept of the recording, in fact, we recorded that at the studio EGREM, which used to be the old RCA studios.[1]

FIG. 1.1: Yosvany Terry. Photo courtesy of Petra Richterova.

Terry dropped this stunning detail into conversation while negotiating the uptown traffic and interviewer and summer heat. I heard his comment not as an accidental remark upon, but as recourse to this and many other collaborations present during the recording of *Cuba Linda*. His recourse to the Davis/Evans sessions to approximate his experience came so quick it felt automatic. Even with its stealth delivery, Terry's recourse maintained the heft of its many meanings. It was "an act or the action of resorting or turning *to* a person or thing for help, advice, protection, etc." and a "habitual or usual visiting of a particular place."[2] By turning to and revisiting a familiar place under the sign of jazz—a sign as elusive and robust as Cuban music—he made other geographies and bodies from across the eras present in the Havana-based sessions. Terry enlivens jazz and Cuban music by evoking them simultaneously. One is not the inclusion or exception or derivation of the other.

Here Terry offers a method of writing about the centuries of collaboration and contact embedded in Afro-diasporic creative traditions that unceremoniously breaks the laws of time and space. He remarks upon but does not elaborate on the seizure of RCA and the subsequent nationalization of the music industry by the Cuban government in 1961.[3] His statement was not accompanied by some customary context that would make its implications clear. Instead we are left with some perceptible and hidden continuities. The delivery of his citation of Davis and Evans was striking for its ease and ordinariness, even if the Davis/Evans and *Cuba Linda* sessions happened decades apart from each other, even as they came to life in different geographies. Terry marks many musical precedents, not as verifiable points of contact between populations, but as collaborative events actual and imagined. What Terry urges here is a way to feel influence without a map or reliable proof. He presses us to get beyond our surprised reactions to such points of contact and to assume their frequent and well-established assembly.

Although I begin with Terry's jazz recourse to tune up for what follows, and I am awestruck by the work it does and does quickly, I recognize that much rehearsal is required before one can make such recourses of their own. Musicians prepare you all the time, whether you listen as they talk or listen as they play. There are so many suggested assignments that arise in song and elsewhere. In this case, Terry offered a few exercises that lead my interaction with *Cuba Linda* to the page. More than just a way in, there is something of a baroque scaffolding supporting his conversational detail that calls us into its folds and folds us into other calls. These calls are partly musical. Consider Terry's encouraging return to Davis and Evans and to the many sounds that came before and after them. They are partly geographical. Picture how he makes the studio a palimpsest of revolutions old and new. The calls are also methodological: how might it be possible to version his response into a form of criticism? Terry spurs a return to others who have made such recourses in writing and emboldens you to make some of your own—all at the same time, one microphone.

Cuba Linda is a creative laboratory that troubles the modes and methods of analysis that determine what Cuban music is, where it comes from, and to what and whom we might have recourse to in order to listen to it more closely.[4] On the last page of the liner notes for *Cuba Linda*, Alfredo Rodríguez tucks this spare though expansive acknowledgment: "Thanks to all of the musicians, also to those who in one way or another contributed to this work." To listen in detail to *Cuba Linda* is to imagine those who, in one way or another, contributed to the work. This chapter plays in Rodríguez's citational excesses to offer an association of performers and locations as contributors to *Cuba Linda* and to Cuban music. To help assemble this association, I turn to critics and performers who have boldly modified the scholarly fields and formats used to comprehend the migrations of bodies and the performances they carried in the twentieth century. By tracing the tandem rise of the literary anthology, revue, and record album, I propose a provocative trajectory for the writing about these bodies and performances, especially their failed attempts to cohere them. It is through a few wayward details found in these iterations of the anthological project that I find, as the conclusion of the chapter suggests, modes for performative composition.

These performers, locations, and critics encourage recourses to how one might approach, and approach differently, the structures and effects of Rodríguez's *Cuba Linda*. My work with various anthological formats—the literary anthology, revue, and album—is an extended rehearsal for listening in detail to the album. *Cuba Linda*, I argue, is an alternative iteration of the anthological project that resists coherence, demarked influence, and authoritative closure. I perform a close listening of it at the end of the chapter not because it is secondary or exemplary to what comes before it. My groundwork reaffirms a few critical precursors for the writing about race, nation, and music and also suggests the potential of *Cuba Linda* to alter the past, present, and future of scholarly fields. I record the winding paths that have led to my writing about the album as a way of honoring *Cuba Linda* as an object and experience that one has to go through a few things for. There is no direct access to this or any magical musical detail in the greater Cuban musical catalog.

My choice to put the album at the chapter's end might frustrate if read as an act of withholding or a slapdash stylistic. Resistance to transparent interpretation remains a tricky operation for some. Even when up-front access to the why of the work is made available—for whatever reason of material survival—reproach is often a response when recourse is made to the personal. It is through my willful demurral of this predicament that I offer the following: I defer *Cuba Linda* until the end because it has been something that has taken me a long time to find words for. My keyboard has had to be dabbed dry on too many occasions. It has made me read and listen and read and listen. It has forced the private relationship I've had with it public. Its details have motivated countless talks, conference papers, discussions with musicians and their critics and collectors, congregation with those whom find a parallel tone to their own fractured togetherness. It has pushed me to find funding so that I could travel and touch my own history. Part of the deferment was getting familiar with the larger oeuvre of Alfredo Rodríguez, which also meant some time for the work of mourning as he passed away right before I got hip to the album.

My interaction with *Cuba Linda* is a conclusion I defer, here and everywhere, because it is an active influence on my everyday. To evoke Danielle Goldman whose work makes recourse to Alvin Ailey, "I want to be ready" for the open and attentive commitment to the writing about and enactment of this performance.[5] To write about Rodríguez and his *Cuba Linda* is to bring a most moved and tireless state of homage to the page. To honor the details of such a life lived and how they were put together as this album requires constant preparation. While I insist upon this time in my own research and in this chapter, I acknowledge performers as agents that we can never know fully. One must be willing to fall and fail. I know that I will never be ready and not just because of my age. I will always be unprepared to talk about this album because it is one of the most powerful arrangements of Cuban sound ever put together.

II. FORMATIVE PRELUDES: BETWEEN HAVANA AND NEW ORLEANS

Alfredo Rodríguez was born in Havana in 1936. His mother was his first music teacher. His father was a builder. On the weekends, his father would make repairs on the Loynaz mansion, one of the most famous and elegant of Havana's residences. Young Alfredo would tag along and spend many hours with the two remaining sisters that lived there. One sister was Dulce María Loynaz, one of Cuba's most important and prolific poets active in twentieth-century Latin American literary circles until 1959. After the revolution, she remained in Cuba but lived out an internal exile by remaining silent. Her sister, Flor, was young Alfredo's godmother.[6]

FIG. 1.2: Childhood photograph of Alfredo Rodríguez, age unknown. Courtesy of Michelle Charroppin.

FIG. 1.3: Esteban Rodríguez and Julia María Acon, the parents of Alfredo Rodríguez, date unknown. Courtesy of Michelle Charroppin.

Rodríguez came to music as a singer, and as was a common practice of the time, started entering in radio contests when he was five years old. He eventually turned to the piano after puberty took his voice. Like so many other Cuban musicians, Rodríguez was classically trained.[7] His dream of becoming a concert pianist began after he saw Arthur Rubinstein, the Polish-American virtuoso pianist whose interpretations of Chopin and Brahms are the stuff of legend, perform in Havana when he was not yet ten years old. His teen years—rife with youthful distractions—turned him away from his practice and into other kinds of revelries. In 1960 at the age of twenty-seven, Rodríguez left Cuba for New York and had to relearn how to play the instrument, this time with the help of the popular Cuban music records that he had grown up with. He studied with jazz pianists Albert Dailey and Bill Evans to reacquaint himself with the instrument and eventually sessioned with some of New York's most notable musicians of the twentieth century: Dizzy Gillespie, Vincentico Valdés, Willie Rosario, and Joe Cuba. He was a presence in bugalu and performed some of the most innovative work on

FIG. 1.4: Alfredo Rodríguez.
Photographer: Sophie Charlotte
Ludin, 1997. Courtesy of Michelle
Charroppin.

the Fania Record Label. He worked on Patato Valdés's *Ready for Freddy*, an album recorded in one take and considered a favorite of many jazz musicians such as Art Blakey and especially, Cecil Taylor. After a brief stint in Miami where he worked with Fajardo, the Cuban flautist, he permanently settled in France in the early 1980s. While there, Rodríguez's recordings found successful reception not only in New York, but also in places such as London, French Guiana, Amsterdam, and Dakar.[8]

These figures and locations all form part of the "one way or another" that contributed to *Cuba Linda*. Their impact is palpable in Rodríguez's biographical and played notes. I pause on his tutelage with Baltimore's own Albert Dailey, the luminous if undercelebrated jazz pianist who worked with Damita Jo DeBlanc, Sarah Vaughn, Stan Getz, and Freddy Hubbard among many others.[9] At a certain point in Rodríguez's playing you will be confronted by an irruptive flourish, a particular furious rolling rumbling of notes packed into a short space. Though this played detail is unique to Rodríguez's work it bears an unmistakable trace of Dailey.[10] These flourishes belong to and in both. It is a möbius detail. And just one of the possible effects that these two players—only two years apart in age—might have had on each other. We can never know where one begins and the other ends.

Together with Terry's recourse to Davis and Evans, this trace of Dailey offers a nuanced sense of the jazz intersections that have long been sounded between the United States and Cuba, and that resound strongly in *Cuba Linda*. These and a chorus of others confirm what we should all know by now to be true: jazz is also Cuba's music.[11] As the pianist and bandleader Arturo O' Farrill once put it, "the music that we call jazz is Cuban and the music we call Cuban is jazz."[12] Terry, Rodríguez, and O'Farrill urge us to think harder about how these recourses are made especially when considering jazz's nationalistic function, however unwilling, as "America's music." Consider also the embargo and how Cuban and US music, musical commodities, and musicians have not been officially allowed to be a part of one another since the twentieth century's midway. Even in destructive conditions of fragmentation, such recourses are still made.

To make recourse is also to make refuge, and I believe that jazz is capacious enough to not turn its neighbors away. I reiterate a premise of this book: music has been made of the convergence of Cuba and the United States for several centuries even if we don't have all the recordings to use as evidence, even if the affinities were made before they became official nations. As we imagine those sounds—and as we detect them in the music of the here-and-now—it is necessary to recall New Orleans as a thriving matrix of such gathering.[13] That special city, like Havana, is one of the central creative hubs of the New World. It is a city, like Havana, that has long been both a prized possession and primary problem for the colonial occupiers of its past and the disastrous managers of its present. Like Havana, it has been a portal for the collecting and expulsion of bodies, commodities, and living ephemera from both the Old and New Worlds. Both are taken up as domestic anomalies at the same time that they are also called upon to stand in for the nations in which they dwell.

Given their geographic intimacy and the mutually formative histories that have passed between them, New Orleans and Havana might be better described, together, as the front porch of the Americas; an intergulf threshold that can only be written as science fiction given its difficulty to grasp in the present moment. The cities' futurity has perhaps always been their danger. It is why, with inspirational urgency, that Ned Sublette always signs off his public talks with a call to end the embargo of Havana because it is also the embargo of New Orleans. He forlornly notes, "with the embargo still in effect as of this writing [2008], the more than forty years of communications blackout between New Orleans and Havana has clouded our memory of how important that link was, from Spanish colonial times through the 1950s."[14] This clouded memory is tragically present in many minds and hearts on both sides of the gulf, from scholars to musicians, critics and schoolchildren. That music has continued to thrive in spite of this seemingly broken link is the stuff of wonder.

Sublette is among a chorus of scholars who have rightly turned our attention to New Orleans at the end of the eighteenth and beginning of the nineteenth centuries as a cultural crossroads, especially in the rough temporal bookends that incorporate revolutions in Haiti, North America, and France. The specific commercial and cultural linkage to Cuba was further facilitated by the city's Spanish occupation, which lasted from 1769 to 1803.[15] Sublette writes, "The Spanish/Cuban period in New Orleans in one of the most important moments in African American history. For the intensity of its African culture and the relative freedom with which it was practiced, Spanish New Orleans was unique in North America."[16] The ease with which Sublette slides in this period as formative to an African American history is in step with its sound: there is no way one can mention the city-as-milieu without that decisive trespass.

Sublette finds wonderful company in his emphasis on this formative interstice and its impact on music. Thanks to the labors of love by critics such as Leonardo Acosta, Raúl Fernández, Radamés Giro, and Natalio Galán such impacts have been well documented.[17] Leonardo Acosta's indispensible *Cubano Be, Cubano Bop: One Hundred Years of Jazz in Cuba* is one of those books that has made this one possible. It is deservedly legendary and admirable for the specific attention paid to the results of such crossings. Beyond the shared experience of a colonizing presence of Spain, Acosta refers us to several historical "parallelisms" that brought Cubans into contact with African Americans in the port cities. Acosta notes the profound importance of migrations of free blacks who left Cuba for New Orleans after the abolition of slavery in 1886; the presence of African American troops who were sent to fight in the Cuban Independence War of 1898 (aka the Spanish-American War), and the effects of the early twentieth-century US occupations of the island (which I discussed in the introduction).[18] Raúl Fernández reminds us of the economies of and enabled by music, particularly in the early nineteenth century. As a global port, whose various market lives were echoed by Havana's own, New Orleans brought multiethnic populations together to perform in its diverse venues. From theaters to restaurants, hotels and port saloons, the city facilitated the material living for many musicians. There were also informal, public venues that brought together the port city's itinerant bodies. Fernández points to the city's Congo Square, a performance space that featured drumming by slaves and former slaves from Africa and the Caribbean. These performance practices had been otherwise outlawed in most parts of North America. Other historical ephemera track a Havana opera troupe that had moved its base of operation to New Orleans as early as 1836.[19]

Another critic who has spent a lifetime dropping jazz recourses in his writings is Radamés Giro who dedicates an elegant entry in his *Diccionario enciclopédico de la música en Cuba* to the history of jazz in Cuba.[20] The entry begins and ends in New Orleans. He opens with the turn-of-the century cornet player Manuel Pérez. Beginning in 1903, Pérez led New Orleans's legendary Onward Brass Band, a group that included Joe "King" Oliver, Lorenzo Tio, and Louis Armstrong among its ensemble.[21] Giro concludes with the tribute to Louis Armstrong at the Jazz Latino Plaza Festival in 2000 (held annually in Havana). The effervescent Natalio Galán, the critic, composer, and dancer, wrote his moving *Cuba y sus sones* while living in exile in New Orleans from 1974–1979. For Galán, New Orleans did not only have a vital effect on Cuban music, but in his effort to write about it: the city and its residents literally made his research possible. From its first pages, he graciously acknowledges Tulane University, the librarians at New Orleans Public Library, and the University of New Orleans (UNO) for their help and support. By way of these scholars and the music and musicians they have studied, we learn that the traffic between the ports is not merely made up of the movements of musicians and their audiences, but of other kinds of currents that carry their sounds, if not their actual bodies.

There are too many intersections to mention regarding what Acosta calls the "prehistory" of musical exchange between Cuba and the United States. But following his lead, I cannot resist his reference to the touch and go movements of the Louisiana-born Louis Moreau Gottschalk who involved Cuban and African American musicalia in his compositions. Acosta notes other musical parallelisms. He observes how musicians from jazz and Cuban popular music emerged from brass bands, particularly military bands organized by colonial governments. He traces the mirrored incorporation of instruments such as the trombone, clarinet, and cornet to the dually developing sounds.[22] As Acosta also stresses, it is not only official historians who are aware of such parallelisms. He cites the words of Frank Grillo ("Machito," a musician who will make a cameo in chapter 2) who stressed, "When Cuba was a Colony of Spain there were so many supporters of independence who escaped to New Orleans, among them many musicians; that's why New Orleans was always so important."[23]

The Cuban impact was made on W. C. Handy as he toured the hemisphere with Mahara's Minstrels. His visit to Cuba in 1900 would provide him the habanera material for his "St. Louis Blues."[24] Nor did it escape the sharp ear of Jelly Roll Morton who famously theorized the effects of influence brought together by this geographical location. In an interview with Alan Lomax, Morton defined the distinction between jazz and ragtime with the following, "Now in one of my earliest tunes, 'New Orleans Blues,' you can notice the Spanish tinge . . . In fact if you can't manage to put tinges of Spanish in your tunes, you will never be able to get the right seasoning, I call it, for jazz." The "Spanish" to which he refers, includes the musical references brought by Cubans to the Crescent City, including the habanera and the contradanza. Morton's adage also takes into account the added impacts brought by other Latin/o musicians such as the Mexican musical legacy of the Tio family and the impressions that arrived via the Argentine tango.[25] This conversational detail has provided a critical heuristic for many, notably John Storm Roberts's *The Latin Tinge: The Impact of Latin American Music and the United States.*[26] Still, I'm not sure Morton's statement has been adequately theorized. I believe that he was aware of the excesses of tinges as he evoked them; for "tinge" is both a verb and a noun. It can "impart a trace" and be "a modifying infusion or intermixture."[27] In other words, we have more work to do beyond the accenting of our jazz historiographies—or, for that matter, any New World historiography. They do not need to be corrected, but modified.

It is an urgent project, not without precedent, to continually remind scholarship of the relationship between Havana and New Orleans, which is not merely a linking up of subjugated histories of race and empire, but also of the setting forth of righteous musical currents. This relationship helps us to get at the excesses of the jazz story, its criticism, and its institutionalized study. I needed to make a deeply felt, if brief mention of New Orleans—even as I'd rather like to linger there—for a few reasons. For one, it is called jazz's cradle, and because it is so commonly (and, in too many ways, deservedly) made the holding place of jazz's origins, its sister port across the gulf is an obvious and intricate part of its sonic convergence. Coupled with the intimate musical conversations that New Orleans has long held with Havana, and given that the Cuban effect on jazz has been contextualized ad infinitum (in writing and song), one would hope that the Cuban presence might be understood as something beyond additive to, not simply derivative from, the larger story told of jazz in the United States. This story has, in one way or another, been beautifully and experimentally told in writing, say, in and by the work of Jayne Cortez, Toni Morrison, Ralph Ellison, and Langston Hughes. And it has, of course, been beautifully and experimentally told in music.

Cuba Linda is a powerful reminder of the intergulf threshold. It intervenes in how the signs of jazz and Cuban music have been used as entities imposed from the over there and taken from the over here. I argue that analysis of the album can assume the copresences and coabsences of these muddy origins. By this assumption, I am not reifying those neat narratives of Latin jazz that trade in myths of even exchanges or felicitous marriages between different musicians and styles. It is not my intention to erase the complex and difficult encounters between musicians from different traditions of performance, notation, language, and overall sound. The album, to my ear, brings to life Jairo Moreno's thoughtful description of Latin jazz as, "a tense and dynamic syncopation of sonic and social histories and temporalities."[28] The album makes jazz and Cuban music mutually operative and open spheres that refuse limits on who, where, and when one came to be a part of the other. *Cuba Linda* reminds listeners of the relationship between these sister ports through the facts of its material locations; including where it was recorded and by whom. Many, if not most, of the musicians that worked on *Cuba Linda* came of age as jazz musicians. The album—like the intergulf threshold—encourages us to listen in detail to the relationship between jazz and Cuban music, to the historical binding of Cuba and the United States, to how blackness moves in the Afro-diaspora, and to the ways that music gathers this all together at once. This gathering together is palpable in *Cuba Linda's* overall sound that I will describe soon, but not soon enough.

The above is a very small part of what's compressed in the meaningful details that are Terry's jazz recourse and in Rodríguez's irruptive flourishes. In addition to my short lifetime of close listening, the work of the above scholars supplement my own critical instruments to think carefully about what's at work in what Terry and Rodríguez have left behind. In what follows, I make recourse to a few other critics who have helped to shape the ways that I bring my listening in detail to *Cuba Linda* to the page. My habitual and usual visitation of their work reveals how the album and Cuban music treads within but slips beyond scholarly protocols that attempt to contain it.

III. THE STUDIES PROTOCOL

To evoke the relationship between the sister ports of Havana and New Orleans is to enliven how we might approach, and approach differently, jazz and Cuban music. It asks for us to approach, and approach simultaneously, the vitalizing potentialities that trouble the signs of the African American and the Cuban. It is also an invocation to approach, and approach imaginatively, African American and jazz studies. I hope to search for other ways into those fields while also recognizing that other ways have always been a part of them. *Cuba Linda* is a force that troubles any tendency to calcify either field on nationalistic lines, specifically those borders both infringed and maintained by the legacy of US empire. The album also alters those dependable rubrics scholars turn to in order to freeze cultural objects for an argument's sake. *Cuba Linda*, by which I'm also suggesting Cuba, is impossible to turn into a fixed curricular object for any academic program.

In the last forty years, traditional scholarly disciplines have been supplemented by a seemingly endless proliferation of interdisciplinary studies, through which subjects and objects that have not been accorded prominent status in the disciplines have taken center stage. But these studies almost always develop their own disciplinary protocols.[29] Hortense Spillers writes,

> It is not customary that a studies protocol discloses either its provenance or its whereabouts. By the time it reaches us, it has already acquired the sanction of repetition, the authority of repression, and the blessings of time and mimesis so that, effactually, such a protocol now belongs to the smooth natural order of the cultural.[30]

Spillers traces the phenomenon of the "studies protocol" to the institutionalization of Black Studies in the American academy, specifically of the late twentieth century. By calling our attention to how the black movement became the "cognizable object" of Black Studies, Spillers gives us a verdant pause to reflect on how "theories of African-American culture and its manifold contents are partial and incomplete."

I understand Spillers's "studies protocol" as the authoritative formulae that seek to make legible and transparent those materials that cannot be made legible and transparent. Part of this forced making evident occurs through those sanctioned discourses with which one is supposed to describe and theorize culture. The assumption that subjects are complete conspires with hierarchies of keywords and authorized methodologies to promise that objects can be known.[31] Such assumptions, found across the disciplinary spectrum from the humanities to the social sciences, both obscure and clarify that Afro-diasporic culture anticipates and exceeds such knowing. As Spillers maintains, "the culture, because it locates a synthesis, as well as a symptom of resistance, shows all the instabilities of definition and practice." Although studies protocols are impossible to escape completely, for all of us in the academy must reckon with how we are trained, it is the instabilities of definition and practice that productively puncture them. Spillers encourages an embrace and (through her own writing practices) an aesthetics of these instabilities to sustain the health, movement, and necessary difficulty of the illegible and obscured.[32]

The details of *Cuba Linda* made tangible, but not capturable for this chapter, inspire a different kind of critical writing experiment, one that escapes studies protocols and reawakens what Spillers calls the "mystical qualities" that elude them. Mystical qualities are tangible obscurities that cannot be grasped without recourse to some sort of spiritual means. They require leaps of faith, especially one's familiar sense of sense. Funny that I should first feel for such mystical qualities in the project of collecting known as the anthology, an object relied upon to calibrate truth and proxy History. Even as they are supposed to contain them, I suggest that anthologies might paradoxically help us to get closer to the excesses of the racial logics premised by US empire, especially as they are tracked and collected, upheld and debunked in scholarship and performance. To engage the anthological trains one to seek out possibilities: to listen for what is muted, to look for who goes missing, to pry open a singular vision that, more often than not, tries to deny that which for whatever reason it can't include.

In the following section, I begin with the literary anthology to architect a mutually formative relationship between the page and music and to reveal how studies protocols are both upheld and broken. I trace a few key characteristics of the anthology and its importance in racial and musical knowledge production through James Weldon Johnson's preface in *The Book of American Negro Poetry* (1921), and a cluster of anthologies that began to appear in the mid-1990s heralding the new Jazz Studies. Though separated by wide stretches of time, it is possible to follow a few threads that connect these projects to questions of race and empire in relationship to the musical. By emphasizing the performativity of their composition, and their relationship to aesthetics of performance, I argue that these anthologies are not definitive collections but are provocative invitations for criticism. By using these anthologies as rehearsals for the writing about *Cuba Linda*, I call attention to the album's prehistory and the many uncognizable objects, both heard and unheard, that have always resisted studies' protocols.

IV. THE ANTHOLOLOGICAL IMPULSE

The anthology is the idiom of the corrective.

Anthologies can make persons, objects, and phenomena present and available that have seemingly gone forgotten, overlooked, underestimated. Its form entrusts verification and affirmation. An anthology can offer a respite for things that have had to struggle to simply breathe and provide a safe house for those authors made susceptible to violences big and small. Sometimes they are keepsakes to be passed among families, actual and invented.[33] Materials are considered important enough to put in one place so that they can be circulated with more ease. They are a strategy to order and make sense of difficult things, to make the scope of history portable. They are traded as touristic, compact guides for short visits to unfamiliar places. And quite often, anthologies bear a tricky erotics (not unlike speed dating) by offering just enough of an impression to see if the relationship will take. Authoritative, and just as often, groundbreaking, the work they are made to do in the world is formidable. As Kobena Mercer succinctly put it, anthologies must fulfill the premise that "exclusion can be rectified all at once."[34]

The word anthology comes from the Greek word *anthologia* meaning to gather flowers.[35] The term later became a way denote other kinds of "literary collections. . . . esp. of paintings, songs, etc., and other art forms." And later, the anthology also came to mean collections of music, or the assemblage of an artist's greatest hits. To anthologize is also a legitimate verb meaning the compilation or "yield" of materials for an anthology, in addition to an action being done unto another, that is, "the anthologized poet."[36] Textual anthologies have long been critical instruments for the select crafting of literary tradition in the old world, a gigantic trajectory that I'm unable to address here.[37] As early mercenaries for the calcification of canons and fortification from any threatening invaders, many a composition teacher and overlooked writer can tell you: anthologies can and do cause pain. Edward Mullen succinctly sums it up this way: "once in, always in." For many authors, the logic has too easily worked in the reverse: once out, always out.[38]

In the New World, the anthology became an idealized tool for conquered territories as they were to assert their independence and later, for anticolonial ribbing as they became official nations.[39] Pronounced especially in, though not exclusively to, Cuba and the United States, the anthology became a vehicle to define nation and national culture apart from its colonial occupiers, especially, though not exclusively through its literature.[40] They were called upon to order the disorder of founding narratives and to come up with traditions anew. As a way to showcase the accomplishments and skills of a select citizenry, literary works were cast as heroic partners in the making of nation. The anthology has been an enormously effective tool in the formal and informal education of a nation's population.[41] The form was and is a way for an editor or small consensus to make nation a cohesive entity with an agreed-upon past, a fixed present, and an imposed future. National anthologies continue to traffic in the possibilities and dangers of this is who you are and who you will become.[42]

Principally used as vessels for literary objects of the Americas such as poetry, their organization was preoccupied with the documentation of black populations, even if such anxiety was made manifest by their complete erasure or conditional inclusion.[43] These terms of publication would begin to shift in the early twentieth century.[44] Because of the sustained and willful neglect of the contributions of populations of color in both the United States and Cuba, some writers and editors found a most urgent project in anthological upheaval. It was a necessary activity for and on behalf of those disappeared from national collections. It would be a mistake, however, to assume that its compilers were always driven by some version of: to exist means to be read. This would reduce too many labors of love into the failed fodder of representation. Rather, some corners of the anthological enterprise were raising difficult questions about black futurity: how can reading publics be nurtured? How can little sisters be taught? How can a book offer company? What happens when survival strategies are put together in print? I'm reminded of Elizabeth Alexander's gentle reminder, "In many cases, the anthology is an act of love. It is an object that someone *has* to take on."[45]

One needs to look back to the moving trajectory of anthologies of Afro-American authors in the United States, particularly when put together by those who bore witness to Reconstruction, to get a sense of such urgency. In his 1947 essay, "The Anthologist and the Negro Author," John Nash reminds us of Alice Dunbar Nelson's *Masterpieces of Negro Eloquence* (1914) and especially, James Weldon Johnson's *The Book of American Negro Poetry* (1921) as significant examples.[46] As early assemblages of black poetry and American literary experimentation, their texts made generations of writers and readers.[47] Through their curatorial moves, they also modeled ways of approach and study to African American expressive culture. In Nash's words,

perhaps the greatest service which Johnson's essay and anthology performed for the Negro author was their establishment and demonstration of a theory of "Negro literature" which, in view of the outburst of expression immediately following, was fructified and extended.[48]

With *The Book of American Negro Poetry*, Johnson playfully revealed the fissures of the anthological form. Through his opening preface, Johnson modifies the form as one that might enable the critique rather than the edification of history. For Johnson, the corrective anthological impulse can easily let readers off the hook—their job is done by simply owning the book or being vaguely familiar with its contents. Notice how he directly confronts the dangers of corrective finitude:

> the matter of Negro poets and the production of literature by the colored people in this country *involves more than supplying information* that is lacking. It is a matter which has a direct bearing on the most vital of American problems. [emphasis mine][49]

What's more, what Johnson does with most agile care is to address those things that the corrective—particularly that which in some way directly involves the racial question—would like to mute. For Johnson, crevices were not necessarily threatening lapses to the anthology's order. Echoing Dunbar-Nelson's editorial and international openness through the inclusion of works on Haiti, Johnson's incorporation of the extranational into a collection on American Negro poetry begs for permanent notice. At the same time, through his forward and curatorial style, Johnson demonstrates that Aframerican literature must be considered as deeply connected with the extraliterary.

The whole of Johnson's preface is one of the richest examples of the written interface between the musical and the literary in American literary history. It is astonishing to read his love of Aframerican musics and their makers as he unapologetically overwhelms the preface with sound. He begins the essay and then proceeds at some length to discuss the vitality of ragtime, blues, and dance forms *as* the Aframerican literary tradition. Note this example—¡a habanera recourse!—made without fuss and fanfare: Johnson listed the "tango, a dance created by the Negroes in Cuba and later transplanted to South America" as part of the power and promise of Negro artistic and intellectual production; as part of the "Negro stamp" on, quite literally, the ways America moves.[50] In addition, one of the preface's more provocative details is the substantial chunk that Johnson dedicates to the Cuban poet Plácido.[51] While Plácido does not make the official table of contents (his "Mother, Farewell!" is translated by Johnson and provided in an appendix), his placement as a primary figure involves Cuba in America beyond a foreign influence.[52] He did not relegate Cuba to the distance, but instead made recourse to it.

Immediately following his meditation on Plácido, Johnson takes pause: "This preface has gone far beyond what I had in mind when I started."[53] I am so drawn to the way that Johnson is overwhelmed by his intentions, his willingness to go "far beyond" what he set out to do. To reveal the excesses of one's own project is revel in the incompleteness of things. To do so in a preface marks a great degree of courage. Of the anthology's preface, Brent Hayes Edwards offers this lovely passage,

> A preface is always early or late, always a mask or a coda. . . . . As a formal device, the preface speaks double in this way: it is outside, it marks what is not within the book, it precedes the book's "speaking," but it is also the very force that animates the book, that opens it for us and shows its contents.[54]

Alongside Edwards's influential work on the anthology and *The Book of American Negro Poetry* which is at the heart of this passage, I am inspired to consider how Johnson's preface did not only speak double in the book itself, but also in the greater foundations of African American studies in the United States.

Part of what I read as the speaking double of Johnson's preface, is his yearn to take up aftermath of the golden age of US empire and the continued development of cultural productions by Aframericans regardless of national affiliation *at the same time* that he offers a domestic theory of not only American Negro poetry, but also of the American Negro. That Johnson offered this theoretical contribution only twenty-three years after the war of 1898 shows that there was an instant precedent set for African American literary theory to go "far beyond" what it set out to do. To go "far beyond" is to risk not being considered complete in a way that nation demands. After any reread of the prescient and tardy interruption that Johnson enacts in this preface, I find myself wondering aloud, what happened to this precedent of going far beyond? How was such a precedent of openness shut down and made into a governing studies protocol?

That anthologies would gain renown as racial compendia should come as no surprise. Because their didactic nature makes them particularly useful for the study of race in the Americas, their development alongside the rise of the social sciences is less than accidental. When used as pragmatic tools, racial anthologies have much to reveal of the tension between the cultural and the empirical in scholarship. No longer the domain of literature, the anthology would perform the interlinking of social science and culture. Part of this, Edwards argues, has to do with the rise of the *vogue negre*, the internationalization of black radicalism, and the new generations of scholars who were coming of age and sharing ideas in the early twentieth century. Of course, this was also the very trouble that some racial anthologies sought to contain. To do so, some questions were raised. Where should this newly acquired knowledge about the Negro go? Or, alternatively: where could this knowledge be sent? And finally, the most pressing of all: is the Negro knowable? While the sociological enterprise—and it could be argued, its intersection with the New Negro enterprise—seemed to answer in the affirmative, many cultural workers (even within the social sciences) did much to frustrate the violent transparency of the question.[55] It is Johnson's prescient and shameless going "far beyond" that serves as a vital foundation for this frustrative activity, especially via the extranational and protointerdisciplinary work he compresses into this written detail.

If, as I argued in my introduction, to listen in detail to Cuban music is to enliven Cuban music's relationship to aesthetics, rather than solely to the ethnographic, I find in Johnson a unique opportunity to explore this relationship in *Cuba Linda*. His elegant fusing of a specifically African American literary culture alongside its musical culture does not depend upon a comparative framework that decontextualizes the populations and influences involved. The force of Afro-diasporic culture is not siphoned into proper contextual protocols of geography, history, form, and function. Instead what Johnson offers is an open, far beyond aesthetics to gathering African American culture that willingly and necessarily moves to the excesses of any intention. What I take all this to offer for scholarship is how Cuba and

Cuban music form part of African American and jazz studies not as foreign comparatives, but as elemental parts of their aesthetics.[56] On the ground level of this chapter, Johnson emboldens a listening in detail to *Cuba Linda* that goes far beyond what I had in mind when I started. The album is not only a portal into the life of Rodríguez or the Cuban musical catalogue, but also an occasion to open up the frameworks of how we even come to approach them in the first place.

Cuba Linda extends the wondrous, mystical qualitied, far beyond foundations of African American studies. It also supplements the foundations of jazz studies even as that field has had a studies protocol that forecloses the far beyond. Many of the anthologies that have made jazz studies Jazz Studies—for "the anthology" and anthologies have played a key role in the institutionalization of the field—seem keen to extend the impulses found in Johnson. On the one hand, there is a going "far beyond" by making the case for jazz as intellectual work (no small feat considering the hostility that the academy has generally had toward popular music); by boldly showcasing writings that are interdisciplinary in actual substance and not just in name; and every once in a while, some small gesture is made toward international "influences." And on the other hand, there is also palpable disavowal of the "far beyond" due to the continued investment in jazz as African American exceptionalism. Some writings in Jazz Studies have a tendency to extend imperial understandings of influence; to exclude the excess pieces that might not be legible as jazz, including women musicians, critics and listening publics; and to understand the international as interchangeable with the foreign. The territoriality of US empire, therefore, is not registered in sight and sound.

I admit to some dependence upon a distinction between Jazz Studies and jazz studies. By Jazz Studies, I mean the proper curricular unit and associated accompaniments that often desire and depend upon a nationalist paradigm to claim legitimacy as a critical enterprise—even as it fronts internationalist leanings.[57] Such a paradigm does much to account for the international by discourses of jazz's spread across the globe; influence moves imperially.[58] By jazz studies, I gesture to more than a century of writings and associated ephemera that keep close to the music. There are so many key figures of jazz studies, say Ralph Ellison and Langston Hughes, who become codified and collected as Jazz Studies stars even as their projects punctured nationalist paradigms. And just as often, there is work being published as Jazz Studies that is not invested in a possessive claim over the sign of jazz.[59] Then there are others such as Gayl Jones who tend to haunt both of these categories as she generally eludes and is eluded by them.

The anthology has done important work for Jazz Studies. It has been the primary vehicle for the findings of working groups, actual and virtual; put into circulation scholarly work that would otherwise be considered out of place; and played a significant part in what has made the field legible as scholarship. The reach of Jazz Studies anthologies is particularly vast given their use in countless seminars and other immeasurable publics.[60] Beyond all the vital work they have done, however, an alarmist position with respect to Jazz Studies anthologies is easily available. Here I am thinking specifically about four principal anthologies. Two have been edited by Krin Gabbard (*Jazz Among the Discourses* and *Representing Jazz*); both published by Duke University Press in 1995. And two to emerge from Columbia's Center for Jazz Studies, *The Jazz Cadence of American Culture*, edited by Robert G. O'Meally in 1998; and *Uptown Conversation: The New Jazz Studies*, edited by Robert G. O'Meally, Brent Hayes Edwards, and Farah Jasmine Griffin in 2004; both published by Columbia University Press.

As Jazz Studies begin to take important forms in many contemporary locations, I would like to take into account a few key concerns. The Jazz Studies anthology—as genre and contemporary collection—can induce states of paranoia in one's scholarship. I admit to counting and sorting contributors, indexical citations, and content by gender and the locations considered. However tedious this work is, it does make a few things strikingly clear. Despite the amazing feminist voices that have long made Jazz Studies and jazz studies possible, particularly in black feminist criticism, they are still made a false minority in these volumes. For example, out of the seventy-eight possible contributions in these anthologies, only eleven are authored by women. Alongside this excision of women from the canonical texts of new Jazz Studies scholarship, and perhaps not accidentally, there is a dire inattention to locations outside of the United States. The scant attention paid to Latin tinges is continually troubling, especially as I and many others have argued, Latin jazz is not merely additive to or derivative of US countercultural traditions. Even in the New York-centric mindset that, for better or for worse, dominates Jazz Studies anthologies, Spanish Harlem is glaringly absented. This happens even as there is a refreshing self-consciousness the editors and contributors perform around the canonization of jazz in scholarship. It is not enough, I'm suggesting, to be cognizant or upfront about the pitfalls of canonization. I recall Johnson who reminds that this isn't a matter of simply adding on information that is lacking. It is a matter, rather, of reconfiguring how we gather and understand our information in the first place. One current effort of this can be found as Nichole T. Rustin and Sherrie Tucker's important volume, *Big Ears: Listening for Gender in Jazz Studies* that keeps our vital attention to the critical legacy of black feminism and its intersection with jazz studies and is a model for the gathering together of new voices to imagine its futurity.[61]

Christopher Washbourne writes,

> For many in the jazz establishment (i.e., the community of jazz musicians, promoters, educators, writers, DJs, industry people, and consumers), Latin jazz represents something alien, a continual disruption, which is paradoxical precisely because it shares a common origin with mainstream jazz, yet has undergone several stages of disassociation along the road.[62]

I reiterate that the aforementioned anthologies have done important and groundbreaking work for scholars working in the academy's jazz furrows, so my critique of them is not merely to call attention to what they have left out. What they offer are opportunities to reconsider the alien and continual disruption made by "Latin" (whether that sign means Cuban, Puerto Rican, Dominican, Brazilian, or Spanish Harlem). Such opportunities if and when taken up can nuance the nationalistic paradigms that do not only govern studies of race in the academy, but also of US popular music.[63] Part of this work means continuing to confront how we understand the "international" in relationship to the United States. Review the involvement between the United States and the rest of the Americas, and how the "international"—particularly the antiassimilationist international and the languages still spoken there—has been messing with domestic claims to jazz from within US borders since its first generative notes were played. Such a reconfiguration of the international makes disassociation impossible for musicians and scholars alike.

If inclusion is not my aim here, why insist upon arranging my interaction with *Cuba Linda* alongside impressions on African American and jazz studies? Its sound reaches out to and finds company with the mystical qualities of those fields. For a critic, there is a need to make recourse to the centuries of Afro-diasporic literary and critical practices that have engaged those qualities. To hear it apart from this company would be to turn it into an isolated object of novelty—an exceptional additive. *Cuba Linda* bears all the tension, love, disagreement, difference, and humor experienced through this congregation. There are embraces, waves, nods, raised eyebrows, smiles, moves made and returned on the album. It is a vital and living antiphonal partner in the greater American sound. The musicians on the album offer so many of these conversational details—a few of which I will describe at the chapter's end. What do the musicians *sound* like? In order to keep preparing my responses to this question, I turn to a detail in the jazz studies anthology *Uptown Conversation* written by the musician and critic Vijay Iyer. This detail—a version of Johnson's "far beyond" that extends the anthology's coordinates—does much to undo the pressure for narrative coherence often enacted by the anthological form and by the jazz story.

In *Cuba Linda* I hear many of what Iyer calls "traces of embodiment" felt in African American music, particularly through the practice of improvisation. For Iyer these traces reveal "how musical bodies tell us stories." These stories, however, aren't the cohesive narratives that the anthological form depends upon. Instead, Iyer argues, to talk about African American music is to engage in a different kind of critical experiment:

> I propose that the story that an improvisor tells does not unfold merely in the overall form of a "coherent" solo, nor simply in antiphonal structures, but also in the microscopic musical details, as well as in the inherent structure of the performance itself. The story dwells not just in one solo at a time, but also in a single note, and equally in an entire lifetime of improvisations. In short, the story is revealed not as a simple linear narrative, but as a fractured, exploded one.[64]

Iyer's proposal does much to advance what might be at work in playing in detail; a musical practice that accounts for and moves far beyond multiple structures, temporal registers, and lived dimensions to create something new. There is something crucial here about honoring performers and their practices as central to Iyer's formulation as it is they who put their bodies on the line, whether on a stage or in a studio. Still, his proposal also offers a crucial something for listening in detail that helps to break open the national, gendered and racialized narratives depended upon to cohere America, African America, jazz, Cuba, Cuban Music, *Cuba Linda*. He urges us to unburden performers from "top-down notions of overarching coherence to bottom up views of narrativity."[65] I take Iyer's important intervention into the anthological form, jazz, African American music, and listening in detail to imagine the performed trajectories that both structure and explode Rodríguez's narrative project. The story that Rodríguez tells as *Cuba Linda* is a fractured one that can and can't tell the paths his ancestors were forced to make, the dynamic musical education that began with his mother, to the events both major and minor that he encountered throughout his refugee wanderings across the globe. Perhaps Rodríguez knew that he would never find a home, but could improvise one as *Cuba Linda*.

V. PERFORMING ANTHOLOGY

Many congregants in the back alleys of performance studies are keen to the invitation that Iyer extends in the above. Alongside what I read as Iyer's gentle guiding back to performers and their practices, I'd like to ask: what if we were to understand performance as another form of the anthology?[66] Performers have long offered modifications to that determined question: is the Negro knowable? To perform is to anthologize. Performance is always far beyond the grasp of the critic's intentions or organizing structure, whether the structure is understood as nation, milieu, scholarly discipline, genre, narrative, or venue. Performers' negotiation of these structures reveals other kinds of fractured, exploded stories at work in the larger anthologizing of populations of African descent. They propose other compositional traditions. Musicians are particularly adept at arranging practices picked up in waking and dream life, from centuries ago to yesterday. And even as they mark the contributions of others in legible ways, they can just as easily slip by unnoticed.

A palpable nexus for this kind of performance activity can be found via the revue, the textual anthology's counterpoint in the early twentieth century. The revue is another form that can't quite get a handle on what it hopes to frame. A critical specter has now been conjured, for to turn to the revue means, in some ways, to turn to liveness. For some, a turn to liveness— meant here as a temporal condition and discourse—means automatic access to spectacle and the unchecked consumption of it. It presumes that living and breathing bodies make themselves available on demand, even and es- pecially if those bodies are no longer with us. Because there has historically been a valuation of the live over and against the recorded in performance studies—a studies protocol that insists on an easy corporality—it is no se- cret that the field has historically trafficked in the bodies of others. To insist upon an intelligible liveness of curricular objects in this studies protocol is to also insist on their death.

We have many alternative models that give us the tools to consider per- formance's hereafter. The turn to liveness can mean an admission of the wonderful lapses of one's project. There's a healthy and not-knowing qual- ity of liveness that always reminds: you were not there.[67] You cannot simply jump into history's lap and conquer the laws of time and space. You cannot subjugate that which you were not a part of, as performer or spectator. Re- covery of the historical live, is always a, if not the, problem that confronts our reengagement with the past. We can see the incredibly creative and nec- essary ways that many have had to imagine the live—especially from those who also bear a historical, embodied relationship to its more horrific mani- festations.[68] Because we were not there, we have to depend upon whatever ephemera are left behind rather than belabor our lack of access to the actual enactment. We have to listen harder for its trace in the performances to fol- low. I operate under the assumption that the live performances of the past announce themselves in the recordings of the present.

The early twentieth century saw an upsurge of activity on the hemi- spheric revue circuit, a mobile performative format popularized both in the domestic, nationally specific sphere—to transnationally assembled revues, whose itineraries ran up and down the Americas and also reached transatlan- tic audiences in interwar Europe. Permit me to give you a sense of this move- ment and format by giving you a six-year career snippet of one performer's career. In 1926, the Cuban vedette and national icon Rita Montaner worked

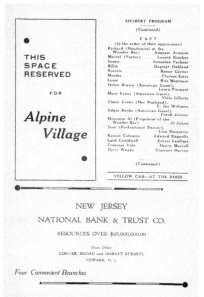

FIG. 1.5: "The Wonder Bar" revue program, 1931. Courtesy of the Shubert Archive.

FIG. 1.6: "The Wonder Bar" revue program, 1931. Courtesy of the Shubert Archive.

for the Shuberts and appeared in bit parts in revues at places such as the Apollo Theater. Her appearances in other revues in places such as Mexico City—which has its own, intense cabaret and revue history—to Buenos Aires, where she graced the stage of the famed La Comedia Theater is exhaustive.[69] In 1928, she recorded her version of "El Manisero" (The Peanut Vendor) with the Columbia Label in New York, one of the earliest global hits of modern recording. This is the same year she had been a transatlantic sensation at the Palace du Paris, where, alongside Josephine Baker, she was at work continuing the import of Cuban sound into the Parisian revue tradition. And also the same year she was featured in dozens of revues in her native Cuba. Let me leave you at 1931 where Montaner came back to New York as a star performer in Al Jolson's famed "Wonder Bar" revue, whose featured roles modulated from a man in blackface to wayward ingénue. This revue did not only find success in the New York, but also Washington D.C., Los Angeles, and Newark.

Like all origins, those of the revue format are difficult to pinpoint. According to the *Oxford English Dictionary*, the word emerges from mid-nineteenth-century France to mean, "A theatrical entertainment presenting a review of current events, plays, etc; hence also an elaborate musical show consisting of numerous unrelated scenes." Its French etymological provenance is echoed by theater historians such as Robert Baral and Lewis A. Erenberg who trace its earlier iterations to the cafes and music halls of late nineteenth-century France where performers would make comedic sketches about politicians and their "foibles."[70] Developed as a genre in the United States as early as 1907, the format began to take on a set of formally shared characteristics. As Erenberg notes, "the revue focused impulses toward vitality, presenting them in an organized manner with a common theme." These themes could include such banal experiences as "Girl Behind the Counter" or "Day in the Big City." Through recourse to the thematic, the revues departed from the haphazard variety-show effect of vaudeville by organizing and unifying seemingly disparate music and dance numbers.[71]

Even while revues attempted to stage a banal everyday, they were often in line with certain attitudes formed by a history of bodily spectacle in the Americas. For example, in *The Scene of Harlem Cabaret*, Shane Vogel traces a line from Saidiya Hartman's study of "antebellum amusements" to consider the revue during the Negro vogue at places like the Cotton Club in the late 1920s and 1930s. Vogel writes,

> The revue was an ideal form for . . . offering blackness as spectacle and surface and allowing white audiences a carefully choreographed and controlled access to blackness and black sexuality under terms that were ultimately unthreatening to their own social position or sense of self. As kinetic, spectacle-driven performances, with neither narrative nor psychological realism, there was little need for interpretive work from either the spectator or, sometimes, the performer, who often saw such gigs as nothing more than a job."

Vogel understands the revue as a format that links processes of racialization to a forced interface with spectacle.

I'd like to extend Vogel's analysis to also say that the revue lent itself not only to index a slave past and present, but also became a vehicle to display certain colonial spoils during the climate of American expansionism in the early twentieth century. At the same time that there is this upsurge in revues that trafficked in the display of Afro American bodies, there is also a rise in revues that put the "out there" within US audiences reach. Revues did so not only by bringing those bodies to the stage but also their signifiers. For example, revues were particularly invested in "things Hawaiian" in 1916 and onward. The "Hawaiian craze" was among the revue's earliest imperial tendencies that made the spoils of empire available for novelty and consumption.[72] Take the double billing of the musical "Daniel Boone" and the "Imperial Hawaiian Revue" in 1936. And in the 1926 advertisement Rita Montaner's tour "A Spanish Musicale" is printed just below "A Night in China."

Although the revue format had impulses toward racial, ethnic, and gendered containment, performers perpetually troubled it. For one, we need to think about the power of performers to puncture the conditions of their display. So even though Rita Montaner might have been featured in the complicated racial imaginary of Al Jolson, she was also importing Cuban sonic traditions in her own way. That she performed a number in male blackface in the "Wonder Bar" revue also puts all kind of pressures on New Negro ideology that had its own revue iterations. In addition to the back talk wrought by performers to the revue, counterrevues were staged.[73] As Joseph Roach once wrote, "To perform also means, though often more secretly, to reinvent."[74]

Consider the performance history of Katherine Dunham, whose lifetime of work has raised persistent challenges to the anthologizing of blackness. A student of Melville Herskovits, Dunham was awarded a Rosenwald Fellowship in 1936 and traveled to the Caribbean. This early fieldwork provided the material behind her books such as *Island Possessed* and *Dances of Haiti*. But she also recorded her migration throughout the Caribbean (and other areas off the black Atlantic map) in her actual dancing. Let's imagine her *Tropical Revue*.[75] Here, note the ways she was presented for consumption. As you do so, also imagine the import—the recording—of her migration throughout the Caribbean into her movements. Among the first dancers to incorporate Cuban drummers on performance stages in Paris and New York City, Dunham sneaked in dance forms such as the nineteenth-century Brazilian quadrille and Martiniquean-influenced choreography to her reper-

FIG. 1.7: Promotional handbill for Dunham's "Tropical Revue" featuring a watercolor by Al Hirschfeld. The show premiered at the Martin Beck Theater in New York City in 1943. The revue toured North America before once again returning to New York for a three-week run at the Century Theater in December 1944. © The Al Hirschfeld Foundation. www .AlHirschfeldFoundation.org. Al Hirschfeld is represented by the Margo Feiden Galleries Ltd., New York.

toire.[76] Dunham often traveled to Cuba and is usually attributed as being on of the first dancers to incorporate Cuban drummers on performance stages in Paris and New York City. She also collaborated with the prolific Cuban composer Gilberto Valdéz on her "Rumba Trio," "Son," and "Ñañigo" performances. Imagine all that she was able to sneak in to the performance repertoire of the Americas.

As an anthology, the revue offered physical proximity between its contributors that might not have happened or been possible in the textual. Sometimes proximity meant a shared stage, as was the case with Baker and Montaner in the Palace du Paris. Or a shared headline, as in the "Harlem vs. Havana Revue" staged at Harlem's Apollo Theater in 1935. This early battle of the bands featured Luis Russell (aka Harlem's "Old Man River Orchestra") and the legendary Cuban musician Alberto Socorrás (billed as "Cuba's Duke Ellington"). It makes one generally wonder how these contributors met, rehearsed together, mingled backstage, and got involved in those ways that only theatrical casts can. The closeness could also mean a shared venue. Take, for example, the program line up of Washington D.C.'s Belasco Theater in 1931: Rita Montaner in "The Wonder Bar" was loaded in just one week after "Rhapsody in Black" starring Ethel Waters. It's impossible to know if they were acquainted, or if there were any performative vibes left behind by Waters and picked up by Montaner as she took the stage. And yet, even if their encounter was a near miss, I believe that it is these near misses, brushes, and actual mergers between these touring performers that have provided much of the substances for the recourses made between them.

Even if the gathering together of these performed intersections are impossible to fully locate but possible to imagine, there is a palpable, creative accounting for all of this and more in the singular object of *Cuba Linda*. To my ear, *Cuba Linda* finds correspondence with the musical revue form, that in some ways goes back to its French provenance. It does so literally, given that Rodríguez is part of the Cuban émigré scene that settled in Paris's Montmartre district. The pianist hitched on the route of a centuries-old Cuban path, one initiated by travel on oceanliners not for leisure, but for musical work.[77] This particular population has its roots in cultural industry, one that was absolutely tied to the legacy of revues, whether as fixtures in their more transnational assemblages, to recall my example of Montaner and Baker, or as touring groups of Cuban cultural emissaries who found considerable audiences between the wars. Cubans *in* or *as* revues made a certain kind of space possible for radical, creative work. Today, of course, Paris is one of the gravity spots of the contemporary Cuban metropolitan migration where, with the sounds that they bear, continues to not only shake up Europe, but also keeps jamming with other itinerant bodies brought together by empire. As I move to a brief meditation on final anthological format of this chapter, the album, I would like to pause on all that I've gestured to this far: the dynamics of the revue's framing, its historical stagings, and most important, the performed histories of its radical reoccupation. My turn to liveness—which here I reoccupy as a term for a productive not-being-there, rather than as a term for easy access to bodies on theatrical stages—means a turn to recording.

Album. Record. Record album. The terms come to work interchangeably, or they are combined to reiterate each other. Album's etymological ground is "a blank tablet for entries," where, "the prætor's edicts and other public notices were recorded for public information." Its governmental, bureaucratic function was later altered for keepsakes. Ben Johnson had album as "a book in which foreigners have long been accustomed to insert the autographs of celebrated people."[78] Assuming literacy, it was a place to jot down notable, elevating brushes with the social world. With the development of photographs in the nineteenth century, the album became a repository for developed images. In sacramental book form, the album conspired with "registry" to archive the bodies present during those occasions that are difficult to remember clearly: weddings, a new birth, a life-altering funeral. Signing people in is usually a job given to an older relative who has seen the union and passing on of many, who know the importance of such things.[79]

The phonograph would be the machine used to transfer sound into portable objects—or in Adorno's words, used to make "acoustic photographs." Kittler points out that its partial development by Charles Cros, a Parisian poet, wanted the phonograph "to store beloved voices."[80] For Edison, his contribution to the phonograph emerged from experimental play with the telephone; he sought to do away with the wiring necessary for the telegraph to expand the geographical distances for communiqués.[81] "Record" would become the named verb of this of reproduction, a word that bears the linguistic weight of memory and recall and reckoning. In addition, record would become the named object produced by a phonograph, the disc that made the storage of sound portable.[82] I'll proceed by embracing record and album as interchangeable and not get mired in their distinction. Nor will I digress into a discussion on the evolution of media technologies. Regardless of their format—whether long played or single, downloaded or dubbed—these are objects that hold material scraps of life lived.[83]

As trite and cringeworthy as it feels to say it: a record album tells a story. As Iyer reminds, however, that story does not necessarily follow the typical protocols of narrativity. Although the question—what story is being told here?—can overdetermine our interaction with it, it changes each time we enter the scene of the recording (or the scene of the anthology or revue) whether we want it to or not. The story changes as our life changes. We grow up with albums and they come to mean different things as time passes. Sounds come into focus or move into the periphery in ways that we can't foresee. The record changes with each telling and each listening.

There are temporal warranties to the anthology, the revue, and the record album. The contributions have been edited, gathered, rehearsed, enacted in the live, recorded, and put into one place. They are supposed to save you time. Many and few have done the work for you to now bring your own kind of work to them. And as much as such formats evidently enable quick consumption, it is their abbreviation that encourages us to slow down and take a closer look. Quite often we don't have the choice but to get held up by them, by what they compress and how. In the preceding pages, I have shown the necessary detours I had to take even and especially given the seemingly authoritative directives of the anthology and the revue. I have had to move between the disciplines even and especially given the seemingly authoritative directives of the studies protocol. What the detours suggest is that the mystical qualities are ever present even in the givens of their teleological determinants.

I had to take these detours before arriving at the object this chapter is "really about" because of a dissatisfaction, even an ethical pause with those well-trafficked routes of the studies protocols, be they of race, ethnicity, empire, music. The object of this chapter is not within my or anyone's immediate reach. Nor is it available to prove some thesis. And this is why I began with Yosvany Terry's jazz recourse. Because although Terry makes it quickly, he also slows everything down. Because a detail—in the form of a conversational aside or a record album—can and should hold you up.

I would like to return to that acknowledgment that Rodríguez extends on the back cover of *Cuba Linda*: "Thanks to all of the musicians, also to those who in one way or another contributed to this work." Here Rodríguez puts forth an incorporative, anthological impulse that allows for the infringement of permission, negotiation of restriction, and the possibilities of closures. There is also an instruction for listening here. *Cuba Linda*, as title and theme and entity, openly acknowledges that the process of assembling Cuban performance into a singular entity, be it revue or what have you, is one that is always already unfinished. Its moves through too many musical traditions to mention—marking too many spaces to count—fleshing out too many performers we have loved and lost. It is also an intervention into what I discussed in my introduction as the packaging of discovery that too often wraps Cuban cultural commodities. A packaging, I argue further, that emerges from the anthologizing of things. The album somehow performs a kind of acknowledgment, and then, an *extraordinary bypass* of the touristic enterprise. It is not designed for the desire to know a culture, particularly a culture that might emerge from a former colony, with the kind of knowledge that can be satisfied by a revue, anthology, art exhibit, tour package, and compilation album.

Cuba Linda is a sonic confrontation of the most paralyzing kind: you are flooded with too many places, bodies, and what they bring with them, all at once. It puts the "far beyond" in the sonic foreground. It is no "Day in the Big City" nor walk in the park. It is nothing less than a movement through forced passages and those fierce scraps of love and survival put into music while there. *Cuba Linda* is a participatory, performing anthology that invites you to not only write about it as I've done in the above, but also to write alongside it as I do in the below. I remember a detail from a conversation I had with Roberto "Mamey" Evangelisti, another musical intimate in the Rodríguez buena gente orbit and touring percussionist for *Cuba Linda*.[84] He told me that when they performed together that he could tell if Rodríguez liked what he was hearing when his smile stretched from ear to ear. His musicians played zealously for it. Here is an attempt to make him smile.

VII. MYSTICAL QUALITIES

José Lezama Lima, the great Cuban poet of the baroque, sang it like this: "only what is difficult is stimulating."

"Tumbao a Peruchín"

The preface. The timbales begin when you're not ready. Emilito del Monte stamps down across the plates of skin making sure the edges are sharp with steady pressure from left to right. Such skin signals put companies in grooving line, send signals across fields, move carnaval. This rollout is what you

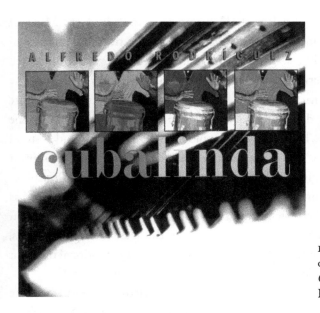

FIG. 1.8: Album cover
of Alfredo Rodríguez's
Cuba Linda. Hannibal
Records, 1997.

hear first; a call that must be kept up with in tone and tempo even when it
ducks into the thicket. It is not a managerial force watch in hand keeping
time. The crisp thudding will soon jump up and out and make other appearances. You're scooped, without enough air, into a tidal wall of horns playing
up and down scales together. It is an opening fanfare that eases the transition
from private to public. Furious and festive at once.

Soon after entering—and yes, there is something of a chivalry to it—
you're led around the room, introduced to everyone. The leader presents the
scene's main players to the outside and sustains the intimacy of the inside.
All those interactions between them before during after the session are here.
We're given names and nicknames and the called sonically abbreviate themselves after they are recognized. El Goyo, Xiomara Larrinaga, Juan Carlos
Gutierrez Mesa all lend their voices to the cues: "¡Jesús florea!" Alemañy's
trumpet—a pelican diving—sails in from the above. He goes first to hang
some urgent holdover from *¡Cubanísimo!* onto the piece.[85] He puts out some
measured outbursts before rolling you into the tidal wall of horns again.
There is an instruction for the rest: provide your signature before the next
surge. Fast.

Another nudge: "¡Toca Perucho!" A start signal to Pedro Justiz Márquez the guitarist who inherited a handle with a generational modification: Peruchín Jr. He picks the strings rather than presses the keys like his father, the great pianist Peruchín royally known as "The Marquis of Ivory." The senior Peruchín spirit not body here Tenderly made jazz recourses before heaven in 1977. He deserves a directive: go and hear how he took his time with "Laura" in 1958, how he made it mambo, gave it humid interludes, stood it up and let it shake.[86] The jazzed séance of the father's spirit and its imprint on the son's hands gives *Cuba Linda's* opening song its name and purpose: "Tumbao A Peruchín." Peruchín is an elder you must care for before and as you go about. The homage is a tumbao—a form of improvisation, a jam off of an established riff. This encounter joins up the ages. Rodríguez tells us, "I've known Pedro since he was a child and it was a very emotional moment for me to play this piece with him, knowing it was for his father."[87]

The roster moves on too quickly. Each acknowledgment must be done quickly and heartfelt. The space for the young folks is left open. Next a clearing is made for Yosvany Terry and his tenored sax. Through his poetic packing I learn part of what's to the skill of making jazz recourses so instant and ordinary. "¡Díselo Terry!" The band's present and not present elders say: what can you do with your sax in this small space in this small time? How can you do it as the rest of us encourage you by chasing you? To ask Terry what it was like to participate in *Cuba Linda* while he drove through Harlem in August was to prompt another version of: what can you do with your sax in this small space in this small time? Remember. As he delivers, we hear one of them shout a proud affirmation "¡Ahora!" Terry's turn sounds like that back-then sensation when a trusted grown up would threaten to tickle you. That thrilled scared laugher stirred by their approach before contact was even made. The horns come in again. They are a relief.

Bolstering Terry's solo is bandleader Alfredo Rodríguez who places himself in the middle of the roundsmaking. The kind of confident move coming from the kind of confident man secure in his ability who would never put himself front and center, or, would most likely feel uneasy if and when he had to. "¡Camina Alfredo!" He takes the instruction literally by taking the piano for a walk through its high and low and major and minor tones. He shows us the strength of its melodic and rhythmic legs. Reveals his Havana childhood encounters with Arthur Rubinstein and Claudio Arrau León. His early New York adulthood with Bill Evans and Patato Valdés who he admired for using the congas like a piano. He was not ambivalent about it in sound or conversation, "the piano is a very delicate instrument."[88] He does not use it to elevate himself, but to teach us respect for the instrument. Nestling himself in the opening number, like this, gives you a feel for his good person.

Without the bass backbone and percussive ribs the song would have nothing on which to hold. "¡Camina araña!" Carlos del Puerto Jr. gently sets down the heavy load. The band hushes and gives him a break. His spider hands spin feather light, a silk carpet for the percussive surround. "¡Tata goza!" Tata Güines's conga interference walks on. As one of conga's kings, his ability to feel time's potential is beyond the capacity of most if not all. He applies his upwards rumbling to the song, the surface and interior come together. "Dave diabla" Dave, devil it out. An action and instruction reserved for the group's resident celestial, a bongosero from the United Kingdom. Funkily precise, Pattman types magpie movements onto the twinned heads. "¡Come Emilio!" We finish what he started, dizzy from the long quick turn around the floor. Fully warmed, he beats out and down hard calling our attention to the work we have yet to do. Emilito del Monte takes it and us to the end.

The preface "Tumbao a Peruchín" does not reveal the album's argument. You are given nothing predictable to make you feel safe, from being lost. You don't know what is coming. But there is something about the group's dynamic—they way they introduce themselves to one another and to us— that you want to be close to, trust. They are called out, introduced, given air. All of the album's musicians are not called out in this preface, but are foreshadowed by the textures that make the song a moveable whole. The last splayed notes sound like a group collapse, as if they jumped off a trampoline together. A cartoon splat. What now.

"Cuba Linda"

For a long time now they leave and don't come back and if they do visit they don't stay. Many were caught in that hard squeeze of the early 1960s. They poured out of the island. Virgilio Martí came to the other island city of New York after fellow rumberos who couldn't get by down there. Not streamlined intellectuals, unshaven bourgeoisie. They lingered with pressed against depended on other dreaded objects of trade before the revolution. They were too much a reminder of those queer black dangerous parts: dirty cabarets, decadent nightclubs, unwanted street corners, and unseen solares.[89] It was never easy for them. Still isn't. But music there here always happens. Virgilio Martí—whose name bears the lyricism of poets from the earliest and latest empires—turned scores into guaguancós, those bare percussive boned songs where singers flutter through the drummed beats. Sacred secular dance songs made for roostered and other get-down movements. Songs for the transitions between dropping and rising up. For Martí, emerging standards were among the most pliable; he made a rumba out of Brasilian Jorge Ben's samba "Mas Que Nada" and transformed the Peruvian waltz "Todos Vuelven" into a dance floor for fast rumberic feet.[90]

Martí wrote the guaguancó "Cuba Linda" from the New York of the 1970s. He was not only rumba there but also a link to other islands to help turn out what they call salsa. We don't and can't know the sad gulfs of his exile, but we do know that he never returned before his death in 1995. He is one of the many that stay forgotten there. A year later, Alfredo Rodríguez made him return—in spirit material—by recording his song on his natal island. He took what was left behind of that subtle conversational buttery voice to engrave an epitaph. This album. The song needed to go second after Peruchín's tumbao because joy needs a place in a dirge. The tumbao allowed Martí that euphoric step off the plane into tropical lungs, the best and hardest part. Rodríguez opens the piece by keeping his melody spare and extends a few musical lines that are our collective sincerely felt melodrama. He presses the keys like smoothing bandages on skin, in a curative way, on that which gave Martí that faraway look, that which kept him mad enough to refuse to go home. Rodríguez and piano then temporarily step aside to allow for the guaguancó takeover. A two/three clave cracks light into the anguish.

Gregorio "El Goyo" Hernandez never left it. Only occasionally as a Cuban emissary for rumba with the others who can and must support self and family and nation. María del Carmen Mestas got this kernel from him,

Al dedicarme al canto no paré más, le fui cogiendo tremendo amor y participaba en cuanta fiesta podía; esto es como una fiebre que se apodera de ti y no hay pastilla que te la quite [After I started singing I couldn't stop. I had fallen in love with it and was going to every single party I could. It's like a fever that takes over you and there's no pill that can cure it.]⁹¹

With his first sung notes of "Cuba Linda," we do not meet Martí's timbre, but a barreled roomy voice with a heartening scratch at its edges. The voices here—the live and dead—eclipse perfectly. El Goyo gets at the wet of Martí's sad gulfs that we don't and can't know. Even as he always stayed. He funnels all this voluminous matter into a microphone. Before the stanzas, an invocation and a plea: "¡Güiro!" And then:

Cuba linda de mi vida	Pretty Cuba, love of my life
Cuba linda siempre te recordaré	Pretty Cuba, I will always remember you
Cuba linda, Cuba hermosa	Pretty Cuba, beautiful Cuba
Cuba linda siempre te recordaré	Pretty Cuba, I will always remember you
Yo quisiera verte ahora	I would love to see you now
como la primera vez	Like the first time I saw you
Cuba linda, Cuba hermosa	Pretty Cuba, beautiful Cuba
Cuba linda siempre te recordaré	Pretty Cuba, I will always remember you
Cuba linda, Cuba hermosa	Pretty Cuba, beautiful Cuba

El Goyo drags open the last word of each line and leaves plenty of slack for other voices to tighten after him. When they do, they rustle the pores in that way that only choirs can. They make perfect lyrical copy of El Goyo's call. They are not in the same place as him or even one another, but they dwell in complimentary notes together. So many hours of rehearsal.

El Goyo then delivers the gut hurt lament:

Te recordaremos, te recordaremos	We'll remember you, we'll remember you

> Cuando llegamos a La Habana   When we get to Havana
> nuestra tierra besaremos,   we'll kiss the land

Martí wrote it from the faraway. The song sung and recorded from Cuba says: we need you here. I also hear: we'll impress your feet into the sand, you are already back. The return is given comfort, made unscary. Hands are held. The song-in-return does not refuse Cuba of the here and now even as it was written in longing. Rodríguez's arranging hands puts the song in contact with the port's actual unfathomable antiquity contemporaneity futurity together. When the chorus comes in to repeat El Goyo's last summons, the piano and bass and Alemañy's trumpet come too. They make space for the hilarity and gravity of group dance. The coupled might take fast turns they're too drunk for. The chorus lifts our arms up to the sky in a motion we do to give them company up there. Feel our hands under your feet.

Rodríguez takes a needed solo to mourn a friend whose eulogy can't be well-tempered. It has its surprise eruptive moments—the reenactment of many lives lived in music's scales. The tightly ordered confusion inspires an epiphany. Martí is "Cuba Linda" is *Cuba Linda* is Cuba, which is also, partly, our collective sincerely felt melodrama. What are we going to do. Rodríguez and El Goyo reserve the final stanza to budge this hopeless and helpless stasis. El Goyo "Si tu quieres gozar, ven a Cuba guarachar."[92] (If you want to have a good time, come to Cuba and get down.) Cuban humor with its throwing up the hands is a blessing even if it can cause emphatic harm. Here it is restorative not fracture or corrective. The funny impatience makes this spare but full instruction possible. I went.

"Cuando vuelva a tu lado"

It can't continue in those gulfs, in that way. And this is when *Cuba Linda* offers a working intermezzo. It extends the elegance of the guaguancó by lengthening and slowing down the notes. The violin and flute become the song's featured performers. The composer María Grever, a prodigy that stayed prolific even while living on the road, shifts us, delicately, into another melody of return. Her birth and death happened in different places, born in Mexico's León, Guanajuato 1885 and died in New York City's Manhattan in 1951.[93] She saw Europe as a child with her family, made lonely homes in other outposts as a young diplomat's wife, and became a part of everywhere else while on that revue circuit. She wrote more than eight hundred songs and many scores, sang and or directed and or taught them all. As a teenager she absorbed musical advice from the Hungarian composer Franz Lehár.[94] She performed in New York's Princess Theater in 1919. She made "novel" revues in 1927's Little Theater.[95] She made Mexico a musical theme.[96] She dealt too often with the assault on her compositional grace. Of her revue at 1939's Guild Theater they said, "Some of the music was of a type not to be taken too seriously."[97]

Any archeology of María Grever needs a book of its own. Heard here she is one "who in one way or another contributed to this work." Grever as revue as Mexican as composer as New Yorker as the compositional primary text through whom so many have passed has "in one way or another contributed to this work," this *Cuba Linda*, this book, that now asks that we remind ourselves of her "Cuando Vuelva a Tu Lado" (otherwise known as What a Difference a Day Makes). It is a song that we know by so many. Nat King Cole, Esther Phillips, Aretha Franklin, Coleman Hawkins, Gato Barbieri, Pepe Delgado, Django Reinhardt, Libertad Lamarque, Sarah Vaughn, and a beautifully overwhelmed Olga Guillot. In Rodríguez's version we don't get vocals. It is an invitation for us to pick whomever's grain we recall with his version. I can't help it if for me it's Dinah Washington who made a storm clearing of this song in the up north of 1959 while the down south was going about another kind of revolution, just a few years after her singing of Bessie Smith. She made a day-after voice sound clear after a long night of work. She altered Grever's bolero—a form for that last dance before during after love eros separation—into a tinged torch song.

Rodríguez turns Grever's bolero into a danzón-cha. Talk about capacious. Danzón has admitted so many outsides and far beyonds, its baroque structure has allowed baroque citations even the "Well-Tempered Clavier."[98] The crystalline violin threads spun by Dagoberto and Lazarito González keep it sugary. Other admittances: bodies have many options in the danzón even as it is tightly controlled. You walk in to be presented, to present one another to the out there. This can lead you from tight together turns to an open promenade across the floor. Show the way your skirt can swish move its material in a watery way. Finish with an elegant flourish.

Standards resurrect their multiple coverages. Rodríguez's setting of "Cuando Vuelva a Tu Lado" between the neighbors "Cuba Linda" and the "Canto de Palo" to follow, makes Grever take tradition to its intended provenence. For Adorno, tradition "recalls the continu of generations. What is handed down by one member to another, even the heritage of handicraft. The image of handing down expresses physical proximity, immediacy—one hand should receive from another."[99]

"Canto de Palo"

Rodríguez's piano is both clear adhesive and wet drywall and urges physical proximity and immediacy between and inside the songs. A structure both shanty and solid. In "Canto de Palo," the planet that arrives after Grever's, he tunes up El Goyo and his chorus, Xiomara Larrinaga and Mario Dreque "Chabalonga." El Goyo nudges them to attention—an invocation that is also a roll call—so they may begin an offering to Severina, the priestess of the elderly in the Palo Monte religion.[100]

Rodríguez puts the piano and vocal offerings alongside the congas, bass, and other percussives. Now Yosvany Terry channels his saxophonic impulses to the cowbell that hallowed brass medium that suggests a wayward animal and most endearing metronome. He finds a scale in it swiftly taps a stick from its hips to its shoulders and back again. He accompanies his father Eladio Terry González who long ago won the deserved title "Don Pancho" because he plays the chekeré like no other.[101] The chekeré is a bead-covered gourd. Don Pancho always plays it while wearing a wide-brimmed straw hat. To give it shade? The mechanics of its handling are tender and impossible. He cradles it, bumps its underside, makes an orchestra of it as he turns it a few unperceivable degrees at a time. The vessel makes the beads vibrate and the beads make the vessel vibrate. It is an up-tempo rattlesnake. The trout mouth of the chekeré is also the instruments eye, a cyclops that forges the music onward.[102]

I met Don Pancho when I had too much energy and almost melted the screen door of the house in the neighborhood my dad was raised and that I was not supposed to be in without him. I woke him up from his nap. His lovely wife put the fan on my face and gave me some cold juice. As he rubbed his eyes, I tried too quickly to ask him questions. He asked for a moment to collect himself, and for me to collect myself before we began. He taught me the importance of a deep breath, especially in the presence of someone or something that you admire so much, before that someone or something wants to be engaged. I took two years of deep breaths before I could write him write this *Cuba Linda*.

"Tumba, Mi Tumba"

Which also meant breathing to better hear revolution. Not the one they market and mismanage and use suspiciously to clamp down and stop those things that made and make it beautiful and extragalactical and dangerous. I mean those always and forever rumbles that have long helped to cast off and out, to get from here to there, in the catastrophic beginnings of that mass that became known as the New World. Rodríguez opens us up to an inaugural rumble: Haiti's uprising in 1791. Its echoes brought populations of slaves and their owners to the Cuban coast. Slaves formed Sociedades de Tumba Francesa and made magic out of their owners' easily corruptible minuets. They put drums in the parlors and shook them hard while keeping its stem glasses unshattered. They kept colorful skirts in perfect semicircles as they curtsied and turned in elegant line to the drumwaves. There are two societies that still exist by some official's record, there are likely many more.

The Tumba Francesa La Caridad de Oriente is from Santiago de Cuba, a region that Roberto Faz once sung as the "cuna de Florida" (the cradle of Florida). They still stretch the skins between Cuba and Haiti and keep moving after earthquakes. They maintain part of what Leonardo Acosta called the "'primary magma' of Afro-Caribbean polyrhythmic framework or foundation."[103] Rodríguez makes us read all of this, feel Saint Domingue's blood-soaked ground, before the flutes, bulá, and bass drums begin to move the dancers. I found out from Miké Charroppin that the woman listed as composer, G. Yoya Venet Danger, was the godmother of the tumba francesa. She gave dozens of original melodies to Rodríguez to make versions of. She died before she could hear his realization of "Tumba mi tumba."

"Merceditas, yá me voy"

Because its progression is the stuff of philosophy, I became curious as to the arranger of the next song, "Merceditas, yá me voy." Arranging is that

FIG. 1.9: Michelle "Miké" Charroppin with Patato Valdés, 1994.
Courtesy of Michelle Charroppin.

most vital and overlooked musical labor of love, musical women's work. The
song's assembly is among the most powerful putting togethers of past, present, and future. I learned through an online review by Maya Roy that the
arranger, Miké Charroppin, was also Rodríguez's wife. The liner notes credit
her with the artistic and musical concept of the album. Her idea! I found her
after hours of virtual searching when I stumbled upon a comment she made
in an online forum thanking everyone for their sympathies after he died. I
located an Alfredo Rodríguez in Paris's white pages and the coordinates for
where they lived and loved together. She had to move out after. Too much. I
couldn't locate a Miké, but a Michelle Charroppin. I called this number not
expecting an answer. She answered gruff and properly suspicious. Many have
used her for access to his ghost. I choked on my words and only managed to
blurt out: creo que "Merceditas, yá me voy" y "Para Francia flores" son dos
de las canciones mas importantes en la historia de la música cubana.

She agreed to meet me in Montmartre. Getting there I thought of Rita
Montaner and Josephine Baker. And Graciela and Langston Hughes and Florence Jones. And so many others who had lived there to congregate,breathe,
make music, read things. I retraced their footsteps after years of following

their sound steps. I met her in front of the easel she used to display her paintings in the Place du Tetre. Behind her easel I saw pictures of Rodríguez gently holding their horse's muzzle (his name is Ramses) in his hands. His head is tilted downward as if to offer Ramses a secret. She can look at him all day like that as she waits to sell one off. We walked through the tourist throngs to eat together. She's a priestess of the neighborhood that still gives a break to its working artists. We only got charged by how much of the bottle of wine we actually drank. They kindly put the chocolates I bought her in the refrigerator so they wouldn't melt.

Mercedes Martín, the song's homage, was Miké's closest friend and a painter who had her easel set up on the other side of the square. Even though I had always heard that song as a sung memoriam to Merceditas Valdés who died the same year of the album's release. Miké lost the Mercedes of the song too early just before they went to the island to record *Cuba Linda*. And that piano bit he plays quickly was intended to remind everyone of her footsteps when she would climb up the stairs to the square, right under their window. I found out some of the other unspoken loss in the album. Rodríguez lost his little brother three months before they went into the studio.

The song begins with El Goyo invoking Obatalá, the elder orisha of disability and imperfection, morality, the deity who brought mankind into being. The chorus once again follows him and the walking drums. They stop. Rodríguez offers an invocation of his own: a piano figure that the rest of the instruments will follow. Three chords three times each upward. The rest boldly enter the scene at the same time, in their own way. It doesn't make sense until the violin strings start to pull it all together. It is a ball of fire and smoke, the sound of the shadows inside your head. A break. And then it swings so ferociously releasing those muscle knots of grief, the stomach that has remained clenched and hungry since their passing.

| Para ti va mi inspiración | I give you my inspiration |
| Con todito mi corazón | with all my heart |

They return to this chorus throughout as El Goyo improvises about and celebrates the life of a woman he did not know. We get to know a feel for the magic of Mercedes as she is put into song on an island far westward from the Place du Tetre. Alfredo takes a solo and plays his and other losses. It asks why them and why now? It returns to son swing before speeding up at the end. It mimics spirits passing upward and we get to imagine them turning around to wave and smile. The way Charroppin put it all together—the invocation, piano outline, the inevitable furious swing and chorus lament, his solo, their fast ascension—makes you understand how she makes things possible for others even as she harbors her own body aches. She showed me pictures of her Martinican mother his Chinese mother his baby pictures.

"Drume Negrita"

We are given another standard intermezzo when it feels like moving on would mean taking to one's bed. "Drume Negrita," a lullaby composed by Eliseo Grenet, has been done over the decades by Merceditas Valdés, Xiomara Alfaro, and a most affectionate Bola de Nieve. Grenet was the composer who would write the songs that Rita Montaner would take around the world. Mama Inés. Espabílate. They were part of what made her mobile. His compositions engraved those routes of the revue circuit between, during, and after the great wars. They carried the revue's performers and gave them songs to make parts of themselves.

Those early records that made those first global rotations were emissaries of Grenet's larger repertoire. And he was a nascent part of the jazz scene that formed simultaneously in Havana and New York. Leonardo Acosta reminds us that in 1925, Grenet formed a jazz band that played at the Jockey Club and the Montmartre Cabaret (the island other).[104] In 1934, he played piano for a jazz group organized by the trumpet player Julio Cueva.[105] And in 1930, at a sold-out performance at New York's Palace Theater, his "Mama Inés" was played by Don Azpiazu's orchestra, the first time a full section of Afro-Cuban percussive instruments ever played on a formal stage before the American public.[106] "Mama Inés" was no doubt in the ear echo of Francis Picabia as he made a graphic of her in paint.

Rodríguez's version is calming. It slow rolls you should you need an embrace or something soft to put against your cheek. The song is transitional—it gives your bones a chance to settle back into their joints, the reflex to a calm state. El Goyo easily alters his register to accommodate Grenet's tip-of-the-tongue standard.

"Para Francia Flores y Para Cuba También"

The final song of *Cuba Linda* is a powerful reminder that we need to deserve and defer what the album makes possible. It reminds that listening to history requires a willingness to give phenomena time to reveal itself in small ways. This willingness is a long rehearsal between those rare intervals when it can flood you all at once. This final song begins by taking you through this kind of practice. It lets you hear its parts, gets you familiar with the details of its whole. It slowly eases into Cuba's past present. That is, until the song resists its own order and reveals an instant portal into history's future extension. Its trail is the highest modern, science fiction, and spaceship transport to possibility. By its amputated end, the song floods. It brings the detailed register of this book to its knees: "Para Francia Flores y Para Cuba Tambien" is one moment among many in the history of Cuban music where you can hear it all at once.

Charroppin later told me that the song was necessarily improvised. A condition of their loss of Alfredo's little brother, which meant the loss of compositional time before entering the studio. I've been living in this first take for years.

Her arranging hands provided the song's spine but also orchestrated their coming together. From the studio in Santiago, she instructed Alfredo to begin playing, anything. Their dear friend Luis Mariano "Nene" Garbey was to vocally follow what he left behind. And ever slowly, as if it was an actual comparsa rising over that hill on the horizon, the Conga de Los Hoyos would enter the scene and make carnaval. The Conga de Los Hoyos is a group of musicians from downtown Santiago de Cuba. With an ocean of percussive noises, they provide structures for the winding lines of dancers during carnaval. Congas include bells and drums and a shrieking whistle. The instruments are often made from other things: scraps of metal that fell out of cars, other hollowed-shaped findings that made good noise. They are played all at once, a thundering order punctuated by the corneta china, the Chinese cornet, an object soaked up by the conga after they arrived in the nineteenth century. To hear a conga is to hear an approaching battalion, an invocation, third, and fourth, and fifth comings. Makes you want to be a part of its bold swinging shuffling forward.

Programming is another kind of women's work. Miké Charroppin was behind the musical introductions made here. It was she who first brought La Conga de Los Hoyos to Paris in the 1980s. For some of the musicians, that appearance was their first time outside of Santiago. How did she get the resources together, organize meals, how did she get them to the airport, and tend the grounds for their first steps in that other cultural capital? And it is said that this is the first song in which La Conga de Los Hoyos were recorded inside a studio. And the first time the conga and piano came together in song. They joked about hitching Alfredo and his piano to a wagon come spring in Cuba's Oriente.

Alfredo played. Who knows how the melody came to him how melodies come to them. It is a strong epic beginning with hands spread octaves wide. On the piano's upper reaches, he makes out the song's figure and then shows how it can be altered. He taps the high notes to cue the singer. Those introductory taps say: you can take it where you want to. With scorched larynx Nene sings:

Estando yo en mi casa/yo recibí un telegrama	I was at home when I got a telegram
Estando yo en mi casa/yo recibí un telegrama	I was at home when I got a telegram
que en el foco de los Hoyos	In the center of Los Hoyos
una rumba se formaba	A rumba was born
Francia yo voy a cantarte	France I am going to sing to you
y que me importa tu lujo	and I don't care about your opulence
Francia yo voy a cantarte	France I am going to sing to you
Y un cariñoso saludo	and send you a loving greeting
que yo mantengo en mi escudo	that I keep on my shield
Y mi música y mi arte	And my music and my art
Francia yo voy a cantarte	France I am going to sing you
mientras mi alma se agite	While my soul is beating
A Miké y a Dominique	To Miké and to Dominique
Cantando me desespero	I am overwhelmed as I sing
un Saludo para Alfredo	A greeting to Alfredo.

As Garbey sings, Rodríguez accompanies. They finish each other's thoughts, give the other space, come together when they need to. It is a most ethical call and response, a model for how to be and work with each other. Garbey's is a wise elder statesman voice, aware of its swaying and swinging ability. It is strong and vulnerable, unhesitant, and makes you shiver. An emphatic lump forms in your throat. Miké told me it was the first time he sang into a microphone and that he started to weep soon after he began. Consider the improvisatory dimensions: melody and lyrics, tears and technology, all while also setting the song for the claves chorus and others to follow.

| Para Francia flores (y para Cuba también) | Some flowers for France (and for Cuba too) |

Bouquets are laid at the foot of island stages. Stems are gently tossed from balconies. Throughout the choral repetition of the line, Nene continues to make things up as they go along. He lets others join in and take center stage. His vocal becomes yet another instrument in the sea of things.

A foreshadowing bell begins to ring down in the square. It is a church bell moved to bring you gently out of the half sleep at dawn. It also signals a funeral or wedding procession or the passing of a saint on a raised platform held up by believers. You are folded into whatever mass it is moving. And then there is no palpable directive but suddenly, intuitively together, drums beat out a hard sputtering start. The bells are alarms now. Rodríguez plays the keys as if an ordinary part of the procession — even if it is not now or ever was an actual and portable accompaniment. We have fun alongside him as he figures out — in real time — how to make it all fit. It is a fast gallup of noise. Kamau Brathwaite says that the hurricane does not roar in pentameter. It instead roars like this. It is a skyscraper and plantation and seaside. It is a street in Santiago and New York and New Orleans. It is a concert hall, cabaret, sacred room in someone's house. The quake is a good time and battle cry, an ideal inebriation and threatening armor. It makes you want to follow it, be a part of its tail. Imagine them together in that studio channeling all this through tiny microphone planets. Miké said that it went on like this for another ten minutes, but the producer cut it short. He faded out the track for its inability to fit in time. They went

FIG. 1.10: Alfredo
Rodríguez at
the piano, 2004.
Photographed by
Michelle Charroppin.
Courtesy of Michelle
Charroppin.

far beyond the capacity of the machines of recording, time, space, history, these pages, Cuba, *Cuba Linda*. Listen to its how it continues, like this, the kite-like phrasing of the corneta china flying up and away, the bellows of the drums, Alfredo's rolling rumbling, the steady bell clanging calling in from everywhere, those who in one way or another contributed to this work. . . .

Chapter Two

"Una Escuela Rara"
The Graciela School

After all, the subversive intellectual came under false pretenses, with bad
documents, out of love. Her labor is as necessary as it is unwelcome. The
university needs what she bears but cannot bear what she brings. And
on top of all that, she disappears. She disappears into the underground,
the downlow lowdown maroon community of the university, into the
Undercommons of the Enlightenment, where the work gets done, where
the work gets subverted, where the revolution is still black, still strong.[1]
—Fred Moten and Stefano Harney,
  "The University and the Undercommons: Seven Theses"

I am going to get involved with a few subversive intellectuals and some of
the labor they have left behind. I do so not to render visible those supposedly
invisible from the record—by which I mean official knowledge, and later, an
actual material object. The subversive intellectual might disappear from representation but moves into other temporary locations. Such shanties do not
get the privilege of permanency, but their foundations are always detectable.
Moten and Harney push us to understand her disappearance as strategic,
as flight that is not only forced but also chosen. She is a runaway who does
not want to disclose her whereabouts so that she can become part of your

epistemological real. And while she vanishes, her acts cannot be erased. Her work is somehow and somewhere always recorded, maintained, and circulated even when left on a dusty bookshelf or in that free crate of records left over from a garage sale. It is left behind in details, not in and as monoliths of scholarship or prized objects of musical collection. Her escape from the sanctioned places of scholarly capital and value demands that you, always the student, be schooled in a different kind of way.

I begin with the university in part to recap music's place in it. Music is often relegated to anecdote, used to fluff one's prose, or made to propel a decided-upon argument. When it is taken up as a primary object of inquiry, it can be made alien and technical. Some attempt to make property of it. Such are the consequences of abandoning it to experts, of leaving it at the door of the conservatory in the middle of the night. And yet, for all the attempts made for its quarantine, it does not stay put. Because of music's capacity to be many places at once, it walks through the academy's walls. Josh Kun writes, "music does not respect places precisely because it is capable of inhabiting them while moving across them—of arriving while leaving."[2] Like a stealth party guest that can be at once there and not there, any space is irrecoverably altered by music's traverse. Even if it is undetected and erased, corralled and controlled, music turns up in locations, disciplines, and archives without a proper visa. Music has always been a nurturing, shifting ground for the undercommons of the Enlightenment.

I begin with the academy, in this way, not so I can make metaphor of Moten and Harney's undercommons, but to humbly dwell in its generous shanty structure. The undercommons and subversive intellectuals featured in this chapter have left behind a few critical details to reconsider the relationship between gender, pedagogy, and music. When listening to Cuba, such a relationship is a tangible one. For example, La Lupe and Celia Cruz are two of many who fled to performance after being trained as schoolteachers. Even Ignacio Villa (Bola de Nieve) was set to be a professor of mathematics before, "his love and unique talent for singing his native music 'snowballed' him away from pedagogy."[3] This anonymous writer of sleeve notes might have confused such a career shift with an abandonment of pedagogy. I like to think that Villa's instructional skill instead changed shape and sound.[4] His teacher's training was long in the making, his methods a result of a lifetime of experimentation. As a child, Villa would peek through the bars of a doctor's mansion to hear and witness one of its residents playing Chopin.[5] Consider too all those unsung music teachers who might not have had the luxury of a proper education but are still called upon to produce one for others. Remember all those lessons given in private homes, of making music into bread and butter. All of these teachers signal a tradition of musical seepage out from institutional spaces. Their contributions demand to be thought of beyond the finitude of the recovery project.

One cannot rely upon nor even ask for some prescriptive that will enable passage into the downlow lowdown. There are no prescriptives because the subversive intellectual leaves none behind. Which is not to say that there are no house rules. Openness seems to be inarguable condition. One has to go beyond reliable critical locations, listen a little harder, feel comfortable with flexible theories. A willingness to become trained in their methods of insurgence, escape, and risk taking is required. To proceed with such methodological vulnerability requires a bit of patience and a lot of trust, especially when confronted with the broken lines of their movements or their mercurial participation in your project. No matter what or who you encounter, you can (and must) return to their work, their music.

I'm going to bring a musician into focus who emerges through a variety of schools—so many, in fact, that she is not easily identifiable to any one of them. By becoming involved with a musician like Graciela Pérez, known as Graciela, or the "First Lady of Latin Jazz," I assumed that any careful attempt to think through her contributions was going to hurt a little bit. I'm grateful that such work was and continues to be difficult. Some of the difficulty has had to do with becoming familiar with the multiple creative geographies she has occupied; but more so for the appearances and disappearances she makes in archives, her necessary and unwelcome influence, and especially, the effect of getting to know her. What follows is an attempt to reflect on some of the ways she has documented herself even as she has been forced and chosen to disappear from familiar timelines about popular music. Such documentation is left behind in the music itself, but also appears in other forms such as her oral histories and in face-to-face meetings.

To attend to such proceedings is daunting for its historical expansiveness, for Graciela had been musically active for almost eight decades. I can only pause on a few moments from her extraordinary oeuvre, including the undercommons quality of her early career in Cuba, a few of her global performance migrations, and finally, her presence in the New York scene starting from the mid-1940s. Even through this select shortlist of stops on her performance itinerary, Graciela leaves behind a marsh of material to get lost in. Because of the voluminous luminosity of her life and experiences, she demands that we reflect on her contributions in details and in a detailed register. She encourages us to actively and alternately select, listen closely to, and get lost in the universes she leaves behind in her songs and stories. She asks us to listen to her songs as stories and to her stories as songs.

Subversive intellectuals do not, cannot work alone. I'd like to loop back to the university so that I can set up a contextual frame for Graciela's early career and to give some sense of the Cuba in which she came of age. Such a return takes me to an actual university and to a specific undercommons. Permit me to venture back several decades, 23 degrees north and 82 degrees west (to be confused with a Stan Kenton song by the same name). In September 1930 the doors of the University of Havana were slammed shut by the repressive Machado dictatorship (1925–1933). Nurtured by the aftermath of Spanish colonialism and corrupt policies developed through decades-long US political and financial domination of Cuba, President Gerardo Machado—known as the "President of a Thousand Murders"—first emerged as a democratically elected leader. Later, he would come to be known as the front man for one of the more violent and repressive eras in Cuban history.

Among the many of Machado's notable acts was his changing the constitution to extend his stay in power. A highly organized secret police, called the Sección de Expertos (literally, the Expert Section) was enlisted as his brute-force cosigner. This action was to further safeguard the political and economic elite, ensure the continued US dominance of Cuba's economy, and attempt to control the population through corruption, violence, and fraud.[6] But the regime could not operate in isolation from its surroundings. For all of Machado's seeming control, Cuba was at the mercy of global market forces, devastated by the Great Depression and the consequential fallout from its neighbor to the north. With hunger came action. The desperate and mobilized masses began to push back against the regime through mass labor strikes in both the rural and urban sectors. This mass resistance was not due to the violence of Machado's regime alone—to attribute such activity solely as a response to state violence does not account for the larger coming of age of a post-independence Cuba. Instead, imagine the political cultures—the frustration, opportunism, and disappointment—developed by those born after Spanish colonial control and who came of age in the era of American occupation. As Louis Pérez argues, "By the 1920s the first republican-born generation of Cubans had reached political maturity and found the republic wanting."[7]

The island on the whole was at the brink of revolution. The University of Havana had become a hotbed for oppositional thought and was one of the government's most uppity targets. Machado closed the university in September of 1930 as a disciplinary response to the early rumblings of protest shaped within the walls of its student lounges.[8] Shutting it down, it seemed, was the best method of containment of dissent for the upcoming November elections. Or so he thought. The evident subtext behind the university's lockdown was to render the student body, their faculty, and many of the administration as one guilty unit regardless of participation or ideological particularity.[9] To be in the academy made you an automatic accessory to criminal activity. Participation in marches made one a target for either arrest or murder, as in the infamous assassination of a student named Rafael Trejo and the arrest of almost 50 students during a demonstration.[10] The university's closure did not, in fact, foreclose spaces of learning. As Carleton Beale's curious first-person account of the era announced, "A generation of Cuba's youth is growing up in darkness, schooled only in violence and murder."[11] To be outside of the academy also made one implicitly criminal, schooled in the hard knocks of darkness.

Nevertheless, Cuban techniques of adaptation were mobilized as a response to the material and psychic effects produced by the closure. These long-forged adaptive traditions create a temporary outside from an immediate and binding set of conditions. These techniques often revise an object's given form thereby revamping its intended use. A few examples of these adaptive techniques are always worth repeating, especially as they doubly help me to get to music: the switch up of wood for claves, a gourd for a güiro, Santa Bárbara for the chorus "Que Viva Changó" pig fat for

"Manteca," the six-stringed guitar to the three double steel-stringed tres. Such adaptive techniques are as musical as they are migratory: the kind of improvisation that can reconstruct a score by Ernesto Lecuona with a tropically rotten piano and/or turn a '57 Chevy pickup into a full-functioning boat.[12]

The 1930 closure of the University of Havana would contribute to the sorts of conditions that enabled the revamping of a student's intended use. For many students, a closed university simply meant a switch in venue, and many took their struggle directly to the streets of Havana and engaged in urban guerrilla warfare.[13] For a privileged few, education would commence by way of study abroad, a mere oceanliner trip away. For others, there was commercial potential. In Cuba, this can often mean the move to music in order to survive. It was at this moment that a woman named Concepcíon "Cuchito" Castro, a dental student, slipped out from a back door of the University of Havana. After her exit, Castro conceived an all women musical group with the help of her seven sisters in 1932.[14]

Castro's group was baptized the Orquesta Anacaona, named after a Taíno queen who lived on the island of Quisqueya (Hispañola) and was most famous for her poetry, songs and areitos.[15] The sound of the slamming doors of the University of Havana somehow resonated with the Castro sisters. Four centuries prior, Queen Anacaona's attempted overtures at diplomacy in the face of a rapidly approaching genocide were answered by a Spaniard's noose in 1503. Queen Anacaona's legacy was and is familiar as a resistant trope in the archipelago. Some might understand the recovery of Queen Anacaona as part of a problematic form of Taíno revivalism, one that privileges a fundamentally native past at the disavowal of African ancestry. Or, some will invoke Anacaona as a way to feminize a Caribbean landscape and too easily reproduce the discourses of a metaphorical (versus actual) rape. However, Queen Anacaona, as I understand her in the space of Quisqueya, could perhaps be understood as the instructive and insurgent ground under Toussaint Louverture some three hundred years later, what Edwidge Danticat has requiemed as, "the first flow of blood on a land that has seen much more than its share."[16]

The formation of Orquesta Anacaona was set into motion after its founder was purged from the university. The traces of her covert musicianship were thus always there, under the very surface of the academy, even in the seemingly sterile rooms of its dental school. But it was not musicianship alone that emerged. The naming of Castro's group in itself entails a defiant gesture, a homage to an ancestral past from a land often locked away in the more anxious quarters of Cuba's national (and racial) conception of itself.[17] The assembly of young women musicians, as I will discuss below, was (and often still is) in itself a defiant act against the proper, official comportment required by gender, racial identification, nation, and institutional belonging of the times.

This defiance was further facilitated by sheer necessity. The Castro family patriarch, Matías, was a bodegüero (grocer) who had lost virtually everything on Black Friday and was eventually persuaded to grant his permission.[18] These assemblages became common and the Orquesta Anacaona was one of the many all-women groups of the era whose numbers were never again reached in Cuba.[19] Diverse in repertoire, composition, and outfits, the Orquesta became a mobile musical undercommons that played in outdoor cafés and toured extensively around the Caribbean, United States, and Europe in the late 1930s. Although they might have been consumed as novelty, they were still doing deep musical work. They were heralded for their considerable fluency in a variety of genres: son, guaracha, rumba, and bolero. They also adopted jazz compositions like foxtrots and swing numbers to keep a competitive edge for business with North American tourists.[20] While recordings of the original group are scarce, a variety of photos of the women exists, lined up (according to height) in smart tailored suit sets, hula skirts, and even full Mexican señorita regalia.[21]

The members of the Orquesta Anacaona have contributed a vital part of musical labor in the larger texture of Cuban *and* Afro-American music—by their conditions of formation and (rather obviously) as material part of this ongoing musical conversation by their very presence, location, and history. Considering their dates of formation (1932) and onward, they belong and have contributed to that cavalcade of jazz traditions assembled in and between the United States and the island from the turn of the century to the present.[22] They have picked up the musical conversations set into motion by the contact made between Afro-American and Cuban soldiers during Cuba's independence wars at the end of the nineteenth century. With a few

FIG. 2.1: The Orquesta Anacaona at the Havana Madrid in New York City, circa 1937. Courtesy of the personal archives of Ingrid Kummels, author of *Queens of Havana* and niece of Alicia Castro.

notable exceptions the group is absented from even the most comprehensive of musical bibliographies—a glaring omission, as the members of the Orquesta Anacaona were regular players at the venues, cabarets, and performance spaces (both mainstream and underground) where the most heralded of these musical convergences took place. These venues include the Havana-Madrid and La Conga clubs in New York and Les Ambassadeurs on the Champs-Elysées in Paris.

The original Orquesta Anacaona had a revolving door policy in terms of membership. It has been a musical school that launched musicians such as the vocalists Omara and Haydée Portuondo and Teresa Carturla. A few cameo appearances by male musicians also made their way into some performances such as the presence of trumpeter Felix Chappotín, the Cuban Louis Armstrong, on a radio program in 1932. Members had been continually replaced by new voices as the older move on, due to offers with other musicians, death, exile, retirement, and infighting. This versioning of the original group has provided its own intergenerational flourish, adapting to context with each grouping. The existing members of the Castro sisters performed in Cuba until 1989, performing in theaters, urban high schools, and rural secondary schools.[23] Even as it proceeds without the Castro sisters, the Orquesta Anacaona has had stunning career longevity. As of the writing of this chapter, the orquesta is a slickly produced ensemble that plays salsa and reggaeton-inflected timba. Their 2009 song "Mentiras" (Lies) is a swinging and meaty soundtrack for those who have been done wrong by another. While Orquesta Anacaona's music (both then and now) has been described in tourist friendly, cute, and gimmicky terms, I cannot help but to think of the actual Queen Anacaona's last gasp of air as she caught a final glimpse of her people and land in this world before she was forced into the next.

If, as I insinuate, the founding members of the Orquesta Anacaona are subversive intellectuals, their labor was and is both necessary and unbearable to the masculinist thrust of musical timelines and their sanctioned greats. Predicated on discourses of female absence, it is no secret that music's firsts are typically male ones. So too are the critics, whose gendered relationship to the archive remains unchecked. Still, if we just look a little longer and a little bit harder, which is to say, if we move beyond the despair produced by the supposed absence of groups such as La Anacaona, it becomes clear that their presence and influence is far from exceptional and beyond terminal. I have referred to the Orquesta Anacaona as a mobile musical undercommons because their effect, musical and material, lingers. Taking their presence seriously can offer exciting modifications of how we come to know and inevitably not know music. They offer grounds with which to complicate how we come to know and not know genre's master narratives. By situating La Anacaona as a rudimentary and righteous musical foundation for Graciela, I hope to contribute to Frances Aparicio's refreshing call for "careful and attentive listening" that can enable the move "toward a feminist genealogy of Salsa music."[24]

Graciela emerged onto the musical scene in 1932 when she was recruited at age seventeen to be the singer for the Orquesta Anacaona.[25] Though not directly pushed out of higher education by Machado, Graciela is implicitly an unregistered member of the university's undercommons by virtue of contact and collaboration with La Anacaona. She was professionally pulled into a life of performance by her metaphorical upperclasswomen the Castro sisters. Graciela had a somewhat part-time enrollment status with the group. Subsequent assembly of Graciela's brief tenure with La Anacaona proves to be a productively clumsy affair due to the inconsistencies in the few documents, mostly in the form of liner notes and brief textual passages, that haphazardly indicate or erase her collaboration.[26] This erasure or removal is widespread, even by the Castro sisters themselves. For example, in Kummel's documentary, Graciela is dismissively referred to by Ondina Castro as "that singer who left." Nevertheless, even at ninety-two years of age, Graciela remembers her introduction to the Castro sisters with stunning detail, including their ages, what they played, and nicknames. Ondina, she recalled, was always "majadera" (capricious).[27]

Although I begin Graciela's story as she comes of age with the Orquesta Anacaona, I want to acknowledge other musical callings she heard in childhood. Her father's whistling is the first detail she mentions when asked about her family's musical background. It is his sound that she has always tried, and failed, to reproduce. There was also, of course, the encouragement of her older brother Frank "Machito" Grillo, who was already active in some of the most influential groups on Havana's musical scene as a singer and maraquero.[28] And take this detail that is the stuff of storybooks: Graciela attributes her official musical call to Maria Teresa Vera, one of the greatest figures in popular Cuban music of the twentieth century. Vera used to spend the afterhours singing with her guitar in Graciela's childhood home. Graciela was the only one of her siblings who would wake up to become part of the intimate audience. It was because of this early apparent commitment that Vera pegged her as a singer in the making.[29] Feminist musical genealogies are as ordinary and commonplace and material as we might dream them to be.

Graciela was the perfect fit for the Orquesta Anacaona. She did not only know how to sing and play the claves—those wooden sticks relied upon to keep the time—but she also literally fit into the costume of the woman who she replaced. The former member, in Graciela's words, was "gordita como yo" (chubby like me).[30] While new to public performance, Graciela immediately discovered a set of untapped skills. In one of her first forays with the group, she found herself performing on a double bill with the famed Cuban flautist Fajardo to promote a discount store called Precio Fijo (Fixed Price). Later that evening, she accompanied La Anacaona as they played in an open-air cafe on the Prado. At that time, the Prado was a central gathering spot for nightlife and North American tourists. Graciela quickly discovered that she could seduce and taunt her audience with her playful and heavily accented English. As she performed novelty she would also thrust a tip plate in their direction. In the span of twelve hours the band went from a fixed price to a hot market commodity. When Graciela shared this story with me, she tied it all together with this characteristically Cuban denouement: "Descarada siempre fui. Si tu no eres asi, tú no vas a llegar a nada" (I was always shameless. If you're not that way, you don't get anywhere).[31] Loud guttural laughter, foot stomping, and fist knocking then take over the recording.

One has to appreciate Graciela's shameless shamelessness during her adolescence, the very stage in life where shame can be paralyzing. Such shamelessness was necessary given the hungry times that they and so many Cubans found themselves in at that moment. I'd like to consider Graciela's performance mode, her shameless shamelessness, through a few details she shares from her early performance life. I argue that Graciela's mode—a quality that I align with fearless adaptation—has not only taken her beyond the comportment required by gender and genre, but also offered necessary protection while on display. Her fearless adaptive mode has always been behind her impressive vocal reach and flexibility. It is the gumption behind her career's durability. It is the tricky way she positions herself in history. In what follows note how such fearless adaptation changed locations, and with such movement, changed forms.

I first came to hear something about Graciela's early performance life through a three-hour interview she recorded for the Oral History Program of the National Museum of American History. The interview was conducted by Raúl A. Fernández and Rene López at her home in New York on September 19, 1998.[32] In the recording, Graciela performed the familiar and unknown at once. The familiar: that girlish crackle felt at the ends of her words, the narrative lilts in her storytelling, the flirtation with the people in the room, that reassuring, beautiful, difficult Cuban humor. These vocal, technical traces are well established in her greater discography. The unknown: those behind-the-music stories, the right dates and full names, the details behind her performances that you might have detected but of which you never knew the particulars. The theoretical possibilities to be heard from many oral histories—especially those by musicians—are in the creative ways they respond to the questions. Throughout the interview, there is the slightest palpable struggle detectable as López attempts to get the record straight in ways, to recall Naomi Schor, "more congenial to male epistemological models."[33] But Graciela handles them with aplomb. She insists that we listen to her in detail. This is partly to do with her incredible memory and mostly to do with her gift at improvisation.

I consider the recording as a living and breathing document, and one that can be used as a methodological guide with which to analyze her actual music. The interview is not necessarily an object that ossifies her presence in the musical record, a common ideology that accompanies reproduction and discourses of el legado in general. Nor do I understand it as the static as opposed to the live object of her performance. Certainly, the interview prepares us for the eventual ephemerality of her material body. For example, while her tone is mostly playful throughout the interview there are moments where one feels her age and fatigue in a visceral way. The document should not be taken up as Graciela's last will, but as another in a long series of clues to her undocumented career. The aural testimony is not only a record of her history, but also at the same time a sonic interpretation of that history. The recording, in short, is a musical one, and its resonances are altered (among other things), by the context of the here and the now. That is to say, the infinite present occurrence of the recording produces a set of perpetually shifting responses.

In a formal sense, the dynamics of Graciela's voice, the details she selects, the pauses she takes and those she does not, and her interplay with the interviewers are among the most impressive displays of improvisatory technique. These perpetual twists create open and infinite systems of meaning for the critic. Further compounding this interpretive play happens through the comparative bridging of her recorded music and the interview. Graciela's soprano has always had a tender and gentle lilt to it. It is at once sweet and playful, and always bolstered by a strong, well-supported vibrato. The wavering always rounds out her notes in a gentle, floating movement from one measure to the next. In the midst of this highly melodic voice, there has also been an ever-present hoarseness—a scratchiness—that you could hear coming in the earliest recordings made in her late teens. It is humbling to follow this particular development, one that has been earned and crafted for more than seven decades, even in the album that Graciela recorded in 2004 (pushing ninety years of age) with the famous conguero Cándido Camero.[34] The interview greatly accentuates Graciela's powerful vocal rasp; it is the laying down of a voice that has learned, loved, lost, and gained with age.

For these reasons, listening to Graciela's interview feels like the experience of a jazz recording rather than an ethnographic exercise in data collection. The body becomes carried by the sound and dynamics of her voice and gestures. Working in the mode of repeated play (literally sitting, listening, and pressing pause) carries its own kind of labor and is far from passive spectatorship or disembodied practice, as some critics might argue. The recording itself demands a kind of running or chase without end as it always avoids capture. Graciela's vocal filigree and nuance takes hold, and then takes flight. These details flee in that very moment when you arrogantly think you can freeze frame them while pressing pause.

I further argue that this recorded interview occupies what Yolanda Broyles-González, in her essay on the oral history of the Tejana singer Lydia Mendoza, has termed the "borderlands of print culture and oral tradition."[35] Certainly there are fundamental differences between the Tejana and Cuban body in the United States. However, in both cases these borderlands are both material and methodological. In Graciela's specific case, her body and work in diaspora, is always rendered as foreign regardless of her current US citizenship status or her sixty-two-year residence in New York City. As typical fall-out, her work remains unimportant to American expressive culture. Cuba and its diaspora (particularly for Afro-Cubans like Graciela), has often been forced to perform a tenuous and outsider relationship to Americanness, even in its more inclusive formulations.

What I'd like to reemphasize here—in keeping with the undercommon atmosphere of this chapter—is to understand Graciela's labor as unbearable and necessary in relationship to Americanness. Hard evidence of all of her appearances with and influence on musicians is hard to trace out—especially as most of the records (in all forms) do not even use her correct last name. She is also often caught on the border between the milieus of Cuban and Afro-American sonic traditions. Not quite identifiable to either, she is subsequently disappeared from both. Graciela's work in the interview thus performs and bears the burden of fulfilling two functions: it falls within Broyles-González's feminist translation of *historia*, the Spanish word that means both history and storytelling.[36] It also allows for Graciela's particularity as an Afro-Cuban woman coming of age in the United States and her place in its larger trajectory of female minoritarian musical performance.[37]

For her part, it would be a grave error to assume that Graciela is not well rehearsed in the trappings and possibilities of her documentation or testimonio, especially when witnessed by recording technology, particularly if it must somehow rectify years of her ignored oeuvre. A prime example of this happens in the first minute of the interview—a moment traditionally used for the obligatory banal greeting and listing of the parties involved. While she greets her interviewers, the Nuyorican music critic Rene López and the Cuban scholar Raúl A. Fernández, with Spanish pleasantries, she greets the young sound engineer with a notably different approach. Upon introduction to Matt Watson, Graciela did not hear (or pretended not to hear) his name. Without dropping her smile, she affectionately hailed him as "y el señor Americanito, ¿cómo te llamas mi amor?" (oh, and the little American gentleman, what is your name my love?).[38] Here Graciela (who knows English) demonstrates the use of not only a greater strategy of bilingual code switching, but also that technology of resistance offered by the Cuban linguistic love affair of the diminutive. Severo Sarduy understands this behavior as manifested by Cubans' "innate aversion to the monumental."[39]

The monumental, for Cubans, is both a theoretical and material concept. It is understood as institution, establishment, and class as well as seriousness, severity, and altruism. One could probably pinpoint death as the highest form of the monumental—typically responded to with callousness both biting and playful. In this sense it is often a method of loving that doesn't (on the surface) love too much. Performances of grandeur in any form become minimized so that they can be contained, jousted around, deflated.[40] Undoubtedly shaped in part by Cuba's captive and colonial legacies and itinerant occupations (including dictatorships) the "innate aversion" can nevertheless be turned into a utility in the face of power, both seen and unseen. In this sense it is often a method of combating what doesn't (on the surface) hurt too much.

Graciela demonstrates that the diminutive can be used in the face of certain patriarchal, racial, and institutional coordinates, both direct and/ or implied. Note that the monumental in this specific case is rendered as either the form of Watson, an Anglo-American man; the National Museum of American History, an institution that has a history of ossifying cultural objects, or as the sign of Watson who for Graciela might signify the technological recording devices in and of themselves. Artfully, her diminutive ("el señor Americanito") manages to indicate all three in tandem, scaling them down to bite-sized versions. But she also seduces in a way specific to the Spanish-speaking Caribbean and its diaspora in that interpolative use of "mi amor," which is typically extended to an object of care at the same time that it is deployed as a cog to disrupt uneven power relationships. Graciela immediately places her hands on the controls set to record her history with this minute linguistic gesture.

This kind of move—at once subtle and disruptive, and most crucially, charming—is one exemplary instance of the work that Graciela does throughout the oral history. To closely listen to and reflect upon the interview in the tight space of this chapter is a difficult feat, for each detail demands infinite critical play. It demands a book of its own. Somewhat undaunted, I would like to consider a particular detail in the interview that has altered my project in significant ways. My hope is that such profound impact will not be trapped locally or be read as merely exceptional. I argue that such a detail has the capacity to alter the larger coordinates of the study of music, race, migration, and especially, the coterminous histories of Cuban and African American performance traditions and the places where those histories intersect. I will now focus on a detail—and its delivery—from one of Graciela's trips with the Orquesta Anacaona in 1938.

Soon after its formation, the Orquesta Anacaona would tour the global performance circuit that had renewed energy after World War I. This circuit, you might recall from chapter 1, featured musical groups and revues and stretched between the Old and New worlds. In her oral history, Graciela recalls a few of their stops. They first played all over Cuba's open-air cafes (the Aires Libres), traveling between Camaguey, Oriente, Santa Clara, and Matanzas. Between 1933 and 1934 the group secured a contract to play in San Juan's historic Hotel Condado and eventually toured all over the island. She recalls other gigs like slightly delayed fireworks. In 1935 they performed in Panama, Baranquilla, and Venezuela. And in 1937, the Orquesta went on a contract to the Havana Madrid in New York City. While stationed in New York, a promoter came to hear them and quickly recruited them to play at Paris' Ambassador Hotel. They were sent to Cuba to rehearse under the direction of Alberto Socorrás before their departure.[41]

While in Paris, the women secured a gig at the Chez Florence cabaret on the fingers of Montmartre. The Chez Florence was a cabaret named after its proprietor, Florence Embry Jones, who was an Afro-American cabaret performer and star of Paris' Montmartre district in the 1920s and onward. At the cabaret, La Anacaona were featured as the alternate line-up with Django Reinhardt and Stéphane Grappelli's Quintett du hot Club de France.[42] Graciela explains that on this particular venture, the orquesta's upright bass player was unable to make the trip, as her husband didn't allow her to travel. Graciela was then called in by their musical director of the time, Alberto Socorrás, who incidentally had affectionately nicknamed her "la loquita," to quickly fill in for the now-captive member. He figured her solfeggio training could easily transfer. With Socorrás as her guide she had to quickly familiarize herself with the instrument for the tour.[43]

She recounts the moment with a teenaged vocal quality, vulnerable and sweetly abject. As she sonically accesses this past self, Graciela talks about the challenges of learning this instrument as she had difficulty in understanding the logic map of the bass. The low notes are played by holding the strings at the top of the instrument. The high notes are sounded by pressure on the lower part of the instrument. And as she learned, Graciela's greatest challenge was keeping this playerly compass straight. As she explains this, she phonetically reproduces her struggle by vocally miming the actual sounds that emerged from the instrument. The sounds were shaped by directional words: "Pa' arriba abajo, para arriba para abajo." Up and down back up and down again.

FIG. 2.2: Advertisement featuring the Orquesta Anacaona at Chez Florence, Paris, 1938. Courtesy of the personal archives of Ingrid Kummels.

Graciela then moves the tale to La Anacaona's actual performance time on the stage of the Chez Florence. As she does so, she vocally and gesturally demonstrates her confident and feigned mastery of the bass. Much like the repetitive refrain in the Cuban musical tradition of son montuno, Graciela repeats the phonic reproduction of her method we heard just a moment earlier albeit with a bit more bravado and exaggeration. She performs the real-time seriousness for us. It is a comic reprise. After the performance, a French musician who had played in the proceeding house orchestra approached Director Socorrás and questioned him on Graciela's playerly method. The musician asks Socorrás if "esa muchacha" (that lady) is from some kind of "escuela rara" (a strange school). While he pulled over Graciela's technique and form, he conceded that the sounds produced nonetheless came out just as they should have. Ducking responsibility for this phenomenon, Socorrás replied that in actuality, Graciela learned to play from "un viejo Cubano," an old Cuban master and that was his peculiar method handed down especially to his young protégée. As he recounted this to Graciela (who is recounting it for us—playing each part with a different vocal register), Socorrás playfully admonishes her for having made him lie for the first time in his life. As a response and through laughter, Graciela retorts that it was Socorrás who got her in this mess in the first place.

Graciela's musical dictée in this detail contains several intense layers that

I'm going to construct into a lean-to. I'd first like to address the question of venue and personage. You might recognize the name Florence Jones from her venerable cameo in the chapter "Don't Hit a Woman" from Langston Hughes's episodal autobiography *The Big Sea*.[44] My use of Hughes's text here, and in this way, might raise some eyebrows as to its verifiability—it is, like all written accounts, his version. I nonetheless rely on Hughes and his written wanderings because his intersectional being and belonging was an intimate part of Paris' interwar nightlife.

Hughes tells us about the night that Jones stood up to defend a coworker— a pregnant and liquored up French danseuse named Annette—who was being violently manhandled by the owners of the Grand Duc. As one of interwar Montmartre's star performers, Jones's fierce intervention was one for the history books. He describes her reaction in slow motion:

> Then it was that Florence, the famous entertainer, that same Florence who snubbed millionaires nightly, arose from her table near the orchestra to defend the poor little French danseuse in her troubles. Florence wore an evening gown of gold and a spray of orchids in her hair. She swept across the floor like a handsome tigress, blocking the path of the waiters, who, at the bidding of the management, rushed to eject the little danseuse. Florence said: "Don't touch that woman! She's a woman and I'm a woman, and can't nobody hit a woman in any place where I work! Don't put your hands on that woman."[45]

This passage does many things. I'd like to point out how Hughes makes this space of nightlife public. He puts important figures and venues in print, for example, a sense of Jones's celebrity that might have been unknown to American audiences. Jones's interruption serves as a catalyst, a break before the scene (and story) turned tumultuous. Hughes described its unfolding— with the sort of novelty used to describe girl fights—as a "battle royal" between the women and the management.[46] Onlookers picked sides and got involved. Fists were thrown. Empathies and angers aroused. As the chapter comes to a close, Jones ends the scene with the pronouncement, "You men ought to be proud of any woman that has an *enfant*, 'cause it takes guts to have an *enfant*. None of you men ever had a baby! *Ecoutez! Je dis*, it takes all kinds of guts to be a mother! You hear me?"[47]

According to Hughes, Jones's relationship with the owners of the Grand Duke continued to sour after the incident. It was then that she partnered with Louis Mitchell to open the Chez Florence cabaret, a place that "became, and remained *the* place in Montmartre for a number of years."[48] While we can't know what Jones was really like or what her motivations were for opening her own place, there is something of her fearless, bilingual gumption in this passage that allows us to imagine what she eventually made possible, musically and spatially. Jones is too often ignored in the larger history of black transnational performance and is most familiarly known as the influential pathfinder for the notorious Ada "Bricktop" Smith as both a model of performance and entrepreneurship. She has been left off the radar of many histories of transatlantic performance but Hughes nevertheless reminds: it takes all kinds of guts to get to be a woman and a cabaret owner.

Both Jones and her Chez Florence were fundamental to the processes of those nudged movements of American jazz into the space of Paris and its nightlife. As Graciela teaches us, however, it is not only jazz or strictly Afro-American performers who shared a forum in the Chez Florence. Jones was also partly responsible for providing a venue for other musical traditions found throughout the Americas, namely those for which the Orquesta Anacaona were noted for: the son, guaracha, and rumba.

Stepping in the footsteps of Florence Jones, or as Graciela puts it, not only into her actual space but also her éxito, are the ladies of La Anacaona who are thus marked in the transnational wanderings and formulations of jazz music and its poetics.[49] This specific lived instance is one among many that testifies against the black/white and domestic/diaspora binaries that have been vigorously upheld in some jazz practices and scholarship.[50] Both musicians and critics have historically used a set of first-world lenses to consider or contextualize those bodies and techniques coming in from the third. The off-site corroborations that have long taken place between performers such as Jones and Graciela must still be made as they are a formative partnering behind American jazz. While many point to Duke Ellington and others as planting the seeds for the radical traditions later performed in bebop, what might be made possible with reimagining Jones and Graciela as also central? As Geoffrey Jacques argues, bebop formulated, "a certain conscious internationalism that found its reflection as an aesthetic concern within the music

FIG. 2.3: The Anacaona Sisters in Paris, 1938. Garciela is pictured far right.
Courtesy of the personal archives of Ingrid Kummels.

itself."[51] It is no secret that this conscious internationalism, while rooted centuries prior to the 1940s, could be considered already articulated by Florence Jones while beboppers were entering puberty.

Through her oral history, Graciela provides us with a crucial moment of collision in order to rethink the so-called excess moments or performances often disregarded as simply additional to, on the outside of, or as adornment to the "heroic individualist" narrative of jazz, which in turn readily replicates the dominant narratives of modernity.[52] Through Graciela's shared memory, performances such La Anacaona's make themselves felt as necessary labor, unwelcome though they might be. Here, through the *Anacaona-as-within* the space of Florence Jones's particular performative intervention—and it should be underscored that its racialized and gendered spatiality was in itself an intervention—we have an opportune moment to theorize those exchanges between Cuban and Afro-American women.[53] This moment is the sort of specific flash of contact often put on the most wanted posters by critics, feminist and nonfeminist alike—in the form of a performative space of transnational feminism.

According to Jody Blake, venues such as the Chez Florence (in addition to Le Grand Duc, Bricktop's, and the Temple Club) were the go-to places for those workers recently clocked out of other sectors of Paris' nightlife economy. Musicians and performers from the other clubs in Montmartre would gather at these sites during late night hours to relax, share gossip from their respective places of work, take their bodies on or off the market, and to participate in informal jam sessions. Much like the white bohemian fixtures that became commonplace in Harlem's renaissance, many of the poster figures for the surrealist movement strategically found their way to these venues in Paris. No longer cabarets, but "surrealist discoveries," the performing and otherwise milling bodies that occupied these spaces became objects of an imposed sense of primitive time. As Blake writes:

> This issue was a crucial one for the surrealists because of their own conviction that African-American musicians "instinctively" achieved what they had to learn how to do, which was to express themselves spontaneously, unhampered by exterior considerations and drawing upon inner sources of creativity. The surrealists' enlistment of jazz in their cause typifies their practice of validating their own approach to creativity by appropriating the work of "uncivilized" and "unsocialized" artists.[54]

Demystifying the instinctive veneer of her performance produces a set of questions regarding what could be construed as Graciela's surrealist model of playing the upright bass (when her hands went up when she should have gone down). Here I'd like to think about her grafting of technique of playing as a way of jolting not only the provisions of surrealism's relationship to music, but also its conditions of institutional validation for third world bodies generally speaking.

Graciela illustrates that a "surrealist aesthetic" is not so much a privileged exercise of spurting or expounding the subconscious, as it is a necessary improvisation or strategic repositioning in the face of being on display—or as strategic performance in the face of the monumental. Shameless shamelessness. Her method, when rendered as "non-form" fits well within the overriding versions of European surrealism. This version typically understands certain formal methods as extractable and codifiable from the primal Other. In the same narrative, that primal Other remains unnamed, overlooked, and also generally unaware of what it was enacting or performing. What might it be like to imagine Graciela's adaptation—making the sounds come out by way of an alternative form or technique—as shaking down these assumed methodologies borrowed (or stolen) by many within the European surrealist movement of its colonies?[55] Graciela might play the wrong way, but she also manages to smuggle out the notes *and* she performs virtuosity as she does it.

I turn now to the French musician's query. An attempt at interpellation of Graciela and her attendant techniques become hailed through the third party of Socorrás. The French musician's provocative naming of her training out from an "escuela rara" provides us with a spectrum of possibility. According to the *Vox Compact Spanish and English Dictionary*, "rara" can mean scarce, seldom, odd, and/or strange. On the one hand, Graciela is potentially rendered as emerging from an exceptional institution (exceptional colony?), one that houses and sends forth special-talent individuals. While on the other hand, perhaps she was preemptively let loose from another kind of institution, the mental variety.

However, "rara" in some instances (and by vernacular definition) could also be code for what he perceives as the Orquesta's queerness. Though not mutually exclusive from the exceptional or other kinds of institutions I noted above, the French musician's speech act calls out women who play instruments, make music, and travel together as in some ways always already queer. One wonders if the musician was in some way using the question of Graciela's form to sneakily out her and her compatriots for a variety of personal reasons or desires.[56] Or perhaps he can be read as simply marking a gender nonconformity—a rareness—that in some important ways resonates beside what many critics today theorize as queerness. To do so is not to unveil some epistemological truth about the artist.[57]

I'd like to now think through Socarrás's playful admonishing of Graciela as he recounts his response to the bassist as "making him lie" for the first time in his life. Here there is an amazing interplay that begs to be contextualized between Socarrás and Graciela. Socarrás must navigate his own gendered and racialized place within the economy of Chez Florence as a black Cuban man traveling abroad. He is figured by the musician as the de facto voice for and over the women and also as a kind of chaperona for the ladies in La Anacaona. But in his response to this bass player he also plays with a kind of strategic primitivism of Cuba in the international imaginary by chalking up Graciela's training with an authentic Cuban viejo. In his marketable exotic genealogy, Socarrás assigns a false authenticity to her method, one that he knows will be consumed with ease and fascination.[58]

The Graciela who performs in the Oral History Program adds the final twist through her reproduction of these two historical accounts at the same time: the true behind-the-music story and the other, somewhat muddier version. The twist happens by the way in which she appropriates and imports an imagined institution of learning (the "escuela rara") into a strategic and literal one (the National Museum of American History). Part of the way in which Graciela plays along is through her perpetuation of the existence of this particular school, her "escuela rara," in the act of vocally reproducing and recording it.

Through the lecture of sorts to both interviewers López and Fernández, Graciela documents her own musical undercommons by way of the circulation of this detail. And she manages to sneak it into the institutional monument that is the National Museum of American History. Graciela is undoubtedly conscious that her oral history interview will be used to narrate the larger, unwritten history of Latin jazz in the United States. The context of the recording is thus explicitly pedagogical: it will be used as an instructive document for the curator, historian, critic, and visitor alike. But this alumnus of the "escuela rara" takes care to situate her school in an undertheorized and overlooked space made possible by another undocumented performer, Florence Jones.

Enter the dynamic of the actual geographic location named by Graciela in the story above. I read the Chez Florence as a material stand-in for feminist transnational spaces of exchange; spaces often kicked off the maps that delineate migratory routes, landmarked sites, and even proper disciplinary fields. In following the implications of Aparicio's evocation of the transnational within Latina sonic recordings, the North/South American binary to Latino/a transnational identity becomes pressured here by the site of Paris—a location not automatically listed as a place of convergence and confluence of Latino/a experience.[59] Both Florence Jones and Graciela together trouble not only the concept of nation but also of migration. Jones for her part, as moving far east of the Great Afro-American northward migration at the turn of the century. Graciela moves beyond the Americas and far out of reach of Cuba, still an unofficial US protectorate. Their performances run as counter to myths of stasis and domesticity in that they press far beyond them. They move outside of both parlor and sewing room, those spaces of intellectual exchange sometimes documented. Though it should be noted, that even when written about, these sites are too easily written off as bourgeois iterations of the real deal.[60]

Far from being shipwrecked on some domestic shore, the link between Jones and Graciela not only swells the scope of who is constituted by the black Atlantic but also how this greater who has adapted its typical coordinates. Likewise there is also an altering of the terms of a greater conception of latinidad—one that considers Florence Jones in its flexible structuring. Along and within Paris, Graciela's stopover demonstrates supplementary modes of contact made with other bodies who carried their own specific histories of racial formation. I argue that it is those lessons picked up and cross listed between folks like Graciela, the members of La Anacaona, and other subversive intellectuals that formulate a pedagogical underground—railroading between maroon encampments such as the space made possible by the Afro-American Florence Jones.[61]

The Chez Florence thus emerges as a material site that has housed what Chandra Mohanty has named "imagined communities of women . . . with diverse histories and social locations, woven together by the *political* threads of opposition to forms of domination that are not only pervasive but also systemic."[62] In the particular context of this cabaret, I read Mohanty's "political threads" as performative ones. Musical performance, in this specific case, is the chosen medium. Picking up an end and following this performative thread back to the Americas, I want to think about Graciela's form of delivery and her storytelling of this fact of contact as providing the critical tools with which to approach her actual music.

I believe that Graciela offers a method of performance theory in the telling of this anecdote. I'd like to emphasize and hone in on the motif of adaptation that runs through each of the aspects I've underscored through her inclusion of this particular story. By "performance," I include not only her entire body of work that predates this moment in the interview. I also feel it important to reiterate her immediate adaptation of the conditions of her historical reproduction in this document—one that insists upon certain boundaries at the same time that it maintains a loving generosity (that is, the diminutive "Americanito" alongside "mi amor"). Graciela choreographs the archivists to proportions that befit the intimacy of her home, and one could argue, interior life.

Graciela also refashions the story of the Chez Florence itself in its telling, using different registers and vocal shifts to reproduce the narrative in the here and now of the recording. It is through her refashioning of the actual story that adaptation itself takes center stage in her recounting of her method of playing the bass instrument. Most important, Graciela instructs those of us who listen to this story to adapt our own methodological preoccupations or borders, those who seek to posit blackness and latinidad as both processes and ways of being that can be somehow understood in isolation from each other.[63] She does this through her attention to the detail of Jones, a fundamental cameo that acts upon not only the larger texture of her interview, but also the mobility of music in and beyond the Americas.

In a later moment of the interview both Fernández and López ask Graciela for her thoughts on and words of advice for young musicians. I, however, would like to adapt and adopt this as advice for young critics. For Graciela, lesson number one: "Que se visten bien" (They should dress well) and second, "¡a aprender! (to learn!) or as she clarifies," "hay que oír a los viejos para aprender" (One has to listen to old people to learn). Some could read dressing well as some shameful, internalized notion of proper public comportment that in turn carries its own set of gendered, xenophobic, and racialized nuances, especially when uttered by an Afro-Cuban woman performer. Instead, I'd like to think that Graciela is trying to instruct us to not only talk about music, but also how to move through it—how to move through the undercommons and perform virtuosity even in the face of being on display—another helpful hint on how to try and avoid detection even when your material body might immediately give you away.

In 1945 Graciela introduced "Mi cerebro" (My mind), a bouncy son montuno by José Blanco Suazo to the New York scene. The song was one of the first that Graciela recorded after making the permanent move to the United States as a member of the seminal orchestra Machito and His Afro-Cubans in 1943.[64] Frank "Machito" Grillo, her older half-brother, was already making a name for himself in the United States after migrating there in 1940.[65] The Afro-Cubans was founded together with Mario Bauzá, one of Cuba's most important jazzmen who put down roots in New York as early as 1926, and later settled there in 1930 to play trombone for some of the most notable Big Apple–based Cuban orchestras such as Don Azpiazu's and the Cuarteto Machín. He eventually switched to the trumpet and played for groups helmed by Chick Webb, Noble Sissle, Fletcher Henderson, and Cab Calloway. Bauzá directed, played trumpet for, and arranged many of the numbers for the Afro-Cubans. Many of these compositions and arrangements were later taken up by Charlie Parker, Dexter Gordon, Flip Phillips, and most famously, Dizzy Gillespie.[66] Bauzá was a principal and primary artery of the bop sensibility.

There is much to linger on when recalling Machito and His Afro-Cubans. I'm grateful to the many scholars, artists, and fans who have insisted on this group's importance to the larger history of New York's jazz/Latin/dance music scene.[67] It would be easy to digress here, but I understand my contribution to this vital documentation as keeping the focus on Graciela. Before proceeding however, I would like to call attention to the group's name. Like the adoption of the name Orquesta Anacaona, the name Machito and his Afro-Cubans is a bold and defiant gesture, particularly when considering their national reach in the Jim Crow era. The band is one of the mambo era's "big three," part of the trinity that also included Tito Rodriguez and Tito Puente. They were the marquis names not only on multiracial venues such as New York's Palladium Ballroom, the Savoy, Park Plaza, and Royal Roost, but also in venues on the Borscht Belt, the global touring circuit, and especially, radio programs broadcast throughout the United States.[68] The work of the sign "Afro-Cubans" adapts Cuban, island-based racial descriptives such as cubanos de color, or simply, cubanos, to a US context. Its passage to from Spanish to English, from Cuba to the United States was a fierce and courageous act of self-determination. The Afro-Cubans might have sounded as a confrontation for some, but was a rallying point for others.

The Afro-Cuban's recording, "Mi cerebro" begins with an announciary horn section that sounds like a warm up exercise. While they are technically in time, the orchestra has a feeling of being slightly out of step. After patiently waiting her turn throughout an interminable intro, Graciela and her blushing soprano enter. From the first sung measure, one can hear a voice bolstered by a strong, supported posture, sitting upright in a rather uncomfortable chair. One imagines Graciela singing this song with her chin raised and her hands folded in her lap, the sound picture of a proper woman performer. Perhaps she permitted a fanning gesture of the hand from time to time—to feign being overwhelmed and/or overheated—especially dur-

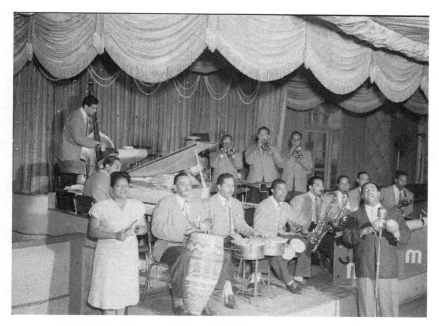

FIG. 2.4: Machito, Jose Mangual, Carlos Vidal (?), Mario Bauza, Ubaldo Nieto, and Graciela Pérez, Glen Island Casino, New York, NY, circa July 1947. From the William P. Gottlieb Collection, Library of Congress.

ing her stabs at spoken improvisation. But before I proceed to more of the performative dynamics to the song, let me give you a sense of the basic lyrics of "Mi cerebro." They go like this:

Mi cerebro es lo último	My brain is the best
mi cintura es lo último	My waist is the best
que mi cerebro es lo último	My brain is the best
yo no quiero que me digan	I don't want anyone to tell me
que lo último no sirve pa' bailar	I can't use that last one to dance
sabroso	sabroso
No (ay que me pasa adios mio)	No (oh my God what is happening to me)
No-ni-no (que polito se me fue-ay)	No-ni-no (that Polito left me- ay)
No (ay)	No (ay)

No ni no (¡mira!)	No, nor, no (look!)
No. Sí. Ay.	No. Sí. Ay.
Anda que quiero morirme	Come on, all I want to do is die (climax)
Mi cerebro es	*coro*: lo ultimo
Como yo gozo con	*coro*: lo ultimo
Y vacilo con	*coro*: lo ultimo
Que me cerebro es	*coro*: lo ultimo
Que yo mi vado con	*coro*: lo ultimo
Que yo me pierdo con	*coro*: lo ultimo

yo no quiero que me digan
que lo último no sirve pa' bailar
sabroso[69]

The interchangeability of the mind and the waist is only one element of poetic play that Graciela performs in the song. Through this most ultimate challenge to Descartes, Graciela positions her mind and waist as not only the definitive, up to date, but also more nearly, the last word on what serves her best to dance. In the midst of this triple or even quadruple entendre, Graciela subtly lobs cries of "si" and "no" to enact the sort of coquetry that masquerades as indecisiveness. A simple piano plays musical straightman to her improvisatory play, adding an oopsie element to the song. The piano adds to the comic business of these improvised bits.

In the 1945 recording, there is something of a resonance de ser buena, to be good, or a good-girlishness, in her rendition of the song. While I'd like to reiterate that Graciela's voice is, as always, well supported and musically self-aware, her performance evokes that feeling of clomping around the house in the high heels of your mother or older sister. The Graciela in this recording plays with permissiveness by placing gentle, if steady pressure on the comportment expected from her. This is most explicitly heard through her improvised asides ("si" and "no") that provide a welcome texture to a rather unsurprising score. She charms the composition by repeating some of the gimmickry of the asides. For example, the repeated iterative "se me fue" and "ay" make you feel that these are all she has in her repertoire of sexual innuendo. And while Graciela's asides don't explicitly seduce in the way of Mae West with those corner-of-the-mouth zingers, its tentative boldness announces something else on the horizon. For the asides are also the locations where she shows a vocal top and bottom. Here she alternates and conflates the mind (cerebro) with the waist (cintura) to also demonstrate her experimental reach into both extremes of a soprano's range. While this is a voice that might be mature for its years, it still doesn't feel as if it has grown into itself.

My hearing of her work here should give you immediate pause. For lest we forget, Graciela is in her late twenties at this point, having already traveled the world with La Anacaona, and is especially fluent in the ambiance of innuendo found in such places as interwar Paris. And recall the young Graciela and her powers with the tip plate in Havana of the 1930s. Young women who perform publically require this fluency and facility with innuendo. You might even say that such skills are required of women (young and old) who leave the house generally speaking. My hearing of this voice could (on the surface) be read as overdetermining Graciela's sound with innocence and her body as a naive object of novelty. This is not what I am after. Instead, and as I pointed out earlier in the chapter, we can be certain that Graciela has a well-honed technique of posturing (by which I also mean, a vocal posturing) in front of audiences who would falsely assume access to her interior.

As I mentioned above, Graciela was no stranger to New York City. She had performed a lengthy three-month stint with La Anacaona at the Havana Madrid nightclub in 1937. One has to appreciate a young Cuban woman of color beginning her recording and performance career in the United States with a ditty like "Mi cerebro." Perhaps the feeling of a not-yet quality to her voice had to do with the fact that this was one of her first cuts as a solo vocalist without La Anacaona to accompany her. It is doubly evocative to see what gets carried over into "Mi Cerebro" from her days with La Anacaona. While she demonstrates a bit of improvisatory experimentation in the piece, she in many ways adheres to a musical and gendered standard.

It feels as if Graciela retreats into her early La Anacaona vocal sound—a teenage just starting out sound—in these early US recordings. One has to remember the conditions of this voice: it had to sneak performance without her father's permission.[70] At the same time, however, "Mi cerebro" is in vast company with a hemispheric vocal quality shared by many women singers of the Afro-diaspora in the 1930s. While very different in overall effect, Brazilian Aracy de Almeida ("Rapaz Folgado" 1938), to Billie Holiday ("Strange Fruit" 1939), and Graciela ("Mi Cerebro"), all shared a girlish vibrato that began to show some evocative cracks as the decade came to a close. These singers who shared the same approximate birth year began to reveal early signs of a material, which is to also say, vocal moving far beyond.

"I wasn't selling anything with that," Graciela told me when I asked her about the older version of "Mi cerebro."[71] To her, the recording's weak returns required some shameless shamelessness. It was thus that she transformed "Mi cerebro" into what is known as her signature song, "Sí, Sí, No, No." The 1956 studio recording of "Sí Sí, No No" has circulated widely on mixtapes, compilations, and makeshift listening salons across the globe.[72] The song's initial recorded debuts, however, happened several years earlier during the great Symphony Sid's live broadcasts from the Royal Roost, a venue the esteemed DJ located at, "the Metropolitan Bopera House on Broadway between fortything and forthythoom . . . right near bop city."[73]

The first version was performed on March 19, 1949, for almost seven minutes, the second on March 29, 1949, for just over eight minutes. When the two versions are heard chronologically, it is wonderful to hear how Graciela became a seasoned veteran of Sid's antics in just ten days. It is also apparent how she quickly exploited the live radio format to demonstrate her vocal reach and performative playfulness. For example, in the first broadcast Sid introduced her as Gra-see-ello. In the second session she boldly corrects Symphony Sid when he repeats the error. "Graciela," she interjects. It is an interruption that sounds like the sonic iteration of a hip thrust. You can hear the roll of her eyes, the get-it-right already sense of exasperation. This vocal hip thrust was sustained and accentuated throughout duration of the performance.

In all recorded versions of the song—whether in the studio or in the live—the formerly coquettish "no" of "Mi Cerebro" becomes: ¡NO! ¡NO! ¡NO! no no no no baby no ¡No!. The "si": Yes! Yes! ¡Sí! ¡Sí! No longer equidistant instructions, she brings them together to make an art form of the mixed signal: ¡Sí! ¡Sí! ¡No! No! ¡Sí! no ¡Sí! In the Royal Roost recordings she screams at orgasm's precipice before having one at song's end. She scats when you least expect it. She makes grace note of "ay." But she always makes a choral return to the charged uncertainty of Sí sí no NO no Sí Sí. Such feigned indecision should not be mistaken for a lack of control. Instead Graciela's role in this staged sexual encounter smashes the familiar charges made of women's sexuality: as not knowing what it really wants. The uncertainty, in other words, is commanding. It is part of the erotic.

Graciela directs more than the tricky sexual narrative in the song. As you listen, it becomes clear that Graciela is not only in command of where hands and lips are allowed to go, but she also guides Machito's orchestra by way of her improvisatory play. The musicians must move around her timing, cues, and willingness to turn up, turn down, speed up and slow down the *entire structure of the song itself*. It is not simply a humorous (and for some, very recognizable) foreplay being performed here. There is virtuosic interplay between sexual performance and musical experimentation that is as much a legacy of great blues singers such as Bessie Smith and brilliant Cuban vedettes like Rita Montaner.[74] Such interplay demands that instrumentation and vocality act reciprocally. Vocal protagonists can and do move accompanying musicians along in dynamic temporal ways.

The bop sensibility—which we might think of as musicality without capture, as fugitive performativity—is too often conflated with male instrumental prowess. As Eric Porter writes bebop, "mark[ed] the emergence of the figure of the modern black jazzman as a defiant, alternative, and often exotic symbol of masculinity."[75] While she is far from an exception in this regard, Graciela augments this jazz teleology. Her adaptation of "Mi Cerebro" into the sustained sexual and experimental irruption and interruption of "Sí, Sí, No, No" is just one instance of how to rethink women's musical responses to modernity, to the form of composition, to their place on the stage. To think of Graciela performing this song in the live, as the front woman for the Afro-Cubans, without a producer in control of its timing, volume, and cadence, opens up an almost twenty-five year gap for the song that is generally agreed upon as the first woman's orgasm recording in popular music, Donna Summer's "Love to Love You Baby." She does much to lend history to that important vocal legacy.[76]

When asked about it in conversation, Graciela would offer an exhausted dismissal of "Sí, Sí, No, No" because of its stubborn persistence as her signature song. Not unrelated, her dismissal perhaps came from the frustration felt from having her body and work treated as a novelty. Artists themselves don't necessarily choose signature songs. They are often the imposed and predetermined will of a selfish audience who demands a performer to be that self and no other. Signature songs make artists recognizable and their request often insists that the artist freeze themselves in space and time. Such forced stasis is of course impossible. One need only recall the incredible diversity of Celia Cruz's lifelong performances of "Bemba Colorá" to be reminded that signature songs are not, like the artists who sing them, safe from revision and reversion. They also have an incredible reproductive life of their own. It is virtually impossible to know how many recordings or enactments of a signature song are actually put out in the world. To say nothing of karaoke renditions or living room sing-a-longs. Signature songs—however overplayed or overdetermining—offer the possibility of their own renewal and upheaval. Rather than putting them to reductive use, they can provide infinite listenings and interpretations of an artist's body of work.

I'd like to recap some of the layers that Graciela has helped me to put down in the foregoing: there is the adaptation of "Mi Cerebro" into "Sí Sí No No"; a modification of a song, and possibly, a self into new national and musical and orchestral and racial contexts. The shameless shamelessness of making one of the earliest recordings of a woman's orgasm, faked or not. There is the certain uncertainty of one of her sexual personae staged in public. There is the experimental work of her timing and voice to difficult musical effect. Finally, we have her willful dismissal of "Sí, Sí, No, No" as her signature song, which is to also say, her signature. Fearless adaptation. Shameless shamelessness. Certain uncertainty. Willful dismissal. At the beginning of the chapter, I refused to name stable prescriptives required for working in the undercommons. Still, after spending years with this particular song and artist, these qualities have had necessary and bearable effect on my scholarship.

Such qualities have been especially necessary and useful to adopt when working with the thorniness of any biography, but especially, her biography. Biography, even if that means a few details of a life, cannot be taken up with a phasic whimsy or messianic ethos. It is not merely an endurance test, but an enduring state. There is a quartet of biographies that gave me much needed company and I must pay brief homage to them in the textual body. They have recorded the songs of others in beautiful ways and means. Instructions for writing have been provided by Yolanda Broyles-Gonzalez's inspirational *Lydia Mendoza's Life in Music*, a training manual for being intimate with an artist without fear of also interpreting that artist. George Hutchinson's work on Nella Larsen reminded me that the perceived "invisibility" of an archivally elusive figure is "a precise marker of unresolved contradictions, of moral, political, and imaginative failures endemic to American society."[77] Jamer Hunt's gently frustrated exiges on Sylvia Lacan, the former movie star and wife of both Bataille and Lacan, encouraged my scholarly project to be misguided and frustrated by its person/object of inquiry. Hunt instructed me to see how such frustrated work is in itself *work*—that the most fulfilling access to a person is, in many ways, lack of access. As he writes of his ethnographical failure, "It was the potential dynamics of face-to-face encounters that challenged my illusions of theoretical control."[78]

Finally, there is Farah Jasmine Griffin's work on Billie Holiday. I have long been heart-struck by Griffin's use of Rita Dove's poem "Canary" and its final line as the title and ethos of the book: "If you can't be free, be a mystery." Griffin writes, "Mystery is the thing we do not know, cannot solve."[79] Holiday's life was like her musical line—with the exquisite difficulty of not knowing where it will go. She created too many possible melodies, too many possible routes to make her life and music reducible to one version. Graciela once told me that Holiday would often ask her to hold her dog when she performed on stage. I dream of the two of them sharing the same space and the intimacies that might or might not have passed between them. In my imagination, I envision them as two beautifully illegible musical figures in a teacher's lounge of which we will never see the inside. There is too much these two veteran colleagues in the undercommons continue to teach us.

After spending so much time with Graciela's recordings, it was a wonder to discover how much of her nuanced performance techniques were carried over into one-on-one conversation. The difficult demands she makes in her music were also made in off-stage and outer-studio contact with her. Graciela is one of the first artists who generously gave me the honor of several sit-downs. She came along in those last years of graduate school and followed me throughout the writing and revision of this book and until I had to change her from the present to the past tense. Throughout, Graciela trained me to move past questions of access, to methodologically improvise, and to see vital intellectual diversions made by all of the subversive intellectuals who have not only shaped this book, but also its author.

I was always uncertain as to how to be with her, what my place was, if she would ever trust me. There were so many important tests. Graciela would often pretend to be someone else when you would call her up on the telephone. Such masquerades could happen before and after she came to know you; whether she was suspicious of you or not. Her reasons for doing so were impossible to know. Perhaps it is what she did when she was too tired to engage, when her arthritis was torture, when she needed to deflect that person who dared to call during the afternoon telenovelas. For someone who had lived most of her life in the public, it was a tested method to get some privacy. Or maybe it was the quickest vetting process of the person on the other side of the line, the unknown. Because her voice was unmistakable and recognizable even in its ninth decade of use, those performances required your complicity. You played your part in the exchange and didn't reveal that you know to whom you are really talking. Sometimes you would have been handed over to the actual Graciela, other times you hang up without being put through. Such rejection was instructive but frustrating for those of us who hoped for her approval. You never knew.

There was a beautiful undercommons quality to those exchanges: you are not given direct access to your teacher. She required you to do the work of getting past your personal agenda and desire for her. The actual and hidden vocality of these conversations made Graciela present and absent at once. She did not exactly hide out. She chose to answer the phone. But there was that reliance upon your complicity. Such abject orchestration of you meant that any possible exchange with her would have happened on her terms. It was a generational schooling: she snapped you into a respect-your-elders state of mind. Her unrequited interest could hurt, even if you knew she was old, even if you knew it was not about you. Right before you would lose hope, however, she would give you other bright telephonic moments. From time to time, you might find a voice mail from her out of nowhere, wishing you a happy Valentine's Day, wanting to know how the wedding went, what your plans were for a happy Halloweens. These are messages that can't and won't ever get erased.

I linger on the telephone as it was a proxy for her unpredictability and a mode of her protection. It was also the primary instrument of my seduction. Weeks of phone calls could lead to an actual appointment with her. I always dreaded calling her when the day would come because she never felt well, didn't have her hair done, couldn't get out of bed. When I was able to see her, I had the nerves of an awkward suitor: get her the right present, bottle of whiskey, flowers. Blow out your hair and dress well. I would arrive at her tiny Upper West Side apartment too overwhelmed to charm. My bilingualism— which can deform both languages with nervousness—would fail me here as it would fail me in other important elsewheres. I came to understand that she would make me wait for just the right moment to see her because she wanted to be, hear, and look her best.

Her apartment was an altar; a few compressed square feet of a rich musical life. Photos covered every inch of wall space. There they were, like old friends: Bola de Nieve, Mario Bauzá Olga Guillot, and Dizzy Gillespie. A signed headshot from her dear friend Miguelito Valdés would catch your eye when she would drift off to the television. There are family portraits that feature nieces and nephews that she would immediately point to when asked if she ever had any children. There were all kinds of traces of how much she meant to many. There were cheap commemorative plaques for the important contributions she has made to music, to New York and touching collages made by fans. Yolanda Maldonado gave her a full-length acrylic painting of the Taíno queen Anacaona. It was placed so that she could preside over all the goings on in the cramped household. Queen Anacaona kept watch over the dearly beloved and departed: below her there were pictures of her parents, sister and brothers, and loved ones who continued to keep her company. A candle was always lit beside them. Perpetual vigils.

She lived in a scrapbook. Not so that she could stay in the past, but so that she could enliven the present. It is no wonder that she protected her selves and surroundings. Many scholars, journalists, and fans had gotten close to her to write about her more famous brother or to be able to capture the last living legend from the great mambo era. Others wanted to use her so that they could subjugate her and her oeuvre to argument, to vulgarly use her to speak to race and gender and then leave her behind. Others signed up to write biographies, make documentaries, and program tributes. Sadly, many have not followed through on their promised projects. Some stole beloved materials; some hangers on hoped to acquire her archive as private property so that subsequent critics must pass through them. But to be fair, one also came to learn that Graciela made follow through extremely difficult. I tried hard—but not hard enough—to orchestrate campus visits, to raise resources so that she could make her materials safe and accessible to the public. I wanted more people to take her musical contributions seriously. I wanted for people to know how much she mattered. Perhaps her wish—forever unsatisfied—to see the right project in the right hands was to keep singing, stay relevant, mean something.

I recall one reunion with her when she leaned forward in her brown leather chair to get closer to my recorder. She asked, "Que cosa es música? Tu sabes lo que es música? Que es la música?" While similar in gist, there are actually three different questions being posed here, approximately translated as: What is this thing called music? Do you know what music is? What is music? The quick switch-up of interrogative pronouns punctuates the raspy fatigue of her voice. It was a characteristic of hers I came to anticipate toward the end of her interviews and stories.[80] After a too-long pause, she delivered the following dictum with an index finger: "Es el arte de combinar los sonidos" (It is the art of combining sounds). This recitation is possibly a leftover from her years at Havana's Academia Musical where she studied solfeggio and theory in the 1920s.[81] It could have been a response her father once gave when asked about his virtuostic whistling. Or maybe it had always been an agreement between her and fellow musicians while touring the world, one that enabled them to live and work together. Then again, perhaps it was simply her go-to mantra when describing the proper ways to do things, a sense of protocol that solidified her reputation as the "First Lady of Latin Jazz." The phrase was another instance of Graciela leaving something unbearable and beautiful behind in recording. Through Graciela, I came to learn that to get at music, I have to hear the combinations of sounds in multiple forms, be they details, interviews, ephemera, or songs. After having dwelled in Graciela's underground, I've come to know only a few ways she combined sounds, and I continue to think about how she pieced them together. To

FIG. 2.5: Graciela Pérez
and Machito, Glen Island
Casino, New York, NY,
circa July 1947. From
the William P. Gottlieb
Collection, Library of
Congress.

do so means to be committed to the enduring state of biographical work. I
don't or can't move on from Graciela.

When she passed away in April 2010, Graciela reminded all that she was
also one of the great models of Cuban vanity—she wouldn't sit down to
an interview without a visit to the beauty salon first. So of course, defying
Catholic convention, she asked to be cremated so she would be remembered
prettily. But before she moved on from this world to the next—when her
material form was complete—she asked for her claves to be placed in her
hands. I think of her beautiful brown hands, with their innate commentary
and humor, and with their under-the-surface robustness, as dusty matter.
They are now reminders and remainders. To leave the body behind while
keeping the beat is an instruction for living and a model of dying that I don't
have the right to speak about for a while. And so I resort to the great leaving
unsaid channel of the song dedication and will end by dedicating one of her

signature songs back to her, César Portillo de la Luz's "Contigo en la distancia" ("With You In the Distance"). [82] The bolero, a hopefully melancholic genre Graciela had always had a special grace and dexterity in, was a languid and dynamic showcase for her voice. In lyrics and sound, this touching homage to an intimate and distant, close and far away longing, refuses time and space as conditions of togetherness. This bolero allows for longing to be a sustained refrain, forever rehearsable. I leave you with a detail in the song that, like Graciela, asks for your adaptation:

> No hay bella melodía/ There is not a beautiful melody
> En que no surjas tú/ If you don't appear
> Ni yo quiero escucharla/ Nor do I want to hear it
> Porque me faltas tú/ Because I am missing you . . .

> Contigo en la distancia,/ I'm with you in the distance
> Amado mío, estoy/ That's where I am, my love.

Chapter Three

Itinerant Outbursts

The Grunt of Dámaso Pérez Prado

In the song "Locas por el mambo," the sonero Beny Moré answers one of the great, unsolvable mysteries in the history of Cuban music. To the question, "Who invented Mambo?," Moré replies, "Un chaparrito con cara de foca" (A shorty with the face of a seal). Unnamed but described, the person behind the description is Dámaso Pérez Prado, the pianist, composer, and bandleader long heralded as "El Rey del Mambo" (the "King of Mambo"). The figure registers in the memories of many, whether as the orchestra leader in Mexican movies of the golden age, a Cuban additive to the American standard-bearers, or the musical visionary who made a continuum of the tuxedo and the mod suit. He is embedded in the popular cultural imagination and an understudied anomaly; a visitor from a familiar but distant elsewhere. Even Quincy Jones described his first childhood sighting of Pérez Prado like "seeing *Star Wars* for the first time."[1] As the author of some of the most sold instrumentals of all time, you might not know what else he's musically responsible for, but you know the Pérez Prado sound when you hear it.

Moré helps turn Pérez Prado into a recognizable figure we can evoke by singing along. In what follows, I engage a persistent vocal detail found in his performances that is a bit more difficult to intone. While much—but not enough—has been written about Pérez Prado's prolific career as an arranger and performer, his performative signature is often dismissed as a too idiosyncratic, which is to say, too difficult object of serious study. To try and stabilize it into noun format might render it motionless. But because it is forever running out of discursive reach, and especially, these pages, it might not matter how I qualify it. The vocal armament and ornament is found in most recordings made by the artist. It partly functions as a conductor's tool, but is not a dependable or monolithic sound. It is a grunt, a yell, a battle cry, a reaction, a direction. It is often a permutation of the Spanish word *dilo* (say it), but sounds like an impossible variety of *ugh*. Other times it feels like the kind of noise that escapes if and when you get punched in the stomach. It can sneak attack from the edges of the musical measure and is therefore both playful and terrifying, like being tagged "it" in a game of freeze tag. It is a grunt that is meaty, loud, sometimes jarring and abrasive. It recedes into the air of the recording as quickly as it emerges. It does not stick around, but its spirit lingers. It is an irruption, radiant outburst, and electrifying current that runs from the belly of the earth through the escape hatches of the fingertips. Pérez Prado is both its conductor and conduit.

Even as I try and qualify this phenomenon, its inscrutability encourages me to try and leave it unnamed but described. And to never tire of describing it. I will never be able to solve the sound's enigmatic trouble, but I can stretch the potential of my prose. It is not my choice of words, but the act of stretching that gets me closer to it. Engaging Pérez Prado's noise has precedent in the aesthetic traditions that span the continents. Through his work on African script systems, for example, Timothy Simone suggests a letting go of discursive control:

> Imprecision, fuzziness, and incomprehension were the very conditions which made it possible to develop a viable knowledge of social relations. Instead of these conditions being a problem to solve by resolute knowledge, they were viewed as the necessary limits to knowledge itself, determined by the value in which such knowledge was held, and the attitudes taken toward it.[2]

Rather than take up Pérez Prado's strange signature as a problem, I'd like to honor the productive limits it presents to naming, writing, and any hope for an epistemological solution. His grunt is a phenomenon that reveals "the necessary limits to knowledge itself."[3] The names by which I refer to Pérez Prado's noise will thus fluctuate throughout the chapter. Because the cadence and iteration of it is so varied, it insists that I be imprecise. The fuzziness of the grunt's logos—its insistent nonclarity—makes it a mobile detail that has the potential to undo many of the assumptions made of music, its movements, and its makers. Our incomprehension of it can take us beyond the situational borders that would seek to bind its theorization.

Permit another of this book's seeming paradoxes: although Pérez Prado's signature detail has all the conditions of imprecision, fuzziness and incomprehension for criticism, it is a precise, clear and comprehensive thing. Pérez Prado once described it this way: "Es un *cue*. Una entrada para trompeta o una melodia de saxofón o para la tumbadora. Así lo tengo todo organizado. Se me ocurrío."[4] (It is a *cue*. An opening for the trumpet or a saxophone's melody or for the drummer. That way I have it all organized. It occurred to me.) Pérez Prado's English recourse to "cue" teaches us that his grunt is a signal and a direction. It is an indication that a musician depends upon to come in at the right time. A cue is the thing you wait for as you get ready. It is a noun and verb, a thing and an action. To cue also means to fast forward or rewind to a specific moment; to drop yourself and others in a desired place in time. By taking Pérez Prado's cue beyond its recorded forms, I'd like to ask: what might such a cue signal and direct in the ways we listen to popular music? What do we experience as we get ready and wait for details such as these? How might these kinds of cue details—and our interaction with them—be instructive portals for transhistorical inquiry? Cues like Pérez Prado's must be taken up with prepared urgency, for as any performer can tell you, a missed cue can hold up the entire production. But then again, missed cues are also creative opportunities.

It is with this sense of urgency that I'd like to follow where the grunt asks us to go and to linger in the moments its drops us in. I'll trace its movement through seemingly uncommon geographies, its interchanges with other musical and critical traditions, and its surprise appearances in the literary lexicon. I'm interested, therefore, in the performative life of Pérez Prado's grunt, a life that moves well beyond its actual recordings or typical interpretive places.[5] What I'm after is not what the grunt seems to be saying, in the axiomatic wording of J. L. Austin, but what it is also doing.[6] By not pinning down and instead following Pérez Prado's vocal signature—through his actual migrations, its generic contours, hemispheric literary instances, and his myriad experiments with sound—we can see that this musical eruption greatly alters the ways we both can and can't know the details of violence, history, and creative collaboration.

Perhaps as a result of this cue that feels both pleasurable and injurious, many studies of popular music cannot avoid the figure of Pérez Prado. Obvious reasons for his presence within the mainstream popular music lexicon are due to his lengthy reign as "El Rey del Mambo," a tenure carried out in one of the most internationally successful and circulated genres in this history of recorded sound. It is thus impossible to step over the bandleader's opus of work at some point in any serious or even not-so-serious study of popular music.[7] Interestingly, however, his grunt remains widely undertheorized. It is usually left alone for fear of disturbing it. To the extent that it has been approached theoretically, some critics have offered theories-in-place through their descriptions of it. Take the following brief example: Pérez Prado's noises were once described as "peculiar burp-like noises" in a 1950 *Newsweek* review.[8] This description teaches us that these sounds do not abide by protocols of bourgeois comportment. They betray potential overindulgence or an inability of self-control. Additionally, the usage of "peculiar" signals a litany of its historical suffixes, including: institution, nation, people, and race. The prevalence of such descriptions makes it nearly impossible to dismiss the grunt as a simple idiosyncrasy.

One vital exception to the critical inattention to Pérez Prado's grunt is found in Gustavo Pérez Firmat's "A Brief History of Mambo Time" from *Life on the Hyphen: The Cuban-American Way*. Pérez Firmat examines old reviews, the musician's different compositional phases, and buried lore to reinvigorate Pérez Prado's varied musical and cultural contributions. He argues that the musician indicates some of the complex negotiations behind the North American circulation of Cuban musical genres and by default, Cuban bodies.[9] I'd like to build upon the rich work that Pérez Firmat performs in his text. I humbly imagine my work in palimpsestic relationship with it—a layering that I hope gestures toward intergenerational continuity in Cuban American studies and the field's continued reorientation. I move into the author's critical terrain not to reiterate his analysis, or to solely reproduce his project on Pérez Prado as the indicative figure of the Cuban American condition. Nor am I content to safehouse Pérez Prado or his grunt within the mambo genre, but what it does in excess of it. Pérez Firmat's work has functioned as another kind of formative cue that has prepared me to keep Pérez Prado deservedly relevant in studies of American popular culture.

I begin with a sketch of his early performance history. I mean sketch in its roughest sense for Pérez Prado had, like many musicians, a wonderfully lapsing memory. It is no coincidence that Leonardo Acosta once wrote that to speak of Pérez Prado is to enter a thick polemical terrain.[10] In interviews you will often read his way of recalling dates with a year and a "por allí" (around there). He is exact and vague. Nevertheless, for a helpful introduction to Pérez Prado's career, I'd like to revisit Pérez Firmat's overview: "As one more representative of the great Cuban tradition of dislodgement, he is another of those Cubans for whom unhousedness and misplacement seem to be the conditions of creation."[11] These conditions, elsewhere described by the anthropologist Fernando Ortiz as "aves en paso" (birds in flight), suggest bodies and aesthetics that are always en route, never solidly here or there, perpetually in between.[12] Tracing the development of Pérez Prado's grunt should thus consider his various flights from one place to the next as shared creative grounds. It is a challenge to pin the musician and his grunt to a specific place of origin as they collected and incorporated substances lost and found in migration. In one extraordinary interview, for example, Erena Hernández noted that Pérez Prado's Spanish was inflected with "typical Mexican expressions." The conversational sprinkling of "híjoles" and "ahorita, pues" revealed his movements in ways that exceed the mere disclosure of tour dates.[13] One is left to imagine what else in addition to that beautiful and uniquely Mexican conversational filigree was picked up and made a part of the music.

Pérez Prado was born in Matanzas (known as "the Athens of Cuba") in his words, "no sé que año" (I don't know what year, but likely 1916).[14] In Matanzas, he studied classical music at the Academia de Música de María Angulo when he was eleven or twelve years old. After speeding through his musical training in double time, he eventually switched from playing classical to popular music so that he could make a living as a musician. His first stint playing popular music was with La Charanga de Senén Suárez, the esteemed dance band based in Matanzas. After moving to Havana in 1940, he briefly sat in Paulina Álvarez's orchestra and later became the pianist and arranger for the Orquesta Casino de la Playa.[15] He eventually put together his own orchestra in 1946 that toured the Americas—the same year he stopped in New York to arrange for Xavier Cugat. In Cuba, however, his reception was acknowledged if lukewarm. Like many Cuban performers of the period looking for employment, different audiences, and more recording opportunities, Pérez Prado moved to Mexico City in 1948. During his time in the capital, he recruited Mexican musicians (as well as Cubans who had migrated to the country earlier) to form what would eventually become his main orchestra.[16]

Pérez Prado recorded more than twenty-five singles in Mexico and became a prominent player in the "época de oro" (the golden age) of Mexican cinema, a period that roughly incorporates the decades between 1936–1956. He appeared (in soundtrack or through cameos) in upward of forty films, providing the musical numbers behind such Cuban performers as Amaila Aguilar, Rosita Fornés (aka "The First Show-Woman of the Americas"), and Ninón Sevilla of "Las Rumberas," as well as Mexican screen starlets Lupe Carriles and Amparo Arozamena. His filmography runs an impressive gamut: from pictures titled *Del can can al mambo* (*From the Can Can to the Mambo*) to *Pecado de ser pobre* (*It's a Sin to Be Poor*) and most famously, *Victimas del pecado* (*Victims of Sin*). Together with the fallen women that make these films great, he shared the live performance labor of their cabaret settings. The significance of the intersection of performers in Mexico City at that time cannot be underscored enough. As Ana M. López argues, this age of Mexican cinema was among the first cultural industries to "consistently circulate Latin American images, voices, songs and history; the first to capture and sustain the interest of multinational audiences throughout the continent for several decades."[17]

With the aid of these movies and the visual familiarization of Pérez Prado's penguin-like figure in Latin America and in parts of the United States, his sound inevitably washed up onto the shores of North America. One of his earliest performances was at the Reverend Pat McPolin's Mexican Youth

Center in Chicago.[18] His migratory movements were often made compulsory by where the work was, in and between different outposts of the cultural industries in the Americas. His difficulty with the music industry, including the unions in Cuba and in New York, illuminates some of these forced routes.[19] In Cuba, he was blacklisted by the Peer-Southern publishing group (a powerful music publishing company) as his compositions were too bizarre and indicative of the increasingly "adulterated" tendencies in Cuban popular music.[20]

Although Prado was an intricate part of the instrumental experimentation that gave mambo its legs, he was often looked upon with suspicion.[21] For example, his work was often rejected for not being sufficiently Cuban. He was unapologetic in his seemingly incongruent influences—a promiscuity with source materials that, in my opinion, is a custom shared by most, if not all of the best Cuban musicians. An adamant devotee of jazz musician Stan Kenton, existentialist authors such as Sartre, and composers such as Stravinsky, Pérez Prado was considered too high art for some audiences.[22] As Pérez Firmat points out, his elevated proclivities were evidenced by his mambo compositions notated with specific numbers (that is, "Mambo No. 5," and "Mambo No. 8") echoing the titles of many compositions in Western classical music.[23] In his interview with the musician Rolando Laserie, Pérez Firmat discovered that, in Cuba, when Pérez Prado would approach, people would remark, "here comes Beethoven."[24]

In the United States the New York unions were hostile to Pérez Prado and often cut him out of many working opportunities for fear of increasing competition. It is partly for this reason he is often excluded from the east coast school of Latino/a popular music historiography in the vein of Vernon Bogg's volume *Salsiology* (1994). Even with his supposedly high-brow pretentions, he was dismissively understood as a commercial hit-maker; a watered-down figure who played the Waldorf-Astoria from time to time.[25] These conditions forced the future mambo king to find other parts of the country receptive to his experiment with sound. Given his success in Mexico, the musician easily found an audience (and somewhat hospitable unions) on the west coast. In August of 1951, he signed up with Los Angeles Local 47 and played an enormously successful eight-date tour of California.[26]

Partly as a result of these movements and struggles regarding his legal right to work, most mention of Pérez Prado is done to shorthand the mambo at the expense of his lifelong experimentations with other genres. Or he is listed as yet another notch on the scene of the Cuban sound. However, as I stated earlier, I believe that his movements (chosen and forced) and the vast circulation of his recordings make it difficult for Pérez Prado's profound imprint to be pegged to one genre or geographic locale. Instead, he is a flickering figure in a larger pan-metropolitan sound be it New York, San Francisco, Mexico City, Rome, Manila, Paris, or Tokyo. Everywhere and nowhere. Like Alfredo Rodríguez and Graciela, his being many places at once has had the paradoxical effect of making his oeuvre not only marginal to popular Cuban music, but also to American and Latin jazz. And yet his contributions and influence can be traced to both stage and page. As Leonardo Acosta writes, "the dominant tendency in jazz since the 1930s was to increasingly combine the sound of the bands, blending instruments from different sections . . . Pérez Prado does just the opposite and establishes different planes with different registers." According to Acosta, by creating different sections where the "high" featured the trumpets and the "low" other brass such as saxophones, Pérez Prado originated a sustained method of "counterpoint and contrast" that had an unprecedented and energizing effect on many arrangers.[27]

His underrecognized contributions are even more difficult to make relevant as Pérez Prado has been forcefully thrown into the musical-kitsch repository. This space of disposable irony reduces his body of work to the instrumental favorites variety record offers once made available on television, or as part of the greatest hits of swinger lounge favorites that gained currency in the mid-1990s. His biggest selling singles were the organ-inflected "Patricia" (1958) and the saucy trumpet stylings (complete with brazen trombone commentary) of "Cherry Pink and Apple Blossom White" (1955). This latter song was featured in the film *Underwater!* starring a bathing-suit clad Jane Russell. It was also one of the highest selling instrumentals of all time. "Nonserious" at best, "cheesy" at worst, his perceived ridiculousness is amplified by his use in many an ice dancing and sport ballroom routine.

His talent at instrumentation often made him the prime additive to a racial other. For example, in 1959 Pérez Prado recorded an album called *A Touch of Tabasco* (with the proper McIlhenny Company Pepper Sauce

FIG. 3.1: Front album cover of Rosemary Clooney/Pérez Prado's *A Touch of Tabasco*, 1960.

trademark) behind the vocals of Rosemary Clooney. The front cover reveals these unlikely partners (in their painted likenesses) exchanging a knowing glance—the kind that adults might share over a dirty joke told in the company of children. Prado was tinted much darker than he actually was. The back of the album pairs small cartoon drawings between seemingly disparate objects; a bowl of beans makes eyes at a smiling apple pie; a *Peanuts*-esque drawing of Prado is costumed in a baseball outfit; the male partner of an average American couple holds a maraca.[28] As these illustrations reveal, Pérez Prado has long been painted as a disparate object to American popular music. His sound begs to be given a forum beyond the island themed mojito party. Its composition asks that we listen and not use it solely to set the mood for some over-the-clothes heavy petting.

The presence of Pérez Prado and his music in the above examples reveal a few situational frames for his reception, particularly in North America. Even though the musician has been circulated in those familiar ways that empire requires (by being made novelty and additive, rendered as outside tradition and history), I believe his grunt intervenes in his own commodification and circulation. In his hit song "Cherry Pink and Apple Blossom White," the music instantly constructs—and makes you part of—a cinematic landscape: you want to saunter toward something or someone with intention. But before you can get too caught up in your own performance, it arises from a deep-sea depth: *dioughh*! His grunt instantly demands recognition and your alterity. It thwarts your expectations. During every subsequent listen to the instrumental you find yourself waiting for it. And even though you might remember each point in the song where the grunt happens, it still catches you unawares.

Such interruptions also have the potential to remind anyone who hears them of the nonsafety of Pérez Prado's musical compatriots. You imagine what they might be enacting through performed details that are not readily legible to you. Meaning, how might they and their instruments be grunting in other ways? How do they demand recognition and our alterity? The grunt's timing, its effect, and its mere appearance in seemingly innocent instrumentals and dance numbers thus intervenes in those user-friendly guides that hope to make Cuban music and musicians definable, which is to say, predictable. This demand has made its ubiquitous presence felt in scholarly travel accounts and record compilations that wink seductively from sepia-enhanced covers.[29] Such demand largely reflects—and borrows from—ethnomusicology's tendency to taxiderm its objects of study. Racial and temporal categories are affirmed to track musical influence in legible ways. It also keeps certain music boxed-set to its proper place. The world music industry's supply and ethnomusicology's demand continue to keep Cuban music scholarship and musical commodities in a mode of trade mirrored in the island's other touristic economies, formal and not. Such trade demands: we want you as backdrop, but we don't want your difficult outbursts.

Ronald Radano and Philip V. Bohlman have coined the phrase the "metaphysics of ownership" to succinctly describe these sorts of attitudes that accompany the consumption and study of music. Forged from the fantasy that music (its makers and origins) can be tracked and mastered, such attitudes have taken many forms in scholarly criticism and in the everyday ways we think and talk about it. Possession is the unifying ethos. The authors helpfully identify a few principal reasons for this. The first, "results from the need to make music understandable . . . achieved through the attribution of linguistic properties to music; that is, to hear communication, signification, and meaning."[30] They attribute the second reason to "technologies of music's production," including the mechanics of recording, instruments used for music's transmission, and the objects that are played. Through this duel system of mastery over the enigmatical and the discipline of machinery, "one acquires the power to own and control the ways in which music bounds the group for which it has meaning."[31] For the authors, "Race is imagined as a component of these issues of music because it is connected with understandability, belonging, and ownership." Pérez Prado's grunt in an instructive menace that reminds any effort to control it (be it receptive, discursive, historical, and racial) will constantly be frustrated.

Radano and Bohlman take special care to reveal the relationship between a thing like Pérez Prado's noise and its vehicles of circulation. They help to make blurry the line between a commodity and a body. They urge a connection between those sepia-packaged CDs or *Rough Guides* and discourses that insist on racial, geographical, and temporal containment. Such work seeks to differentiate the frothy, overlapping waves of ancestry, migration, and racializations that often shipwreck upon a singular Cuban body to make mastery more feasible. With them, I suggest that this attempted arrest of music and bodies—and the immeasurable detailed currents that run through them—does not mean they cannot move into other places, traditions, and genres, or even other sections in a record store. I argue that Pérez Prado's grunt places exceptional pressure on such containment and differentiation by virtue of its extramusical, off the page, and unpredictable, though perfectly timed entrances and exits in music.

I need take a closer look at the mambo, the genre that Pérez Prado is most widely known for and where his grunt arguably took its initial shape. It is not my intention to write a comprehensive history of the genre.[32] Instead, I'd like to echo the astute words of Wai Chee Dimock and call upon genre as

> a self-obsoleting system, a provisional set that will always be bent and pulled and stretched by its many subsets. Such bending and pulling and stretching are unavoidable, for what genre is dealing with is a volatile body of material, still developing, still in transit, and always on the verge of taking flight, in some unknown and unpredictable direction.[33]

Given the volatile, still developing, and in-transit materiality of the grunt, I have long imagined and heard it as a vital organic component to (and infraction of) mambo's provisions. My rehearsal of genre carefully considers Pérez Prado's grunt as a mode of performance that experienced great rehearsal in the mambo.

There is a debate that aggressively haunts mambo, one that is waged over its ownership and its locations. Like all music, its provenance is difficult to sort out and attribute directly to an individual person and place. On a good day, I believe such debates about mambo are less about whom to properly credit and more about earnest efforts to get at what it is. Such efforts have taken innovative forms. For example, the Cuban music critic Radamés Giro put together an exquisite and compact collection *El mambo* that includes photographs of its main players, musical scores, interviews, and polemical meditations on what mambo is. Published in 1993, the book was assembled at the hungriest height of Cuba's Special Period (which in itself begs for a moment of reflection and silence).[34] Giro suggests that one needs to have an undercommons flexibility to enter the scene of mambo even if that scene takes place on a page. Although he begins the volume with the following line, "El mambo es quizás el género más controvertido de la música popular cubana" [The mambo is perhaps the most controversial genre in popular Cuban music] Giro does not structure his introduction (or the larger text) as the final word on the matter.[35] Instead, he incorporates many points of view and argument. As we wade into the volume, he calls our attention to three principal portals into mambo: etymology, musical structure, and location. I borrow his mode of entry here.

There are numerous theories on how mambo entered sound, song, and conversation.[36] Following Giro's cue and Helio Orovio's research (a dream critical tag team), I choose to proceed to mambo's etymological grounds through Arsenio Rodríguez. Rodríguez, the brilliant Cuban musical innovator and instigator of Congolese ancestry, defined mambo this way:

Los descendientes de congos [. . .] tocan una música que se llama *tambor de yuca* en la controversia que forman uno y otro cantante, siguiendo el ritmo, me inspiré y esa es la base verdadera del mambo. La palabra mambo es africana, del dialecto congo. Un cantante le dice al otro <<abre cuto güirí mambo>>, o sea: <<abre el oído y oye lo que te voy a decir>>.[37]

[The descendents from congos[. . .] play a kind of music called drum of yuca. I was inspired by the controversy created between the singers following the rhythms, which is the real base of mambo. The Word mambo is African, from the Congo dialect. One singer tells the other <<abre cuto güirí mambo>>, meaning, <<open your ear and listen what I am going to tell you>>.]

In Rodríguez's stunning conservation of things past, mambo is not a thing but a detailed command. It asks that you open your ear. It asks that you get ready for the song's next steps and reminds you of a transition to come. Said or sung from one singer to the other, it is a direction to listen carefully. They are laying the ground for your what's next.[38] Such provenance reminds of Pérez Prado describing his grunt as cue.

In her interview, Erena Hernández asked Pérez Prado to explain his version of the word mambo. In response, he reminded her of the word's everyday function:

Mambo es una palabra cubana. Se usaba cuando la gente quería decir cómo estaba la situación: si el mambo estaba duro era que la cosa iba mal . . . Musicalmente no quiere decir nada, para qué le voy a decir mentira. Es un nombre. Hasta ahí no mas. [Mambo is a Cuban word. People used to say it when they wanted to talk about what the situation was like: if the mambo was hard it meant that things were not going well . . . I won't lie to you, musically speaking it doesn't mean anything. It's just a name. That's all.][39]

Mixing Rodríguez and Pérez Prado's etymological positions together, we are left with a detail from Congolese dialect that means a command and an object that carries the pulse of things. I am struck by Pérez Prado's refusal to overdetermine the word with meaning that it did not ask for. And that he leaves instructions for how to approach his grunt. He demonstrates how a Cuban colloquialism might name something but leave its actual properties a mystery. The word might not mean anything musically, but it offers a surface for feeling, a roomy platform for a descriptive that says things as they are. How do certain mambos feel hard? I've long been haunted by a Bebo Valdés recording called "Mississippi Mambo," recorded in Havana in 1955.[40] Valdés's piece envelops and expands a geographical and affective South. It is but one instance that testifies to mambo's vast locations and mobility, its ability to carry feeling and history. Its grinding outrage and minor key melancholy feels like a condolence sent to a mourning Mamie Till.

There has been such a tremendous set of responses to the question that Moré posed at the beginning of this chapter: "¿quién inventó el mambo?" which is to also ask, where was mambo invented? To reiterate, I will not offer a firm answer as to the genre's origins. I'll instead proceed with the creativity of the responses. And so, I defer to Leonardo Acosta who famously attributed the appearance of mambo to something that was "in the air."[41] That "something in the air" lingered over a vast terrain, from Havana to Mexico City to New York to Los Angeles and so on. The geographical reach of said air was incredibly expansive. In the above, Arsenio Rodríguez rightly maps its West African roots.[42] Mambo's gestation is generally attributed to occurring in Cuba, but I believe that its shared development between many locations means that any attempt to fix and possess its provenance will fail. There seems to be some agreement, as Elena Pérez Sanjurjo and many others have argued, that it was in Mexico City that the genre really galvanized a massive public.[43] "Buscando horizontes," (looking for new horizons) was how Pérez Prado explained his move to Mexico City in 1948.[44] Put this way, he asks that we think of sound not so much in the margins, but in and as horizons.

Because of the historical exchanges between Afro-Cuban and Afro-American jazz musicians, a historical relationship of contact and exchange that I examined in chapters 1 and 2, and the proliferation of mambo-themed movies of the Mexico's cinematic golden age, the mambo sound and public was further developed in North America. New York City is often understood as the home of mambo in the United States. It is reflexively historicized with what it known in mambo-speak as the "Big Three." The Big Three included the Cuban-born Frank "Machito" Grillo and his Afro-Cubans (as you will recall, Graciela's brother and orchestra) and the famed Puerto Rican musicians Tito Puente and Tito Rodríguez, both of whom had their own respective orchestras.

Featured at important nightclubs such as the Palladium Ballroom, the Savoy, the Cotton Club, the Apollo Theater, Latin Quarter, and Havana Madrid, the Big Three competed among themselves for their cross-cultural audiences. Though these venues attracted predominantly Latino/a and Afro-American audiences, they also lured a large amount of Italian, Jewish, and Irish American dancers, especially on nights that featured mambo.[45] The physical contact between the dancers found in footage from the era continues to be among the most beautiful and stirring in the history of hemispheric performance.[46] However, the circulated mythologies of the Big Three have the unintended effect of erasing the vibrant mambo scene on the West Coast in both San Francisco and Los Angeles. California, as I've already mentioned, was where some of mambo's and Pérez Prado's most adoring audiences resided. The limited view from the East Coast also incidentally shrouds the contributions of Chicanos and Filipinos, as performers and audience members, from mambo's repeated narratives.[47]

For some audiences, the mambo was considered another on the long list of so-called Latin musical booms or crazes (explosions in current lingo) that followed on the coattails of genres such as the rumba, tango, and in approximate tandem with the cha-cha-cha. As the 1954 article in *Newsweek* reported, "the mambo rhythms spread through Latin America and then wiggled their way into the United States."[48] While at first glance this pull quote might be dismissed as highly problematic, it actually offers some provocative analysis. Not lost on the strategic quality of gesture, the sound did not simply walk or ask permission for entry and reception to the United States, but *wiggled*, maneuvered, and finagled its way over national borders. As John Storm Roberts once pointed out, Pérez Prado was a wiggling figure like no other, among the first performers to have immense crossover appeal in North America, and the most visible figures of the mambo craze of the early 1950s.[49]

Mambo's hold on North American popular music was partly made possible by charismatic figures such as Pérez Prado and the Big Three. But I want to emphasize that the migrations the genre made revealed some breathtaking critical moves (to borrow Randy Martin's useful phrase)—with or without the musicians' physical dislocations. Consider the hemispheric timing when mambo was such a beloved (and also reviled) and omnipresent phenomena. The circulation of mambo's sound dovetailed the last postwar vestiges of

Franklin Roosevelt's "Good Neighbor Policy" as increasing cold war para-noia turned into policies of containment. Straddling the mid-1940s to 1950s, mambo happened at the very moment that the movements of bodies and the ideologies they might or might not have carried were increasingly seen as problems to be controlled. Consider, for example, that the 1950 spotlight on Pérez Prado and the mambo was in an issue of *Newsweek* that bore the cover page, "The Soviet Army Has Its Weaknesses: Report from Behind the Iron Curtain."[50] Also consider how mambo was part of the soundtrack for the space race. There is lengthy article titled "Uncle Sambo Mad for Mambo" in a 1954 issue of *Life* magazine behind the cover "The Star Studded Features of Measureless Space," (prompting the editor's note, "Andromeda and the Mambo").[51]

Mambo and its makers were partly understood as friendly exceptions to the increasing and understandable opposition Latin/o Americans had to US hegemony in the postwar era. It is hard to believe that mambo and its musicians could be relied to play good neighborly mascots. Were they as accommodating as the saccharine descriptions given to the music? Pérez Prado's grunts were some of mambo's stray details and their effects couldn't be anticipated by any act of consumption, whether buying a record or dancing. Millions discovered that learning the dance steps from magazine cut outs did not prepare them for mastery over the genre. In Pérez Prado's "Mambo No. 8" for example, the bandleader invites the listener to a game of aural freeze tag. When the song begins, the orchestra sets up the piece by vocally counting-up in unison and in Spanish. In walks a playful bass line accompanied by a cyclical and repetitive horn section. Together they provide a steady and increasingly familiar pattern. In this way, the composition could be described as a typical, dancer-friendly mambo. Immediately after this familiarity offers comfort, Pérez Prado's grunt renders it unpredictable. Just when the dancer might begin to effectively get their groove on and settle into a series of repetitive turns and backs and forths, the orchestra stops playing for several measures. Before one knows what is happening or what might come next, in enters Pérez Prado's "¡ugh!" In short, just when you think you've trapped a particular movement and sound, Pérez Prado disrupts and relies on the listener's power of imagination (and one could argue, bodily flexibility) to find the flow within the spur of the grunt.

The resistance of the genre—even in its global proliferation—likely has something to do with some of the formal qualities of the mambo itself. Even those formal qualities are difficult to make discrete. They resist my summarizing. To try and isolate them means getting controversial, as there are hundreds of theories about what mambo is. It is a genre like most others that insists on multiple theories when explained.[52]

Without becoming definitive about it, it is generally agreed upon that mambo emerges from Cuban dance genres, such as the rumba, danzón, and son. Rumba, with its fundamental rhythmic spines, can be felt in the faster mambo compositions. From the danzón, Acosta tells us that mambo inherits the cinquillo rhythm from the final (and fastest) part of its structure.[53] Pérez Prado himself identified his "new musical style" initially by the phrase the "son mambo."[54] It is as a possible extension from the montuno section of the Cuban son that makes the origin story of the genre even more provocative. The formal properties of the Cuban son are based structurally on a largo repetition (usually two or three stanzas that are identical in form) and followed by the montuno (a refrain space for vocal and instrumental improvisation). The repetitive structure of the formal son sets up the stage for the montuno, a moment for flourish and collective remark. The montuno does not only involve the musicians, but also the audience that surrounds it. As Alejo Carpentier writes of the space of the montuno, "The instruments embroidered, designing 'filigrees,' subdividing the basic notes, working in tandem with the growing excitement of the dancers, who in turn, made their steps more intricate."[55]

To think of mambo as a form that partly arises out of this maelstrom of genres and especially, the montuno section of the traditional son, reminds that though it keeps tempo, the grunt operates in improvisational grounds. Perhaps it is due to the difficult representation of improvisation that the creator and provenance of the mambo are still widely debated among Cuban musicians and aficionados. Perhaps the grunt might offer a model for how we can mark mambo's myriad contributors—a way to listen in detail and record those who improvise in history.

Thus far, I've given a sketch of Pérez Prado's career and movements, the mambo as a generator, and the feel of the grunt from such generative grounds. I'll now take an even closer look at the grunt itself. To do so, I will move through a series of objects left in Pérez Prado's wake. By way of these objects including, most obviously, his recorded music, I'll also pay some attention to how others have engaged the grunt. As I do so, I'll consider the grunt's reiteration comparatively with other modes of outbursts—a necessary methodological move especially considering mambo's cross-cultural conditions of production. I'll first consider a few surfaces of his resonant archive.

The grunt is just one detail in what Dimock calls genre's "volatile body of material." Such volatility wasn't only detectable in his work with mambo. It was the constant in his musical experimentations. There have been so many memorable infractions. Take his 1962 *Twist Goes Latin* album that featured twisted versions of the "Hava Nageela," "St. Louis Blues," and even a song called the "Saigon Twist." By now it was clear to anyone who listened that he would unscrupulously work with whatever sound he felt like taking up and out. In fact, he built his reputation on it. As the sleeve notes ask, "And who is there greater to carry this biggest new dance craze in twenty years to its next logical—or illogical development? The nonpariel Prado, undisputed King of the Latin beat, that's who."[56] The logical and illogical development could also be heard on albums such as *Las novias de Pérez Prado*, which featured twelve songs dedicated to specific women. Their names (Norma la de Guadalajara, Rebeca, Maria Eugenia, Lupita, etc.) are used to title the tracks that ranged from dengue to mambo to Ritmo Italiano.[57]

In Latin/o music criticism, many writers make a waxpoetical habit of positioning certain musicians as politicized and others as merely pop spectacle. Such binaries are often made to correspond with how rare their records are. Disc jockeys are often complicit when they describe their search for source material with hunting metaphors, or using egyptological parlance, call their work "digging." When such rarities are rediscovered by them, there can be a push to rerelease due to increasing demand. The privileging of musicians (and romanticization of) the Fania Records empire is one example. Such efforts at rerelease and critical attention are undeniably important because Fania produced beautiful body-rocking work. The problem is that all others who came before, during, and after, were left in Fania's wake and are dismissed as novelties coopted by the mainstream, derivative, played-out.[58]

Such novelties were reproduced so often that they usually end up in the three-for-five-dollars section. It is in those sections that you will often find Pérez Prado. Such availability can make many grossly underestimate his musical work. Take the words of Richard Gehr, who qualified Pérez Prado as "the act middle-class white Americas turned to most loyally for their mambo fix."[59]

When I shop for records I gingerly move my fingers through the crates like an overpolite guest and wait for them to select me. It was at the Logos Used Books and Records Store in the Santa Cruz, California, of 1997 that Pérez Prado's 1958 album *Dilo (Ugh!)* jumped out and told me to get to work. The surface of the album cover is taken over by a giant close up of his face in mid-grunt. We don't and can't know if he is grunting in the live, what he is feeling, what sound was produced as this image was taken. We certainly can't dismiss his expression as an ironic one. I take in his goatee, a look he was said to cultivate to pay homage to Dizzy Gillespie. I think of this yelling face circulating in the America of 1958 and wonder what kind of effect it had as it was laid beside the turntable, placed on a shelf, left on the floor. I think of its resemblance to that iconographic picture of Pedro Albizu Campos in mid-scream. I think of James Brown. And Aunt Hester. And even Salvador Dali. I think of how Pérez Prado made the Americas dance as he grunted their violent undercurrents. I think of how this record came out a year before the Cuban Revolution, as a trace of how Cuban musician's movements were once commonplace in the United States. His image here shows how the grunt's volatility is felt beyond the sonic and in the visual.

On the backside of the *Dilo (Ugh!)* album, there is a broad-stroke drawing of the bandleader's profile. Out from his mouth pops the stereophonic fontesque *Dilo (Ugh!)*. This graphic rendering of Pérez Prado and this parenthetical (ugh!) illustrates how he was conflated with his vocal trademark. The artist makes the grunt an alternative referent for the musician. Whether it was intended or not, I read the image as keeping with the Cuban tradition of making nicknames out of virtually everything and everybody. In this case, the "ugh!" marks the man. As Severo Sarduy writes, "With sly accuracy, Cubans systematically nickname everything that refers to them; they use nicknames to smash every attempt at solemnity and grandiloquence, throw reality to the *choteo*."[60]

This process of nicknaming as it relates to people (versus other objects in

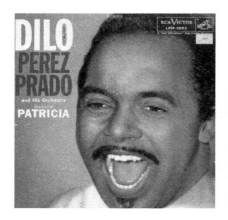

FIG. 3.2: Front album cover of Pérez Prado's *Dilo (Ugh!)*, 1958.

FIG. 3.3: Back album cover of Pérez Prado's *Dilo (Ugh!)*, 1958.

the world) has a tendency to take flight from and exaggerate off of bodily surfaces, racial marks that disrupt the myth of Cuban whiteness, and even animal characteristics. A Cuban with a hint of slant to her eyes becomes China. A man with a large nose is magically transformed and named el Loro (the Parrot). The nicknaming can also work in dialectical opposites as the case when an overweight man is rebaptized as Flaco (Skinny). Whatever the case, these nicknames adhere for life regardless of rhinoplasty, weight loss, or even death. Nicknames throw reality to the choteo in that they retain past truths, underscore what is in front of you, or excavate what might be concealed. This drawing makes it possible to imagine that in one way, Pérez Prado's grunt functions much like the shorthand of his performance: the musician becomes defined by the "ugh!" Or perhaps it helps to imagine how the grunt might be understood as the nicknaming of unspeakable pasts—those that can't be spoken but can be shouted, grunted, screamed.

As I noted earlier in the chapter, the theories-in-place on Prado's grunt are typically found through its written descriptions. Many of these theory-descriptions offer much on the dynamics of the grunt's reception. On the same *Dilo* album, the critic Watson Wylie takes on the grunt in the sleeve notes. His words are so earnest and spirited, I've decided to include them almost in-full. Wylie reports:

Perez Prado waves the only vocal baton in music. The urgent bellicose grunts that appear like punctuation marks in Prado's performances are no haphazard outbursts. These grunts are Prado conducting his orchestra in his own unique and fantastically effective way . . . To the uninitiated ear, the Cuban bandleader seems to be saying, "Dilo!"-a Spanish word meaning "Say it!" or, in the context which Prado uses it "Give out!" . . . In Prado's throat, it becomes part of the number. It provides accents, it produces a shock that bursts a pool of calmness . . . Not the least intriguing aspect of Prado's musical war cry is how he manages to make "Dilo!" sound like "Ugh!" the exact technique is his own secret, but it would appear to the analytic ear that he accomplishes the transition by removing the vowels and the consonants from the word before exhaling.[61]

The who or what that comprises either of Wylie's "uninitiated" in unclear. The uninitiated could mean those who are unfamiliar with the Spanish language, as the qualifying verb for this particular category is based upon hearing a particular word. Nevertheless, this uninitiated ear still hears what Pérez Prado "seems to be saying" by the word dilo. This ear hears the word, but perhaps refuses or is incapable of translating it. The uninitiated descriptive also suggests that there is some unspoken rite not yet participated in. Perhaps the hearing of the grunt is based on something even further indefinable. Note that there is no diametric opposite to the uninitiated ear posited in Wylie's notes. There is no follow-up regarding what the initiated ear might do with the grunt.

I'd like to conjecture what an initiated ear might mean and what it might have to do with the "shock that bursts a pool of calmness." To do so, I'd like to take a moment in Afro-Nuyorican/Cuban Piri Thomas's autobiography *Down These Mean Streets*. Thomas poetically chronicles his experiences as the darkest member of a family that does not acknowledge their blackness; caught in what Raquel Rivera has termed "between blackness and *latinidad*."[62] It documents first loves and losses, the "first hired, last fired" mantra of capitalism, drug addiction, and his stint in prison. The narrative is replete with mambo references. It is the text's soundtrack. In one scene, a young Thomas enters a candy store while waiting for his girlfriend to get ready. From the jukebox, a mambo played. Thomas writes, "Mambo! My feet automatically reacted and I danced the last few steps to the door."[63] I read this automatic reaction of Thomas as an improvisatory one. Danielle Goldman has argued that improvisation is too often deployed to, "impl[y] a lack of preparation, thereby eliding the historical knowledge, the sense of tradition, and the enormous skill that most eloquent improvisers are able to mobilize."[64] Thomas's automatic reaction is not some dehistoricized natural phenomenon. It is a wise, trained, adaptive, and instantly articulate response to what surrounded him at that given moment.

Pérez Firmat offers his own linguistic examination of the grunt, "Pérez Prado's disarticulation of *¡dilo!* into 'ugh!' makes evident the mambo's logoclassia, its tendency to reduce speech to sound, communication to expression."[65] He contends that "mambo's laconism," its minimal use of words, or in the case of Pérez Prado, the refusal of words, neither necessarily requiring translation, worked to diffuse the music on an international scale. In this way, the author continues, it is neither decidedly Spanish nor English. The terms of those who might be potential initiates are productively made more flexible than the more clumsy forms of in-group nationalism allows. I would nevertheless like to trouble Pérez Firmat's juxtaposition of "communication to expression." I argue that this false opposition made between precision of language (communication) versus ambiguous feeling (expression) does not allow the grunt to do both at once. This eludes its potential power.

In another episode in *Down These Mean Streets*, we follow young Thomas as he flees a school dance after being assaulted by a racist remark. He ran out in the midst of a mambo that had been playing. Thomas writes, "My lungs were hurting-not from running but from not being able to scream."[66] What would it be like to imagine the grunt as both indexing his frustration in all its complexity, at the same time that it addresses the violence of that given moment? Moreover, that Pérez Prado's grunt screams for Thomas and offers relief as it keeps the time for the actual music? The grunt's production of "shock that bursts a pool of calmness" makes available places in mambo where the listener can insert their tale of events through a dance move, find protection in assault, raise a fist of solidarity, offer a reprieve from the racist everyday.

In Wylie's account, the "analytic ear" is offered as a kind of counterpoint to the uninitiated ear. Moreover, it uses a different sensory register than utilized by Thomas in the passages above. To the analytic ear, the grunt appears, an appeal to sight to turn sound to sign. Pérez Prado's removal of the vowels and consonants from the word before exhaling reveals Wylie's quandary: to try and turn the grunt into a sign is made impossible by the musician's secret technique. Such a technique reveals the challenges faced when trying to represent what we hear. It reminds that noise is already articulate and doesn't need linguistic orients.[67] It reveals that musicians can intervene in their documentation in and outside of song, especially through details such as these. When taken from the heard to the written, Pérez Prado's secret makes the grunt's capture impossible. We are left to speculate in the way that Wylie began to do back in 1958. Pérez Prado made himself an unsolvable riddle.

Whatever Pérez Prado is saying or how it is made to look (for any attempt to make a word of it is provisional) the grunt is an integral part of the musical structure even if it can't get represented in words or marked on a five-lined score. Performing this unscored score thus makes clear a kind of irreproducibility of Pérez Prado's musical intervention. I've nonetheless seen and heard how the grunt gets reproduced in many a forum, even in (and it could be argued, because of) its impossibility. Pérez Prado grunts leave open, for the musicians in his orchestra, the dancers in the club, the academic ensconced in her headphones, marked gaps for collective interplay.

My thinking about Pérez Prado's grunt as an indexical noise, or as that which makes possible a space of reprieve, is particularly indelible when considering the cross-cultural reception of Prado and his grunt. The spaces of reception I take into consideration in the following pages are a few dance floors. Although these scenes do involve Pérez Prado himself, they also gesture toward what else might be indexed by the grunt. While the grunt is Pérez Prado's signature, and its "exact technique" escapes written representation, it can nevertheless be reproduced. It is a material signature left open for the penmanship of multiple hands, indicating the mobility and fugitivity of hemispheric performance.

The Latin music producer George Goldner of Tico Records and concert promoter Irving Schact inaugurated 1954 as the "Year of the Mambo" by putting together an eleven-city tour named "Mambo, U.S.A." It was billed as the biggest musical tour to date and featured forty performers from the international mambo circuit. Musical headliners such as Machito and his Afro-Cuban All Stars, Tito Puente, the Facundo Rivera Quartet, and the Joe Loco Quintet, were featured alongside some of mambo's famed dancers such as Horatio and Lana, Aura San Juana, Tybee Afra, the Mambo Aces, and others whose moves graced the Palladium Ballroom in New York.[68] The roster also included Tun Tun, a performer billed as a "midget Mexican comedian."[69] In the documentary *Palladium!*, an interview with Michael Terrace, an Irish-American dancer from New York City, offers a remarkable memory from the tour. Terrace describes the company's departure from New York City as the performers being "all in love." They opened in Brooklyn to unprecedented success. The tour then traveled to Connecticut where they were welcomed with arms and feet open to the not-heard-before rhythms. At this moment in the story, there is a break in Terrace's voice as it changes from excited naivety to one soaked in melancholia. Terrace reflects on the day the tour arrived in Baltimore:

> That's where the Mason-Dixon line is, and then we had a rude awakening . . . when I was doing "In a little Spanish town" there were about 15 black kids sitting down front. Young kids—maybe 14, 13—maybe up to twenty. And, the number goes [Terrace claps] Ba ba babadaba, Ba Ba Babadaba OOOOOOOOOOO WAH [*Author's note: this is an attempt to phonically reproduce Terrace's sounds—it is a citation of Prado's grunt.*] That was a Pérez Prado number. Well, those kids picked up on it—and whenever it came to that climax of a crescendo, they would all chime in "OOOOOOOOOO WAH." And, in the middle of that rehearsal—Machito was playing the number. . . . rehearsing the number, two cops come up to me and they say "Hey boy, you get those niggers out of there."

Imagine what might have ruffled the policemen as they emerged on the scene. Perhaps their reaction would not have been much different had these young black onlookers been sitting quietly. Their gathering together could be criminal in and of itself in the Jim Crow south. It was the perfectly timed collective grunting, however, that made their union a disciplinable offense. I imagine that trying to chime in was a good deal of fun for both the children and the performers. It was a game that included grunting both familiar and foreign, and outbursts both anticipatable and elusive. For the police the moment was unbearable; both spectacle and spectator formed a temporary, in-unison whole. It needed to be pried apart and shooed away. To do so they resort to plantation antics. Terrace, addressed as "boy" in keeping with the paternalistic signifier of folks of color, is implicitly racialized by his contact with the musicians and the young men and/or by the ways in which he moved. Although he was not quite saved by the color of his skin, Terrace was supposed to inflict discipline.[70]

The collision of multiple grunts emerges here. Although Terrace's story is not explicitly about Pérez Prado as performer, it says something about the grunt's reproduction beyond him, beyond a recording and into live performance. Live performance in a formal sense via Machito and his Afro-Cuban All Stars, and in the everyday sense with the "15 black kids." While Pérez Prado is the primary text of the piece, Machito is his interlocutor. The boys and girls in the audience layer multiple textures onto Pérez Prado's grunt. On the outskirts of the stage, we have Michael Terrace "In a Little Spanish Town" bridging (albeit romanticized with pastoral Spain) the Iberian Peninsula and the moves that stem from his Irish American body to the performance.

The layered senses of timing, form, and cadences to Pérez Prado's grunt in this scenario brings to the fore a field of meanings and usages. Although Machito and the children share a sense of time, it would be an injustice to flatten out their vocal outbursts to being the same. Referencing the work Amiri Baraka, author Nathaniel Mackey dubs the phrase "cultivation of another voice" in order to describe part of the "fugitive spirit" of Afro-American aesthetic practices. Mackey reads Baraka's work as adopting the poetic fugitivity—formal and felt—enacted in the music the poet was listening to at the time. He describes the mode through which Baraka submerges sound into his work as "the cultivation of another voice, a voice that is other than that proposed by one's own intentions, tangential to one's own intentions, angular, oblique-the obliquity of unbound reference."[71] I like to think of how Pérez Prado's grunt offered another voice to the young kids. It was not imposed onto them by Machito, but was instead made available as another mode of performance, which is also to say, another way of being in the world.

The word "cultivate" according to *The American Heritage Dictionary* means: "1. To improve and prepare (land) for raising crops. 2. To grow or tend (a plant or crop). 3. To foster. 4. To form and refine, as by education. 5. To seek the acquaintance or good will of."[72] I am particularly caught on the fourth and fifth definitions. The children cultivate the grunt in that they form and refine it from their place at the edge of the stage, and they educate it to the realities of their experiences as young folks of color who reside on the edge of the Mason-Dixon line. As Mackey continues, "A different medium is a different voice, an alternate vocality."[73] I also hear the import of an alternate locality here—which we might say is Havana, or Mexico, or New York. Rather than make locality singular, I prefer to think of it as that "something in the air" described by Acosta to encompass the vast geographies and influences in mambo. Even if points of contact are not made transparent to us, that something is deeply historical and it is shared, across water, languages, land.

By bringing in an alternate vocality and alternate locality, the children's revision of Pérez Prado's grunt happens geographically and generationally and affectively. That they use the grunt to "seek acquaintance" of, or identification with, the musicians on the stage, opens up Pérez Prado's sonic practice as a place of dwelling, a place for kinship, a site of mutual release across the Americas. As demonstrated by Terrace's story above, Pérez Prado's grunt is an opportunity to think through the preciousness of this shared past that is not limited by access to language or attention to national borders. There are, of course, other arenas where receptive access to the grunt has produced altogether different effects. The process by which borders are crossed, whether they are linguistic, musical, affective, or geographical, depends upon who is doing the crossing. In themselves, the archival borders that Prado's music is made to cross are dizzying. Therefore, it should come as no surprise that he makes another appearance in the guarded catalogue of canonical American literature.

New editions of Jack Kerouac's *On the Road* are generally labeled with the ubiquitous superlative, "The novel that defined a generation." The inclusion of Pérez Prado in the novel generates some interesting speculations. Most obviously, his insertion into the text—however brief—works as a counternarrative to the privileged wandering of young Anglo men in Jim Crow America. Prado's presence partially signals other kinds of migratory figures for whom movements are less about the sowing of oats, adventure, or other rites of passage that certain masculinities often require. These rites described in one way or another throughout the book, often depend upon the passing through and over others found not on the road, but seemingly in the road to some existential truth. As readers we are allowed to travel on what are compulsory routes for many ghosted others. In the most notable case, the text documents movement across the scar that is the US-Mexico border. Sal Paradise (the narrator) and his road buddies cross from San Antonio and into La Gregoria, a town 150 miles south of Juárez. As often happens in border crossing from the North *to* the South, there is an automatic transition to things deviant. Soon after such a crossing in the book, we are introduced to Pérez Prado's music.

The musician is not just included in some haphazard moment in the text. Instead, he is used to provide the soundtrack for the novel's notorious brothel scene, the climax before the inevitable denouement of the journey. In a closing chapter, Dean, Stan, Victor, and Sal go to a Mexican brothel. Immediately after laying eyes on the "girls," they sent the bartender to procure some mambo records. The bartender returned with many Pérez Prado records that were then played as "loud as we wanted." Delighted with both the control of soundtrack and its volume, Paradise muses at length after being confronted with the sounds of mambos such as "Chattanooga de Mambo" and "Mambo No. 8" (which I described earlier):

All these tremendous numbers resounded and flared in the golden, mysterious afternoon like the sounds you expect to hear on the last day of the Second Coming... The mambo beat is the conga beat from the Congo, the river of Africa and the world; its really the world beat ... The cries of the leader were like great gasps in the air. The final trumpet choruses that came with drum climaxes on conga and bongo drums... froze Dean in his tracks for a moment till he shuddered and sweated; then when the trumpets bit the drowsy air with their quivering echoes, like a cavern's or a cave's, his eyes grew large and round as though seeing the devil, and he closed them tight. I myself was shaken like a puppet by it; I heard the trumpets flail the light I had seen and trembled in my boots.[74]

This passage is a classic example of a Kerouacian attempt of mimetic reproduction of music. Here the proclivities of mimesis, especially when describing music, often reveal more about the desires of the author rather than what the music itself is formally doing. My critique here is not intended to foreclose any interpretive space, even from Kerouac. However, the music of the other, or the "world beat" broadly defined, has an unfortunate repository of automatic significations and terms that critics too easily rely upon. These kinds of descriptives too frequently overdetermine other musics with racial anxieties. That said, there is something refreshing (or even reassuring) about Paradise feeling something along the lines of fear regarding the Second Coming via Africa and Prado's grunt.

For Kerouac, a description of Prado's music and grunt indexes a different mode of release on an individual and collective level than those that I've described in the preceding pages. His music provides echoes that "quiver" in vaginal-like caverns and caves. The grunt is no longer a grunt. Instead it is a reversal of a grunt, a gasp, an action that is desperate for air rather than that which expunges air. By fault of the instrumental signifiers of things African, the congo and bongo, the trumpets "came." Dean "shuddered and sweated" and Paradise "trembled." It is important to note in these instances that the "girls" do not directly produce the orgasm. Prado's music is that which coaxes this visceral reception and release. For Paradise, the grunt rendered as gasp, and functions as the receiver to his receptive pleasure. The music does certain kinds of work (historical, racial, and gendered) for Paradise. But this is not enough. The narrator also needs to be reassured that its worker is enjoying it. In this way, the musician's labor bears some kind of important relationship with that of sexual work.

For the rest of their time in La Gregoria, Prado's mambos pipe in and out of the happenings at the brothel. The mambos offered no reprieve and "frenzied on like an endless journey in a jungle."[75] The gang eventually turns their attention to where "they found the girls."[76] Of course, these women most likely sensed their arrival hours prior to their supposed discovery. It was only through dancing with the women to "Mambo Jambo" that Paradise and the boys were able to "discern their varying personalities." Through this dancing, a formerly undifferentiated group of women's bodies were now identifiable as discrete entities. Here there is a productive fissure in Paradise's narrative that does two important things. For one, their dancing disrupts Kerouac's discursive control over them and the actual situation. In this brief instant, the women also disrupt the grunt as a male-only domain. For Paradise (and likely, for Kerouac himself), their mambo dancing brings the unbearable traces of their respective personhoods. This is not to say that they become transparent though mambo or by way of Prado. What eludes Paradise is that their dancing is quite possibly a performed mode of the working self.

While they might have been discernable, they were not yet individuals in Paradise's mind as their names, not even their stage names, were asked for or documented. Instead, the women were given racial nicknames. A heavy drinking bi-racial (half-indigenous/half-white) woman was named "Venezuela." Others are simply referred to as "my girl" or x's "girl." The main object of Paradise's affection was a sixteen year-old referred to as a "the little colored girl-not colored, but dark." I read Paradise's recognition and subsequent refusal of her raced skin as resonating in the same way that the mambo just will not "let up for a moment." It toggles between the background and foreground.

Nor do the visible conditions of the employee's living let up for a moment, even in the narrator's desire to deny them. Paradise reflects upon "the little colored girl" whom he couldn't keep his eyes off. After staring at her for a time, he adds, "Mexicans are poor. It never, never occurred to me just to approach her and give her some money." Her potential scorn that she would give in return for his gift was too much for him to bear.[77] His great fear was that she would not enjoy it. She would not gasp with pleasure. After spending a "lot of money" (thirty-six dollars), Paradise and his crew leave Gregoria. Their next stop was the nearest bathhouse. As they left, the "haunting mambo followed us a few blocks." Indeed. The mambo and its maker haunt Kerouac's work as much as it does a whole genre of literature, and it can't be washed off.

As Kerouac makes decidedly clear, the mambo and Pérez Prado are not stains that can come out in America's wash. Bearing this in mind, I'd like to draw attention to the grunt's appearance in one more literary instance that takes place in a very different America, this time in the Cuban American writer Achy Obejas's *Memory Mambo*. The novel follows the travails of Juani, a young Cuban lesbian who must navigate her coming of age in exile in the United States. What's more, she must do so while working long hours in her family's laundromat. Through Juani's eyes, we come to know her family's memories of both their past Cuba and present Chicago. They are disjunctive and conflicting entities, residual products of cold war politics and the painful separations that they conceal. These afflictions are felt from the outset, as Juani starts off the novel, "sometimes I wonder if we know where we each end and the others begin."[78] It is hard to resist mentioning that Pérez Prado shared this similar predicament in the most literal way. In the mid-1950s, he discovered that his younger brother Pantaleon Pérez Prado had been touring Europe under the billing "Pérez Prado, King of the Mambo." The elder Pérez Prado procured a restraining order against the fraternal imposter, eventually suing him for $500,000.[79]

In the midst of the intimate collisions throughout *Memory Mambo*, Juani must learn to survive her first loves and losses, to publicly modulate her sexuality between the space of family and its outside, to move past failed expectations, and make a joke of those existential disappointments that often define one's early twenties. While Juani attempts (and ultimately, fails) to discern those gaps between where each member of her family "ends" and "begins," there is one private impenetrable space: that which holds each character's secrets.

In a later moment of the book, Juani takes a trip in order to air a few of her confidences accumulated throughout its temporal arc. She had certainly collected her fair share: from harboring doubts of her father's claim to the invention of duct tape, the horrific behavior of one cousin's problematic husband, and some ideas on a distant family member who is not as straight as the rest of her family would like to believe. But more than anything else, Juani is haunted by her recent hospitalization. This forced admittance was due to a violent altercation and consequential break up with Gina, her Puerto Rican nationalist girlfriend. Her injuries were not the result of a politically or poverty-motivated crime as her family supposed.

Juani thus flees to Miami to visit her sister Nena, a stay that had been conceived as a transitional layover between Chicago and her first return trip to Cuba. Upon their reunion, the two sisters begin the process of taking stock of each other's lives by sharing their privileged information. Juani relays her theories about family gossip, including the unknown father of their cousin's baby. Nena unloads her clandestine life in Miami with a half-Jewish, half-Afro-American boyfriend, one she long kept out of reach of her family's gossip and racism. Juani, however, withholds the tragedy behind her broken heart and injuries. In a brief pause in conversation, Nena put a Pérez Prado CD on the stereo. When confronted with his music, Juani thinks, "The hyper-happy sound filled the room. Trumpets struggled against saxes, saxes against trombones. '*Unnngh!*' grunted Prado. I couldn't take it."[80]

Juani's inability to "take" the mambo, especially punctuated by the grunt, is a reminder of the life worlds of secrets and their desire for reprieve. Although Juani does not want to make her episode with Gina public, the shrill, saccharine sounds of the mambo might have created *too* much volumic cover for the event's unspeakables. Perhaps Juani wanted to acknowledge her secret without revealing its particular details—a quieter moment where she could simply sit and let the secret lay in the company of her sister. Or maybe it was the realization, or a reminder, of the violence she had once thought herself incapable of. But Juani's listening detects a set of internal rips within the song. The music is described in terms of struggle over being heard, one instrument is pitted against the other, "trumpets against saxes, saxes against trombones." The grunt sounds like an umpire's call in the way it rhythmically enters the prose. And perhaps it was this that pushed Juani to realize that she "couldn't take it." One wonders if the grunt interrupted the instrumental struggle either too early or too late. What would have happened had Prado withheld the grunt, or if the CD was left to play, for just a moment longer?

More secrets are unveiled between the sisters, including the sexuality of a family aunt whose face Juani once described as a "map of a sealed island, surrounded not by water but by an invisible, electrified barbed wire."[81] In the aftermath of this veritable storm of disclosures, Juani eventually asks her sister how she explains their family to the outside. Nena answers that everyone has their own stories and that the variants come together to form an incomprehensible whole. As Nena puts it, "Its sort of like singing 'Guantanamera'— everybody gets a chance to make up their own verse." Juani immediately picks up the beat of Nena's gist and adds the second part of the musical metaphor, "Memory mambo . . . one step forward, two steps back-*unngh!*".[82] The sounds that Juani couldn't take just a few moments prior, now provide a moment of discovery. They reveal the method to her family's madness. Unlike *On the Road*, the music of Pérez Prado is not simply left to briefly haunt *Memory Mambo*. Instead, it becomes an integral part of the book. The dancing of mambo and its interruptive grunt partly constitute the characteristics of Juani's various dilemmas. They also mark *Memory Mambo* as a whole—the grunt is even used to issue the novel's denouement. Juani and the text then proceed, quite literally, to face the music.

A meditation on Prado's grunt requires another kind of conclusive gesture. The grunt slips away from any attempt to turn it into function; it resists being cast as a cohesive solution. It asks to be left as an unresolvable detail. Because it would be a disservice to contain the grunt within any genre, musical and literary, and to these pages, I close by opening up one of Prado's own unresolvable narrative structures: the 1962 composition piece titled *Exotic Suite of the Americas*. The album sleeve describes the suite as "an inspired 16-minute tone poem." I'd describe it as a sonic map that charts different musics of the Americas onto one score. The performance moves the listener through several movements that feature instruments or specific sounds that stem from a particular people and place. The movements are as follows: "Theme of Two Worlds," "Amoha," "Criollo," "Theme of Two Worlds," "Uamanna Africano," "Blues in C Major," and finishing the structure is another version on the "Theme of Two Worlds." These worlds are difficult to assign strict spatial boundaries upon their hearing. The segues between them make their separation impossible, whether the transitions are gentle or jolting. The main theme is epic and long-winded, replete with strings galore and long, sustained notes. It is further layered by the horns of the forty-member orchestra, including performances by Shorty Rogers on trumpet. The wandering quality of the main theme is slow and deliberate, like footsteps carefully stepping through a terrain that gives.

The main theme hovers, and might be lazily misunderstood as melodramatic. Upon repetitive listening, the theme is better described as saturated, the perfect soundtrack for the looking elsewhere gaze commonly found on the melancholic. The theme is tweaked into different variations as it weaves itself into and out of the four different movements. It tries to carry the weight of the entire score. The album sleeve instructs us that "Ahoha" is the signifier for the indigenous peoples of the continent; "Criollo," the com-

FIG. 3.4: Album cover of Pérez Prado's *Voodoo Suite/Exotic Suite of the Americas*, 1962.

ingling of the son and West Indian string and flute instruments; "Uamanna Africano" is the record of those "African origins of Americans" brought through the middle passage; and "Blues of C Major" as the presence of Afro-American musical traditions "expressed by Jimmy Nottingham's trumpet with dark toned, stabbing deliberation."

Failing the qualifications of entry for Roland Barthes' parlor game, "talk about a piece of music without using a single adjective,"[83] the unnamed author of *Suite's* sleeve notes uses a wide spectrum of provocative adjectives to describe Pérez Prado's work. The piece is "spiced with brilliant flares of brass, saucily buoyant saxophones" and the trumpet section in "Blues in C Major" is "a hair raising descending smear" that finally arrives "to some brassy ululation."[84] Accompanying this "stabbing deliberation" in different variations throughout the piece are Pérez Prado's grunts, suspiciously few in such a long piece.

I'm drawn to the suite for the reserved places and ways that the grunt appears and disappears. As a whole, the score maps the musical effects produced by conquest, the formal shifts in the music and, it could be argued, the rough temporal eras in the history of American empire. The grunt is altered and modified to the texture of each movement. In "Amoha," the lone grunt arrives toward the end as a way to singularly witness a genocidal occurrence. "Criollo" gives out a few of the most playful grunts of the piece, celebratory and articulate "dilos," or grunts said in clear linguistic terms. The grunts are most frequent and dynamic in the "Umanna Africano" section, which is also the suite's most percussive. The outbursts in this movement emerge warrior-like. Where the main theme is withheld is also hard to miss. There is no thematic segue between "Amoha" and "Criollo," nor between "Uamanna Africano" and "Blues in C Major." The quick shifts in the score at these moments are announced by way of the percussive and are left to overlap, falling on top of one another. Overall, however, it is noteworthy to see where the outbursts are absented, for the "Theme of Two Worlds" does not produce one single grunt. The main theme evokes a space of rest and reprieve: a break between the collision and forced overlapping of colonial histories.

In just over sixteen minutes, the listener is moved through the epochs, environments, and collisions that made the Americas. Although the suite is necessarily selective of the musical elements included, it does not feel like a sampler. It does not provide travel from the comfort of an armchair; it does not remove the dangers of other climates, bodies, and terrains. We don't and can't know if there was any intended kitch involved here. The musical details Pérez Prado chooses to include do not feel like the exceptional, sonic darlings of the hemisphere. Instead, the suite strings together the picking up of frequencies on a radio dial that runs from north to south. The *Harvard Dictionary of Music* defines the "suite" as, "A series of disparate instrumental movements with some element of unity, most often to be performed as a single work."[85] Experiments with combinations of sound and put together as objects like the *Exotic Suite of the Americas*, are often looked upon as haphazard and without order. His grunt—even and especially in its imprecision, fuzziness, and incomprehension—is a unifying and yet ever-changing detail that orders and disorders his larger oeuvre. It echoes the ordering and disordering noises of the New World. Because the grunt is left open for stretching, variation, and possibility for interpretive play, this New World unspeakable will continue to be grunted by others.

Chapter Four

Visual Arrangements, Sonic Impressions
The Cuban Musical Documentaries of
Rogelio París and Sara Gómez

I've come to wonder how Pérez Prado's grunts—those everywhere interruptions in the American midcentury soundscape—can prepare us for other modes of listening in detail in the rupture that now divides Cuba and the United States. His grunts train dancers to sustain movement in the break. They remind that past violence might be unspeakable but it is not mute. It has resonances: the grunt's reproduction in the mouths of others reveals that outbursts are far from finite. It presents, then and now, the opportunity to recognize that there are some things that will remain illegible and inscrutable to us as much as we might want (or don't want) to know them. Part of the critic's challenge is to resist treating such resistant sounds with suspicion and containment and to instead alter our approaches to them. Pérez Prado's grunts are challenging rehearsals: how do they demand to be heard, and be heard again, and be heard differently? Such are the properties and powers of the grunt, another, and far from exceptional detail in Cuban music that instructs our interactive experiences with history.

An event that never fails to offer interactive experiences with history—for "History" is wielded so strongly in the discourses about it—is the event of the Cuban Revolution of 1959. Here I revisit it as another occasion to ask that enduring question: What do the United States and Cuba have to do with each other? I've discussed in prior chapters how the query has been played with musically, from the exchanged experimentations with jazz aesthetics starting from the early twentieth century to the circularity of mid-century mambo. This chapter moves into the cinematic register to introduce more nuances the question and to offer another set of performative modes to respond to it. After a brief discussion of a few effects on Cuba and Cuban music after 1959, I turn to two documentary films produced on the island about Cuban popular music after the revolution, Rogelio París's *Nosotros, la música* (1963), and Sara Gómez's *Y . . . tenemos sabor* (1967). I listen to the films in detail—and argue for the detail's generative ability—to imagine other kinds of relationships to Cuban music, and to the revolution, beyond the bombastic, within or against positions that have long taken hold over the discourses of both.

These films, I argue, do not prescribe what Cuban music is, but use it as a flexible medium to document lived experience; a porous documentation that remains open to other visions and versions. Unlike many films that use the documentary form to collect and preserve, *Nosotros, la música* and *Y . . . tenemos sabor* resist the ethnographic impulse to fix Cuban music and instead offer other kinds of creative tools to listen closer to it. I decenter comprehensive formal readings of the films and instead focus on, describe, and take elsewhere a few of the films' details and the performative modes to be found in them. By doing so I hope that my readings will offer impressions of the films' structural entireties and the worlds they compress. Impressions are not faithful to an original, nor can they ever hope to be. They can be blurry, out of focus, misguided, captivating, wrong, or lend a different view of the object in question. An impression can be a noun or a verb, "the action involved in the pressure of one thing upon or into the surface of another; also, the effect of this."[1] This chapter is a response to the pressure that *Nosotros, la música* and *Y . . . tenemos sabor* put on the signs of Cuban music and the revolution. It is also a documentation of the effects such pressure has had on my own scholarly practices.

After 1959, to engage what the United States and Cuba have to do with each other through official discursive channels means getting involved with a host of obstinate polemics. Here and everywhere, I want to resist them. And yet, their platforms are impossible to deny: the relationship between the nations had long been determined by their proximity, their intertwined if uneven economies, those unwanted interventions, and the shared flows of people and objects. The post-revolutionary antidiplomacy by the leadership of both nations has been disastrous. The division of families, the suppression of dissent on and off the island, and the broken channels of communication are just some of the heartbreaking broad strokes. These painful divisions, however, tend to cloud some hopeful particularities in the rupture made official by the total trade embargo imposed on Cuba by the United States in February of 1962. There have been continuities sustained in the break that demand our attention. They demand to be heard and be heard differently.

Music, as one of Cuba's primary exports and touristic lures, as a sign for the island itself, was clearly not immune to the diplomatic snarling between the nations. It is fascinating to note how many of those early ruptures were sonic, both in quality and instrument. The US government quickly turned the radio waves into an ideological front. The hijacking of radio frequencies by the United States to interfere in Cuban domestic affairs is as old as the media itself.[2] After the revolution, however, there was an upsurge in interference after President Eisenhower approved of anticommunist broadcasts to Cuba breaking the NARAB (North American Regional Broadcasting Agreement) in 1960. Sponsored by the US government, Radio Swan (later known as Radio Américas) became a forum for well-known Cuban radio personalities, now in exile, to provoke the Cuban government. The game of one-upmanship continued when Cuba responded by jamming Radio Swan's signal, and strongly, with the CMBN's "La Voz del INTRA" (The Voice of the National Institute for Agrarian Reform). And so on and so on.[3]

Signals were distorted and broken at many levels. One example from the higher reaches was unearthed by Dave Tompkins who discovered that during the Cuban missile crisis, President Kennedy channeled his conversations between the White House and the Kremlin through a vocoder—a machine that sped up communication, but that also verbally deformed the voice, making directives unrecognizable.[4] Consider the stakes of such sonic distortion during one of the most frightening displays of brinksmanship on record. This distorted channel, one that routed over Cuba to the Soviet

Union, was part of the new machinery that set the tone for how Cuba was to be spoken to and heard.

These conditions help to set up some of the stakes behind the creation and consumption of music after the revolution. The Cuban recording industry and its outlets were affected at the level of both production and distribution. As early as 1960, many independent radio stations were put under government control, others shut down completely. Cuban record labels that had experienced something of a renaissance during the 1950s were eventually folded into a nationalized unit called EGREM (Empresa de Grabaciones y Ediciones Musicales). The early revolutionary government gave important support for research on national culture, especially in 1961 what was decreed as the "Año de la educación." There was a wealth of musical materials made available about music to be used alongside Cuba's literacy campaign (*Campaña nacional de alfabetización en Cuba*) that same year. The Departamento de Ediciones Musicales published sheet music that revealed a new and optimistic nationalism, from printing updated versions of the national anthem, choral arrangements of Latin American songs, and musical scores that valued Guajiro and Afro-Cuban forms.[5] By 1964, the Cuban government controlled all official channels of musical production, recording, and distribution.[6] Musicians, along with their repertoires, who chose or were forced into exile were removed from the Cuban airwaves as punishment.[7] Leonardo Acosta recalls that the vinyl of their records was often melted down to provide raw recording material for those who stayed.[8] Some Cuban labels closed for good, others went into exile and firmly based their operations in places like New York and Miami. They quickly released recordings that directly responded to (and created an industry out of) the rupture.

Take the case of Panart, Cuba's largest independently owned label with established ties to studios and channels of distribution in New York.[9] As early as 1962, Panart put together a series of records for those who were already suffering from exilic blues. The album collection *Asi cantaba Cuba libre* quickly made nostalgia operative.[10] For the increasing numbers of Cuban exiles who chose or were forced to leave the island, Cuba instantly became something to be mourned. The album includes, "songs of rebellion and hope that in another era of oppression, sadness and bitterness, guided another generation of Cubans to conquer liberty."[11] It includes anthems from

FIG. 4.1: Album cover of *Asi cantaba Cuba libre*, 1962. From the Ramon S. Sabat (Panart) Collection. Courtesy of the Cuban Heritage Collection, the University of Miami Libraries.

past and present, unofficial and not, including the hymns, "La Bayamesa," as well as "El son se fue de Cuba," (The *Son* Left Cuba) which would become the Cuban exilic refrain of the 1960s even if it was the Dominican-born and Venezuelan-based Billo Frómeta who wrote it.[12]

Other channels of distribution and reception were significantly altered. One of the early moves by the Cuban Revolution was to prohibit jukeboxes ("vitrolas" in Cuban). The vitrolas had long been prized objects of Cuban musicking; they were an ingrained part of the scenery of neighborhood bars, bodegas, and other gathering spots. They were also one of the primary and most effective channels of distribution for Cuban music. Cubans chose which artists got traction in the recording industry by voting with their coins, a kind of democratically chosen hit parade. As Cristóbal Díaz Ayala notes, the jukeboxes created audiences, informal venues, and—most important—markets for Cuban records.[13] They were sonic arteries for Cuban popular music throughout the island. Such was their popularity and omnipresence that there was even a makeshift genre called "música de vitrola," which brought together the soundtracks behind the torn throats and sanguine events of everynightlife.[14]

The jukebox was a fixture in those locations of underground economies of love, desire, and escape; it was the domain of the bolero. They were prohibited as part of the purifying efforts of the revolution, which in the name of post-Batista renewal meant shutting down all signifiers of vice, corruption, and unseemly patriotism. Alongside casinos, nightclubs, and brothels, the vitrolas suddenly stood accused as objects of unsuitable influence. There was also justifiable fear by some musicians that the machines would outmode live music completely. But the outcry against their prohibition was such that it occupied pages in both *Bohemia* and *Revolución*, a veritable scandal in February of 1959.[15] As one commenter put it: "¿Por qué tratar de hacer de nuestra Habana, ciudad naturalmente jacarandosa, un cementerio . . . ? Las vitrolas no hicieron nada. Las vitrolas son inocentes."[16] (Why make our Havana—a city that is naturally joyful—into a cemetery? The vitrolas did nothing. The vitrolas are innocent.) The outrage was such that the new government allowed the vitrolas to remain, but with conditions. None were to be played near hospitals, churches, and schools. None would be heard during inappropriate hours.[17] The creation of these kinds of conditions, here and everywhere, would severely alter what was the bustling and glittery midcentury Cuban nightlife.

The closure of and/or nationalization of Cuban tourist sectors greatly altered conditions for performers and, just as critically, the countless many who worked behind the scenes to make Havana a show. Some left the island unable to find their way in the new regime.[18] Some were left destitute and unemployed. Some were provided means of survival by receiving a paid living as artists and found ways to keep performing in the new system. By 1968, musicians were required to belong to the Musician's Union for a guaranteed salary and pension, and all gigs were coordinated through it. Performers were dependent upon the state for work.[19] Many others, especially poor Cubans of color, found opportunities not afforded during the Batista regime, from performing on stages once prohibited to them, to becoming a part of new conservatories and other forums for musical life established by the revolution.[20] One side effect of the noble expansion of musical education, however, was the disregard and devaluation of self-taught musicians, who have forever been vital to the invention of and experiment with Cuban sound.[21]

During this period of adjustment, the US embargo made Cuban musicians (and their recordings) illegal to import. Globally established routes of circulation were suddenly closed, rendering outlaw the most important developments in Cuban popular music in the second half of the twentieth century. Because a substantial number of musicians chose exile, the Cuban government imposed strict conditions on mobility for those who chose to stay for fear of a musical brain drain. Permissions were subsequently required for any movement, domestic and international. As Robin Moore writes, "The normal movement of performers in itself became a statement about one's relationship to the cultural hierarchy."[22] Such relationships have, of course, their own performative elements: one must be able to convey a degree of loyalty and fidelity—whether sincere or at the very least, the appearance of sincerity—to the revolution in order to perform in more formal arenas. Access to global performance venues depended and depends upon the absolute certainty of musicians' return to the island. To tour domestically means that select musicians are, for the revolution, worthy of the resources afforded to them. Those musicians who have more visibility and support are often confronted with charges of political opportunism, whether deserved or not.

Although there was a proliferation of music (and scholarship on music) on the island after the revolution, there is an insidious finality that many lay listeners and critics use to claim 1959 as the death knell of Cuban music.[23] Many examples can be found via the Cuba nostalgia variety record compilations that market themselves as the golden era of Cuban musicality. By suggesting a temporal end to the island's musical creativity, the isolation of Cuba from modernity has less to do with desiring its discovery and more with the protocols of cold war containment. As of this writing other channels have been developed to access Cuban musical recordings after 1959, including its production and distribution through European record labels.[24] However, it cannot be understated that the embargo has made it very hard to get acquainted with the work of Cuban musicians and scholars working after 1959. One unfortunate consequence has been that many North American and European critics assume that work, musical and scholarly, has not been done. Such effects reached considerable heights with the *Buena Vista Social Club* enterprise that in too many ways depended upon myths of Cuba's musical time freeze.[25] It is perhaps for these reasons and more that Adriana Orejuela Martínez titled her marvelous book on the decades following the revolution with a fact and an outcry: *El son no se fue de Cuba* (The Son Did Not Leave Cuba).[26]

I've offered these historical specifics to suggest the totalizing way that Cuban music was affected after 1959. And to introduce a few other contours to the question: What do Cuba and the United States have to do with each other? The refusal of the other's sounds was enacted in policy, the recording industry, on objects, in scholarship, and most intensely, on actual bodies. I begin this chapter with these specifics to offer a few contextual coordinates. However, the work that I do in these pages should not be confined by said context; such historical recognition is not made to rigidly stage what is to follow. As I move to a set of films, productions that cannot be contained by history, I would like for the foregoing context to be read as flexible supports. I do so not merely to *show*, once again, the kinds of difficult work we're asked to do as a result of the conditions of the rupture. But in what follows, I am also firmly committed to try and *live* out a different relationship to it. Listening in detail to who and what falls out of these entrenched ideological worlds is a primary strategy for living outside of them.

I hear the kinds of sounds that emerged on the island in the decades following the revolution as the past, present, and future. I cannot turn them into dead monuments and pawns for those obstinate polemics. What I'm trying to avoid, in other words, is for the "post-revolutionary" to overdetermine these pages. To do so can often prevent their extension backward to the there-and-then and into the here-and-now and onto the now-and-not-yet. Nor do I want them to carry the burden of representing a singular time and place even as they consciously reflected them. Because the Cuban Revolution has inspired all kinds of attachments, from within and without, there is a certain fixity to discourses that recall its earlier periods. Instead, I wonder what it would mean to experience Cuban musicalia made in the decades after 1959 in dubbed time, to both hear where the objects have been and where they might be going. I do not use the films that follow to unlock some obscured secret to what the early revolution was "really like," but instead work with them as introductions to new modes of being and feeling as they intersected with Cuban music. I experience these films as musical productions that emerged from Cuba in the 1960s as things that do not signal closings but openings; as things that are not lost in the rupture, but can be heard in rapture.

To gently wade into some of the stirring and breathtakingly experimental work of the period, I proceed to the documentaries: Rogelio París's *Nosotros, la música* (1963) and Sara Gómez's *Y... tenemos sabor* (1967).[27] The documentary form is a commonly used idiom for the exposé, for the capture of endangered objects, animals, or cultures, and for the instruction or indoctrination of citizens. When used as a form of evidence, it is often put to work as an objective truth about a historical event, or as supposedly unfiltered documentation of the event in question. It has been relied upon as an ethnographic tool: recall the wealth of footage taken of native dances from many an elsewhere, and how such footage has been used to explain said natives in said elsewheres. The documentary-as-evidence model disregards aesthetic choices, the politics of the frame, and whomever is behind the camera. Bill Nichols challenges the false mythologies about documentary that upholds it as a static form or its ability to render representation directly and accurately:

> Documentary is what we might call a "fuzzy concept" . . . [it] is an arena in which things change. Alternative approaches are constantly attempted and then adopted by others or abandoned. Contestation occurs . . . They push the limits and sometimes change them.[28]

After the revolution, many burgeoning Cuban filmmakers found documentary practice, as a fuzzy concept, uniquely able to work alongside the lived experiences of the moment. The aesthetics of the revolution were experiments in history and form, and in these early films, contestation did occur. The documentary genre was also thought of as the ideal training grounds for apprentice Cuban filmmakers after the revolution.

Both París's and Gómez's experiments with documentary, and the ways I analyze them here, are far from ethnographic proof of cultural practices. There is no stale preservation of music—past and present—in either film. There is nothing about them that suggests Cuban music as endangered. There is no temporal distancing of the included performers and their inherited traditions. Although they are so fully present in their place and time, the rootedness and intimacy with their subjects make the films experiences rather than explanations. Far from nostalgic relics, the films' rich immediacy make such experiences palpable in the here and now. París and Gómez as filmmakers push the limits and sometimes change not only the approaches to documentary practice, but also to music. *Nosotros, la música* and *Y . . . tenemos sabor* do not define what Cuban music is for outsiders, but rather invite all to experience what it can do. By placing music and playing with it in a different idiom—rather than translating it for more widely available consumption—they encourage us to feel for music's potential effects on all forms of expression.

A turn to the visual Cuba is of course fraught with imperial undercurrents. In her "Picturing Havana: History, Vision and the Scramble for Cuba," Ana Dopico reminds that Cuba as a visual field has long been served up for the project of empire, from the conquest of Columbus to William Randolph Hearst's famous role in the US intervention for the Spanish American War ("Get me the pictures and I'll get you the war"). Dopico's work excavates the island's myriad representations in ethnographic studies and touristic trade, its post-revolutionary visual promises of uplift, and its ubiquitous and often violently decontextualized representations of its present ruin to remind how the image has and continues to play a driving force behind affective attachments to the island.[29] Always out of place and time, the old car, hungry body, and crumbling building operate in a visual economy with the desiring precedents of the past. I turn to the cinematic partly because the contemporary (and voluminous) circulation of Cuban images—specifically those that enjoy it as a cold war relic, as political fantasy, and as aestheticized poverty—can make the island present in the here-and-now. However, such visual narration continues to render Cuba's bodies and buildings as empty, stuck in time, and as always at the service of the spectacle. Although bodies are made present in certain visual terms, they are safely absent and out of reach. I believe that making Cuba physically absent but visually available finds direct corollary to the island's representation in a US weather report: it is an unnamed grey landmass that is the frontline for a hurricane's path. It is there but not there. It suffers damage but not for us to see.

Many Cubans who live abroad feel that this and other kinds of damage are often overlooked and underheard. People are left to wonder if their family is safe, if their child is well protected in their grandparent's house, does their old school still stand. Then there are those of us who can only imagine and inherit the effects of such damage. Outside of the island we might have been raised in households never seeing or hearing the Cuba of the present. We might have been too scared to ask about our parents' past because their delivery and our reception of it made us weep or angry or bored or frustrated or all of these sensations at once. And while it might not sound like a big deal to many, for Cuban youth brought up with the rupture, wherever they reside, we often don't get a chance to know what our peers are doing, what they're wearing, what they're listening to, what the everyday feels like. Whether through the accidents and the privileges of migration, or the courage and necessity it takes to stay behind, we wonder, together and apart: how is it that some of us are here and some of us are there? The shared curiosity often leaves us with the simplest of questions that we always want, but are too afraid to ask. I once met a young Cuban visiting New York for the first time who asked me: "But did you guys eat rice and beans too?" Much of this has thankfully become outdated as more of Cuba's recently migrated populations maintain strong ties to the island.

My turn to the visual register of music by way of these films helps to open up the category of musician, to include filmmakers, editors, dancers, and on-lookers. As Daniel Goldmark, Lawrence Kramer, and Richard Leppert affirm, "What still needs saying, and is beginning to be said, is that film is also a musical medium."[30] Opening up the category of participant in the music of the era is especially important for Cuba during this period partly because creative play with music was everywhere. For example, some of the most interesting, yet overlooked examples of experiments with graphic design in post-revolutionary Cuba were done on sheet music.[31] In addition to this flourishing of the arts, both films' inclusive sense of what makes a musical practitioner helps to muddy and make productively ambiguous the use of the collective pronouns found in their titles: the "we" (nosotros) and the "we have" (tenemos).

By incorporating, in film, Cuba's participants in musicking, the filmmakers prevent the reduction of the project of making music (or nation) to a select few and open it up to a heterogeneous societal whole. The worlds incorporated in the films place pressure on the tyrannies, ideological and otherwise, that often overdetermine the "we." As Ana M. López has written:

Of course, the Cuban Revolution has had a great stake in producing a vision of Cuban identity that is singular, unified, coherent, and identical to the nation-state. . . . However, even in the glory days of the Revolution, when the stakes for national unity and hegemony were greatest, "Cuban" nationness was already fractured and unstable, precisely because of the impossibility of remapping the necessarily transnational and imprecise space of "Greater Cuba" onto the confines of the geographical island.[32]

The films I discuss are two rich examples that documented such impossibility and imprecision. In the films, however, such challenges to the singular "we" demanded by the early revolution are not presented as problems to be solved. Instead, the filmmakers figure the excesses of Cuba's unstable geographies and identities as making possible a more flexible and adaptable revolutionariness. Such ways of being did not suddenly appear with the triumph of the revolution of 1959, but have been enacted in music for several centuries.[33]

Finally, by turning to the visual, I want to reiterate the real, material presence that bodies have in my studies on sound. For those of us who did not grow up on the island, the embargo has worked well to cloud musicians' physicality. Which is not to say you can't hear, or at the very least sense, the amped-up musculature of a group like Irakere or the knowing glances of Elena Burke in recording. Because both films document and resurrect many Cuban musical notables in live performances, they offer a sense of homecoming. Such an experience feels less like a return or a reunion and more like a feeling of meeting a dearly loved pen pal for the first time after decades of correspondence. The films allow us to put faces to the sounds. They help to put Cuban musicians' shapes and gestures above ground, images that have long had to be imagined in waking and dreamlife.

Nosotros, la música flickers in the space of waking and dreamlife. It was directed by Cuban filmmaker Rogelio París and was released in 1964. After setting up some of the film's conditions of production, I focus on two details that open and close the film. I emphasize that these heart-stopping details are techniques found in and by way of music. These details remind how performance is able to impress hopeful particularities in times of difficult transitions. Although these details are, once again, so firmly rooted in place and time, they are portals to other worlds, times, and places. They do not speak only of the difficult transitions experienced during the revolution of 1959, but also of other events in Cuban history still carried in the notes and bodies of many. The details encourage many influences and references to rise to the surface in the mere description of them. They can't help but be treated associatively—and so by following some of the details' associations, I try to emulate the documentary practice modeled by París. For París's incredibly inspiring work, nothing seems to be external or excessive to the frame, he rather seems to invite all that couldn't be included or represented.

The title of *Nosotros, la música* itself presents a challenge in both language and feeling. A felicitous translation might convert the title to *We Are the Music*. The Spanish version, however, withholds the present indicative active plural of "to be" from the phrase. It is rather, *We, the Music*. The title allows for both readings. *We, the Music* have x to say and sing. *We Are the Music* makes the we and the music interchangeable terms. Both senses of the title evoke other rallying cries and inaugural manifestos that marked those first years of the revolution. Over time, the "we" and its uses would change. Yet the film encapsulates a creative dilemma posed to many young artists of the period: What does documenting self-definition in a rapidly changing nation look, sound, and feel like? This conundrum was not only particular to Cuba but also indicative of larger concerns and constraints in the new Latin American cinema.[34] As the film unfolds, it becomes clear that the "we" is not prescriptive, but spacious, unsure, cautious, impulsive, mournful, and celebratory all at once.

Nosotros, la música is among the cavalcade of documentaries that flourished in Cuba in the early 1960s. As Michael Chanan argues in his excellent and foundational *Cuban Cinema*, the upsurge in this mode of filmmaking both anticipated and was influenced by cinematic movements on the other side of the Atlantic, including Italian neorealism and the impact of the British New Wave, particularly its claim on "free cinema." The film's debut was announced in an issue of *Cine Cubano* featuring a smoky image of the Cuban film actress Daysi Granados on the cover.[35] The brief commentary on the film shared space with a feature on the Cannes Film Festival of 1964, an essay titled, "Un Bergman doble: Anotaciones sobre el rostro y el séptimo sello" ("The Two Sides of Bergman: Notes on 'The Face' and 'The Seventh Sign'") and a highlight on the Dutch activist filmmaker Joris Ivens.

While further critical attention should be given to the relationship between cinematic avant-gardes on both sides of the Atlantic, a trajectory that Rogelio París's movie decidedly occupies, there were other factors at work. París was part of this transatlantic conversation and the cadre of filmmakers who redefined the urgent role of cinema for the revolution. For example, in the same issue of *Cine Cubano*, there is an expository article titled, "Para filmar la zafra" ("To Film the Sugar Harvest"). Cameras were vitally necessary to record the revolution as it happened, its unexpected and unprecedented successes and failures. As José Quiroga contends in his remarkable and aptly titled chapter, "A Cuban Love Affair with the Image," "the state knew that history needed to be documented in order to become a living presence, as well as to reinforce the historical import of all decisions taken since the very early years of the revolutionary process."[36] As a state-sponsored collective, Cuba's Instituto Cubano de Arte y Industria Cinematográficos (known as ICAIC, Cuban Institute of Film Art and Industry) was especially vital as a pedagogical force for the revolution.[37]

Although many documentaries were commissioned by the state, several filmmakers took advantage of the early flexibility of the ICAIC by integrating their technical development as artists with their sponsored work. In many films there appears a mass reparative urgency to examine and speak openly against Cuba's colonial past. In 1964, París's documentary emerged alongside an early Sara Gómez film titled *El tabaco rubio* (Blonde Tobacco), Santiago Villafuerte's *La Enmienda Platt* (The Platt Amendment) and Nicolás Guillén's biopic on the iconographic Cuban performer Rita Montaner. It should be noted, given its current cinephilic cache, that Mikheil Kalatozishvili's *Soy Cuba/Ya Kuba* the Soviet-Cuban coproduction also premiered the same year to little acclaim on the island. One wonders if this was perhaps a result of the movie's prophetic quality, one that (even if unintentionally) dramatized the awkward, colonial and vexed relationship that would come to pass between the two nations.[38]

By tragic coincidence, the filming of *Nosotros, la música* occurred at the time of the death of Beny Moré, the great Cuban singer and bandleader who succumbed to cirrhosis of the liver in 1963.[39] If you ever find yourself in the company of Cubans, Moré is the voice that immediately cues sacral nods of some unspoken agreement. You will probably confront prolonged melancholic glances. A few might leave the room to tear up in private. Others shrug from that feeling of having lived too much. El Beny's vocal skating through multiple octaves—through its back-of-the-throat highs and lows—is the stuff of what is often called "música de borrachos" (music of drunks) the substance of which was the very thing that took him away.

Undaunted by the inevitable jolt this would have on París's footage, the movie inaugurates the post-Beny moment by beginning with a nod to the beloved "Bárbaro del Ritmo." The movie opens on Julieto Figueroa Alfonso, a member of the Conjunto Folklórico Nacional de Cuba, who diverts questions about his line of work (his exprofession as a decorative painter) to heap praise upon the beloved singer. As the initial credits of *Nosotros, la música* begin to roll, we learn that the film is dedicated to him. The movie is thus partly a homage that fits within the repertoire of songs made to Moré after his untimely death, including Miguelito Cuní and Félix Chappotín's tender musical requiem: "A Beny Moré." As the object of the film's homage, Moré is both present and nonpresent in the documentary. He is a primary force and specter that is vitally necessary to the "we," a sonic bookend for what is to follow.

Soon after the dedication to Moré, the viewer is taken along as the camera side-winds through different soundscapes of Havana, at one point taking a rich detour to el Oriente, the eastern part of the island that bears the seedlings of Cuban music from past, present, and future. As it moves between each scene, the camera records these landscapes at the same time that it documents a series of musical performances. It lingers at certain genres, for example, stopping by to check out a lengthy performance by the Quinteto Instrumental de Música Moderna at a jazz club immediately before arriving at small cabaret featuring the performer Ana Gloria dancing to a rumba. The camera moves along with a comparsa in Santiago before quickly returning to the urban landscape of Havana. It even manages to include a plucky version of "La Bayamesa," before sliding into the performer Bola de Nieve and his foundational rendering of "El Manisero."[40]

En route to each musical stop, the camera collects shots of a few landmarks of the Cuban landscape in its everyday use. In montages that both reimagine and refashion in tandem, the film moves through the Parque Central, a jazz club, a cabaret, a courtyard of a solar, a public beach, the Gran Teatro, and various outdoor venues. The streets of Havana are characters unto themselves: the viewer is driven and shown the city by day and by night from the vantage of being stuck in traffic. These other stages in the film might not include formal performances, but they nevertheless make noise and rustle and add their own riffs to the movie's soundtrack. They are not external to, but an intimate part of the event.

At and between these locations throughout *Nosotros, la música*, the film introduces the viewer to a few other artistic heavies and the contemporary landmarks of Cuban music. They are introduced to us casually. We are put into conversation with Bola de Nieve as he empties a liter of whiskey into a glass with the abandon used when shaking a stubborn ketchup bottle. As he does so, he relays his nickname's origin, taken from a remark about his black skin by Rita Montaner. We meet up with them after hours of rehearsal. In three-inch-high white heels that manage to escape unscuffed by the endeavor, Celeste Mendoza performs a rumba on the patio of a solar. We are introduced to their stage personae. Elena Burke tunes up with a guitarist during a farewell concert and banters informally with the audience before asking them to forgive her being "insoportable" (unbearable). We meet them on the land where they stand. Chappotín and Cuní pronounce their greatest hits at La Tropical under those heavy tropical clouds that whisper thunderstorms.

París's documentary generates a living and breathing comic book, layered with pregnant pauses that allow worlds to exist and collide, rub up against, and dance with one another. The film is a fantasy superlative section of Cuban musical glitterati. Seen in the here-and-now, the movie enables contact with the bodies of all of these musicians who have been ravaged by time, some by disease, age, the embargo, and overall forgetting.[41] What París's documentary fleshes out is not only those bodies that are materially lost in the present, but also those bodies often left undocumented and unnamed in the circulation of Cuban musical commodities, including a few of which I will discuss below.

Nosotros, la música was present for many of the critical shifts and fractures occurring on the island in the early 1960s. There are too many to mention but I review some of the following: an overall renaissance of the arts after the fall of Batista's regime, including cinema but also music, the graphic arts, and letters; the gradual disappearance of privately owned to state centralized live music venues; and finally, both the return of folks to the island, post-Batista, and those who began to leave in 1959. During these profound fractures in the film, both transparent and obscured, many moments arise that disrupt the visual imperative of uplift in early post-revolutionary Cuban photography. According to José Quiroga,

> the lens was always focused on changes taking place in Cuba, and images were a general project of "uplift" . . . The photograph had a duty to perform; it was a document and, as such, it contained a certain kind of *knowledge* that would be used to produce more *knowledge* in turn.[42]

Alberto Díaz Gutiérrez or "Korda's" ubiquitous portrait of Che Guevara would be the de facto example.[43] The circulation of that portrait by the state (to the dismay of even the creator himself) suggests that the revolution had reached some finite arrival through this iconographic figure, a fixed model who paradoxically keeps its eyes forever scanning toward the horizon. This image, later plastered worldwide, was one of prescriptive revolutionariness, one that apparently captured its authentic essence, or what would become the formative mantra for many: "Seremos como el Che" (We Want to Be Like Che).

While I do not want to conflate the similar and divergent histories of photography and film, a critique that reaches as far back as both media, there was nevertheless a similar impulse behind some Cuban films of that early post-revolutionary era. However, the wonderful vitality of some Cuban cinema immediately after the revolution was its attention to those messier moments often made static, definitive, or generally coopted by the state in many photographs of the time. This had much to do with the early ICAIC and its quasi-independent status with the state afforded by what Chanan describes as, "a de-facto autonomy because of a privileged relation to the source of power and authority" as with the technology itself.[44] In the case of both *Nosotros, la música* and *Y . . . tenemos sabor*, all who had a hand a making in the film—in front of and behind the lens—skillfully performed nuanced relationships to what was happening around them. There was a kind of mobility performed that spoke to the time's potentiality—multiple versions of what went down exist; that all are not subject to dogmatically positioned historians.

The first detail I examine in *Nosotros, la música* takes place in the composition itself. The first music that one actually hears in the film is a piece that skates the highs and lows of an instrument: the first prelude of Bach's *Well-Tempered Clavier (Das wohltemperierte clavier)*. The piece opens two books of short compositions by Bach—better described as pedagogical texts—that essentially flex the formal constraints of a keyboard instrument. Written at the height of the baroque period, its forty-eight preludes and fugues document the various musical passages of Bach's career for more than forty years. As Davitt Moroney explains, the compositions worked "to train reluctant fingers to feel at home in unwonted corners of the instrument."[45] They are comprehensive attempts to arrange sounds through the correctly "tempered" instrument, that is, one that is tuned so that all of its keys may be put into play. Bach's combinations of sounds, it should be noted, were not only tonal but also temporal. The work does not necessarily demonstrate how different sounds can collide, but also *when* they can meet and depart from one another. This playful and often deceptively dissonant arrangement of sounds is called "counterpoint" (the same concept, I note, that powers Fernando Ortiz's landmark study of transculturation).[46]

Immediately after Alfonso's remembrance to Beny Moré, a piano begins to play Bach's familiar prelude, that is, until a güiro starts to hiss in from the sidelines. After watching Cubans, lots of Cubans, walk down a busy sidewalk to that familiar, pedestrian repetition of Bach's melody, a jump and musical cut interrupts its familiarity. We are suddenly moved to a group dancing at a beer garden party. They are instantaneously recognizable as Cuban at the same time that the instrument enters that instantaneously transforms Bach's music into Cuban: into the prelude flies the playful flute that peeps unexpected notes—those bird noises that sneak attack between and above where they are supposed to fit. As accompaniment to this musical sneak attack, the title of the movie appears in bold white letters, in uniform font: *Nosotros, la música*.

Odilio Urfé, the pianist, composer, and musicologist, is the author of this particular composition, or the performed decomposition, of Bach's score.

A performing figure among the transatlantic symphonic elite, including the British conductor Leopold Stokowski, Urfé was also a vital force in the greater education and transmission of Cuban popular music.[47] On an institutional level, Urfé founded the National Institute for Folkloric Research (first called the Center for Music Research) in 1949, an archive that has facilitated scholarship for generations of musicians and scholars. In 1963, the name of the institute was changed to the Seminario de Música Popular Cubana and was transformed into a conservatory to provide formal academic training to musicians who had none.[48] Other highlights include his participation as the Cuban delegate to the first Pan-African Culture Festival in Algiers in 1969. In additional forums, as demonstrated by his version of Bach, Urfé's work does not simply solidify corrective inclusions of Afro-Cuban forms into musical history. As the headlining song of *Nosotros, la música*, it does not steal the prelude and tape it under another, melodic streamer. Rather, the performance uses Bach as an introduction so that he can be interrupted, in the casual way you would with a close friend. By gently interrupting Bach, Urfé makes room for the horse-trot sound of charanga that moves the prelude into a different direction.

A facile hearing of Urfé's *Well-Tempered Clavier* would portray it as a singular performance of virtuosity on both musical fronts, the "classical" and the "popular."[49] It might use the song as an example that reveals a surprising ability to switch styles and influences. Ability, seen as such, would figure Urfé's work as an exception to a Cuban given. Instead, Urfé plays out the longer history that Afro-Cuban musics and musicians have had with its objects of training through his *Clavier*; the classical must itself be made to work and tread within the "unwonted corners" of its own history. I hear Urfé's rendition of Bach's text as an undercommon lesson within a pedagogical text, one that partly folds the "unwonted corners" of Cuba into classical instrumentation. This schooling marks both techniques and actual names of too many musicians pushed out of the historical fold. Here I'm thinking of Teodora Ginés, the emancipated slave who wrote the first son in the fifteenth century, a detail difficult to verify, that many musicologists prefer to disavow a bit too quickly and easily.

The tricksterism that defines the prelude form must briefly be mentioned here. Moroney continues,

The difficulty of talking about the prelude, however, largely evaporates once we have understood its magpie nature: its ability to seize upon anything and appropriate it, with complete license to drop it immediately if something more interesting comes along.[50]

Other kinds of impulses can be recovered from Moroney's observation. I would disagree with Moroney by reiterating a (by now—one hopes) well-known line of thought: although the magpie might have the "complete license" to let one of its objects of influence "drop" it nevertheless retains the traces of the thing it once appropriated. Moroney adds that Bach was, "the great magpie himself." Admittedly pushing the metaphor, what said magpie collects becomes part of its nest, feeds it, gives it company. As Radamés Giro theorizes, the Cuban musician has, "una fuerza capaz de absorber todo lo que toma en préstamo" (a force capable of digesting everything it borrows).[51]

In his scholarly life, Urfé perpetually reminded the "we" about the modulations that Cuban musicians have exacted on concert music for centuries. He prefaced a 1956 essay written on nineteenth-century virtuoso violinist Claudio José Domingo Brindis de Salas Jr. (nicknamed the "Black Paganini") with the following: "There is much need for a calmly revised, well-documented history of music and its principal exponents to be undertaken and published."[52] Born to a musical family, Salas's father was a musician and composer later imprisoned and tortured during Cuba's "Conspiración de La Escalera" (the Ladder Conspiracy) in 1844.[53] This conspiracy is history's shorthand for the brutally repressive measures inflicted by colonial authorities to execute, imprison, intimidate, and exile hundreds of free persons of color. This bloody period of Cuban history ushered in this series of repressive measures for fear of emancipatory movements and rebellions, in addition to the growing presence of a black bourgeoisie on the island. The violent discipline was also enacted to contain the Afro-Cuban majority of professional musicians. Its atrocities included the assassination of the great poet Plácido and countless other artists and musicians.[54]

Although Brindis de Salas Jr. emerged from conditions put into place to stop his mobility (in addition to his forebears and decedents), he trained in the Paris Conservatory and toured internationally to huge acclaim, particularly in Milan, Berlin, and London. For reasons that are unclear, his sound eventually fell out of favor to global audiences. Salas later died of tuberculosis in a hostel in Buenos Aires. Poignantly, Urfé calls for a calm revision of Cuban musical history through a figure whose only material object left behind is a silk corset.[55] Describing Salas's musicianship, Urfé writes:

> As a rule he always played the same composition differently; at times he was like a fourth-year student, playing out of tune and in disarray because "he was upset or apathetic" and at others he was the veritable colossus of the violin with a finesse of interpretation and absolute dominion of the technical aspects of his instrument.

Urfé reads Salas's technique beyond his tinkering of actual compositions. Here the playing of difference is also determined by mood (or temperament) and its effect on performance. But it would be a mistake to think of this as unconsciously letting his interiority out without mediation, thought, or control. Such a performed effect was likely strategic and planned for a musician with "absolute dominion" over his instrument. Playing his instrument did not convey some facile sense of mastery, or that the instrument could even be mastered completely. I hear Urfé's reading of Brindis de Salas—his claim that he could both perform and withhold his virtuosity, that though his instrument could be correctly tempered, it could not be fully controlled—in his rendition of the *Well-Tempered Clavier*.

As the musical consultant for *Nosotros,* Urfé makes us wonder why he begins with this prelude to prelude the film. His first move in the larger soundtrack was to alter Bach before moving through various stops of Cuban musicalia. By departing from a piece that was written to demonstrate all the available keys of an instrument and thought to be one of the more important rites of proper musical training, Urfé reveals the power of any composition's instability. Rather than pathologize or panic in the fact of such instability, Urfé makes music of it. His version instead thrives in the transition of the stable classical text into the new world tropical of the danzón.[56] That he turns Bach into a danzón in particular is striking. The danzón is a genre that often derived its melodic riffs from classical music (residuals of conservatory training) and Tin Pan Alley songs.[57] It is a genre, as musicologist Grenet points out, that was once regarded as the "degeneration of the *danza*," a square dance rhythm first popular in the mid-nineteenth century. However,

Grenet understood that the danzón was a necessary (and actual) next step of the danza. Grenet states that the danzón, "not only becomes slower but introduces a pause or rest for the dancers who stop during the introduction repeated at the end of each part to recover from effects of our warm climate."[58] The danzón genre not only acclimates to the climate but also to the movements of its dancers. In the film, the genre is not only acclimated to the climate, it is acclimated to the nosotros.

The second detail of *Nosotros, la música* that I examine involves another kind of embodied composition. In the closing chapters of the film, París introduces us to Silvio and Ada, a dancing couple who carry their own notoriety in the larger history of Cuban dance. The setting takes place in what was before the revolution the Miramar Yacht Club, one of the most exclusive social and athletic clubs on the island. In a predictable move of militaristic opportunism, it was later made into a club for the armed forces (Fuerzas Armadas Revolucionarias).[59] In the film, its use seems not to have been determined one way or another—it looks and feels as if it is in transition, and the transition is stunning. To see people living out an ordinary Sunday in all its delicious leisure is moving, hopeful, and reassuring. We see people from all walks gathering in the club's common areas. There are older folks enjoying the sun, kids playing, young men hoisting themselves onto gym equipment, lovers gathering into one another on the club's piers to watch the horizon. Outside of the club there is a spacious dance floor on the waterfront. A giant compass is inlaid at the center. It is to this aid of orientation that Silvio and Ada emerge from a crowd, take their places, and begin their dance.

Silvio and Ada begin their elegant performance with some gentle turns in the middle of the compass. It is not the typical pas de deux of romantic love. They hold each other up with respectful tenderness. They are not playing familiar roles, but work together to keep the balance. Their introductory spins in the middle of the compass do not require or cause discomfort. It is fine that we do not know where they'll go; they make our inevitable adjustment something to look forward to. As they turn, they play with indirection, teasing the approaching onlookers. They instantly put the spectators (the audience that surrounds them and the unknown ones who follow along on film) to work—the positions that the onlookers might occupy must consider the multiple directions to which their bodies might turn or surprise. It is in this dizzying grasp toward orientation that Silvio and Ada would have us join with their performance. Defined, present, but also poised on that ambiguous precipice between restraint and release, Silvio and Ada morph a stable grid of being into a flexible dance space of becoming.

The camera follows the dancers as they move their dance to various locations throughout the club. They are in constant movement and always moving toward an uncertain something. However, they do not move across the locations in straight lines. Instead, they gently proceed toward that uncertain something by taking the time to make a series of turns together. Rather than taking a direct route from point A to B, they allow the space for subtle flourishes. Although the routine is dubbed over by the soundtrack of Ignacio Piñeiro's "Échale salsita" (to which I will return to below), their footsteps wouldn't be audible anyway. They do not stomp or march and barely seem to touch the floor. Grounded and suspended at once, they will get there in their own way and time.

The camera continues to follow Silvio and Ada as they create one of their defined but unpredictable lines on a pier as the sun begins to set. The camera films them from the far away shore, not so that it can voyeuristically capture their performance, but so that it can give them the space they need to do their work. It is on the pier, with their figures cutting shapes into the tangerine light, that the dancers fold in a dramatic interlude. Ada takes Silvio's hand and begins to spin around him. He allows himself to be turned. They move in concentric circles around each other without a break to change hands. As he slowly spins inside of Ada's circle, Silvio begins to move downward. On the way down he removes his hat with his other hand. Throughout the course of being turned, Silvio alters his body from the upright, to a crouch, and finally to a low horizon. They look like they are dancing on top of the water. As he puts his body in a vertical plane, and with only one foot touching the floor, he places his hat on his foot, which offers the perfect perch as his toes are now pointed skyward.

All the while, Ada still turns him. Ada, it must be pointed out, is solid in her support and the reason he is able to make this incredible move. As he begins to pull himself upright again, Ada takes his hat and puts it on top of her head. It is a gesture that does not claim, but delicately asserts a coauthor-

FIG. 4.2: Silvio and Ada in *Nosotros, la música*, directed by Rogelio París, 1963.

ship of what has just been made possible. After completion, the dancers are slowly edited back to their original starting point as the song comes to a close. It is a reverse mirroring of the first half of the song. The brilliant editing by Nelson Rodríguez allows for the dancers, the song, and the series of locations to finish in perfect time.

The song behind Silvio and Ada's performance is Ignacio Piñeiro's famous son entitled "Échale salsita" (Give It Some Sauce). The son is both genre, and in Spanish, the third person plural of the present indicative "to be." The sonic architecture of the song itself is built around the pregón, which is a public announcement that generally involves commerce in the street. As relayed by Cuban musician Roberto Torres, this particular pregón recalls a popular street vendor who would stand near the Central Highway in Havana with a cart of sausages.[60] In his recollection, the members of Piñero's septet were fresh off of a late night gig at a club, famished by their exhausting performance. Driven by an impossible desire for these sausages, the band was disappointed to not find the vendor in his habitual turf. They sought out this man, having mapped his steps by word of mouth, and eventually went to his home. In exchange for food, Piñero and his septet promised to compose a song about him. "Echale salsita" was composed as gratitude for sustenance and circulated as a homage to pedestrian hospitality. Though he remains unnamed, this son memorializes the street vendor and his seemingly finite speech act is extended into new worlds, spaces, and dance floors.

In the opening and closing shots of Silvio and Ada on the club's dance floor, the large crowd (including the septet that plays behind them) is made to disappear. The interpretive readings of these cuts are infinite. Perhaps this editorial move is a nod to the felt effects of a small part of the population having already left the island—an ephemeral remainder of bodies that were once there. The occupants of this dance floor are not erased but rather bracketed momentarily, phantom presences that continue to orbit around the dancers. However, I'd like to allow my experience of the film to spin beyond the pre-s and post-s, and offer another possibility. Perhaps this cut into community allow Silvio and Ada a more intimate space of being, one that is undoubtedly informed by but does not necessarily have to report back to an official "public" or an official "nosotros" or "we." This space of being is within and at the same time gestures toward the possibility of being outside of the "we."

Because it is often evoked to muffle difference and dissent, and because it has been employed to repressive effect in regimes everywhere, the "we" can be intolerable. This is especially true in Cuba where each generation is continually called upon to sacrifice mind and body for the national "we."[61] It is partly for these reasons that I am struck by what these filmed details do to any facile sense of collectivity that might be evoked by the "nosotoros" of the film's title. The film urges a recognition, and not a paving over, of the past and all of its pleasures and difficulties. Review all of the neglected names, bodies, and traditions that are brought to the film's surface so that the "nosotros" it hopes to document can include and be altered by the past as much as the present and future. It is not static. It does not insist on straight lines. Nor does it shorthand the complexity of Cuban music for convenience and expediency. The film does not offer a tidy way for the viewer to capture what and who Cuba is. And while the "nosotros" might be ambiguous—it is not the ambiguity of power whose interests masquerade as the greater good.

Before we depart from this film for the next, I'd like to briefly but thoughtfully consider the larger nosotros captured in the background and foreground of the film, those who sat in the editing studio, and the audiences of the time who were all, in one way or another, navigating the shifting terms of nation and belonging.[62] Urfé's stunning transformation of Bach into a danzón, and Silvio and Ada's intimate dance, offer porous modes—ways of being in transition—at a time when ideological positions were increasingly becoming calcified. Their elegant indeterminacy, eager playfulness, experimentation with time, adaptability to the larger film, allow us to revisit those moments after the revolution that found strength in an uncertain future promise, even as the "we" became increasingly bifurcated along within or against lines.[63] These performances were (and are) not only singular manifestations of a more open, more time taken "we," and perhaps this is part of their power. The song and the dance both offer an oppositional softening of that steely cold war feel that has come to dominate discourse, aesthetics, and diplomacy wherever Cubans reside. They are reminders that such moments are always taking place and deserve to be remembered and learned from. What we learn from these details can occupy our present and future as much as they offer an alternate view of the past.

It is once again in the spirit of openings that I'll introduce Sara Gómez, the director of *Y . . . tenemos sabor*. In my analysis of this film, I focus more on Gómez's handiwork as a filmmaker—as a weaver of details—because she allows us to see documentary practice as a form of musicking, which to recall Christopher Small's definition, "is to take part, in any capacity, in a musical performance, whether by performing, by listening, by rehearsing or practicing, by providing material for performance (what is called composing), or by dancing."[64] As I reveal below, I am particularly interested in how Gómez makes possible a slippage between filmmaker and arranger. As a director, Gómez bears the honor and burden of being many firsts. She was the first woman, and first woman of color, to direct a feature length film in Cuba. This feature, called *De cierta manera* (1974) was one of the first to deal explicitly with the intersections between gender, race, and class in the new Cuban society. She also broke new ground by playing with formal conventions from a spectrum of film genres, from documentary to melodrama.

Gómez, in print and affection, is often called a pathfinder and has been an inspiration to young filmmakers all over the world. Gómez passed away too early, from acute asthma, at the age of thirty-four. Her many unfinished projects are still mourned. There is an iconic image of Gómez that frequently

FIG. 4.3: Sara Gómez and Julio Valdés, circa 1973, taken from the set of Gómez's *De cierta manera*. Courtesy of the Cinemateca de Cuba, Instituto Cubano del Arte e Industria Cinematográficos.

circulates in the virtual world.[65] For some, it is an anomaly: it shows a black woman in control of a movie camera. For others it is an image of reassurance, righteousness, and pride. It shows Gómez sideling up to the camera in a flowered tank top and jeans. Her thighs grip one leg of the tripod as she braces the camera with familiarity and confidence. She is looking through its lens and I wonder what it is she is setting up, searching for. What does she hope to include, block out, set under a different light? It is a posture she must have assumed hundreds of times to help share and translate her vision to the crew, and ultimately, to her audiences.

This image offers a deep opportunity to think hard about what it is to see the world as framed by Gómez. What is it about her vantage point that stirs so many and make her films among the most immediately and intimately felt in the history of Cuban cinema? And the loss of her among the most immediately and intimately felt losses in the history of Cuban popular culture? It is perhaps because immediacy and intimacy are two of the descriptives that best describe her cinematic aesthetics, in feeling and technique. The great Cuban filmmaker Tomás Gutiérrez Alea (Titón) once described her this way,

> a Sara le hubiera gustado hacer cine sin cámaras, sin micrófonos: directamente, y eso es lo que le da esa fuerza, y esa cosa única que lamentablemente, no creo que haya sido suficientemente valorada con los años.[66] [Sara would have loved to make films without cameras, microphones. She wanted to be direct and that's what gave her that strength, that unique quality that, unfortunately, has not been sufficiently valorized over the years.]

In the iconic photo we get a behind-the-scenes glimpse of this raw directness even, and especially as it is made to pass through the intermediaries of the camera and crew. She was always "Sarita," the affectionate diminutive of herself, and the name she chose to credit in many of her films.

To move through Gómez's legacy properly would require decades and volumes.[67] Here I will necessarily get more specific and consider Gómez's framing of Cuban music through her 1967 documentary *Y... tenemos sabor*. Like *Nosotros, la música*, *Y... tenemos sabor* is another puzzle for translation. It roughly means "And... we have flavor." Sabor finds more familiar company with the American colloquial "flava." It is a superlative that can arise in the everyday, say, when someone (usually a sexy woman) or something (usually good food) is described as saborosa/o (flavorful). But it is a required quality in dance and especially music. As Raúl A. Férnandez notes, it is "the sine qua non of Cuban musicianship: a musician who does not play with *sabor* cannot play Cuban music well."[68] Sabor is a quality, an attitude, and an overall way of being with rhythm and sound that is technically, incredibly sophisticated. Sabor also connotes a more indefinable but present swagger and bold sense of experimentation that has been honed over centuries of musical development.

Y... tenemos sabor might read something like "And on top of it all, we have flavor." One wonders: what precedes the "And...."? What was on this list before coming to this final assertion? Many possibilities are allowed by this title; it is an opportunity ripe for Cuban autoaggrandizement. Whatever came before the "And," the title lets you know that the "we" invoked here has it all, that it is more than complete, so much so that it *even* has this ambiguous but palpable flavor. Like in París's film, the "we" is both exacting and indefinable. Does it refer to Cubans after the revolution? The aim of the documentary refuses a temporalizing of the "we." In the opening titles, we are informed that the film is, "un documental para hablar de los instrumentos de la música cubana" (a documentary to discuss Cuban musical instruments). Given the ways that instruments were developed by indigenous populations and introduced to the island via migrations from Africa, Asia, and Europe, such a discussion must account for Cuba from before the conquest and onward.

Y . . . tenemos sabor is a fascinating documentary for many reasons. It plays with and subverts the authoritative vocality often assumed of the documentary form. It is a refreshing example of a pedagogical film made during the revolution that is not prescriptive or pedantic. For the larger project of Gómez studies, we are given a chance to feel her extensive training from Havana's music conservatory imported into her work, which is to also say, she gives us an occasion to think through the relationship between the visual and music in novel ways. Such a relationship was an early preoccupation of hers. The visual and musical eye was even integrated in her journalistic forays. For example, in 1964 Gómez wrote an article in *La revista Cubana* titled, "La rumba." The piece includes an essay about rumba's basics, its lyrical refrains, histories, and photos of then popular, if not formally well-known performers taken by Mayito (the nickname of Mario García Joya), who would also collaborate with her on *Y . . . tenemos sabor*. The article's layout is more akin to a musical score than journalistic convention. The pictures and text move from their familiar positions and into a graphic arrangement that recalls rumba's repetitions, both its percussive patterns and lyrical refrains.[69]

I understand this article as a rehearsal for *Y . . . tenemos sabor*, which reveals Gómez's gift with musical arrangement.[70] The thirty-minute documentary essentially interweaves three tracks or musical lines. The first is an extensive and oftentimes hilarious lecture given by Alberto Zayas, an important rumba composer and singer known for making the first commercial recordings of rumbas.[71] He was an important educational emissary for Afro-Cuban musical forms and influences. He was also, incidentally,

Quiero aprovechar esta oportunidad para decirles a ustedes como una pequeña historia del Guaguancó, que a través de los años, el que les habla a ustedes, un servidor, Agustín Pina, que desde muy pequeño me dicen mis amigos, cariñosamente, Flor de Amor.

Flor vive en el barrio de Luyanó. En una de las casas a la entrada del solar que forma la esquina de Municipio y Atarés. Allí Flor escribe sus memorias.

Como primer punto de partida para conocimiento de todos ustedes, soy Rumbero de Fundamento, y digo esto porque desde pequeño no he hecho otra cosa que cantar y tocar Rumbas y Guaguancós y Claves. Por mi casa han desfilado todos los grandes Rumberos de la República.

En el Yambú no se "vacuna"   Su ritmo es lento   y acompasado

LA RUMBA

POR SARA GOMEZ YERA

FOTOS MAYITO
CUBA/59

FIG. 4.4: Sara Gómez's article "La rumba" in *La revista cubana*, 1964.

an informant for the renowned Cuban anthropologist, Fernando Ortiz. In the film, Zayas lectures directly to the camera (and to Gómez who can often be seen crouched in the foreground of the frame). He talks through the principal instruments of popular Cuban music by offering short glimmers of their histories and locations. Zayas insists on the criolloismo (the uniquely Cuban born quality) of the instruments by asserting their New World inventiveness. Of the güiro (a hollowed out gourd instrument with ridges) he states,

> este instrumento es puramente cubano . . . la calabaza, o sea, el güiro es africano y se va a toda América . . . pero el sistema de tocar y de hacer ritmo es totalmente cubano" . . . [this instrument is purely Cuban . . . the gourd or the güiro is African and went all over the Americas . . . but the *system* of playing it and making rhythm is completely Cuban].

And the timbales are "puramente Cubano" (purely Cuban) even if Italian opera companies had introduced them in the nineteenth century. No geography is left untouched, even if the expansiveness of it overwhelms. By the time he gets to the corneta china (the Chinese cornet), his teacherly composure shows signs of pleasurable wear. With a loss for words that such an instrument demands, he says, "para divertirnos tenemos hasta la corneta china. Que esto ya . . . figúrese usted." . . . [And as if that wasn't enough, to have a good time, we even have the Chinese cornet. This thing is, well. . . . you'll have figure it out.]

The other track of the film that is used to interrupt, accentuate, underscore, and even anticipate the movement of Zayas's lectures are a series of performances by some of the most important Cuban musical groups of the past and then present, including the Conjunto Changüí, Conjunto Típico Habanero, Conjunto Clave y Guaguancó, the Conga de Santiago de Cuba, Trío Los Decanos, Trío Virgilio, Almenares y Márquez, Orquesta Estrellas Cubanas, and finally, a young Chucho Valdés and his combo featuring Amado "Guapacha" Borcelá on vocals. Gómez orchestrates these clips as points of departure and release for Zayas's words. The clips of the bands also function to showcase the undervalued, underrecorded, and rising stars in Cuban popular music. It makes the rich variety and sophistication of music at the time visible and more alive than ever. Zayas's lecture does not function as the contextual information for the music. His words are also made into part of the film's soundtrack, for example, by being left to play under scenes of musicians gathering or while he constructs a set of bongos from skin and wood. The lecture and songs bleed into the other. And finally, these two lines are woven together by spare narration by Isa Mendoza, who offers another layer of contextual orientation. The lecture, music, and narration do not compete but compliment one another.

Gómez left the Havana conservatory because, in her words, she did not want to be "a middle class black woman who played the piano."[72] Perhaps we can interpret this as Gómez's rejection of the historical path of many Cuban women of color in the performing arts. Perhaps she needed her work to mean something beyond the space of a music lesson given in a family home or as the entertaining background for social gatherings. We will never know. I do not think, however, that her statement can be easily read as a wholesale rejection of music or her training in it. As I stated earlier, one of the many unique qualities in Gómez is her talent at arrangement. I use this musical labor to describe her work because of the musical feel she brings to her films that cannot simply be explained by excellent editing (though she was more than capable of that too). By musical feel I mean that watching her work is like being on the inside of a song. Her films carry you away in that unique way that music can; like the swirl of time experienced on a dance floor.

I say that Gómez is an arranger because there is such a musical quality to much of her work and I believe that it was a skill found in and/or heightened by her experience with music. Arrangers are among the most overlooked creative participants in music even as they are responsible for tapping the potential of any song. The *Oxford Companion to Music* defines an arrangement as,

> The adaptation of music for a medium different from that for which it was originally composed. . . . Such a process, if undertaken seriously, involves much more than simply transferring a score from one medium to the other, since many passages that are effective in the original would sound much less so in another medium. [73]

An arrangement is not a simple transfer of an original song into a different instrumentation, for example, by exporting a melody from a solitary piano and expanding it into a full orchestra. Rather, to arrange requires having a sense of all of the multiple ways in which instruments can be made to sound and made to carry the work that keeps it close to the original, and to also take it into unforeseen directions.

When arrangers are not the authors of the work, their labor is often invisible, their craft thought of as derivative from the original composer. When credited, their name might stand after the composer, post hyphen. But what of this signature? How does it credit? Peter Szendy writes:

> I love them more than all the others, the arrangers. The ones who sign their names *inside* the work, and don't hesitate to set their name down next to the author's . . . it seems to me what arrangers are signing is above all a listening. *Their* hearing of a work. They may even be the only listeners in the history of music to *write down* their listenings,

rather than *describe* them (as critics do). And that is why I love them, I who so love to listen to someone listening. I love hearing them hear.[74]

Arranging implies adaptation, choice, and the movement of an object from one mode into another. Some would insist on a strict division between arrangement and adaptation; arrangement as somehow faithful to composer's intentions (as if those intentions can ever be known), and adaptation as understood almost pejoratively as taking license with an original work.[75] I stay with arranging—and include adaptation as part of it—because the structure and feel of *Y . . . tenemos sabor* takes place *inside* music rather than a distant commentary or interpretation of it. The edits and jump cuts do not happen simply when there are predictable breaks or rests in the music or in Zayas's lecture. The cuts add and create a rhythm and musical texture of their own. They are arrangements of what Zayas and the musicians present to the camera. The film is not a transcription or translation of music into another medium which suggests a once-removed intimacy from the music itself. Such a reading would also neglect the direct intimacy that Gómez uniquely created with her productions and audiences (as Titón reminds us). By allowing the back of her head to be in many of the film's frames, Gómez signs herself next to these musical authors, and she reveals that her body and directorial hand are no anomaly to the history of Cuban music, but are part of the music itself. She is music's student as much as music's director.

Back to the iconic photo I discuss earlier: we are given the occasion to wonder what it is to see the world as framed by Sara. *Y . . . tenemos sabor* offers the opportunity to wonder what it is to hear the world as heard by Sarita. The film is, as Szendy suggests, a writing down of her listenings. And I love hearing her hear. It is an ear that hears in parts and then cumulatively. For example, after Zayas has lectured about most of the instruments, the film arrives at a performance by the Conjunto Típico Habanero. It is here where all of our instruction comes into focus. They are all there: the claves, güiro, quijada, bongos, coming together for a finale. The camera zooms in on each so that we can see what we've learned and how such parts come together. So that we can see how they fit perfectly, so that we can sense their ingenuity.

Gómez's listening makes jumps that take past and present, different

FIG. 4.5: Alberto Zayas and Sara Gómez in *Y... tenemos sabor*, directed by Sara Gómez, 1967.

genres, and locations as all part of the other. For example, at the end of the film, Gómez puts two final performances side-by-side that might seem historically and geographically incongruous. During the first we are dropped into a comparsa moved along by the Conga de Santiago de Cuba, on the far eastern part of the island. The carnaval line moves through the street with the barest of instruments: hubcaps, sticks on boxes, homemade bass drums, bells from scrap metal, the Chinese cornet. It is music stripped to its most essential, even as it also feels, given the perfect synchronicity between the makeshift and the sophisticated, as the future sound. She reveals that the "we" might inherit, but doesn't necessarily require, all of the instrumental inventions outlined by Zayas. Here she shows that sabor suffices.

Right after the clip of the passing comparsa, the narrator takes us to the finish: "Pero ahora nos vamos alejando de la música tradicional y los más jóvenes trabajan en algo nuevo, distinto pero conservando nuestro sabor" ... [but now we will move from traditional music to the young folks who are working with something new and distinct, but that nevertheless conserve our sabor]. The final clip of the film includes a performance by a young and gangly Chucho Valdés—the virtuoso pianist and orchestra leader who has become one of Cuba's most visible musical emissaries—and his combo vocally helmed by scat sensation Amado Borcelá "Guapacha." The film ends on this "something new." What does this "something new" sound like? Valdés and the young musicians that occupy the stage extend the jazz furrows that remained uninterrupted even after the rupture of 1959. Many of the instruments featured in Zayas's lecture are present alongside a piano, guitar, and upright bass. In Guapacha's vocals you hear Ella Fitzgerald and Louis Armstrong. Although Valdés was trained extensively in classical and popular Cuban music, Dave Brubeck first turned him on to piano improvisation. Although his famous father (the pianist Bebo Valdés) was a pioneer in the Cuban jazz sensibility, it was Brubeck who Valdés credits as the gateway into jazz experimentation.[76] In this final scene, we are given Valdés's hearing of Brubeck. The song that the combo plays is called "Chachacha Bebop." It is an urgent, up-tempo chase of instruments that tries to keep up with and provide ground for Guapacha's scatting; it is a funnel cloud of rumba, mambo, blues, big band, and swing.

Given the lengthy and prolonged impressions of Cuban musicians in the jazz furrows—a few of which I offered listenings of in my previous chapters—it is fascinating to note how their presence in the film is offered as the "something new," the musical send off for the next generation. It is doubly fascinating considering how many in the early decades after the revolution considered jazz as the sign of an imperial occupier. It was often regarded as a hegemonic US power structure affixed to music and a problem to be dealt with through disciplinary measures. Leonardo Acosta, who in addition to being one of Cuban music's most important critics, is also a musician who played alto sax alongside many jazz musicians at the time. Immediately following the revolution, he recalls a time when agitators violently interrupted a jazz performance at the Capri Cabaret. "This kind of agitator," Acosta remembers, "carried away in the anti-imperialist sentiment of the time, was capable of creating an atmosphere of fear and witch-hunting under the pretext that jazz was 'imperialistic.'" He also recalls when a few of the best students were caught playing jazz and summarily suspended by the Escuela Nacional de Música. Acosta believed this kind of discipline to be less uniform than totalizing, and attributed it to "the particular idiosyncrasy of one or another acting bureaucrat." Still, he also sees how such measures had profound impact, for example, in the dozens of jazz musicians who left the country during the revolution. The exodus included some of Cuban jazz's brightest stars including Juanito Márquez, Bebo Valdés, and Cachao.[77]

I hesitate to use this detail in Gómez's film, or the oeuvre of Chucho Valdés, as proof (though it certainly could be) that the rupture between the United States and Cuba could never break this continuity of sound that exceeds geography, policy, and national identity. However, it can't be overstated how profoundly such co-collaboration and influence has been rooted in the Cuban musical scene and how it continues to play such a role in its perpetual reinvention. To reiterate: I do not see Cuban jazz as derivative of US practices. It is impossible to separate who was first on the scene. It is especially impossible given the different corners it has come to play in many genres of Cuban music from straight jazz to popular dance genres such as timba that would emerge in the 1990s. By signing off with Chucho Valdés, who would become one of the most critical players in the jazz furrows for the next fifty years, I believe that Gómez was trying to send us all a hopeful signal: Cuba might be cut off, but music's ability to sustain continuities makes it more than complete. And on top of it all, all its myriad participants will continue to have, and add, flavor.

I began this chapter with some consequences of the rupture that would take place between Cuba and the United States. I also promised a few hopeful particularities. Through their details, performed modes, and their overall arrangement, *Nosotros, la música* and *Y . . . tenemos sabor* offer some of the hopeful particularities that would come to pass in the rupture. With the help of the performers of their films, and the musical traditions they came from and would continue to shape, they revealed the impossible project of forging a coherent or singular "we" for the Cuban nation state, by which I'd also like to append, Greater Cuba. It is in these performed responses that I see great possibility for any reparative work in the post-rupture. To abandon a coherent or singular Cubanness, and to find other kinds of models in music, these films and filmmakers have offered comfort and company and methods. They have left behind experiences that, in the words of José Esteban Muñoz, enable us to "see the past and the potentiality imbued within an object, the ways it might represent a mode of being and feeling that was then not quite there but nonetheless an opening."[78] París's and Gómez's documentaries are objects that could be read as artifacts fiercely situated in time and place. Their stunning and transitional quality of being "not quite there," however, continues to equip us for listening together and apart. They are openings that have allowed me to shine light into the chapter that follows.

Chapter Five

Cold War Kids in Concert

for Patty Ahn, Van Truong, and Georgina Ruiz

In 1987, a doe-eyed and chubby seventh grader named Alex Ruiz wrote a song called "What Happens . . ." Here is an excerpt:

> Have you ever thought about what happens in Cuba/ It's not a pleasant thing to hear/ there's been killing ever since communism hit this beautiful land of mine/ It is a big issue something you just can't ignore/ life has gotten so bad that everybody is poor . . . what do we say to that.
>
> *Chorus:* what happens when your homeland crumbles/ what happens when your homeland dies (*repeat*). . . .

Alex was not born in Cuba. His father, like my father, was sent alone to the United States when he was a teenager. They both came by way of arrangements set up by the United States at the start of its cold war with Cuba in the early 1960s. Alex's father arrived as part of a project called "Operation Peter Pan," a well-known, if hushed, partnership between the US government and the Catholic Church that placed Cuban children in adoptive families throughout the country.[1] My father's journey was, like many other uncounted young Cuban refugees, an informal copycat version of Peter Pan.

FIG. 5.1: Ana Mendieta's *Untitled (Silueta Series Mexico)*, 1973/1991. Estate color photograph; 20 × 16 inches (50.8 × 40.6 CM). © The Estate of Ana Mendieta Collection, Courtesy Galerie Lelong, New York.

The routes between Cuba and Florida were well traveled by many families, particularly of the middle class. It was a challenge, but not impossible, to facilitate temporary homes for their children through church and other mutual aid organizations. During those first years after the 1959 revolution, many Cuban parents sent their children away out of real and perceived fear of Soviet entanglement. They couldn't bear the uncertainties or what the swift changes happening around them would mean for their children. So they sent them, alone, to a strange array of US cities. The separations were supposed to be temporary. Some families were reunited. Just as many were not. The lucky ones were placed in Miami. The artist Ana Mendieta was sent to Iowa where she spent her coming of age trying to implant herself in foreign landscapes.

Alex's song, which was written when he was just ten years old, was composed on notebook paper in serious pubescent cursive. The song suggests how such permanent separations have been inherited and responded to. Born and raised in Miami without having ever set foot on this "beautiful land of mine," Alex's song indicates a pervasive practice found in many children of Cuban immigrants. It incorporates a short lifetime of listening in detail to a family's difficult displacements and creates new structures to process it. I don't, and sadly, can't know what those exact details were. But I recognize some familiar contours. To be forced to imagine skeletal Cuban children, by one relative or another, when throwing food away. To want to understand why they cried while watching the dramatic reunification of families on the local evening news.

There are many of us who might recognize ourselves in songs such as these. Throughout our childhoods, we made them up to try and cure those faraway looks in our parents' eyes, help them breathe easier. The responsibility of making them better was and is the greatest charge put upon children of immigrants. However distorted Alex's vision of that land might have been from reality, his song can be heard not as a calcification of but an earnest negotiation with the ideological templates of Cuban Miami. Many would easily dismiss and vilify this song and these fantasies as the typical disenchantment expressed by privileged and right wing exiles. Such simple, safe, and outdated narratives have come to dominate understandings of Cuban communities in the United States. What does not bear worth repeating but must: much of mainstream Cuban exile politics and its myriad manifestations have historically been odious and discouraging.[2] However, to leave assumptions like these untouched contributes to the silencing of some rousing disruptions that interfere in those assumptive taxonomies of migratory waves.

"Have you ever thought about what happens in Cuba?" is a relentless question—even if it goes unasked—for children of Cuban immigrants born abroad. It is not surprising that Alex's vision bordered on the nightmarish. Submerged in the Reagan era, the dearth of cold wars of position in popular culture, and a city dominated by an angry and wounded population, it is easy to see how a sensitive boy was so haunted that he spent nascent reparative energies trying to approximate and heal such anger in song. His feelings might have been misdirected, and his fear misguided, but his real attempt to think about "what happens in Cuba" is nevertheless heartening because it surfaces strong preoccupations that many of us shared and shared early. These preoccupations did not only include inherited familial pain, but also those children who were us and not us.

In this chapter, I explore some of the qualities of such shared preoccupation—with all its inherited distortions and recuperative possibilities—signaled by Alex's song and in other musical repertoires. I reveal how many like Alex have turned to song to articulate the inarticulable condition of coming of age with the embargo, and who have used music as a place of fractured togetherness. This place—attuned to multiple differences—is made in music partly to camouflage itself from the frozen ideological and spatial positions allowed to Cubans wherever they reside.[3] Music also allows this place to exist and move. Although Greater Cuba is my primary focus, I necessarily turn to performances outside of it that have enacted unsanctioned musical visitations during the cold war. The performers I examine suggest music as a powerful gathering spot for company and communion, one that also acknowledges reunion or return or reunification as an always incomplete remedy. The structure of the chapter itself hopes to model hopeful movement on a treacherous ideological route; it begins in Miami and concludes with some deeply funky knowledge by musicians in Havana.

Although this chapter hopes to open up the coordinates of Cuba, it is admittedly Miami and Havana centric. However, my wish is that it is porous enough to be moved to different locations and epochs. Cuban American studies—whether performed by those from inside or the outside the academy—is often done on generational and regional lines. These demarcations are made in the scholarship itself, for example, with familiar and oft-repeated descriptions of distinct Cuban migratory "waves" to the United States. Each wave is understandably, though totalizingly, racialized, classed, and pegged with an assumed politics. As these familiar narratives go, the first wave of Cuban exiles to arrive in the early 1960s were privileged, conservative, white; the second wave brought the disillusioned petit bourgeoisie in the mid 1960s; the third was the Mariel exodus of the 1980s, a more economically, racially, and politically diverse group; and finally, the fourth wave, referred to as "balseros" (rafters), washed up in makeshift boats as a result of the hardships endured after the Soviet collapse in the early 1990s. There are clear generational positions felt and taken on behalf of these different waves, each with representatives in scholarship.[4] What these waves tend to obscure are the circumstances of those who arrived before, in between, and after those temporal coordinates, who spent time in third countries before arriving in the United States, who arrived under conditions not formally counted by official statistics, and those who generally don't fit into the neat sociological profiles assigned to them. The early migrations of Cuban musicians in the 1960s, as just one example, do not heed the racial, classed, or political assumptions too often made of that first wave.

In addition to these obscured exceptions to the empirical rule, these orientations tend to cause inattention to the thereafter: the newest populations of Cuban immigrants who have arrived in the late 1990s and 2000s. Many are currently working in these crucial networks.[5] But a larger trend in Cuban American scholarship has been a turn away from those who arrive and how, to focus on the transition soon to come on the island—and how those living abroad can prepare for it. Conferences and compendia are put together to discuss possible options for the changing economy, policy, and demography that will result in the death of Fidel Castro, or the fall of his brother Raúl who is currently in charge.[6] What of those who are currently arriving and adding their own cadences to the Cuban migratory landscape? There is thus a lot of catching up that Cuban American studies must do, and these later migrations to the United States are of primary concern. Another gap of particular concern to this chapter is the rarity of scholarship—beyond demographic surveys and sociological profiles—on or on behalf of the children of Cuban immigrants who were born and raised in the United States. I am not speaking of what Gustavo Pérez Firmat theorized as the one-and-a-half generation, those who were born in Cuba, spent formative time there, and then emigrated to the United States at an early age. I refer to those descendants of Cuban immigrants who only know their parents' temporary locations as home, for whom exilic memory and experiences of return are once-removed, who live out fantasies and nightmares without their own reference points. I refer to those whose lives were shaped by a place unseen, but who are not fully beholden to it. This rich gap is an underinvestigated delta that holds the legacies of migration and their possible effect on the future.

Alex's song is one object that washes up in this delta. It reveals some of the effects of growing up as a divided population, and how it has affected ways of being. These ways are and are not of our own choosing. Some of these tangible intangibles are said to make us monstrous, paranoid, short-tempered, politically misunderstood, underwritten, and trapped in the polemical register. Because of those leftover residuals from hasty departures and final goodbyes, there is an evident callousness toward any state of permanence, especially death. Contrary to myths that cast some into model minorities, many have informally noted a detectable proclivity to living life on its toxic edges. And given the disorienting distortions that made the us and the them: a general state of being messed up. I wonder what would it mean to try to import something of all this into scholarly research and writing, and to see how it can be put to the difficult work of transformation. By "all this," I mean these indescribable but present symptoms of being messed up, the inherited distortions of past and present, and the formations of self in cold war settings to argue for its transformative usefulness—because part of the despair caused by displacement and a divided nation are feelings of uselessness. From the outset, I refuse to transform the difficulty of "all this" to a smooth political utility, to a singular and pragmatic program to correct a situation that demands flexibility and multiple forms and forums.[7] I'd like to avoid, in the words of Ann Cvetkovich, "too easy assertions of a 'political' solution to the affective consequences of trauma in which politics becomes a phantasmatic structure that effects its own forms of displacement." I'm after something that is much less prescriptive and much more participatory, which will mean turning, once again, to music.

I am far from the first to try to transform and import the "all this" into critical practice.[8] Being messed up in this way bears qualities that are not only shared by generations of Cuban Americans but also by other populations who have inherited and responded to permanent separations in the cold war. "Cuban exceptionalism" is a charge leveled at Cubans and Cuban American studies. While it can be argued that Cuba's history, particularly in relationship to the United States is indeed exceptional, the worst forms of this ethos have insisted on setting Cubans apart from other populations, which tends to dovetail with racist and chauvinistic sentiment. This has been particularly true with the well-known but far from general hesitation of Cuban Americans to identify under the sign "Latino." From within Latina/o studies, Cuban Americans are too often tagged as model minorities and its diverse class, racial, and political affiliations are ignored. Criticism of some Cuban Americans refusal, hesitation, and resistance to Latina/o, and the field's refusal, hesitation, and resistance to Cuban American studies has been well explored in live forums if not in actual publications.

There remains, however, other links to other fields and structures of feeling that beg to be examined further.[9] What would be made possible if we thought of Cuban Americans alongside other immigrant populations—those who don't share such seemingly easy unifiers like language or geography—whose arrival to the United States were direct consequences of policies enacted during the cold war? In what follows, I encourage Cuban American studies to move beyond its familiar academic coordinates and reconsider its exceptional status as a rather ordinary replication of other experiments made during the cold war. I argue that doing so might enrich more nuanced understandings of their consequences and closer listening to the songs they have inspired.

As Alex's song reveals, fleeing to song is a strategy that can be present early, and for this reason offers considerable hope: the sounds have potential to transform and change shape with the privilege of time. It is by way of this potentiality that I recognize childhood as not a place of innocence, but as a mode of willful experimentation. Such a mode exceeds the real time of coming of age and can be cultivated in maturity. Objects like Alex's song are inscrutable—it would be impossible to peg, with any accuracy, what it is. It does, however, suggest a recognizable condition. Cold war kids often share this condition. Cold war kids is a playful taxonomy I let loose with equal parts pain and humor.[10] It is not my own: I took "Cold War Kids" from the band of the same name after seeing their poster plastered all over hipster Brooklyn. I took it, or I should say, took it back, because its ironic stance felt ripe for a reckoning.

"The cold war" has for too long sounded like scholarship built with icy metal.[11] The discourse has a buzz cut uniformity that can't manage to escape—at least to my readerly eyes—the stern voices that dub documentaries for public television, or the Sam the Eagle voice. Think of all those Barnes and Nobles hardcovers stamped with capital letters in some terrifying font. Even the scholarly publication dedicated to the cause, *The Journal of Cold War Studies* bears an alarming detachment in both design and content. Then again, perhaps detachment is the appropriate register to deal with such disturbing material. The cold war is most often used to both fix and avoid feeling history, to frame general policy shifts, and not linger on the details of their consequences. It is my hope that looking into linkages between cold war kids can help to articulate some of the sensations produced by what Jodi Kim calls the "protracted afterlife" of the cold war, its enduring presence in the lives of its casualties, and a few interventions that have the potential to repair such sensations and sustained presence.[12]

I propose kids is a vital suffix to the cold war because we've got to the point where there is a *need* to give up on the steely not-going-to-talk-about-it frozen positions of our elders. By kids, I mean to suggest a willfully experimental grouping that asks to be listened to as purposefully provisional, not as a fully formed or finished thing. Part of this willful experimentation involves holding on to an unpolished rebellious quality. Cold war kids, as a category and a position, is along the lines of giving the finger, the punk rock kind we might have casually thrown during adolescent rebellions. For example, in 1992 the still doe-eyed, but sinewy high school version of Alex Ruiz put together a recording three short years after writing "What Happens." Take his homemade music demo "Cuban Missle Crisis" (*sic*). Note the radical shifts he made in the transition from 'tween to teen, in particular, the bold placement of our situation in a urinal. In the liner notes he "Would like to thank the American work ethic for making him a miserable teenager." That a fifteen-year-old kid was so articulate to the discipline of assimilation—*and articulate in performance*—should give us great hope, especially as there are so many who have derived such thrill and unchecked privilege from being exceptional.[13] Though it is always changing forms because of time and age, I hope that something of Ruiz's *Cuban Missle Crisis*, something of that urinal and middle finger might be learned from and raised to the hopeless political impasses in which we're still made to participate.

We are all, by default of being alive in the twenty-first century, cold war kids. However, in what follows, I wade into a specific interrelation that has far too often gone overlooked as an exciting theoretical and experiential prism. I insist on specificity here, as countless countries are too often made

FIG. 5.2: Outer cover of Alex Ruiz's *Cuban Missile Crisis* cassette, 1996.

FIG. 5.3: Interior cover of Alex Ruiz's *Cuban Missile Crisis* cassette, 1996.

present in cold war discourse solely in the parenthetical. It is much too common to read some line about the modern age of American empire that is quickly followed by parentheses that includes a long list of places. Those of us who actually have a stake in those places perk up at our mere mention, but become deflated knowing that we are only made mere mention. Each interrelation and grouping requires its own work. It is impossible, in other words, to simply insert nations x, y, and z here. And while I insist upon the specificity in these pages, I acknowledge that there are so many different argumentative threads, groupings, themes that a critical category such as cold war kids can take. There is nothing I'd like to make prohibitive to or outside of it.

I imagine some possible links between the children of Cubans, Koreans, and Vietnamese who reside in the United States. Those for whom exilic memory and experiences of return are once removed, who live out fantasies and nightmares without their own reference points.[14] The reasons for my grouping these locations might seem obvious. Sequencing forges intimacies. Recall that Cuba was a rehearsal, suspense movie, and hinge between the US wars in Korea and Viet Nam. Parallels exist in mainstream refugee politics in that we share populations of powerful conservative hardliners who have long been made to singularly represent and misrepresent dozens of politically diverse perspectives. The nations are divided in real and unreal ways, through borders, policy, and restrictive ideological positions. There are parallels on the larger immigrant taxonomies in the United States for which these populations are forced and/or chosen to catch the undertows of model minorityhood. I will reflect on other, less transparent reasons, below.

By placing the children of Cuban, Korean, and Vietnamese immigrants into conversation, I resist the muscular model of the "comparative" study. There is something unwieldy about the comparative project. It can too often follow the compare and contrast model; the mechanical methods by which differences between populations are explored do not get at some of the less transparent but material linkages between them.[15] Comparative, by definition, insists on setting the contents apart (and then a few corrective stitches) for the purposes of argument.[16] The work often demands an official body of evidence whereby one can compare experience via collected data. As Vijay

Prashad has observed, "rather than an active model of mutual interaction, there is a tendency to move toward a static model for epistemological judgment."[17] The protocols of the comparative project can also incite easy, if well-intentioned questions about the dangerous conflation of histories. Permit me to address these concerns here. I do not and cannot argue for facile comparison between populations that have experienced brutal ground wars, the deaths of millions of citizens, and the vast destruction of their lands to those that have not. I recognize that the violences inflicted on and within the Koreas, Viet Nam, and Cuba are different and uneven, and require altering tools for reflection. There is no way that I can work comparatively with these different experiences. That does not mean, however, that those who have inherited such violences—violences that directly implicate the United States and its posturing during the cold war—cannot exchange a few stories and trade survival mechanisms.

How do you engage conversations that might not appear in official surveys? How do you engage commonalities without shorthanding their complexity under "empire" or "hegemony" or "collective trauma"? To work through these large questions will partly mean being attuned in spaces both official and not, that do and don't make sense to the "comparative." I propose that listening in detail might be a way to unearth a camaraderie that is felt if not exactly named. To listen in detail suggests an alternative way to engage phenomena across populations that does not strive to make large claims, build an immovable artifice, or forge static rubrics. To listen in detail is a practice that makes small moves; to lend attention to those powerful minute anomalies that disturb the surfaces of not only music, but also history and the ways we study it. To think through the possible affiliations between cold war kids, I have listened to conversations already happening in those underrecognized symposia put together by junior faculty members across the country.[18] The conversations have happened over cocktails between colleagues brought together at scholarly conferences. They have happened in the real worlds of friends and new acquaintances in too many possible meeting places to mention.[19] Sometimes conversations happen without any actual contact but are carried along in creative drifts, especially in music.

Before returning to the Cuban music scene, I listen in detail to a few critical and creative interventions made by Korean and Vietnamese American artists and scholars, not as comparatives, but as colleagues to lean on because they encourage that lifelong project of trying to find the way and the words. These details have helped me to create provisional practices to approach Cuban musical activity during the cold war. A common process of scholarship is to make a connection with someone—whether picking up the phone, reaching out via e-mail, or making a song dedication—to work through an idea. It is often the only way an idea eventually makes it to the page. What follows then is my reaching out to a few pioneering voices that have enabled me to begin working through "all this."

If part of the reason why we write books is to make up the scholarly practices of our dreams, to "imagine otherwise" as Kandice Chuh beautifully put it, I present a model in the footsteps of which I can only hope to follow. In 2009, I received a California care package sent by Christine Bacareza Balance. In it was an exhibition catalog borne over army-based stew in LA's Koreatown. I refer to the lunchtime origins of Yong Soon Min and Viet Le's *transPOP: Korea Vietnam Remix*, a model of cocuratorialship. Min and Le assembled a group of sixteen artists from Vietnam, Korea, and the United States to work through other kinds of "all this": to model collaborative practices, to share memories too difficult, to turn to pop culture as an unforgotten and sometimes, unforgiving conduit, and to come together even as the world wants and needs them to be apart. In the catalog, Min and Le write a stunning contrapuntal dialog. Their work was not imagined as a final corrective or comparative monolith, but as an invitation for a hopeful future. As Min writes, "it is my hope that the discursive framework of *transPOP* provides a fertile and resonant ground upon which the viewer and the works engage in an extended conversation."[20] Part of their conversation I'd like to extend here could be strategic and restorative to cold war kids writ large.

Viet Le ends the conversational essay with a recent memory of having visited his uncle in 2006 in Duc Hoa, his first return to Vietnam after a twenty-year separation. His uncle gives him some photographs of his mother before the war. I cannot paraphrase him. I will quote him at length:

> One is a black and white photograph of my mother, almost unrecognizable—exactly my age now, thirty one—smiling radiantly on the beach with four friends, all in an informal line at the edge of the water,

FIG. 5.4: Catalog cover of *transPOP: Korea Vietnam Remix*, curated by Yong Soon Min and Viet Le, August 7–30, 2008.

all giggling at the unknown photographer. She is the furthest one on the right. Wearing a plain white cotton sundress, my mother is slender and carelessly beautiful, holding an umbrella.

Holding the photograph, I suddenly sob deeply and uncontrollably in front of my uncle. He is gently quiet. I cannot stop. I am unable to reconcile the gaps in history and memory. I have been looking for my mother's ghost, a tracing, even though she is still alive. I have been haunted all my life by her ghost, and ghostly memories. What has happened before, after, in between? Where is she? I am grieving for the woman she once was, for the woman she is, for the years of pain indelibly writ upon her face, body, psyche. Before after in between. I barely recognize her. I am grieving for my uncle, for the wars then and now, for the limits of my comprehension. I cannot explain it—my sorrow, my rage. I am crying as I write this now. I cannot stop, before, after, in between.

I've been working with Le's passage for a long time now and it is still difficult, if not impossible, to not cry alongside him. It is one of those details that hold you up temporally and physically. For cold war kids, Le helps to reveal how our limits of comprehension set the timbre of every line that we write. It shows that our attempts to locate our parents inform our chosen geographies and at those locations, our ways of being. More than anything else, Le gives company to that feeling of not being able to explain and not being able to stop. It is a permanent condition. It will never be corrected.

Allow me to point out a few things about the structure of this passage. In the first part, Le addresses what this thing is. He plainly describes the photograph and the objects it documents. The giggles, sundress, umbrella are melancholic surfaces. In the second part, he writes what this thing does. Through an unforgiving rhythm of prose, and the salinity of his words, he makes us meet him, hold the photograph, see his mother, feel seaside Viet Nam. He drops us in past, present, and future with no clear temporal orientation. He puts us there without putting us anywhere. He refuses to stop and make sense. By performing this all at once, Le offers a model of how we might look to these residual artifacts—that is if we're lucky or cursed to have them—not as places to recreate traumas not ours, but as places to search for our forever unanswered and unanswerable questions. They do not provide answers but can offer vital respites for hidden grief. His passage reminds us that we can and should turn to objects, not as legible and transparent surfaces, but as things that train us to see what we can't see.

There is a letter my father wrote to the US State Department in December 1961 from a foster home on the Florida-Georgia border. They are bullet points requesting visas for his parents. "I have my parents in Cuba. They are in desperate need to leave the country on account of their disagreement with the present government." I want to adopt the second mode of Le's structure, to move to that risky, analytic mode to talk about what this letter does. What I find compelling about his mode is that it does not take an object such as this as an instrument for closure, but instead keeps the object and its moment present and productive, as a place for the not-yet-ready to comprehend. I try to see what I cannot see: my father at sixteen years old, furrowed brow, sitting down to a typewriter, figuring out how to make his parents feel better. I see him figuring out to whom to write, what to say, how

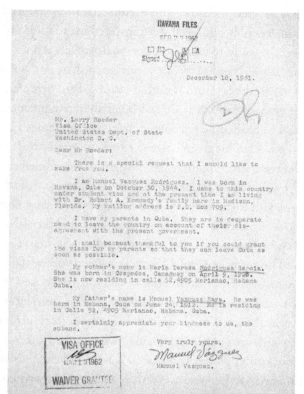

FIG. 5.5: Visa request, 1961.

his guardian Mr. Kennedy sat beside him to help correct his English. The stamp in the lower left-hand corner tells us that the visas were approved in March, seven months before the missile crisis. The letter closes like this: "I certainly appreciate your kindness to us, the cubans." I imagine my grandmother trying to see what she couldn't see: her son in a foreign place without her protection, the food he was eating, his new friends. They couldn't come. His dad had a cancerous lung removed and couldn't be moved. After he got better, my grandmother became gravely ill. I never met her. I see her without the words or the way to prepare my father for her death of a broken heart three years after this request was written. This object is one of the early and devastating signals that my father would be left alone, here.

I am not yet ready to understand the before, after, in between of the separation shrouded by the letter. I can surrender and wonder about the many lives such separation has affected and how. This exercise has not produced stasis or a complacent melancholy but has instead inspired me to look and listen closer to my objects of study, to take those personal artifacts seriously, even at the risk of being labeled narcissistic. Le's courage to share and publish such a reaction to his mother's photo is nothing short of an exercise in the deepest practice of empathy, which is after all a collaborative practice. By making it public and published he encourages us to do the same. The experience of reading Le has led me to embrace the oedipal origins of *Listening in Detail* and its reparative impulse: the thought of my adolescent father—and those like him—who were left alone, here and there, and of my wish to locate them, and with them, to locate Cuba of the before, after, and in-between through music. I want to make them better; to remind them that music keeps locations and relationships alive and present even if they seem not to be. It is the why of listening in detail. Of having to incorporate a family's difficult displacements and the creation of new structures to process it.

For cold war kids, parental ties to the home countries are far from locatable or describable, even as those ties might exist in concrete objects such as photographs and letters and other ephemera. Damages suffered by war, loss, and displacement do not confer proper narrative arcs for scholarship. Nor do they bode well for theories of the subject. As Antonio Viego has written:

> Critical race and ethnicity studies scholars have developed no language to talk about ethnic-racialized subjectivity and experience that is not entirely ego- and social psychological and that does not imagine a strong, whole, complete, and transparent ethnic-racialized subject and ego as the desired therapeutic, philosophical, and political outcome in a racist, white supremacist world. In the process we fail to see how the repeated themes of wholeness, completeness, and transparency with respect to ethnic-racialized subjectivity are what provide racist discourse with precisely the notion of subjectivity that it needs in order to function most effectively.[21]

It is precisely the development of a different kind of language in Le's intervention that I read and feel one answer to Viego's call. By resisting the demand to get beyond, or—as a damaged cold war subject—over, the pain caused by the dizzying disconnect between the image of his mother in the photograph, the wars then and now, and the limits of his comprehension, Le offers a divided, incomplete, and opaque impression that gets us closer to his lived experience than any comprehensive proof. Le reminds that these kinds of inherited violences cannot be explained, but can perhaps be invoked. By doing so, Le presents a way of seeing the subject that doesn't insist on its transparency. Certain things cannot be accessed.

A question remains: how does music relate to the foregoing? As much as Le presents a way of seeing what we can't see, a way with description that doesn't insist on transparency, I also believe it presents a way of hearing what we can't hear. He shows how sonic descriptions might inspire and compliment the limits of comprehension. The recognition and experimentation with such limits get us closer to the lived experience of sound. To get at how Le suggests a way of hearing what we can't hear, I will humbly try to turn on his descriptive mode with another object and location in the *transPOP* catalog. The South Korean artist Bae Young Whan included a piece called "Pop Song-Crazy Love." Two pages of a score are lined up on painted wood. The musical clefs are etched in pencil. The notes and notation are all made up of broken soju and beer bottles. Their edges are left sharp. Some of the lyrics to "Crazy Love," a song made famous by Paul Anka in 1958, are provided below the clefs written in English and Korean. The letters and characters are etched in wood but only some of the English characters are also made with the glass shards. The manicured wood is a palimpsest. Underneath the cream-colored paint are the barely detectable remainders of lyrics that went missing from two stanzas. My eyes and ears are caught by the splintering line: "set me free from this crazy love."

Broken objects make sounds. The sea glass that blows onto peninsular and island shores are the details left from a swept away whole. The sea glass's brokenness, and the suggestion of what it was once a part of, is part of its beauty. Even as the currents smooth some of the sharp edges out, the notes these pieces make are not safe. Even the saccharine sounds of pop songs can tear and cut. Regardless of the shattered vessels and populations in which they arrive, songs wash up and wash out the hard parts. Bae's sonic shards offer new ways to describe the "all this," which is not so much a description, but the invocation of feelings from an old pop song: of fingers being cut by glass, of when it is necessary to cover up the hard parts with music to survive.

FIG. 5.6: Bae Young Whan's "Pop Song-Crazy Love." Courtesy of Bae Young Whan.

The recognition of and insistence on an unfixable brokenness made by Le and his photograph, and Viego and his call for a new language, finds yet another idiom in Whan's piece. Whan instructs that broken found materials can be put together and made anew. These are all mature versions of what I see and hear in the early works of Alex Ruiz. We will have to imagine how Alex's work might have continued to change shape because we lost him too early to some of those toxic proclivities. His gravestone is a cemented anomaly in a Cuban cemetery in southwest Miami. It reads: "Rock and Roll Forever."

Broken cities make sounds too. Miami is the southernmost city in a state that has long collected the runaway, the broken, the refugee. Runaway traces are marked in the ground by thousands of Creek peoples who fled their genocide and the fugitive slaves whose marronage took a turn far south into the Everglades and its rivers of grass. It is the sieve of the United States and the point of entry for many from the rest of the Americas. Talk of the "success story" of Miami tends to attribute the entrepreneurial savvy, work ethic, and "bootstraps gumption" of Cuban immigrants for its transformation into a proper metropolis at the start of the 1960s. Those early waves made it possible for subsequent migrants to find work and shelter there. While this is all true enough, such talk tends to conceal not only the resources afforded to Cuban refugees upon arrival but also the histories of the many diverse communities that have also lived and lost, worked and bled to make the city what it is, especially the early twentieth-century migrations from the Bahamas and other sites throughout black America to the Miami area. Because of Cubans' concentrated economic power in the city, the island's politics has dominated the local legislative landscape, determined elections, and made and broken the careers of many.[22] Historically it has been thus: even if one is fervently anti-Castro, any outward appearance of flexibility, or willingness to renegotiate the terms with how Cuba is dealt with, has been made suspect. These are some of the reasons why Miami is reflexively referred to as a hotbed of conservative Cuban politics in the media and scholarship, even as that claim does its own work to erase the many other populations and points of view housed there. These charges are, as I confront throughout this chapter, not only uncomplicated but also outdated.

Because the embargo is something that is lived—and not merely an inconvenience for business or touristic interests—Miami has been one of the major sites of the wounded and wounding effects of cold war containment. As Roberto González Echevarria wrote, "It is a constant of history: political decisions affect ordinary lives in unexpected and often permanent ways."[23] Cuban Miami has suffered a long history of conflicts over how the embargo should alter the lives of its most implicated people. The familiar narratives are as follows: those who visit Cuba, even if to visit relatives, were considered traitors. Those who visited Miami, even to visit relatives, were considered communist invaders. Such decisions—to go or not to go—have been made with the most determined cores of being. Different gradations of tolerance exist, depending upon when one came over; and such attitudes have steadily and determinedly changed but have not disappeared. The difficulty of the embargo is especially palpable when reviewing how culture has been negotiated in Miami: "culture wars" are not mere metaphors here. When US-based (Cuban and non-Cuban) artists and musicians have visited Cuba, it has often meant their boycott from local radio waves and record stores. Cuban artists and musicians who want to visit Miami in the name of cultural exchange and understanding have been met with massive demonstrations, impressive displays of bitterness, and even terroristic violence.[24]

I wish I didn't have to rehearse the foregoing—but I needed to set up the backdrop for October 1999 when Los Van Van played at the Miami Arena. For those who do not understand the momentousness of the occasion, consider that Los Van Van has been one of the most popular Cuban dance bands in history since its founding in 1968. The group, under the direction of Juan Formell, has had some of the most influential impacts on Cuban popular music. It is a group who has experienced deserved notoriety throughout the globe and most of the United States outside Miami. They have been the sound and the swing for generations of Cubans who came of age during the revolution, providing a soundtrack, a dance floor, and an escape for their hopes, good and bad days, and rites of passage. They are the go-to band who gets played when a party gets dull. For some exiled Cubans, they are known as Fidel Castro's personal band, even as the group has never explicitly aligned themselves with any of those formal or limited political positions available on the island and off. For some, they are communist pigs simply because they are based on the island. When word of Los Van Van's appearance went public this particular sector instantly mobilized to prevent the band's ability to perform and to curtail the rights of those who wanted to attend. In Miami, this has been a predictable pattern of behavior.

What was different about the Los Van Van episode, however, is that the event revealed the demographic shifts in Miami's cultural and generational politics. Many Cubans in Miami—those who arrived in the 1970s and onward—grew up with Los Van Van. The group was, for some, one of the few beloved fixtures of their past on the island. Although there remained that vocal minority ready to orchestrate massive protests and boycotts, there was also a substantial part of Miami's population—Cuban and not—who wanted to attend or, at the very least, ignore the conflict completely. The obstacles were, as always, real, affecting their venue as much as reception. The concert was not originally scheduled at the Miami Arena. They were originally scheduled to perform in downtown Miami's James L. Knight Center but, bowing to political pressure and threats of mob violence that were too expensive for the promoter to insure against, they were forced to cancel and moved to the Miami Arena.[25]

Joining other stadiums built around the United States during the 1980s in the name of urban renewal, the Miami Arena is now demolished matter. It once stood on the same ground of what has historically been South Florida's Afro-American and Bahamian community, a vital nexus of black life and cultural production since the turn of the nineteenth century. Known as Overtown (or Colored Town), it is a neighborhood that used to have a string of black-owned venues and businesses, that was once interchangeably called "Little Broadway" and "Harlem of the South." And also, as a result of all this, the chosen place to impose the construction of the cemented cross that linked Interstate 95 and Interstate 395 in the early 1960s. These two cuts—genocidal in both sign and substance—nearly stamped out the creative force of the area. The Miami Arena sat two blocks away atop the foundations where Sam Cooke once sang.[26] Acknowledgment of this underacknowledged and hallowed ground is just one layer of what it meant to enter the space of Los Van Van at the Miami Arena.

Entering the space of the concert required other kinds of meaningful passages. After weeks of combative battles waged in radio and print, the day of the concert arrived. By 4:00 that afternoon hundreds of protesters set up shop to heckle the concert attendees—by 6:00 that number had reached the thousands. Regardless, the show was to go on. A DVD made of the concert documents some of the action that took place outside of the arena.[27] There were a lot of older folks, some look angry, others look bored as if tired by their own repetitive reactions. There were the usual homemade posters drawn with markers bearing familiar slogans ("Comunistas Limosneros," that is, Communist Beggars) and quotes by José Martí. There are flags galore. Some of the protesters bear the familiar expressions seen in any mob; others are forlorn and present to find company with others. The ugliness of the scene can make your stomach hurt. It is a tragic scene too; its pathos is such that it requires a search for empathy. Clearly these protesters are in a lot of pain. My acknowledgment of this does not make me an apologist. These are folks who have their own sad stories to tell and they must cling to their cold war positions of good and evil to organize the world, their memory, and their loss. I love and share the view taken by the Cuban musician Manolín "El medico de la salsa" at the scene, "I wish there was this type of freedom in my country . . . Look at the demonstrators—look how beautiful it is." He then turned to wave at the concertgoers and said, "Look how beautiful they are. They are going to listen to beautiful Cuban music. This is the way it should be. Respect each other. I understand the exiles' pain. They have suffered a lot and they have a right to be here. But this is also America and the Van Van can play here."[28] His ability to see beauty in this acrimonious scene is both an inspiration and an instruction.

Other concertgoers were equally inspiring and instructive through the survival methods improvised as they passed through the hostile crowds. *Miami Herald* writers Manny Garcia, Jordan Levin, and Peter Whoriskey share this wonderful detail:

> At 6:05 PM, a woman in a miniskirt and black high heels walked halfway up the arena steps, then stopped, waved her ticket and stuck out her tongue at the crowd. She then ascended to the arena's front door, let the breeze lift her skirt, and shook her white lace panties at enraged onlookers.[29]

The mini-skirted woman added a brilliant vaudevillian element to the scene. Her highly choreographed send up of the rigid attitudes of the protestors is all the more astonishing for its spur of the moment delivery (which is not to say that it wasn't rehearsed). Even the elements cooperated to show that she was there to dance in spite of who would prevent her good and deserved time. Its unapologetic quality must have done much to shake off the fear that so many felt at that moment of entry. Her performance, like all performance, lives, and continues to inspire courage in those of us who wished we could have been there. Or who wish we could do the same when confronted by an unruly opposition. It is another version of that middle finger dreamt up by Alex Ruiz through his "Cuban Missle [*sic*] Crisis." It is another fed-up gesture for an intolerable situation.

To enter the scene meant to take a public stance, to put one's body in danger, to shield oneself against epithets, eggs, spit, and bottles. With Manolín and the high-heeled concertgoer in mind and heart, the rite of entry was the cramp before the new growth, as Wilson Harris might say. They lead us into another set of receptive worlds that lurk in the subterranean of overdetermined narratives, whether generational, classed, or racialized forced upon or perpetuated by Cuban Miami. In the DVD we see that once inside the arena, and among the spectators at the foot of the stage are also a population of viejos, virtually indistinguishable from some of the viejos outside—except that the ones at the foot of the stage are just that, at the foot of the stage: they are dancing, crying, having fun, ready to throw their red carnations to the musicians. As the band takes the stage a woman MC takes the microphone to announce: "Buenas noches, good evening. Esta noche se pueden decir muchas cosas. Tonight we can say a lot of things and we're going to say nothing because the music is why we're here . . . por favor una gran bienvenida a Los Van Van!"

The music is why we're here.

Watching Los Van Van take the stage is a blast of oxygen. It is the rush of air desperately taken in after holding a breath for too long. For some in the audience, the musicians are familiar friends they have not seen in some time. For others they are strangers met for the first time after getting to know them clandestinely through headphones. For others the band was a new site and sound brought to them by their curiosity. What unites them is that they all had to make a decision, however tough or easy or banal, to walk through the arena's doors. That this collective passage, and these relationships to the band were played out *in the open*, in the company of thousands, is a seismic thing to witness. It is not simply that the band was allowed to play on that Miami stage. This was not an event in the name of "healing." It was the comingling of the fans and the music who made a decision to come together to get down and have a good time that sends vibrations down many a spine of those who grew up broken. The band began the show with the song "Ya empezó la fiesta" (The Party Has Started), and judging by the shared euphoria palpable even through the DVD, the audience was ecstatic to accept the invitation. To see fans, young and old, sing along and dance to the remainder of Van Van's repertoire is a relief, a release, and a revelation.

Why do some of us weep when we watch this concert? It would be too hard to explain and too hard to stop the reasons from coming. Here's one: an incredible demonstration was made by that mutual agreement of "we're going to say nothing" and to be there, together, with and for the music. This was a new manifestation far from the rehearsed arguments and wars of position relied upon for more than four decades. The melee outside, and what led up to it was better ignored, and better still, acknowledged and then transformed by being sung and danced out. Broken found materials can be put together and made anew.

I would like to describe my encounter with Los Van Van Live at the Miami Arena, but I cannot. Sadly, I was not there. It is one of the shows that one would kill to be at back then, a glitter-inflected dream. But my alternative reception was equally glitter inflected, for I first heard this concert in Brooklyn at an intimate gathering of Cubans who ranged from those of us born in the United States to others who had just arrived less than a month ago. We got to Los Van Van, as we inevitably do, after having gone through the older musical heavies, with whom we, as a whole, are collectively intimate. I've found that when Los Van Van is made to play, some acute differences are revealed between all of us in the ways that we dance. Of course, we all dance, and we most definitely get down and get down together. But I also relish taking quick breaks during some of those twelve-minute jams to sit down, watch, and be taught how to move differently. This is not a spectacularizing enterprise I'm consuming or endorsing—but rather, a recognition of the kinds of work and the kinds of pleasures behind having been brought up on the island. I like to imagine how these kinds of movements would dub with freestyle or Latin house that were the musical staples of South Miami Middle School. And the kinds of work and kinds of pleasures behind being brought up there too.

The album was put on after we had eaten cake, a bizcocho we had bought at the Santo Domingo Bakery. It was supposed to be frosting-inscribed with "Pa' los nuevos Cubanos" (For the new Cubans) but the pastry chef had instead written "Palos nuevos Cubanos" (Sticks new Cubans). Then Los Van Van live at the Miami Arena was put on in Brooklyn with no context or fanfare. And this was one of the best parts of my first encounter with this concert: it was so amazingly, so refreshingly banal and not so overdetermined, or made heavy. There was no difficult passage, only a joyous entry. As the CD played, the concert was imported into the small apartment: the formative texture of Overtown, the Harlem of the South: its undoing and part of its making anew by way of Los Van Van's performance at the Miami Arena. A making anew in the sense that it picks up and reinvigorates that historically entrenched music that skates the arc of the Caribbean archipelago, of which I consider Florida to be an intimate part. And most of all, the playing of the CD carved out another place to sing together: the music is why we're here. During the getting down with "Los Van Van Live in Miami" it was clear to me that here in Brooklyn there was no rehearsal of dated positions and postures, but more nearly, a group of folks who were listening in the distance together. The next day, the sound haunted my ears, and I woke up with the urgent need to find the recording. It is out of print but I found it at Casa Latina, the famed record store in Spanish Harlem. I bought and immediately put on my Walkman. There it was, "The music is why we're here," and the applause exploded in my ears as I rode the train back to Brooklyn.

The events that surrounded Los Van Van at the Miami Arena reveal another condition shared by cold war kids: the experience of people yelling at you from all sides. These events often create the conditions for watershed moments, including political awakenings, signs that call for retreat, reminders of the unrelenting work that needs to get done. Playing a role in or bearing witness to events such as these are a common and even banal part of growing up. The common threads shared between Cubans, Koreans, and Vietnamese in the United States during events such as this are dizzying. They even share an aesthetics and tone. When you compare snapshots of the homemade anticommunist posters, slogans, and gestures across these populations it is easy to be struck by their commonality. Such communion might feel disenchanting and depressing, but I derive great strength and humor and relief from their similarity of spectacle.

Part of the pleasure derives from feeling, at last, that Cubans aren't the only ones behind these enactments. The humor derives from being able to identify the archetypal figures at these protests across ethnic, raced, geographical, and gendered lines. And the relief comes from knowing that there are others who must negotiate and deal with such oppositional in-group violence as they try to find those other alternative ways of living in the ruptures.[30] I wonder what it would be like to try to join forces between cold war kids, to increase our numbers and the spaces we try to create to make conversation and collaboration happen. What would it be like to come together and tell the communities that we understand their pain but with an important difference: we will also tell them that we will not make ourselves conduits and receptacles for such pain.[31] Whether such a refusal is delivered shaking our panties, or dodging a pair of them, we will continue to insist on making the art or the music the central reasons as to why we're here.

"Building bridges" is the metaphor used and abused to describe dozens of exchanges facilitated between Cuba and the United States. They have ranged from shows that feature visual artists, literary collections, and other cultural showcases with Cuban artists and writers based on and off the island. Many of these efforts are heartfelt and moving, particularly when initiated by those who have left Cuba and turn into the island to see who and what they left behind. Regardless of their success, and even if they might be best described as other iterations of the comparative project, such efforts take a great deal of courage. In a divided nation where dialog is among the most treacherous of activities, their production must move through demanding passages and procedures. These conversations have also included a great deal of non-Cubans, particularly African Americans. For example, Amiri Baraka's famous essay "Cuba libre" (1961) is among the first of such documented exchanges initiated by the Cuban government to build support and seek out possible solidarity (and better public relations) with populations of color in the United States. In today's New York, the "Habana/Harlem" is a production company led by Neyda Martinez and Onel Mulet that programs events to evoke,

> a time in American music history when Cuban musicians called Harlem home, and performed alongside African-American musicians, making an indelible mark on American history that continues to inspire and influence artists around the globe.[32]

Other efforts reek of liberal opportunism, for example, when Oliver Stone or Sean Penn visit the island, meet with privileged party leaders, and undertake uncritical political pilgrimages to proclaim, alongside the elite officialdom: down with imperialism.

As "Los Van Van Live in Miami" reveals, musical concerts have been a major vehicle to build bridges between Cuba and the United States especially at the turn of the twenty-first century. There is the always available example of the Buena Vista Social Club, put together by Ry Cooder in 1998.[33] In 1999, the *Bridge to Havana* concert and CD brought an unlikely grouping of one hundred American performers and music personnel including Bonnie Raitt, Mick Fleetwood, Gladys Knight, and Montell Jorden to perform and record on songs with Cuban musicians at the National Theater. The CD/DVD of the concert are nestled in a folded cover that features an old American car as a centerfold. Many of these concerts and collaborative projects tend to cast American performers and production teams as benevolent emissaries, however good their intentions. The tendency is to use such projects to embody a unidirectional carriage of influence into Cuba from the United States, complete with discourses of rescue. There is an assumption that traffic on bridges flow in one direction; they are messianic portals that allow isolates a peek to the contemporary outside.

The presumption of (or desire for) Cubans' naïveté usually disappoints. What can strike many a visitor to the island is how musically in touch much of the population actually is. That the larger population's familiarity with US popular culture is surprising is, to my mind, one of the more condescending attitudes made possible by its colonial history and the formative effect of the embargo. One of my favorite anecdotes that responds to such attitudes comes from a recent trip to Havana that Wynton Marsalis made in 2010 to play with some of the island's most important jazz musicians such as Eladio "Don Pancho" Terry, Orlando "Maraca" Valle, and Roberto Carcassés. Of the excitement (and the inflated altruism that surrounded the event), a twelve-year-old bongocero named Dayrón Rodríguez said plainly, "It's not the first time I've played with great musicians."[34] Nor does pop music familiarity remain on the surface, but runs deep with sophisticated connoisseurship, even of rock and roll's alternative underbelly. Among the most striking of these concert events includes Audioslave's 2005 visit to the island. Featuring the band-amalgam borne from Rage Against the Machine and Soundgarden, the show has the distinction of being the largest production to date by a US-based hard rock group. The DVD of the performance offers salient proof of the stunning legions of hard rock fans on the island, seventy thousand of which were in attendance that evening at Havana's Anti-Imperialist Plaza The audience sang along to songs they weren't supposed to know or have access to. They raised devil-horned salutes without a trace of awkwardness. One woman carried a large sign that read, "Hello Seattle Welcome Audioslave."

As of the writing of these pages, the largest concert to date, is the "Paz Sin Fronteras" event put together and produced by the Miami-based Colombian pop superstar Juanes in August of 2009. It was billed, like so many others before, as an event outside politics, "about the music," and a direct address to the Cuban people. Such detached pronouncements did little to neutralize the news that the concert was to be performed in the Plaza de la Revolucion under the steely outline of Che Guevara and featuring a line up of Cuban musicians long seen as overly cozy with the revolutionary vanguard (i.e., Silvio Rodríguez, Amaury Pérez, and Los Van Van). The other American musicians to perform were Puerto Ricans Olga Tañón and Danny Rivera and Cuban American Cucu Diamantes and her New York-based band Yerba Buena. The remainder of the line up offered an eccentric assortment including the Spanish vocalist Miguel Bosé, the Neapolitan rapper Giovanotti, and the Ecuadorian pop folk star Juan Fernando Velasco. All of the musicians involved were to wear white as a collective outfit for peace.

Soon after the show's announcement, Juanes was predictably subject to the typical, though increasingly tiny opposition in Miami: death threats and the steamrolling over his albums in protest. Many of them gathered at the coffee counter of Miami's Versailles Restaurant, the ground zero of exilic punditry, to raise their voices. But they were confronted by an unlikely turn of events. Achy Obejas reported,

> But a funny thing happened on the way to Versailles last Sunday . . . This time, it was the crazies who were shouted down. And they were shouted down by none other than other *Cubans*—young Miami Cubans who passionately supported the event in Havana. By the end of the evening, the anti-Juanes crowd—mostly older Cubans—had been pushed across the street from Versailles.[35]

For those familiar with the mirrored walls of the Versailles perplex, such a spatial and audible dislocation is nothing less than a historical milestone.[36] Unfortunately, this dislocation did not register on much of the US media. English language networks did not carry the broadcast of the concert even as Cuba gave all-access media rights to whoever should want them. For those of us who could not be there, we could only depend on the strength of our Internet connections and tune into univision.com, the online version of the United States's largest Spanish language network. We watched together and apart, monitoring our friends' reactions on Facebook and e-mail. The sea shimmer of bodies gathered in the plaza took our breath away. Their energy and excitement radiated through our screens. Lots of dance moves were shared through the virtual portals.

I conclude by listening in detail to a moment in the concert: a song by the Cuban musician X Alfonso (pronounced Equis Alfonso) at "Paz Sin Fronteras." His performance, and his positive transformation of the "all this" into his arrangement jolts Listening in Detail with a hopeful futurity. Alfonso was born in 1973 to another of Cuba's great musical families. His parents, Carlos Alfonso and Ele Valdés, were founders of El Groupo Síntesis, the musical group who made daring experiments by combining Cuban symphonic rock and traditional African instruments and forms beginning in 1976.[37] While X Alfonso was completing his conservatory training, he was a key player in the jazz fusion group Estado de Ánimo alongside Roberto Carcassés, Elmer Ferrer, and Descemer Bueno. After graduating, the young Alfonso joined his parents and Síntesis as a keyboardist in 1990.[38] He began on keyboards because that was what the band needed and later became the group's percussionist and vocalist. As Alfonso remembers, "That's how I learned to play the instruments, through necessity."[39] Known as a hugely significant and representative figure for new generations of Cuban musicians, Alfonso is best known for his stirring fluency in multiple genres, from jazz to rock to hip hop, rumba to reggae, funk to rock and roll. His audiences are as diverse as his repertoire; from across the generations they gather to hear him play.

Alfonso brought all this: his training, family, and audiences onstage while performing his breathtaking and body rocking set at the "Paz Sin Fronteras" concert. Visit the clip that lives on YouTube.[40] To watch him take the stage, while the dedicated crowd works hard to shade themselves from the summer sun, adds a renewed sense of urgency to the sentiment "the music is why we're here." Vocally backing him are his parents, the phenomenal singer and rapper Danay Suárez Fernández, and a large children's chorus. After performing his hit "Revoluxion," Alfonso finishes the set with his song "Conga Gospel." The title unites two words that can be both objects and genres. The Conga is a drum or music genre that encourages multiple participants during carnival. Gospel is a written testimonial or sung praise. The original recording of "Conga Gospel" is a talkative and bass heavy dance track, with organ-backed gospel interludes. Lyrically it begins on a ship from Africa and reveals what cannot be lost even in the forceful transfer to the new world. The song testifies to the "reverence and religion" inherited from ancestors who "left us a voice and the truth that love is stronger than eternity." This voice and truth make up the song's chorus and it goes like this:

El amor, puede ser	Love can be
Más fuerte que el sol	Stronger than the sun
Que tú y yo	than you and me
Que el mundo de hoy	than today's world
Que esta canción	than this song

At the "Paz Sin Fronteras" concert, Alfonso transforms his "Conga Gospel" into, among many other things, a homage to Michael Jackson after his death a few months before the event. Alfonso weaves the familiar guitar riff of the dearly departed's 1991 hit "Black or White" into the live version of the song. As that recognizable set of chords takes hold, Alfonso says simply, "Voy a cantar un tema que tiene que ver mucho con la paz" (I am going to sing a theme that has a lot to do with peace). He is partly talking about his own song "Conga Gospel" but it is hard not to also hear Jackson's anthem as part of the theme. Theme is the descriptive here as he does not simply play a cover of Jackson's song, but uses it as an occasional structure. Alfonso uses the optimistic riff to pull together a six-minute performance of genre jumping that not only includes parts of his signature songs, but also sounds from the entire Atlantic world. In this rendition of "Conga Gospel" meets "Black or White" we hear rock, rumba, hip hop, and funk. So much is tucked into the performance that part of the pleasure of hearing it is teasing out its elements while being carried away by the seamlessness of the whole. One can listen and dance along in both detailed and general registers. Just when you think nothing else can fit, there is a citation of the Brazilian Jorge Ben's "Mas que nada" one of the most iconic sambas to draw the song to its conclusion. "Mas fuerte que tu y yo" ([Love] is much stronger than you and me) joins the samba and is sung in relentless reprise for the last minutes of the song.

The physical arrangement of the stage is a homecoming and a making anew. Alfonso's mom, on his right, sings and joyfully shimmies with a tam-

FIG. 5.7: X Alfonso and his back-up chorus. Film still from the "Paz Sin Fronteras" concert headlined by Juanes in Havana, August 2009.

bourine. Beside her, his father beams. On their far side is Danay, who delivers a righteous mid-song rap while backed by the extraordinarily talented drummer, Nailé Sosa Aragón. To sing the choral figure of the song I transcribed in the above, Alfonso enlisted the participation of a large chorus of children, all in the neighborhood of ten to fifteen years old. They are lined up behind him wearing matching white polo shirts and pants. Some are tucked in, some are not; all are spotless. Hairdos have been clearly labored over by their parents. There are braids, buns, ponytails, and half ups. They are kids, in the words of Patti Smith, "just kids." Willfully experimental. And though they are performing in front of such an immense live and televised audience, they do not carry an outward trace of nerves. These kids are pros. Hours of rehearsal are palpable through their coordinated movements and sound, which is a very young version of the sophisticated and mature choruses often seen in Baptist churches.

I hear and see X Alfonso's performance as something different than a building of bridges or an iteration of the comparative project. There is no artifice constructed so that one can move between sides and over the waters that remain, disregarded, underneath it. It is instead an incredibly well prepared, rehearsed, and intimate orb of orchestration with an outstretched hand. The audiences of the then and there and the here and now are invited to take up the invitation, not to cross from a here to a there, but to get down and get down together. The hard work of this performance—and the pain, pleasure, and techniques felt and developed across the generations—is humbling. The incorporation of the creative details that form multiple musical selves and publics, of grandmothers and granddaughters on the same stage, and the "all this" in front of a million live bodies and many unseen millions more, is a model of being together in difference that cold war kids can aspire to facilitate and be a part of.

I hesitate to reduce the children's chorus to the "Greatest Love of All" moment of this book. But then I'm reminded of other kinds of links, to Whitney Houston's formation in the junior gospel choir, and the impact hopeful songs like hers had on our early and future selves across the Florida Straits. And I look down to realize that, out of necessity, I've had to reach through my infant daughter sitting on my lap—her name means both fight and light—to access my keyboard to describe the performance. This reminder and recognition pushes me (and cold war kids) to work through the cynical calluses that harden our political impasses. The detail of the children in the detail of the concert is not a legible and transparent surface with which to attach the pain we inherit. Their performance can train us to see what we can't see, and hear what we can't hear. What we can't see and hear is partly the preparations behind their serious and joyful performance. What we can't see or hear are the forms their creative interventions will eventually take. We can't see or hear what's ahead for them or for us but we can be reassured that they will listen closely to and assemble that inherited lived matter that is both foreign and somehow familiar into something new.

Notes

INTRODUCTION

1. Ignacio Villa was born in 1911 in Guanabacoa, Cuba, and died in 1971. In addition to being an incredible pianist, he composed many beloved Cuban standards such as "Si me pudieras querer" and "Drume mobila." His repertoire also included a stunning multilingual range of standards written by other great composers of the twentieth century (from Cuba, Mexico, France, and many other locations) and they are legendary. Hear his "La flor de la canela" written by the Peruvian Chabuca Granda—or Irving Berlin's "Be Careful It's My Heart." For a biographical impression of him, see Leonardo Depestre's "Bola de Nieve, con su sonrisa y su canción," in *Cuatro músicos de una villa* (La Habana: Editorial Letras Cubanas, 1990). Villa talks about taking on this nickname in the film *Nosotros, la música*, which I analyze in chapter 4.

2. Suárez Cobián's route to New York was less than direct. Note the circuitous journey confirmed in a recent text exchange.

Me: "¿En que año llegaste de Cuba? '92 verdad?" [What year did you come from Cuba? '92 right?] Armando: "Mi cubanita sali de cuba el 1ro de octubre del 91 a las 12 del dia a Merida, Yucatan, el 6 de marzo del 92 vole a Miami a las 2 de la tarde y llegue a NY en la cubana el 24 de marzo del 92 a las 11 de la mañana. J besitos a todos" [Mi cubanita I left cuba october 1st in 1991 at noon to Merida, Yucatan, the 6th of march I flew to Miami at 2 in the afternoon and arrived in NY en la cubana (the name for the famed bus and route between Miami and NYC) on the 24th of march in 1992 at 11 in the morning. J kisses to you all].

Conversation with the author on November 8, 2011.

3. I attribute my honing in on the diminutive directly to Sarduy writing on Lezama Lima. These two Cuban writers are among many who have in some ways

theorized the place of the diminutive in Cuban language. See Severo Sarduy, *Written on a Body*, trans. Carol Maier (New York: Lumen Books, 1989), 64–65.

4. This narration of the field can be found through many of its manuals. See Henry Bial, ed., *The Performance Studies Reader*, 2nd ed. (London: Routledge, 2007); Erving Goffman, *The Presentation of Self in Everyday Life* (Garden City, NY: Doubleday, 1959); Janelle G. Reinelt and Joseph R. Roach, eds., *Critical Theory and Performance*, rev. and enl. ed. (Ann Arbor: University of Michigan Press, 2007); Richard Schechner, *Between Theater and Anthropology* (Philadelphia: University of Pennsylvania Press, 1985); Richard Schechner, *Performance Studies: An Introduction*, 2nd ed. (New York: Routledge, 2006); and Victor Turner, *The Anthropology of Performance* (New York: PAJ Publications, 1988).

5. In Theodor W. Adorno, "The Problem of Musical Analysis," in *Essays on Music*, ed., Richard Leppert; trans., Susan H. Gillespie (Berkeley: University of California Press, 2002), 169.

6. As Alejo Carpentier once wrote, "Cuba's history is also a history of its music." In Roberto González Echevarría, "Where the Singers Come From: Fragments," trans. Vera M. Kutzinski, *New England Review and Bread Loaf Quarterly* 8 (Summer 1985): 569.

7. It must also be noted in the early twentieth century, the sign "Cuban music" was used by US recording companies in many countries around Latin America. See Ruth Glasser's "'Vénte Tú': Puerto Rican Musicians and the Recording Industry," in *My Music Is My Flag: Puerto Rican Musicians and Their New York Communities, 1917–1940* (Berkeley: University of California Press, 1995), 129–68. See especially page 143.

8. Guillermo Cabrera Infante, "Una historia inaudita," introduction to *Cuba y sus sones* by Natalio Galán (Valencia: Pre-Textos, 1997), xi.

9. Here I am of course indebted to Christopher Small's notion of *musicking*, a term he uses to de-center a musical work as the privileged object of analysis. Small writes, "To music is to take part, in any capacity, in a musical performance, whether by performing, by listening, by rehearsing or practicing, by providing material for performance (what is called composing), or by dancing." Christopher Small, *Musicking: The Meanings of Performing and Listening* (Middletown: Wesleyan University Press, 1998), 9. While Small uses musicking to denote precisely these activities at the scene of the event, I am trying to extend its incorporative reach to the documentation of the event.

10. See Simon Broughton, *The Rough Guide to World Music: 100 Essential CDs* (London: Rough Guides, 2000); Scott Doggett and David Stanley, *Lonely Planet Havana*, 1st ed. (Victoria, Australia: Lonely Plant Publications, 2001); Jory Farr, *Rites of Rhythm: The Music of Cuba* (New York: Regan Books, 2003); D. H. Figueredo,

The Complete Idiot's Guide to Latino History and Culture (Royersford: Alpha, 2002); Fiona McAuslan, *The Rough Guide to Cuba*, 1st ed. (London: Rough Guides, 2000); Ed Morales, *The Latin Beat: The Rhythms and Roots of Latin Music, from Bossa Nova to Salsa and Beyond* (Cambridge, MA: Da Capo Press, 2003); and Sue Steward, with a preface by Willie Colon, *Musica!: The Rhythm of Latin America— Salsa, Rumba, Merengue, and More* (San Francisco: Chronicle Books, 1999).

11. Ry Cooder, Ibrahim Ferrar, Rubén González, Eliades Ochoa, Omara Portuondo, and Compay Segundo, *Buena Vista Social Club*, produced by Ry Cooder, World Circuit/Nonesuch 79478-2, 1997, compact disc. The *Buena Vista Social Club* was an album produced by the North American musician Ry Cooder in 1997. Cooder went to the island to record with important Cuban musicians supposedly forgotten over time and erased by fault of the US embargo. However, the musicians featured on the album including Omara Portuondo, Compay Segundo, Cachaito López, Ibrahim Ferrer, Eliades Ochoa, and Rubén González have been well heard on a local and global scale for decades long before Cooder's "rediscovery" of them. Everything written about Cuban music these days seems to be prefaced by the *BVSC* and there is no way to ignore it. This has much to do with the real impact the enterprise continues to have on the production and distribution networks of Cuban music after the special period. Because of the *BVSC*'s incredible monetary success, its follow up projects, including solo albums by many of the featured artists in the original, tend to crowd out many other musicians. This is as true on the island as off.

12. These fantasies were greatly enhanced by the Wim Wenders documentary about the *Buena Vista Social Club*. See *Buena Vista Social Club*, directed by Wim Wenders (Santa Monica, CA: Artisan Entertainment, 1999), videocassette. For a brilliant discussion on the role of the image, and Wender's film, after the special period, see Ana María Dopico, "Picturing Havana: History, Vision, and the Scramble for Cuba," *Nepantla: Views from South* 3, no. 3 (2002): 451–93. For another important *Buena Vista Social Club* critique, see José Quiroga "The Beat of the State," in *Cuban Palimpsests* (Minneapolis: University of Minnesota Press, 2005), 145–72.

13. See Bartolomé De Las Casas, *A Short Account of the Destruction of the Indies*, trans. and ed. Nigel Griffin (London: Penguin, 1992); Christopher Columbus, *The Journal: Account of the First Voyage and Discovery of the Indies*, introduction and notes by Paolo Emilio Taviani and Consuelo Varela; trans. Marc A. Beckwith and Luciano F. Farina (Roma: Istituto Poligrafico e Zecca Dello Stato, Libreria Dello Stato, 1992).

14. See Patrick J. Haney and Walt Vanderbush, *The Cuban Embargo: The Domestic Politics of an American Foreign Policy* (Pittsburgh: University of Pittsburgh Press, 2005); Donna Rich Kaplowitz, *Anatomy of a Failed Embargo: U.S. Sanctions*

against Cuba (Boulder: Lynne Rienner Publishers, 1998); Lars Schoultz, "Benevolent Domination: The Ideology of U.S. Policy toward Cuba," *Cuban Studies* 41, (2010): 1–19; and Peter Schwab, *Cuba: Confronting the U.S. Embargo* (New York: St. Martin's Press, 1999).

15. See Fred Moten, *B Jenkins* (Durham, NC: Duke University Press, 2010).

16. It is beyond the scope of this introduction to adequately address the important work done by countless other scholars, but I would like to honor and mark some of them here. I visit their important scholarship throughout *Listening in Detail*. See Cristóbal Díaz Ayala, *Música Cubana: Del areyto al rap Cubano*, 4th ed. (San Juan: Fundación Musicalia, 2003); Alejo Carpentier, *La música en Cuba* (México: Fondo de Cultura Económica, 1946); Alicia Castro (with Ingrid Kummels and Manfred Schafer) *Queens of Havana: The Amazing Adventures of Anacaona, Cuba's Legendary All-Girl Dance Band*, trans. Steven T. Murray (New York: Grove Press, 2007); Sujatha Fernandes, *Cuba Represent! Cuba 'n Arts, State Power, and the Making of New Revolutionary Cultures* (Durham, NC: Duke University Press, 2006); Raúl A. Fernández, *From Afro-Cuban Rhythms to Latin Jazz* (Berkeley: University of California, 2006); Benjamin L. Lapidus, *Origins of Cuban Music and Dance: Changüi* (Lanham, MD: Scarecrow, 2008); Isabelle Leymarie, *Cuban Fire: The Story of Salsa and Latin Jazz* (London: Continuum, 2002); Adriana Orejuela Martínez, *El Son no se fue de Cuba: Claves para una historia 1959–1973* (La Habana, Cuba: Editorial Letras Cubanas, 2006); Robin D. Moore, *Music and Revolution: Cultural Change in Socialist Cuba* (Berkeley: University of California Press, 2006); Helio Orovio, *Cuban Music from A to Z*, trans. Ricardo Bardo Portilla and Lucy Davies (Durham, NC: Duke University Press, 2004); Vincenzo Perna, *Timba: The Sound of the Cuban Crisis* (Burlington, VT: Ashgate, 2005); Maya Roy, *Cuban Music: From Son and Rumba to the Buena Vista Social Club and Timba Cubana* (Princeton: Markus Wiener, 2002); Elena Pérez Sanjurjo, *Historia de la música Cubana* (Miami: Moderna Poesía, 1986); and Ned Sublette, *Cuba and Its Music: From the First Drums to the Mambo* (Chicago: Chicago Review, 2004).

17. Helio Orovio, *Cuban Music from A to Z*, trans. Ricardo Bardo Portilla and Lucy Davies (Durham, NC: Duke University Press, 2004), 101.

18. The Spanish version, "cuya generosidad ha hecho possible la realización de este esfuerzo por la diffusion de nuestra cultura."

19. Given the timing of its publication, what is further compelling about Grenet's text was that a physical visit to Cuba was not assumed or required. Other kinds of visitations, as I investigate throughout *Listening in Detail*, were facilitated by an upsurge in recorded commodities. Although musical records began to make their presence known at the turn of the nineteenth century, their mass production and

circulation were made further possible by the advent of vinyl in the early 1930s. Sonic versions of Cuba were put within reach on a massive scale. Beyond recordings, however, live Cuban musicians were also in heavy rotation throughout the world. At the same time, many of the musicians featured on said records were also active in the Hemispheric Revue circuit. I discuss this circuit further in chapter 1.

20. Emilio Grenet, *Popular Cuban Music: 80 Revised and Corrected Compositions*, trans. R. Phillips (Havana: Ucar, García y Compañia, 1939), xi. It is worth noting that this text is currently among the most widely available about music for sale in Havana's famous book market.

21. Grenet's recourse to the categorical partly reflects the lingering effects of positivistic debates that included many Latin American intellectuals, especially in the 1920s and 1930s. Grenet relies upon those automatic contextual elements often found in and separated as such by many social scientific texts. Soon after, the author becomes inundated with the tricky labor that arises when trying to distinguish the musical forms themselves. For example, in the text's opening pages, Grenet quickly unloads the influences of the "Aboriginal element," "Religion," and "Specific rhythmic characteristics of our music." Another text that linked musical and racial discourse is the Mexican intellectual José Vasconcelos and his influential essay "La raza cósmica." In his essay, Vasconcelos deliberately utilized music to articulate his own imaginative Darwinism—one that allegorizes processes of miscegenation—to conceptualize a mixed race that will eventually triumph in the Americas. Regarding the sounds of Ibero-American development, he writes:

> They resemble the profound scherzo of a deep and infinite symphony: Voices that bring accents from Atlantis; depths contained in the pupil of the red man.... This infinite quietude is stirred with the drop put in our blood by the Black, eager for sensual joy, intoxicated with dances and unbridled lust. There also appears the Mongol, with the mystery of his slanted eyes that see everything according to a strange angle.... The clear mind of the White, that resembles his skin and his dreams, also intervenes ... Judaic striae hidden within the Castilian blood ... along with Arabian melancholy, as a reminder of the sickly Muslim sensuality. Who has not a little of all this, or does not wish to have all?

His influence on Havana intellectuals is not as far-fetched as it may seem. The essay was circulated in the "Ideales de una raza" (Ideals of a Race) section in Cuba's conservative daily, the *Diario de la Marina*, in 1928. Vasconcelos's first philosophical work *Pitágoras* was written while in exile in New York and first published in Havana in 1916. See Didier T. Jaén, introduction to *The Cosmic Race/La raza cósmica*, by José Vasconcelos (Baltimore: Johns Hopkins University Press, 1997), xxii.

22. As often happens, Cuba's ethnically Chinese populations, who migrated as contract laborers in the mid-nineteenth century, are noticeably absented from the island's musical history. The implications are profound, for it is impossible to imagine the sound of a comparsa without the strident sounds of the corneta china (Chinese cornet).

23. Genre is from the same etymological family as *genus* and *gender*, from the root *generare*, Latin for "to beget." Raymond Williams, *Keywords: A Vocabulary of Culture and Society*, rev. ed. (New York: Oxford University Press, 1983), 285. Debates over genre and its hierarchical ordering (and that are beyond the scope of this book) date as far back as Aristotle's *Poetics*, specifically the distinction he makes between epic and tragic poetry.

24. In Grenet's text, however, it is interesting to note the arc is reversed and the African is placed last. The continent's influence is potentially placed in such a way that recognizes those genres (and the bodies behind them) as modern, experimental, and foundational, in all, the vanguard of Cuban musicality. But this placement possibly betrays the denial of the African, a presence that is an afterthought in the overall texture of the music, one that is merely a contributor to an already in place musical legacy. Or perhaps the "African" for Grenet occupies both ends of the progressive arc at the same time. There is an evocative conundrum that emerges here, one that Grenet performs throughout his text. However, this kind of discursive move is not exemplary to Grenet alone; it is found in different variants throughout the writings on Cuban music.

25. Mestizaje is a widely debated and contested term that has many usages, histories, and implications. For a brief historical sketch of the term, see Lourdes Martínez-Echazábal, "Mestisaje and the Discourse of National/Cultural Identity in Latin America, 1845–1959," *Latin American Perspectives* 25, no. 3 (1998): 21–42. Mestizaje generally refers to the history of racial and cultural mixing in the Americas, specifically those colonized by Spain and Portugal. The term, however, has come to stand-in for a spectrum of ideologies and often changes by national and historical context. Martínez-Echazábal lists three historical tendencies the term has come to signal. It was first used to particularize the conditions of conquest in the Americas—the creation of an alternate discursive mode—for the process of self-definition under colonial regimes. Its second phase was preoccupied with the recognition (or refusal) of the various cultural identities that came together to define "national character." The third usage of the term is often used to mark the cultural and racial hybridity of Latin American nations. Of course, these "usages" are less straightforward then they suggest—it must be underscored that mestizaje was often used, debated, and conceptualized in relationship to positivistic and social Darwinist thought from the turn of the nineteenth century onward. For example,

in her work on Gabriela Mistral, Licia Fiol-Matta problematizes certain conceptions of mestizaje that required the negation versus the affirmation of legacies of conquest, especially for the project of nation building. Fiol-Matta writes, "Mestizaje implies a binary that marginalizes Latin Americans of African descent. At best, they are folklorized as an 'exotic' minority; at worst, they are literally eliminated." Licia Fiol-Matta, *A Queer Mother for the Nation: The State and Gabriela Mistral* (Minneapolis: University of Minnesota Press, 2002), 8.

26. For a discussion on how genre often governs musicians relationships to one another and how it determines music in the marketplace see Keith Negus's foundational book *Music Genres and Corporate Cultures* (New York: Routledge, 1999).

27. Timothy Brennan, "Introduction to the English Edition," in *Music in Cuba*, ed. Alejo Carpentier, trans. Alan West-Durán (Minneapolis: University of Minnesota Press, 2001), 1.

28. Guillermo Cabrera Infante, "Una historia inaudita," introduction to *Cuba y sus sones*, by Natalio Galán (Valencia: Pre-Textos, 1997), xviii (originally written in 1983).

29. Galán, *Cuba y sus sones*, 11.

30. Ibid., 12.

31. I am reminded of a useful phrase set forth by what Radano and Bohlman in the introduction of their volume, *Music and the Racial Imagination* as the "metaphysics of mastery." Ronald M. Radano and Philip V. Bohlman, eds., *Music and the Racial Imagination* (Chicago: University of Chicago Press, 2000), 6. I discuss their work further in chapter 3.

32. Various Artists, *Putumayo Presents: Cuba,* Putumayo World Music, 1999, compact disc; Various Artists, *Cuban Nights,* Narada, 2000, compact disc; Various Artists and Rey Casas, *Cuban Patio: The Music of Cuba,* Music Trends, 1999; Various Artists, *Cuba Si: Pure Cuban Flavor,* Rhino/Wea, 1999, CD; *Putumayo Presents: Cafe Cubano,* Putumayo World Music, 2008, compact disc; Various Artists, *Hecho en Cuba,* La Escondida, 2005, CD. I provide more additions and analysis to this list of collections in chapter 3.

33. For more on knowing nothing as a critical practice, see Alexandra Vazquez, "Towards an Ethics of Knowing Nothing," in *Pop When the World Falls Apart,* ed. Eric Weisbard (Durham, NC: Duke University Press, 2012).

34. Vijay Iyer, "Exploding the Narrative in Jazz Improvization," in *Uptown Conversation: The New Jazz Studies,* eds. Robert G. O'Meally, Brent Hayes Edwards, and Farah Jasmine Griffin (New York: Columbia University Press, 2004), 395.

35. A corneta china is a Chinese cornet, an instrument introduced by the migration of Chinese populations to Cuba in the nineteenth century. I will discuss this song and describe the sound of the corneta china in more length in chapter 1.

36. My encounter with this track was made possible by a homemade CD Graciela Pérez gave to me for Christmas one year.

37. I will discuss this detail in more length in chapter 2

38. Fred Moten, "'Words Don't Go There': An Interview with Fred Moten" with Charles Henry Rowell, in *B Jenkins*, 105.

39. María Irene Fornés with Robb Creese, "I Write These Messages That Come," *The Drama Review* 21, no. 4, Playwrights and Playwriting Issue (December, 1977): 35.

40. I'd like to acknowledge Katherine Hagedorn for the explicit link between listening and rehearsal. Panel discussion, UC Cuba Conference, Irvine, California May 2008.

41. In Timothy Brennan, "Introduction" to *Music in Cuba*, 4. Original quote taken from Araceli García Carranza, *Bibliografía de Alejo Carpentier* (Havana: Editorial Letras Cubanas, 1984), 19.

42. Langston Hughes papers. JMJ MSS 26 Box 485; 12326, "Trip to Cuba + Haiti Notes," no date.

43. This binary might be attributed, as Philip Auslander has argued, to the emergence of the field of performance studies from theater studies and anthropology. This development has had the unintended effect of dislodging musical performance from the field. I think that part of this has to do with the challenges posed by music to the empirical thrust of certain anthropological methods, and the fact that it always slips away once we think we've caught it. Philip Auslander, "Performance Analysis and Popular Music: A Manifesto," *Contemporary Theatre Review* 14, no. 1 (2004): 1–13.

44. In *Dictionary of the Theater*, Pavis calls "incidental music," "Music used in a performance, whether it is composed specially for the play or borrowed from existing compositions, and whether it is an autonomous work of art or exists only in reference to a particular production. The music may be so important that it becomes a musical form in its own right as the text is relegated to second place." Patrice Pavis, *Dictionary of the Theatre: Terms, Concepts, and Analysis*, trans. Christine Shantz (Toronto and Buffalo: University of Toronto Press, 1998), 182. Also see the definition for "Music and Theater," 226–27.

45. Fornés signals a rethinking of the *kinds* of things, bodies, locations, and ephemera from elsewhere, that all form part of what Marc Robinson calls, "The Other American Drama," which is such a useful phrase to imagine the underground rumblings of US empire; or, at the very least, the goings on in some of our households. Marc Robinson, *The Other American Drama* (Cambridge and New York: Cambridge University Press, 1994). For an excellent synopsis of Fornés see pages 89–91.

46. Also see Barthes, especially re: the fragment. The fragment, as Roland Barthes

teaches us, disrupts what he calls "the smooth finish, the composition, discourse constructed to give final meaning to what one says." Roland Barthes, "Twenty Key Words for Roland Barthes," in *The Grain of the Voice: Interviews 1962–1980*, trans. Linda Coverdale (Berkeley: University of California Press, 1985), 210. Here I am also thinking of Michael Wood's line in his review of Zadie Smith's essays, "the affection is in the detail." Michael Wood, "A Passage to England," *New York Review of Books* 57, no. 4 (March 11, 2010): 8–10.

47. For reasons that will become clear in my citation of and homage to Naomi Schor in the work below, it is beyond the scope and intention of this introduction to account for the history of the detail as a mode of philosophical inquiry. Richard Leppert defines critical theory as that which

"draws attention to social contradiction—material existence—*expressed as antagonism and suffering, not only by what I attends to and 'says' but also by how it speaks: in fragments, aphorisms, short forms, in a word, anti-systematically,* and by formulating a negative dialectics, in opposition to the (positive) dialectics of the Hegelian model." (emphasis mine)

Richard Leppert, "Introduction" to Theodor W. Adorno *Essays on Music*, Translated by Susan H. Gillespie. (Berkeley: University of California Press, 2002), 22. Here I provide a short list of the principal thinkers and works most commonly associated with the engagement and mobilization of the detail. See G. W. F. Hegel *Aesthetics: Lectures on Fine Art*, trans. T. M. Knox (Oxford: Oxford University Press 1975); Roland Barthes *Camera Lucida: Reflections of Photography*, trans. Richard Howard (New York: Hill and Wang, 1982); Walter Benjamin *Illuminations: Essays and Reflections*, ed. Hannah Arendt and trans. Henry Zohn (New York: Schocken Books, 1968); Walter Benjamin, *The Arcades Project*, ed. Rolf Tiedemann and trans. Howard Eiland and Kevin McLaughlin (London: Belknap Press of Harvard University Press, 2002); Michel Foucault, *Discipline and Punish: The Birth of a Prison*, trans. Alan Sheridan (New York: Vintage Books, 1995); Theodor Adorno, *Minima Moralia: Reflections from a Damaged Life*, trans. E. F. N. Jephcott (London: Verso Books, 2006).

48. Naomi Schor, *Reading in Detail: Aesthetics and the Feminine* (New York: Routledge, 2007), xlii.

49. The detail, as I understand it, finds company with, but is not analogous to the anecdote as the primary building block—the monad—of New Historicism. Although such work has been hugely influential, I am not as invested in the detail's relationship to narratives. For an overview of the anecdote's relationship to New Historicism, see Catherine Gallagher and Stephen Greenblatt, *Practicing New Historicism* (Chicago: University of Chicago Press, 2000).

50. There are, of course, many exceptions that urgently undo the generalization I make here. I am thinking especially of Lydia Goehr's fierce work. See *The Quest for Voice: Music, Politics, and the Limits of Philosophy* (Berkeley: University of California Press, 1998) and *Elective Affinities: Musical Essays on the History of Aesthetic Theory* (New York: Columbia University Press, 2008).

51. Schor, *Reading in Detail*, xlii.

52. Ibid., xlv

53. detail, n. *Oxford English Dictionary*, 2nd ed., 1989; online version June 2011. <http://www.oed.com/view/Entry/51168; accessed June 20, 2011. Earlier version first published in *New English Dictionary*, 1895.

54. Patricia Leigh Brown, "A Hmong Generation Finds Its Voice in Writing," *New York Times*, accessed December 31, 2011. http://www.nytimes.com/2012 /01/01/us/a-hmong-generation-finds-its-voice-in writing.html?pagewanted=1&_r =1&sq=hmong&st=cse&scp=2

55. See "Greater Cuba" in *The Ethnic Eye: Latino Media Arts*, eds. Chon A. Noriega and Ana M. López (Minneapolis: University of Minnesota Press,1996), 38–58. Of the contemporary moment, see José Esteban Muñoz's "Performing Greater Cuba: Tania Bruguera and the Burden of Guilt" in *Women and Performance: a journal of feminist theory* (New York University: Department of Performance Studies, 2000). López crucially engages the term in other articles, see Ana M. López, "Memorias of a Home: Mapping the Revolution (and the Making of Exiles?), *Revista Canadiense de estudios Hispánicos* 20, no. 1, Mundos Contemporaneos en el Cine Español e Hispanoamericano (Otoño 1995): 6. Lopez defines "Greater Cuba" as "a 'Cuba' that exceeds national boundaries and that includes the many individuals and communities outside the national territory that identify as Cuban and contribute to the production of a 'Cuban' cultural discourse," 15 fn3.

56. From album Orquesta Riverside *Baracoa*. Tumbao TCD 052. "Un besito por teléfono" was written by Marco Perdomo and arranged by Pedro Justiz "Peruchín."

57. Incidentally, "Jeepers Creepers" took its name from the racehorse featured in *Going Places*. In the film, Louis Armstrong's character (Gabe) wrote and played the song for the horse that was the only thing that could sooth him for riding (!).

58. Thanks to Christine Bacareza Balance for this formulation.

59. Louis Pérez Jr., *Cuba in the American Imagination: Metaphor and the Imperial Ethos* (Chapel Hill: University of North Carolina Press, 2008), 1. I'd like to note that this wonderful book should win a prize for the best epigraph ever. Pérez quotes Senator Stephen Benton Elkins who said in 1902, "Somehow we can not speak of or deal with Cuba with composure and without becoming extravagant."

60. Thanks to the many historians who have primed the conditions for my work with details. The literature on Cuba/US relations is understandably vast. For key

readings, see Ada Ferrer, *Insurgent Cuba: Race, Nation, and Revolution, 1868–1898* (Chapel Hill: University of North Carolina Press, 1999); Phillip S. Foner, *A History of Cuba and Its Relations with the United States*, 1st ed. (New York: International Publishers, 1962); Louis A. Pérez Jr., *Cuba: Between Reform and Revolution*, 4th ed. (New York: Oxford University Press, 2011).

61. Luis E. Aguilar, "Cuba, c. 1860–1930," in *Cuba: A Short History*, ed. Leslie Bethell (Cambridge: Cambridge University Press, 1993), 22.

62. For more information on Cuba's various wars of independence, especially the conflicts known as the "Ten Years War" and "Little War," see Ferrer's excellent and indispensable *Insurgent Cuba*.

63. Again, I turn, as we all so often do, to Louis Pérez Jr. who argued that the war of 1898 was "the first postbellum national war effort—North and South together in a common cause against an overseas adversary—fixed permanently how Americans came to think of themselves: a righteous people given to the service of righteous purpose" (Pérez, *Cuba*, 11).

64. It even had a performative counterpoint. Between 1897 and 1901, William Paley shot a series of films of the "Spanish American War" for the Edison Manufacturing Company and the American Mutoscope & Biograph Company; what was to become the United States's first war on film. Some of the footage was indeed shot on Cuban soil as the events happened. However, many of the films were reenactments staged in West Orange, New Jersey, using African American soldiers as Cuban "insurgents." I am grateful to Patty Ahn for calling these films, and their usage, to my attention. See: "The Spanish-American War in Motion Pictures," The Motion Picture, Broadcasting, and Recorded Sound Division, Library of Congress. Accessed March 12, 2009. http://memory.loc.gov/ammem/sawhtml/sawhome .html.

65. Pérez, *Cuba*, 11.

66. The Platt Amendment was a mandatory statute forced into the new republic's constitution (1901). Cuban autonomy was bound to approval and/or discipline. Take part three: "That the government of Cuba consents that the United States may exercise the right to intervene for the preservation of Cuban independence, the maintenance of a government adequate for the protection of life, property, and individual liberty, and for discharging the obligations with respect to Cuba imposed by the Treaty of Paris on the United States, now to be assumed and undertaken by the government of Cuba." President Theodore Roosevelt, "The Platt Amendment," in *The Cuba Reader: History, Culture, Politics*, eds. Aviva Chomsky, Barry Carr, and Pamela Smorkaloff (Durham, NC: Duke University Press, 2003), 148.

67. For a brief overview of treaties and other economic agreements of reciprocity with the United States, see Aguilar, "Cuba, c. 1860–c.1930," 21–56.

68. Vera M. Kutzinski, *Sugar's Secrets: Race and the Erotics of Cuban Nationalism* (Charlottesville: University Press of Virginia, 1993), 136.

69. Willie Perdomo, "Nuyorican School of Poetry," in *Where a Nickel Costs a Dime* (New York: W. W. Norton, 1996), 41–43.

70. Aline Helg, *Our Rightful Share: The Afro-Cuban Struggle for Equality 1886–1912* (Chapel Hill: University of North Carolina Press, 1995), 94.

71. *Lucumí* denotes both Afro-Cubans of Yoruban ancestry and Yoruban religious practices. Many of its practitioners prefer the term to "santería."

72. *Minerva: Revista quincenal dedicada a la mujer de color* (*Minerva: Biweekly Magazine Dedicated to Women of Color*). For the importance and implications of *Minerva*, see Jill Lane's "Racial Ethnography and Literate Sex, 1888" in *Blackface Cuba, 1840–1895* (Philadelphia: University of Pennsylvania Press), 180–223. *Minerva* was a journal founded by Cuban feminists of color and published between 1888 and 1889. It was, as Lane observes, "a commitment to transnational black solidarity, and hence reached out to a wide audience of women of color beyond Cuba's borders and took interest in the progress of black women in the United States and elsewhere" (210). Lane also points out the interdisciplinary ethos of the publication, "*Minerva* authors traced an alternative, if heavily assaulted, social role for mulatas, and themselves modeled alternative relations between literacy, gender, performance, and national belonging, different from any imagined either by the mulata's 'admirers' or her detractors" (182).

73. I see my work as conversant with Lisa Brock and Digna Castañeda Fuertes and how they named such involvements "unrecognized linkages" in their edited collection *Between Race and Empire: African-Americans and Cubans before the Cuban Revolution* (Philadelphia: Temple University Press, 1998). The collection is a quietly pivotal collection of essays edited by scholars Lisa Brock and Digna Castañeda Fuertes. Honoring the endeavors of the US-based Brock and Cuban-based Castañeda Fuertes must begin by not ignoring the tricky material conditions of production (which we should all take a moment of silence to imagine) placed upon them. The editors quite literally stepped up to the plate in their attempts to not only document but also include pieces that *theorize* the exchanged forms of expressive culture between Afro-Americans and Cubans. Too often these exchanges are simply stated, remarked upon, cited as happenstance, called upon to amend the "untold story" or to be perceived as being "in the know" of a factoid-laden "black experience." What was actually produced and mobilized by these "happenstances" often gets left by the wayside.

The title of Brock and Castañeda Fuertes's *Between Race and Empire: African-Americans and Cubans before the Cuban Revolution* in itself makes one pause. While the book deals mostly with Cuban gente de color, it does not utilize the prehyphen

"Afro" as an addendum to "Cuban" within the book's title. Here there is already a marked difference of experience. Namely, that Cuban discourses or identifications of race cannot be flattened or siphoned into North American paradigms. However, the editors were not to be deterred and allowed these differences to exist even within the same title. From the outset of the introduction, Brock refutes the nationalist fueled myths that connections between Afro-Americans and Cubans are nonexistent. As Brock writes:

> Yet, we-the editors and contributors to this collection-knew there existed a rich and diverse history of unrecognized linkages between African-Americans and Cubans. Inklings of them appear in the biographical footnotes of Langston Hughes, in the liner notes of Dizzy Gillespie records, in the political proclamations of Frederick Douglass, and in the bold Havana headlines condemning the treatment of performer Josephine Baker.

Inklings in general tend to pester the more ornery-minded paper pusher as they seep through both sides of the paper—read as indecipherable hieroglyphs when flipped to the other side. Inklings incorporate not only those finely scribed lines but also include those accidental (or intentional) blots and blobs expelled from instruments of documentation. The act of documentation in itself produces these excess forms that stray to the margin, stain the outer crescent of the palm, embed themselves onto your clothes. Lisa Brock, introduction to *Between Race and Empire,* ed. Lisa Brock and Digna Castañeda Fuertes (Philadelphia: Temple University Press, 1998), 1–2.

74. The literature on this topic across the genres—whether in fiction, nonfiction, scholarly work, and journalistic forums—is more than abundant. For the purposes of these pages, I offer a short list of contemporary scholarly publications that have been crucially fundamental to the writing of *Listening in Detail.* Frances R. Aparicio, *Listening to Salsa: Gender, Latin Popular Music, and Puerto Rican Cultures* (Hanover, NH: University Press of New England, 1998); Vernan Boggs, *Salsiology: Afro-Cuban Music and the Evolution of Salsa in New York City* (New York: Greenwood Press, 1992); Paul Gilroy, *The Black Atlantic: Modernity and Double Consciousness* (Cambridge: Harvard University Press, 1993); Josh Kun, *Audiotopia: Music, Race, and America* (Berkeley: University of California Press, 2005); Tim Lawrence, *Love Saves the Day: A History of American Dance Music Culture, 1970–1979* (Durham, NC: Duke University Press, 2003); Adalaide Morris, ed., *Sound States: Innovative Poetics and Acoustical Technologies* (Chapel Hill: University of North Carolina Press, 1997); Fred Moten, *In the Break: The Aesthetics of the Black Radical Tradition* (Minneapolis: University of Minnesota Press, 2003); Ronald Radano and Philip V. Bohlman, eds., *Music and the Racial Imagination* (Chicago: University of Chi-

cago Press, 2000); Jonathan Sterne, *The Audible Past: Cultural Origins of Sound Reproduction* (Durham, NC: Duke University Press, 2003); Gayle F. Wald, *Shout, Sister, Shout!: The Untold Story of Rock-and-Roll Trailblazer Sister Rosetta Tharpe* (Boston: Beacon, 2007); and Christopher Washburne, *Sounding Salsa: Performing Latin Music in New York City* (Philadelphia: Temple University Press, 2008).

75. Américo Paredes, *With His Pistol in His Hand: A Border Ballad and Its Hero* (Austin: University of Texas Press, 1958), xi–xii.

76. See Kevin Moore's incredible analysis of "Yo Bailo de Todo" song at http://www.timba.com/artist_pages/yo-bailo-de-todo-analysis.

77. See note 8.

78. Helio Orovio defines charanga as,

A type of musical group also known as *charanga francesa*. This type of ensemble made its appearance in the early years of the twentieth century as a variation of the typical dance or wind orchestra. Charangas played mostly danzónes, but when the cha-cha-chá appeared in 1951, the new dance style was an ideal vehicle for the charanga-style musical groups. The original instrumentation consisted of flute, violin, piano, double bass, *paila* ("Creole tympani"), and gourd scraper (*guiro*). These instruments were later augmented with a conga drum, two more violins, and three singers.

Orovio, *Cuban Music*, 51.

79. Edouard Glissant, "Introductions" from *Caribbean Discourse: Selected Essays*, trans. by J. Michael Dash (Charlottesville: University Press of Virginia, 1999), 4.

80. Theodor Adorno, "Music, Language, and Composition" in *Essays on Music*, ed. Richard Leppert and trans. Susan H. Gillespie (Berkeley: University of California Press, 2002), 116.

CHAPTER 1

1. Yosvany Terry, interview by author, July 30, 2008, in New York City. EGREM (Empresa de Grabaciones y Ediciones Musicales/Enterprise of Recordings and Musical Editions) is the Cuban government's nationalized unit that deals with musical recording. I discuss EGREM further in chapter 4.

2. *Oxford English Dictionary*, 3rd ed., June 2009; online version March 2011. s.v. "recourse." Accessed June 6, 2011, http://www.oed.com:80/Entry/159918. An entry for this word was first included in *New English Dictionary*, 1904.http://www.oed.com:80/Entry/159918; accessed June 6, 2011. An entry for this word was first included in *New English Dictionary*, 1904.

3. For a good overview of the organizational shifts in the Cuban musical industry

after the 1959 revolution, see Robin Moore's *Music and Revolution: Cultural Change in Socialist Cuba* (Berkeley: University of California Press, 2000).

4. Thanks to Shane Vogel for helping me to clarify this formulation.

5. "I Want to Be Ready" is the title of a solo piece from Ailey's famed dance suite *Revelations*. It is also the inspiration for the title and feeling of Goldman's book. She writes, "'I Want to Be Ready' suggests the need to be prepared, not just for salvation but also for a range of social and historical constraints. In this austere solo, with everything seemingly at stake, dance emerges as a practice of making oneself ready." Danielle Goldman, *I Want to Be Ready: Improvised Dance as a Practice of Freedom* (Ann Arbor: University of Michigan Press, 2010), 104.

6. The early childhood and family information is from an interview I conducted with Miké Charroppin, August 19, 2009, in Montmartre, Paris, France.

7. The intimate familiarity with and creative corruption of so-called Western classical standards have functioned as just one creative spine to Cuban musical tradition. Bits of Grieg, Stravinsky, Chopin, and Mozart are riffs you will hear often in Cuban popular standards. I discuss this kind of creative corruption in more detail in chapter 4 by way of Odilio Urfé's work in the film *Nosotros, la musica*.

8. The foregoing biographical bits are taken from the John Child's interview and John Child's biographical entry in *The Guinness Encyclopedia of Popular Music*, ed. Colin Larkin (Middlesex, England: Guiness Publishing, 1992), 3548–50. I trust this entry as Child and Rodríguez were in correspondence as to its accuracies, what should be included, highlighted, and so forth. To read their correspondence is to note their equal attention to the care necessary for such an entry. My special thanks to John Child for sharing all of these incredible materials with me.

9. Albert Dailey was born in Baltimore in 1936 and died in Denver of pneumonia in 1984. Like Rodríguez, he was also conservatory trained. "Dailey, Albert Preston," entry in *The Biographical Encyclopedia of Jazz,* eds. Leonard Feather and Ira Gitler (Oxford University Press, 1999), 162–63.

10. This kind of flourish is also detectable in the sound of Chucho Valdes, a pianist I discuss in chapter 4.

11. As I write this, I must catch myself from falling into those patterns of demanding inclusion for Cuban contributions to jazz's history, which is not my intention here. To be sure, there are so many of us out there working on jazz perpetually (and frustratedly) armed with factoids that testify on behalf of its Cuban arteries. The manifestos have been written and the outrage recorded, and it is astonishing to realize how scant an impression such work has made. Even the above selection of well-known critics who have long been at work drawing out the fact of this pivot are not routine players in the canon of jazz criticism as it gets codified as Jazz Studies in the United States. To say nothing of the ladies out there always hard at work in the un-

dercommons. See Timothy Brennan, *Secular Devotion: Afro-Latin Music and Imperial Jazz* (London: Verso, 2008); Ruth Glasser, *My Music Is My Flag: Puerto Rican Musicians and Their New York Communities, 1917–1940* (Berkeley: University of California Press, 1995); Ned Sublette, *The World That Made New Orleans: From Spanish Silver to Congo Square* (Chicago: Lawrence Hill Books, 2008); Christopher Washburne, "The Clave of Jazz: A Caribbean Contribution to the Rhythmic Foundation of an African-American Music," *Black Music Research Journal* 17, no. 1 (1997): 59–80; and especially, Jairo Moreno's brilliant, "Bauzá-Gillespie-Latin/Jazz: Difference, Modernity, and the Black Caribbean," *The South Atlantic Quarterly* 103, no. 1 (2004): 81–99.

12. Arturo O' Farrill, "The US-Cuba Jazz Connection," Roundtable panel discussion at the Cuba Project's Cuba Futures Conference, City University of New York's Bildner Center, New York, NY, April 2, 2011.

13. For a vibrant and foundational introduction to the performances of New Orleans—and to the performances that have made it so, see Joseph Roach, *Cities of the Dead: Circum-Atlantic Performance* (New York: Columbia University Press, 1996).

14. Sublette, *The World That Made New Orleans*, 5.

15. Ibid., 4.

16. Ibid., 104–5.

17. The critical literature on and off the island is vast, but I would also like to acknowledge Jack Stewart's "Cuban Influences on New Orleans Music" *The Jazz Archivist: Issue Archive Online*, accessed June 19, 2011, http://jazz.tulane.edu/archivist/ja_online_index; and Pamela J. Smith's master's thesis, "Caribbean Influences on Early New Orleans Music" (New Orleans: Tulane University, 1986).

18. Leonardo Acosta, *Cubano Be, Cubano Bop: One Hundered Years of Jazz in Cuba*, trans. Daniel S. Whitesell (Washington and London: Smithsonian Books, 2003), 2.

19. Raúl Fernández, *Latin Jazz: The Perfect Combination/La Combinación Perfecta* (San Francisco: Chronicle Books, 2002), 14. On the economy of early jazz, please see Catherine Gunther Kodat's astute, "Conversing with Ourselves: Canon, Freedom, Jazz" *American Quarterly* 55, no. 1 (2003): 1–28. Kodat writes,

> The market is also the inescapable horizon of jazz, and not just because jazz is an aspect of life: when we consider New Orleans's Congo Square as the originating locus of American jazz, the connection between jazz and exchange starts to appear more than merely accidental. Marshall Stearns places the beginnings of jazz in the Congo Square dancing and socializing permitted African slaves in antebellum New Orleans; the dances, which records indicate began as early as

1817, became an important tourist attraction for the city. One could even say that the links binding freedom, commodification, and jazz music were first forged in these highly structured and supervised stagings of the musical expressions of "property," and that jazz's later, complex relationship to mechanical reproduction in the Fordist (and post-Fordist) culture industry largely follows from these historical conditions of its emergence.

20. See Radamés Giro, entry "Historia del Jazz en Cuba," in Tomo 2 of his *Diccionario enciclopédico de la música en Cuba* (La Habana: Letras Cubanas, 2007), 261–68.

21. Pérez is one of the many elusive and fascinating figures difficult to verifiably track in the Havana-New Orleans portal. The conflicting reports of Pérez's life demonstrate the difficulty of verifying the movement between New Orleans and Havana. Helio Orovio has his birthplace of Havana in 1863. Writes Orovio, "When he was young, Pérez left Havana for New Orleans, where he studied music." He also states that he later became an owner of a grocery store where he quietly passed away. From Helio Orovio, entry "Pérez, Manuel," *Cuban Music from A to Z*, trans. Ricardo Bardo Portilla and Lucy Davies (Durham, NC: Duke University Press, 2004), 162. Feather and Gilter have his birthplace in New Orleans in 1871 and note that Pérez supported himself with his trade as cigar maker for which he eventually left music. Leonard Feather and Ira Gitler, entry "Perez, Manuel (Emanuel aka Emile)," *The Biographical Encyclopedia of Jazz* (Oxford and New York: Oxford University Press, 1999), 523. Sublette has him born in Havana in 1873. Ned Sublette *Cuba and Its Music: From the First Drums to the Mambo* (Chicago: Chicago Review Press, 2004), 323. See especially Jack Stewart's "Cuban Influences on New Orleans Music" from *Jazz Archivist* 13 (1998–1999). Thanks to Lynn Abbott at the Hogan Jazz Archive at Tulane University for so graciously sending me this article in the mail. Note Sidney Bechet's note of Perez, from *Treat it Gentle*: "Perez, he was a musicianer; he was *sincere*. He stuck to his instrument." Sidney Bechet, *Treat It Gentle: An Autobiography* (Cambridge: Da Capo Press, 2002), 86–88.

22. Acosta, *Cubano Be, Cubano Bop*, 3.

23. Ibid., 4. Also see Larry Birnbaum's article, "Machito: Original Macho Man," *Down Beat* 47 (December, 1980): 25–27.

24. Handy would record "St. Louis Blues" in 1914. Tim Brooks, "W. C. Handy," from *Lost Sounds: Blacks and the Birth of the Recording Industry 1890–1919* (Urbana and Chicago: University of Illinois Press, 2004), 411–12.

25. The Tio family was a trigenerational musical family including the elder Thomas, the son Lorenzo Sr. and Lorenzo Jr. All of the Tios were particularly in-

fluential in reed instrumentation. Lorenzo Jr. is credited with mentoring jazz musicians such as Sidney Bechet and Jimmie Noone. Fernández, *Latin Jazz*, 16.

26. See John Storm Roberts's resourceful and formative text, *The Latin Tinge: The Impact of Latin American Music on the United States* (New York: Oxford University Press, 1979), 38–39.

27. *Oxford English Dictionary Online*, 2nd ed. 2009, s.v. "tinge" (v.) and "tinge" (n2) 1989.

28. Jairo Moreno, "Bauzá-Gillespie-Latin/Jazz: Difference, Modernity, and the Black Caribbean," *The South Atlantic Quarterly* 103, no. 1 (2004): 83.

29. Thanks to Shane Vogel for this observation.

30. Hortense Spillers, "Peter's Pans: Eating in the Diaspora" in *Black, White and In Color: Essays on American Literature and Culture* (Chicago: University of Chicago Press, 2003), 3.

31. For more on the incomplete subject see Antonio Viego's *Dead Subjects: Toward a Politics of Loss in Latino Studies* (Durham, NC: Duke University Press, 2007). I discuss Viego's work in more detail in chapter 5.

32. I cannot continue without offering a difficult side note. Without flattening the differences between them, Latino studies, like African American studies, has also experienced a parallel shift from movement to cognizable object and has been particularly afflicted with studies protocols. The field must continue to honor and adapt to those millions of brown, undocumented bodies that sustain daily life in the United States. They are necessarily illegible and incomplete because to be known can mean deportation, violent separation from one's family, and the reduction of the multiple selves that reside in a singular immigrant body. Although the undocumented (of past and present) might resist being counted in official census reports or demographic studies—studies that are paradoxically vital to their future survival in the United States—this does not sanction their continued silencing and erasure. It means that we must come up with supplemental and imaginative ways to theorize their presence and cultural contributions.

33. Theodore O. Mason Jr. notes familial belonging and tenderness by way of *The Norton Anthology of African American Literature*, the momentous anthological launch by Henry Louis Gates and Nellie Y. McKay in 1997. Mason writes, "A number of my students who have taken the volume with them during weekend visits home describe the difficulty of wresting the book away from family members when it is time to return to college." Theodore O. Mason Jr. "The African-American Anthology: Mapping the Territory, Taking the National Census, Building the Museum," *American Literary History* 10 no. 1 (1998): 185–98.

34. Kobena Mercer, presentation for the Faculty Graduate Seminar, The Center for African American Studies, Princeton University, Princeton, NJ, February 24, 2009.

35. According to Howatson and Chilvers, it initially denoted the collection of short verse. They point to the *Greek Anthology*, a collection that included short poems and epitaphs traceable to the first-century BC, as one of its earliest examples. The verse was of the dedicatory and reflective variety and impressively diverse in its observations about the trials of love, politics, and oddities of daily life. Some entries are said to be satirical, even funny. They also identify the Latin version, the *Anthologia Latina*, which gathered close to four hundred poems written in Africa in the early sixth century AD. See *The Concise Oxford Companion to Classical Literature*, ed. M. C. Howatson and Ian Chilvers (Oxford: Oxford University Press, 1996), s.v. "anthology." Accessed at Oxford Reference Online, Oxford University Press, Princeton University, June 27, 2009, http://www.oxfordreference.com/views/ENTRY.html?subview=Main&entry=t9.e217.

36. *Oxford English Dictionary*, 2ND ed. 1989, s.v. "anthologize, v."

37. On this front, see especially Barbara M. Benedict, *Making the Modern Reader: Cultural Mediation in Early Modern Literary Anthologies* (Princeton: Princeton University Press, 1996) and Leah Price, *The Anthology and the Rise of the Novel* (Cambridge: Cambridge University Press, 2000).

38. Nor can the importance of the anthology in the New World be understated (an equally Byzantine task). But I would like to briefly mention its pamphleteer function for knowledge about the other—whether rendered as landscape, people, and language—as in the case of the Florentine Codex. On the relationship between on the Spanish acquisition and collection of indigeniety, see Diana Taylor's The *Archive and Repertoire: Performing Cultural Memory in the Americas* (Durham, NC: Duke University Press, 2003). The earliest texts about the New World might be thought of as the gathering together and making entries of the unknown into portable form. For example, the early sixteenth-century conquest narrative by Cabeza de Vaca gestures toward the impact between personal reportage and data collection as it was written for the Spanish crown. His prose mirrors the kind of grant-speak whereby one defends the necessity of their findings to funders. The organization of the account carries something of the anthological form. Cabeza de Vaca was one editor of what imperial Spain would come to know about the New World: he put a selection of its fauna, flora, and characters into one place for circulation. See Cabeza de Vaca, Álvar Núñez, *The Narrative of Cabeza de Vaca*, edited and translated by Rolena Adorno and Patrick Charles Pautz (Lincoln: University of Nebraska Press, 2003). Adorno and Pautz's introduction is an especially useful text for a nuanced take on the early American literary scene. Long after their conquest, anthologies were especially interested in documenting what made the New World new. It is here that Mullen offers an interesting paradox: if anthologies are about the preserva-

tion of the past, how was the form adapted from places that supposedly did not have one? This kind of logic defines the anthological project as well-suited for nineteenth-century discourses on the progress of history. On the proliferation of anthologies, especially in a preindependence Cuba—especially as they "collected" black authors, see Edward Mullen's "The Emergence of Afro-Hispanic Poetry: Some Notes on Canon Formation," *Hispanic Review* 56, no. 4 (Autumn 1988): 435–53. For a detailed if admittedly selective survey of anthologies of Hispanic poetry between 1940 and 1980 (an anthology of anthologies as it were), see Howard Mancing's, "A Consensus Canon of Hispanic Poetry," *Hispania* 69, no.1 (March 1986): 53–81. For an early Hispanophile attempt to grasp the new Negro poetry throughout the hemisphere, and an early instance of comparative literary work between Cuba and the United States, see Dorothy Schons, "Negro Poetry in the Americas," *Hispania* 25, no. 3, Coester Number (October 1942): 309–19.

39. See Benedict Anderson's formative *Imagined Communities: Reflections on the Origin and Spread of Nationalism,* especially his chapter, "Census, Map, Museum" (London: Verso, 1991), 163–86.

40. Not only was the impulse to be found in both nations, but scholars in Cuba and in the United States were in documented conversation about the anthologizing of the Negro. One fascinating instance of this interchange was by way of the biannual journal published by the *Sociedad de Estudios Afrocubanos* (Society of Afro-Cuban Studies) whose first issue launched in 1937—and was the textual extension by the group of the same name, founded in 1936 by Fernando Ortiz. Its advisory board is comprised of not only some of the leading scholars on race in Cuba, but also artists and writers. The group is fascinating for several reasons. For one, it gathered an interdisciplinary bunch of scholars and artists into its operational fold. Its first director was Emilio Roig de Leuchsenring (editor at Grafico, Social y El Figaro), and its officers was comprised of poets such as Nicolás Guillén and Emilio Ballagas, and musician/composers such as Amadeo Roldán, Gilberto Valdez, Ramón Guirao, Gonzalo Roig, Alejandro García Cartula, Eusebia Cosme, Ignacio Villa (Bola de Nieve). It was a group that, from the outset, did not mince words: together they came together to get a sense of the other, regardless of racial and ethnic background. Take this from their founding manifesto,

> we Cubans must wage a spirited fight, whatever may be our color or origins. There is an undoubted need for the understanding of the racial factors of Cuba, with no other consideration than objective truth. Whites and Negros must know and understand each other in Cuba; and with a feeling of mutual responsibility for the destiny of this republic, undertake the thorough, intelligent, courageous

and impartial investigation of the consequences in this island of contact between peoples of definite ethnic characteristics.

The *Sociedad de Estudios Afrocubanos* aspires to carry on this work, from Richard Pattee, "Notes" sections from *The Journal of Negro History*, under the title "Cuban Negro Studies" 23, no. 1 (January 1938), 118–19. For the original version in Spanish, see the collectively authored "Los estatutos de la sociedad de estudios Afrocubanos" *Estudios Afrocubanos* 1 (1937). Strangely enough, this journal has escaped the eyes of many scholars. Miguel Arnedo Gomez, however, makes excellent use of it, especially through his attentive studies to the written modes that linger on the limens of poetry and performance in the Afrocubanist movement. See Miguel Arnedo, " 'Afrocubanista' Poetry and Afro-Cuban Performance" *The Modern Language Review* 96, no. 4 (October 2001): 990–1005. Also see his *Writing Rumba: The Afrocubanist Movement in Poetry* (Charlottesville: University of Virginia Press, 2006).

41. Theodore O. Mason Jr. suggests that the anthology is better aligned with what Benedict Anderson has named as the "totalizing classificatory grid." "The effect of the grid was always able to say of anything that it was this, not that; it belonged here, not there. It was bounded, determinate, and therefore-in principle-countable." From *Imagined Communities*, 184. This quote is featured in the epigraph in Theodore O. Mason Jr. "The African-American Anthology: Mapping the Territory, Taking the National Census, Building the Museum," *American Literary History* 10, no. 1 (1998): 192–93.

42. There is something of national becoming that finds counterpoint in disciplinary becoming. See Gayatri Spivak's *Death of a Discipline* (New York: Columbia University Press, 2003); and Benedict Anderson's *Imagined Communities: Reflections on the Origin and Spread of Nationalism* (London: Verso, 1991). I'd like to contribute to the strong legacy of scholarship that has done much to call our attention to the bedfellow antics between nation building and scholarship. And because disciplinary becoming has required proper, authoritative texts to keep its edges clean, anthologies are thus strong parts of our institutional ancestry.

43. In his survey of the Afro-Hispanic anthology in American literary history, Mullen focuses on poetry anthologies in the Cuban colonial and postcolonial period, and calls attention to the work of Plácido as it was modulated through the nineteenth and early twentieth century anthologies. The poet was enlisted by various anthologies as a token, terrible reminder, and nonthreatening presence. One pointed example is his appearance in Marcelino Menéndez y Pelayo's four volume *Antología de poetas Hispano-Americanos* (1893–1895). Plácido was the only Cuban of color included in this mammoth collection published in the final pulses before official independence from Spain. Menéndez y Pelayo framed him this way: "un

poeta espontaneo, ignorante de todas las cosas divinas y humanas, y por añadidura negro, o a lo menos pardo" [a spontaneous poet, ignorant of all divine and human things, and in addition he's black, or at the very least mulato]. The consequences of such an action were manifold, for as Mullen points out, the *Antología* was, "one of the few sources available to the first generation of North American Hispanists and which enjoyed wide circulation through-out the Hispanic world." See Mullen, "The Emergence of Afro-Hispanic Poetry."

44. Keneth Kinnamon agrees that most anthologies of African-American literature were published after 1920. However, he notes *Les Cenelles* (1845) a collection of writings by New Orleans Creoles and Julia Griffiths's *Autographs for Freedom* (1853). See Keneth Kinnamon's "Anthologies of African American Literarture from 1845–1994," *Callaloo* 20, no. 2 (1997): 461–81. The impetus to anthologies was felt across the globe. While I'd like to extend the terms of his periodization, Brent Hayes Edwards points to the upsurge of Negro anthologies in the early 1920s, "For the first time—and in a rush that with hindsight is astonishing—there was great interest in researching, notating, transcribing, assembling, and packaging almost anything having to do with populations of African descent." Brent Hayes Edwards in his *The Practice of Diaspora: Literature, Translation, and the Rise of Black Internationalism* (Cambridge: Harvard University Press, 2003), 43–44. For a well-researched list of examples of such anthologies, *please* see Edwards's footnote 60 on page 331.

45. As Alexander continues, "Anthologies require a tremendous amount of work of a certain kind, and to succeed they must implicitly tell a story. The act of consolidating and then distilling invites aesthetic and political choices at every turn, the kinds of choices that subsequently come to appear inevitable when we read the anthology and the editorial hand is made invisible." Elizabeth Alexander, "The Black Poet as Canon-Maker: Langston Hughes and the Road to *New Negro Poets: USA*," in *The Black Interior* (St. Paul: Graywolf Press, 2004), 25.

46. See John S. Lash, "The Anthologist and the Negro Author," *Phylon* (1940–1956) 8, no. 1 (1st quarter, 1947): 71. Lash's observations have also been taken up by Gerald Early, "Introduction" *My Soul's High Song: The Collective Writings of Countee Cullen, Voice of the Harlem Renaissance* (New York: Doubleday, 1991), 33. And ibid., by Brent Hayes Edwards in his *The Practice of Diaspora: Literature, Translation, and the Rise of Black Internationalism* (Cambridge: Harvard University Press, 2003), 43. I'd like to note that both Johnson and Dunbar's anthologies foreground a historical interamericanism. In Dunbar, a piece on Toussaint L'Overture is featured among its first entries.

47. Considering the general anxiety of publishing houses around the racial question, these editors' bold compilations should be acknowledged in perpetuity. How Dunbar Nelson had to navigate the anxieties and desires from both publishers and

contributors offers a rich exercise in the imagining of black feminist genealogies in the history of US publishing.

48. Lash, "Anthologist and the Negro," 71.

49. James Weldon Johnson, ed. "Preface" from *The Book of American Negro Poetry*, rev. ed. (New York: Harcourt, Brace & World, 1931), 9.

50. Ibid., 11.

51. Born in 1809 as Gabriel de la Concepcion Valdés to a black father and Spanish mother, "Plácido" became one of Cuba's greatest poets of the nineteenth century. Later he was brutally murdered by Spanish colonial authorities in 1844 in an orchestrated racial war called the Conspiración de La Escalera (the Ladder Conspiracy) when hundreds of (mostly) Cubans of color were tortured and/or executed by colonial authorities over fears of antislavery revolts. For more on the conspiracy, see Robert L. Paquette, *Sugar Is Made with Blood: The Conspiracy of La Escalera and the Conflict between Empires over Slavery in Cuba* (Middletown: Wesleyan University Press, 1990).

52. Johnson says of Plácido, "So I think it probably that the first world-acknowledged Aframericanpoet will come out of Latin America. Over against this probability, of course, is the great advantage possessed by the colored poet in the United States of writing in the world-conquering English language" (40).

53. And before Johnson concludes his intro by thanking the necessaries, he writes, "I offer this collection without making apology or asking allowance."

54. Edwards, *Practice of Diaspora*, 45.

55. Here I would like to acknowledge Roderick Ferguson's brilliant work on this tension, specifically with his stunning chapter on James Baldwin and Gunner Myrdal. Using the example of Myrdal, Ferguson nimbly encapsulates his critique of the sociological anthology this way, "The liberal social science addressed culture rather than biology as the site of human difference . . . Gunner Myrdal's classic text *An American Dilemma* was part of this challenge. But by rejecting biology as the domain of difference in favor of culture, Myrdal—rather than neutralizing racism—merely articulated racial knowledge through the enunciations of African American cultural difference." Roderick A. Ferguson, *Aberrations in Black: Toward a Queer of Color Critique* (Minnesota: University of Minnesota Press, 2004), 88.

56. It is not my intention here to keep Cuban studies under erasure. This chapter is intended as a preface for the analysis of Cuban studies that I offer chapter 5. In that chapter, I show how Cuban studies has its own studies protocols that have long refused a going far beyond and the many implications raised, particularly racial and generational ones, at work in that refusal.

57. The emergence of Jazz Studies programs in the United States, alongside academic courses of study of race, gender, and ethnicity were a result of institutional

gains of decades of civil rights activism. Nicolas Evans speculates to the preoccupation with the upsurge in questions of race and national with respect to jazz in the early 1990s. He argues that there are important questions of commerce, for example, the reissue of important jazz recordings. He also points to the shifting place of jazz cultures in policy debates and its public institutionalization (i.e., those decisions made by who he instructively calls the "Lincoln Center Debaters). See Nicolas M. Evans *Writing Jazz: Race, Nationalism, and Modern Culture in the 1920s* (New York and London: Garland, 2000), 3–4. He also mentions the developing curricula found in higher education. Taking Evans's cue, I'd like to point to the upsurge in the textual canonization of Jazz Studies as it emerges especially in the late 1990s. See also the Spring–Spring 2002 special issues of *Current Musicology* dedicated to Jazz Studies. Undoubtedly, the collection and publication of writings about jazz were nobly intended as classroom tools. For other texts that announce "Jazz Studies" see David Ake, *Jazz Matters: Sound, Place, and Time since Bebop* (Berkeley: University of California Press, 2010); Scott DeVeaux and Gary Giddin, *Jazz: Essential Listening* (New York: Norton, 2011); Ted Gioia, *The History of Jazz*, 2nd ed. (New York: Oxford University Press, 2011); Howard Reich, ed., *Let Freedom Swing: Collected Writings on Jazz, Blues, and Gospel* (Evanston, Ill.: Northwestern University Press, 2010); and Tony Whyton, *Jazz Icons: Heroes, Myths and the Jazz Tradition* (Cambridge: Cambridge University Press, 2010).

58. For an important critique on the tendency to view influence along these lines, see Timothy Brennan's *Secular Devotion: Afro-Latin Music and Imperial Jazz* (London and New York: Verso, 2008).

59. *The Jazz Review*, the journal founded by Nat Hentoff, Hsio Wen Shih, and Martin Williams, was one of the first publication venues to explicitly gather jazz in writings in the New York of 1958.

60. For example, the Center for Jazz Studies at Columbia University is one of the tireless initiatives on behalf of jazz as intellectual work. It has housed the Jazz Study Group, originally founded by Robert O' Meally in 1995 with the support of the Ford Foundation. The group has been a vibrant nucleolus of such activity, and has inspired an immeasurable degree of influence on students, scholars, artists and lay critics. Many have said that the group, its conversations, and publications have been life changing. For more information, see: http://www.jazz.columbia.edu/research/the-jazz-study-group.html (accessed July 28, 2009).

61. See Nichole T. Rustin and Sherrie Tucker's *Big Ears: Listening for Gender in Jazz Studies* (Durham, NC: Duke University Press, 2008).

62. Christopher Washburne, "Latin Jazz: The Other Jazz," *Current Musicology*, nos. 71–73 (Spring 2001–Spring 2002): 420.

63. Theodore Mason Jr. gets to the hearts of the matter. In his review of *The Norton Anthology of African American Literature* (1997), he writes: "an African-American anthology rises from an impulse to question previous representations of the American nation in part by advancing the contingent and arbitrary nature of such representations. Yet even as it dismantles racist configurations of nationality, such a volume must find a way to defend its configuration of blackness as somehow necessary and natural, as opposed to arbitrary and contingent. This last move is teleological rather than archaeological in nature, and hence establishes a powerful critical conflict that forms one of the central problems of anthologizing as an enterprise." Mason gets at the "critical conflict" that not only resides at the heart of anthological undertaking, but also at the greater configuration of America as it intersects with music, and the role of the anthology to catalog it. He generously identifies the snafus of the enterprise as the desire for the anthology's purpose rather than the difficult, messy, and residual imprints of the past it gathers. Ibid. Theodore O. Mason Jr., "The African-American Anthology: Mapping the Territory, Taking the National Census, Building the Museum," *American Literary History* 10, no. 1 (1998): 192–93.

64. Vijay Iyer, "Exploding the Narrative in Jazz Improvization," in *Uptown Conversation: The New Jazz Studies*, ed. Robert G. O'Meally, Brent Hayes Edwards, and Farah Jasmine Griffin (New York: Columbia University Press, 2004), 395.

65. Ibid.

66. Here I am also thinking alongside Edwards's closing meditation on Nancy Cunard's *Negro*, where he posits the following question, "What if the anthology enables the articulation of a mood rather than conducting a census, drawing a map, or founding a museum? Neither 'a final thing' (a framing of the past) nor a 'prophecy' (a prediction of the future), but a space of 'new creation' in the performance of reading that takes place in the subjunctive, in a condition of probability . . . Reading the Negro anthology, then, offers a model for that practice, in which diaspora can be articulated only in forms that are provisional, negotiated, asymmetrical." Edwards, *Practice of Diaspora*, 318. For other attention to this passage see Nadi Edwards, "Diaspora, Difference, and Black Internationalisms," *Small Axe* 9, no. 17 (March 2005): 120–28.

67. Here I pay homage to José Esteban Muñoz moving meditation on liveness in his opening pages on Jack Smith. See his *Disidentifications: Queers of Color and the Performance of Politics* (Minneapolis: University of Minnesota Press, 1999).

68. For example, the discursive work of Saidiya Hartman's *Lose Your Mother* and Edwidge Danticat's reimagining of Queen Anacaona; to staged reenactments of Cherrie Moraga's *Heroes and Saints and Other Plays* and Aime Cesaire's *Tempest*; to the sonic descriptions made by Gilberto Gil's "Quilombo" and Billie Holiday's "Strange Fruit."

69. Dates are borrowed from Martínez-Malo's book *Rita la Única*. See Aldo Martínez-Malo, *Rita, la única* (La Habana: Editora Abril), 1988.

70. Lewis A. Erenberg, *Steppin' Out: New York Nightlife and the Transformation of American Culture* (Chicago: University of Chicago Press, 1981). The import of form to the United States is often attributed to Anna Held, a follies entertainer and wife of Florenz Ziegfeld, who encouraged her husband to open his own follies in New York in 1907. For a quarter of a century the Ziegfeld follies staged productions that were elaborately designed, including politically punchy comedians, audience participation, and "most important, beautiful women," (207). As competition between revues pushed production values higher, there emerged identifiable characteristics of the revue format. See also Robert Baral, *Revue: The Great Broadway Period*, rev. ed. (New York: Fleet Press, 1970).

71. In terms of content, early US revues were staged manifestations of a nascent American cosmopolitanism. Through staging the experience of modernity's *flaneur* with the undesirable parts cast into songs, dances, and bright pastels, the revue afforded a privileged wandering through metropolitan locations from the comfort of your seat. An article from 1918 expressed the revue's economy this way: [as] "something razzling and dazzling, of legs and tom-foolery … of productions which introduce plenty of light and color and pretty dresses." Here the use of "legs" indicates how women's bodies emerged as driving forces of revues—what people really came to see as part of a modern spectacle. In addition to flesh-baring outfits, the "I've arrived to the big city feeling" of revues shook up nineteenth-century theatrical conventions, including plot and theatrical time. Erenberg has noted the revue's particular temporality. The revue sped things up. "Pacing emphasized [the structure of the revue]. The essence of the performance was speed" (210).

72. While the revue was also popular in Cuba, it's interesting to note that its stagings were domestically preoccupied. While the United States in many ways looked out and to its captive populations to historically forge an idea of Americanness against an other, Cuba looked inward. Cuban bourgeois audiences in Havana, especially, also wanted to define themselves along cosmopolitan lines. See, for example, Jill Lane's important work on Cuba's *teatro bufo* in Jill Lane, *Blackface Cuba, 1840–1895* (Philadelphia: University of Pennylvania Press, 2005). During the republican era, Cuban bourgeois audiences used race and subjection as metaphors for Cuba's imperial captivity. For example, Cirilio Villaverde's nineteenth-century abolitionist novel *Cecilia Valdés*, was set to an operetta by composer Gonzalo Roig and premiered in El Teatro Martí in 1932 to enormous success. First published in 1882, Villaverde's narrative depicts the tragic story of an equally tragic mulata of an unknown white father who unknowingly falls in love with her half-brother. After being seduced and eventually betrayed by her

brother, Valdés's revenge unwittingly unfolds. While on his way to marry a woman of respectable race and class, Valdés's brother is killed by her mulato paramour. It's translation into the operetta form and its tremendous success gives a great impression of how race occupied the national consciousness. Music would be the reflective vehicle with which to articulate it, even in the realm of "high art." Also consider the prevalence of Cuban revues in the international arena, for example, the Septeto Nacional's 1929 tour of Spain.

73. In his book, Vogel creatively excavates the so-called black cabarets of Harlem, such as the Rhythm Club and the Nest Club, as vital, generative, dynamic nexuses of black performance and social life in the1920s and 1930s. Shane Vogel, "The Scene of Harlem Cabaret: 1926 and After," in *The Scene of Harlem Cabaret: Race, Sexuality, Performance* (Chicago: University of Chicago Press, 2009).

74. Roach, *Cities of the Dead*, xi.

75. For a more extensive reading of this revue see Vèvè A. Clark, "Katherine Dunham's Tropical Revue," in *Black American Literature Forum* 16, no. 4, Black Theatre Issue (Winter 1982): 147–52.

76. See Richard Buckle, *Katherine Dunham: Her Dancers, Singers, Musicians* (London: Ballet Publications, 1949).

77. In the next chapter, through the figure of Graciela, I will take a closer look at and listen to this migration.

78. *Oxford English Dictionary Online*, 2nd ed. 2009, s.v. "album," 1989.

79. Adorno wrote of the linkages this way: the record "is the first means of musical presentation that can be possessed as a thing . . . record are possessed like photographs: the nineteenth century had good reasons for coming up with phonographic record albums alongside photographic and postage-stamp albums, all of them herbaria of artificial life that are present in the smallest space and ready to conjure up every recollection that would otherwise be mercilessly shredded between the haste and hum-drum of private life." From Theodor Adorno, "The Form of the Phonograph Record," in *Essays on Music*, ed. Richard Leppert, trans. Susan H. Gillespie (Berkeley and Los Angeles: University of California Press, 2002), 278–79.

80. Friedrich A. Kittler, *Gramaphone, Film, Typewriter* trans. Geoffrey Winthrop-Young and Michael Wutz (Stanford: Stanford University Press, 1999), 21–22.

81. Michael Chanan, *Repeated Takes: A Short History of Recording and Its Effects on Music* (New York: Verso, 1995), 4–5. I mention this in my essay "Towards an Ethics of Knowing Nothing," Alexandra Vazquez, "Toward an Ethics of Knowing Nothing," in *Pop When the World Falls Apart*, ed. Eric Weisbard (Durham, NC: Duke University Press, 2012).

82. This partly has to do with the increasing reach of recording industry, especially in Latin America. Of the Victor Company, George Tavares writes, "By 1920,

an export department had been established and was an efficient, effective, and aggressive organization. Special records were pressed for the different export areas and instruments were especially protectively treated to withstand tropical conditions. The home office was outfitted with a corps of translators . . . This effort almost immediately resulted in the setting up of foreign subsidiaries in Latin America and other countries." George Tavares, "The Record Industry in Latin America," *Journal of the Audio Engineering Society* 25, no. 10/11 (October/November 1977): 795–99.

83. In this section I am not faithful to the stable notion of what an "album" is. Which is to say, I also consider playlists put together from virtual stores as albums also. I am not hung up on the "album's demise" in this iTunes era in which we currently live.

84. Miké Charroppin, Rodríguez's widow, made my introduction to Roberto "Mamey" Evangelisti. Evangelisti is a Roman-born and -based percussionist whose childhood obsession with (and isolation from) the congas meant that as he taught himself to play, he also had to learn how to build his own drums to get that sound he heard in recording. He was called to it by hands that didn't want the distancing of drumsticks and by the creative work that Armando Peraza did for Santana. I learned about his training with too many Cuban greats to mention and was shown footage of Rodríguez and *Cuba Linda* in the live. Evangelisti is an heir—actual, sonic, soulic—of Tata Güines. As such Evangelisti's is vecchia scuola elegance. His tender structuring held up many of Rodríguez's songs in the live, and continues to do so in recording. Hear him on the virtual whole of Alfredo Rodríguez's beautiful album *Oye Afra*.

85. At the same time of *Cuba Linda*, Jesús Alemañy assembled two album length projects that in many ways inaugurated a new rush of support for Cuban recording endeavors.

86. "Laura" was composed by David Raksin with lyrics by Johnny Mercer in 1945. The song was done over by artists from Charlie "Bird" Parker to Ella Fitgerald.

87. Author unknown, Promotional Materials/Press Kit for *Cuba Linda*, Rykodisc LTD. Courtesy of John Child.

88. Alfredo Rodríguez, interview with John Child, December 15, 1990. Recorded at FM Studios, 26–27 Castlereagh Street, London, W1H 5DL. Child recorded this interview while Rodríguez was in town for a gig at the Bass Clef between Tuesday and Saturday, December 11–15, 1990. Child informed me that the interview with Rodríguez was done for the radio show "Aracataca," which began on London pirate stations and ran for a year on Jazz FM. Unfortunately, the station was axed before the interview got to air. "Aracataca" currently runs as an Internet show via totally radio.com. More thanks to John Child for this incredible material.

89. In Cuba, a solar is a housing project typically built around a center courtyard.

90. Martí is the voice on Patato y Totico's seminal 1968 self-titled recording. See Cristóbal Díaz-Ayala's *Encyclopedic Discography of Cuban Music 1925–1960 Online*, s.v. "Virgilio Martí," accessed August 11, 2009, http://latinpop.fiu.edu/download files2.html. Díaz-Ayala has his birth in Havana in 1919. Martí has a cameo in León Ichaso's 1985 *Crossover Dreams*. In one scene he teaches Rubén Blades—who plays a musician new to the scene—his most famous song "Todos Vuelven."

91. El Goyo was a founding member of Cuba's Conjunto Folklórico Nacional and a vital presence on the Cuban rumba scene for decades. For information on El Goyo, see María del Carmen Mestas, *Pasión de rumbero* (Barcelona: Puvill Libros; La Habana: Pablo de la Torrente, 1998), 99–103. Mestas's book is an indispensible resource for biographical information on Cuban rumberos. Also see the interview with Gregorio Hernández by Patrice (last name unknown), conducted during the Stage International course at Tournai, Belgium, in August 2005. From the blog "¡Vamos a Guarachar!," http://esquinarumbera.blogspot.com/2006/12/interview -with-gregorio-el-goyo.html. Accessed August 8, 2009.

92. A guaracha is a specific kind of dance. As Helio Orovio explains, "A genuine Cuban style of song and dance whose origins are found in the confluence of African and Spanish musical elements. Originally an element of typically Cuban nineteenth-century comic theater (*bufo*), it later moved into the dance halls. Throughout the nineteenth century, the *guaracha's* structure, comprising couplet and refrain, led to a new format characterized by a solo singing section, followed by a response from a chorus. . . . Its lyrics are, in general, picaresque, burlesque, and satirical, mirroring the atmosphere of the time and dealing with popular affairs or humorous events," Orovio, *Cuban Music*, 102.

93. See Grever's obituary in the *New York Times*. "Maria Grever, 57, A Composer, Dies," *New York Times*, December 16, 1951, 90.

94. The song is a bolero. According to the encyclopedic entry in *Grove Music Online*, Grever was born in León, Guanajuato in 1885 and died in New York City in 1951. When reaching thirty, Grever and her husband (an oil executive) permanently moved to New York where she premiered several operettas (as performer and composer). To her name she has writing credit for 850 songs. Her megahits include the Latin standards "Bésame" (1921) and "Júrame" (1927). Her biggest crossover US successes include "Magic in the Moonlight" (1929) featured in the movie "Nancy Goes to Rio"; and "What a Difference a Day Makes" written in 1934, but popularized by Dinah Washington when she won a Grammy for it in 1959. Robert Stevenson, "Grever, María," in *Grove Music Online*, Oxford Music Online, accessed August 12, 2009, http://www.oxfordmusiconline.com/subscriber/article/grove /music/54032. English lyrics were later written by Stanley Adams. For Grever's

performance reviews, see "New Music From Spain," *New York Times*, December 15, 1919, 15.

95. "Presents "Song Dramas," *New York Times*, February 14, 1927, 14.

96. See "Mexico the Theme of a New Musical," *New York Times*, August 2, 1941, 18.

97. "Maria Grever's Works Sung," *New York Times (1857–Current file)*; March 6, 1939; ProQuest Historical Newspapers, *New York Times* (1851–2006), 11.

98. Odilio Urfé turned "The Well-Tempered Clavier" into a danzón and used it as the first song in the soundtrack to the documentary *Nosotros, la musica*, which I discuss in chapter 4.

99. Theodor W. Adorno, "On Tradition," *Telos* 94 (Winter 1992): 75.

100. Miké Charroppin, liner notes for *Cuba Linda*. See Lydia Cabrera and her indispensable work on Palo Monte (Bantu) in the late 1970s. This song brought me closer to Cabrera's work. See her *Reglas de Congo: Palo Monte* Mayombe, 2nd ed. (Miami: Ediciones Universal, 2005).

101. Don Pancho was one of the founding members of Orquesta Maravilla de Florida, an important and body-rocking Cuban dance band. For more on the chekeré and other Afro-Cuban musical instruments see Fernando Ortiz, *Los instrumentos de la música Afrocubana: El quinto, el llamador, tambores de rumba, el taburete, tambores de las comparsas carabalíes* (La Habana: Letras Cubanas, 1995).

102. Don Eladio Pancho, interview by author, August 29, 2008, in Havana, Cuba.

103. Leonardo Acosta, from "On Generic Complexes and Other Topics in Cuban Popular Music," trans. Daniel Whitesell and Raúl Fernández, *Journal of Popular Music Studies* 17, no. 3 (December 2005): 246.

104. Acosta, *Cubano Be, Cubano Bop*, 28.

105. Ibid., 51.

106. Ibid., 93. His artistic activity in New York was especially prolific. Other fascinating stops on Grenet's resume: Grenet's music was featured in the floor show at The Club Yumuri, a club on Broadway and 52nd Street in 1936. See "Night Club Notes," *New York Times*, November 28, 1936, 12. He led the orchestra for a 1939 revue at El Chico Theater at Sheridan Square. Note the following review: "El Chico, at the Sheridan Square crossroads, unleashes a new Spanish revue in its usual spirited and colorful manner. Eliseo Grenet is there leading the orchestra through the intricacies of the Latin rhythm and also furnishing the accompaniment for a show which includes especially Fantasia Novoa, thumping a barbaric drum while dancing about the floor in a manner not demure." Theodore Strauss, "News and Notes of the Night Club World," *New York Times*, February 19, 1939, 124. He was also part of the Ciro Rimac's 1940 "Pan American Revue" at La Conga. Morse

"News of Night Clubs," *New York Times*, June 9, 1940, X2. He did the book for "A Yank in Havana," which premiered at the Havana-Madrid Nightclub in 1942. Louis Calta, "News of Night Clubs," *New York Times*, November 22, 1942, X5. It is interesting that though Grenet died in Vedado, his Havana obituaries were printed in the *New York Times* and the *Chicago Daily Tribune*. Which is to say, even in death, these artists were a presence on both sides of the Gulf.

CHAPTER 2

1. Fred Moten and Stefano Harney, "The University and the Undercommons: Seven Theses," *Social Text 79* 22, no. 2 (Summer 2004): 101–2.

2. Josh Kun, *Audiotopia: Music, Race, and America* (Berkeley: University of California Press, 2005), 22.

3. Sleeve notes, author unknown, *Bola de Nieve con su piano (Cuban Folklore)*, Montilla Records FM-62; (other number on vinyl label: F8-OP-8490).

4. The conflation of musicians and subversives is hardly an original venture. Nor is it without its problems. I am not making automatic links between music and activism, musician and subversive, or demanding a particular politics from those I choose to study. To draw a prescriptive for the qualifications of a subversive intellectual would commit oneself to espionage, and not the good kind either.

5. *Nosotros, la música: The Golden Age of Cuban Music*, directed by Rogelio París, First Run Features, 2008 (originally released in 1964), DVD.

6. It is difficult and somewhat disheartening to reduce the complexities of the Machadato era in the space of this essay. For a few historical overviews and the aftermath of the era (which includes the eventual entry of Fulgencio Batista onto the national scene), see Louis A. Pérez Jr., "Cuba, c.1930–1959," in *Cuba: A Short History*, ed. Leslie Bethell (Cambridge: Cambridge University Press, 1993), 57–94; and Thomas E. Skidmore and Peter H. Smith, "Cuba: Late Colony, First Socialist State," in *Modern Latin America*, 4th ed. (New York: Oxford University Press, 1997), 270–77.

7. Pérez, "Cuba, c.1930–1959," 59.

8. Ibid., 61–67.

9. It is important to note that as many as three hundred of the university's professors openly declared their solidarity with the students. These student movements were formed into actual political parties after the university's closure. Hugh Thomas, *Cuba: In Pursuit of Freedom* (New York: Da Capo Press, 1998), 591–92.

10. "Twelve Hurt in Cuban Riot," *Los Angeles Times*, October 1, 1930, section 1, p. 4. Later, during another demonstration on December 3, 1930, a large group

of students was arrested on the occasion of Machado's reopening the university. The students were protesting Machado's choice of the new president Rodriguez Molina, who had been historically hostile against students accused of "communistic activities." This event was notable because a policeman was killed by a black powder bomb placed under the desk of the dean's office; but more so (indicated by one bold byline) as the demonstration was "Headed By Girls." In the end, a student manifesto emerged describing the rationale of Machado's decision behind the university's restoration: "to create among American bankers an impression of normalcy in the republic so that negotiations for consolidation of Cuba's national indebtedness might proceed." From: "Policeman Killed as Students Riot," *Washington Post*, December 4, 1930, section 1, p. 3.

11. Carleton Beals, *The Crime of Cuba* (Philadelphia: Lippincott, 1933), 281.

12. Ernesto Lecuona (1895–1963) was one of Cuba's most internationally well-known composers. He authored hundreds of songs that have found their way into the standards, including "La Comparsa," "La Malagueña," and "Siboney."

13. Pérez, *Cuba: A Short History*, 62.

14. I initially culled and pieced together a variety of sources regarding facts on Anacaona (the name of Castro's group), all of which conflict with one another. They are nonetheless worth mentioning: Cristóbal Díaz Ayala's entry in the online F.I.U. catalogues, *The Encyclopedic Discography of Cuban Music 1925–1960*; Helio Orovio *Cuban Music from A to Z* (2004); Robin Moore *Nationalizing Blackness: Afrocubanismo and Artistic Revolution in Havana* (1997); Leonardo Acosta *Cubano Be, Cubano Bop* (2003). Two forms of documentation of La Anacaona are included in two excellent sidebars (with photos included) in Raúl A. Fernández's, *Latin Jazz: La Combinación Perfecta* and Sue Steward's *¡Musica! The Rhythm of Latin America: Salsa, Rumba, Merengue, and More.* There is a concise entry in Radamés Giro's *Diccionario enciclopédico de la música en Cuba* (Habana: Letras Cubanas, 2007), 54. The origins of the chapter have much to do with an oral history interview conducted by Raúl A. Fernández and Rene López for the Latino Oral History Project (engineered by Matt Watson. Sound recording, September 19, 1998, National Museum of American History, The Latino Oral History Project). This recording was generously put into my universe by Licia Fiol-Matta. And finally, in this chapter I rely heavily on a series of interviews I conducted with Graciela directly, from early 2007 to the end of 2008. Another invaluable resource has been the documentary, *Anacaona: Ten Sisters of Rhythm*, produced and directed Ingrid Kummels and Manfred Schäfer, 85 min., fulltimemedia Schäfer /Kummels, 2003, DVD. Kummels is the half-German daughter of Millo Castro, the percussionist for the Orquesta Anacaona. The documentary collects stories and photographs from the five then-living

Castro sisters in Havana during Cuba's special period. Kummels later turned her extensive research and family history into a stunning labor of love: a collaborative book she wrote with her aunt Alicia Castro (to whom she gives primary authorship) that I turn to throughout the chapter. See Alicia Castro's (with Ingrid Kummels and Manfred Schäfer) *Queens of Havana: The Amazing Adventures of Anacaona, Cuba's Legendary All-Girl Dance Band*, trans. Steven T. Murray (New York: Grove Press, 2007). Alicia Castro saw her sister's entrance into the university as an explicitly feminist gesture. She notes, "By 1925 she (Cuchito) had taken a place at the University... That marked her as a complete outsider. 'Mujer que aprende Latín no puede tener buen fin... was a riff she often heard. Her dream was to have her own dental practice, lead an independent life." Ibid., 43. Of her family's mixed-race background, Alicia Castro plays down her black ancestry, "On our father's side, we have Chinese grandparents and on our mother's side a Basque grandfather. There may have been Africans involved as well, but no one knows for sure." Ibid., 23.

15. Areito is a word used to describe the sacred musical and dance forms of indigenous groups performed during the Spanish conquest. Queen Anacaona is the disputed author of one of the only remaining areitos, at other times this same composition is attributed by a composer named Sánchez de Fuentes active in Cuba in the early twentieth century. Incidentally, de Fuentes's position in regards to the "Africanist" presence in Cuban music was one of disavowal. According to Helio Orovio, areitos went unrecorded by the Spanish colonial mercenaries. See Helio Orovio, *Cuban Music From A to Z*, 18–19. Thus, little documentation exists on native expressive culture, and the word *areito* was used as discursive convenience to mark their diverse happenings in music and dance. In the Spanish-speaking Caribbean, areito colloquially means a party and/or a celebration.

16. Edwidge Danticat, "We Are Ugly, But We Are Here," *The Caribbean Writer* 10 (1996): 137–41. Anacaona has been circulated throughout the Circum-Caribbean as a genealogical figure, one that Edwidge Danticat names as the instructive forebear for the self-named "Daughters of Anacaona." Danticat has recently written an account of Anacaona's life in the form of the actual queen's diary. *Anacaona Golden Flower: Haiti, 1490* (2005) is intended for young adult readers as part of "The Royal Diaries" series published by Scholastic. Danticat's challenge in writing the text was to recreate the life-world of the Taíno's with little written evidence—using the scant objects left behind as part of her guide. Danticat thus fleshes out this interpretive history with her genealogical imagination. As Danticat writes in the closing line of the text, "in some very primal way, Anacaona has always been in my blood and I remain, in the deepest part of my soul, one of her most faithful subjects." While I hesitate to flatten by comparison, Danticat offers a method of writing about Cuban

women musicians, another set of histories left with little written notation albeit for different reasons. There is also a Haitian women's writing and reading group in South Florida founded under Anacaona's name.

17. Castro's naming also helps to render Haiti as a kind of "Undercommons of the Enlightenment" generally speaking.

18. Kummels and Schäfer, *Anacaona*, 2003. In *Queens of Anacaona*, Alicia Castro notes that their father was initially "dead against us performing in the open-air cafes, saying that there was no way his daughters were going to work at night near the sleezy bars and brothels." She goes on, "I would also have mentioned that we stood our ground in the face of male chauvinists, who believed that a woman's place was in the home by the stove or working in a brothel" (10). Also, she notes that her father was disapproving at first, but Cuchito persistently pushed her father to allow it; he eventually agreed that Cuchito could make it work and then became her and the band's biggest advocate and enthusiast (51–52).

19. Leonardo Acosta notes that this proliferation of all women bands is, "a unique development in our musical history . . . whether they were in jazz bands or not, was a trend that inexplicably died out and has not been regenerated even at times when women's liberation and the fight against male chauvinism . . . are so persistently pursued." Acosta, *Cubano Be, Cubano Bop*, 52. Acosta remarks, "These bands performed for many years in the Aires Libres, the cafes located on the esplanade opposite the Capitolio, contributing to the unique character and touristic attractiveness of this place, from the 1930s through the 1950s, until its disappearance in the 1960s." Leonardo Acosta, *Cubano Be, Cubano Bop: One Hundred Years of Jazz in Cuba*, trans. Daniel S. Whitesell (Washington and London: Smithsonian Books, 2003), 52. In his book *Cuba and Its Music: From the First Drums to the Mambo*, Ned Sublette offers a short list of a few of these all-women groups. Included among them: the Orquesta Orbe, Orquesta Ensueño, Orquesta Social, Las Hermanas Álvarez, Las Hermanas Martí, Renovación, Las Indias del Caribe. Sublette reports that many of these women groups (or orquestas femeninas as they were called), were featured in many cafés on hotel strip on the Prado, a boulevard in Centro Habana, an important site of nightlife for tourists and "Havana bohemians." These groups were present there until the 1950s. Ned Sublette, *Cuba and Its Music* (Chicago: Chicago Review Press, 2004), 426–27.

20. Kummels and Schäfer, *Anacaona*, 2003.

21. There is one easily available compilation of the group for purchase. It contains works by the Orquesta Anacaona from 1937 and recordings by the Peruvian bandleader Ciro Rimac. *Septeto Anacaona and Ciro Rimac (1936–1937)*, Harlequin Records, HQ CD 27, 1993, compact disc.

22. I lingered in and on these traditions in chapter 1.

23. Kummels and Schäfer, *Anacaona*, 2003.

24. Frances R. Aparicio, "La Lupe, La India, and Celia: Toward a Feminist Genealogy of Salsa Music," in *Situating Salsa: Global Markets and Local Meaning in Latin Popular Music*, ed. Lise Waxer (New York: Routledge, 2002), 135–60.

25. Graciela Pérez, interview by author, minute 15:44, February 5, 2007, at her home in NYC. Alicia Castro notes that Graciela replaced group member Elia O'Reilly after she decided to pursue a married life. At first, Martino, the owner of El Dorado objected because she was too "chubby." But he couldn't deny that they, with Graciela, attracted the biggest crowds. Kummels and Schäfer, *Anacaona*, 2003; Castro, *Queens of Anacaona*, 90.

26. The *Queens of Anacaona* only mentions Graciela contingently, at the same time that it seems like she was an integral part of the band when they went international. Alicia Castro speaks of her with nothing but terms of endearment and inclusion; but Graciela does not get written into the story as centrally as the other sisters.

27. Graciela Pérez, interview by author, minute 18:00, February 5, 2007, at her home in NYC.

28. For an outline of his early Havana work, see Acosta, *Cubano Be, Cubano Bop*, 105–6.

29. Both of these formative details ted by Graciela in several different interviews, including my own and the one she recorded for the Oral History Project for the National Museum of American History.

30. Graciela Pérez, interview by author, February 5, 2007, at her home in NYC.

31. Ibid.

32. I'm especially grateful to scholar Licia Fiol-Matta for providing me with this interview. In addition to facilitating Graciela's history in her own words, this oral account was part of the larger data collection for the exhibition "Latin Jazz: The Perfect Combination/La Combinación Perfecta" (also the title of the exhibition's textual accompaniment) in association with the Smithsonian Institution Traveling Exhibition Service. Curated by Raúl A. Fernández, the exhibition was one of the vital initiatives for archiving the development of Latin jazz in the United States in a formal institutional setting. The scope of the bilingual, mixed-media exhibition spans from mid-nineteenth century New Orleans to the current state of Latin jazz and its contemporary players. In both the exhibit and the accompanying text, Graciela and her contributions to this larger history refreshingly occupy an important space.

33. Naomi Schor, *Reading in Detail: Aesthetics and the Feminine* (New York: Routledge, 2007), xliii.

34. Candido Camero and Graciela Pérez, *Inolvidable*, Chesky Records JD 249, compact disc.

35. Yolanda Broyles-González, "Background and Analysis," in *Lydia Mendoza's Life in Music/La historia de Lydia Mendoza* (New York: Oxford University Press, 2001), 180. In Mendoza's case specifically, the borderlands are material in that her actual body has had to tread a border that had rendered her "legal" on one day and "illegal" the next.

36. Ibid., 200.

37. In his work, José Esteban Muñoz uses "minoritarian" as a term to subvert the false empirical hierarchy that constitutes the term "majoritarian." He also defines the "minoritarian subject" in relationship to the majoritarian public sphere in the United States. The public sphere in this sense is one that privileges whiteness, the masculine, the "native born," and the heterosexual. The subject is subsequently left with uneasy (indeed, impossible) modes of identification. Muñoz argues that the minoritarian subject must, "interface with different subcultural fields to activate their own senses of self." The minoritarian subject can be understood as improvising with the world around them—even in its most flawed or false rendering. The word "minoritarian" is particularly useful when thinking about US Latinas/os, whose racial and ethnic identifications often occlude the simplistic terms required by the state. See José Esteban Muñoz, *Disidentifications: Queers of Color and the Performance of Politics* (Minneapolis: University of Minnesota Press, 1999), 5.

38. In Cuban Spanish, "Americano" denotes a visibly Anglo/white person from the United States.

39. Severo Sarduy, *Christ on the Rue Jacob*, trans. Susanne Jill Levine and Carol Maier (San Francisco: Mercury House, 1995), 139.

40. The phenomenon I describe here is often referred to as choteo. In his book *Latin Americanisms*, author Román de la Campa generously offers a clear, rudimentary definition of the complicated phenomena of choteo. He defines choteo as "a tendency to joke around, a dismissal of all that pretends to be profound, or simply a failure to take seriously serious matters, has been historically seen as an inherent defect of Cuba's national culture first articulated by Jorge Mañach in his well-known *Indagación del choteo*." Román de la Campa, *Latin Americanisms* (Minneapolis: University of Minnesota Press, 1999), 97. See also Jorge Mañach, *Indagación del choteo* (Miami: Ediciones Universal, 1991). For an excellent analysis of *choteo*, see Gustavo Pérez Firmat, "Riddles of the Sphincter," in *Literature and Liminality: Festive Readings in the Hispanic Tradition* (Durham, NC: Duke University Press, 1986).

41. Interview conducted by Raúl A. Fernández and Rene López. According to Alicia Castro, they met Socarrás in Cuba, who then brought the girls to NYC where they were adored for their son music. However, because of strict restrictions

imposed by the musician's labor union, they were not allowed to play jazz/dance music, forced instead to only playing son. Socarrás wanted to help them expand their repertoire and market them internationally, so he would regularly meet with the girls at 2 AM after they finished their gig and practiced jazz numbers with them. He then brought Carl Fischer, owner of an important artists' agency who was trying to co-organize a big show in Paris with the head of the International Casino of New York in Paris. They were looking for a band. This is how Anacaona got booked for their gig at Les Ambassadeurs in Paris. Before their trip to Europe, they did indeed stop in Havana with Socarrás to practice for two weeks straight. Anacaona was now an eight-piece ensemble (including Graciela). Castro, *Queens of Anacaona*, 157–64.

42. Kummels and Schäfer, *Anacaona*, 2003.

43. Socarrás was an important flautist and composer, part of the first wave of Cuban musicians to New York City in the twentieth century.

44. Langston Hughes, *The Big Sea* (New York: Hill and Wang, 2nd ed. 1993), 171–75. For an evocative reading of this particular episode see Lindon Barret, "The Gaze of Langston Hughes: Subjectivity, Homoeroticism, and the Feminine in *The Big Sea*" in *The Yale Journal of Criticism* 12, no. 2 (1999): 383–97. For an overview of the presence of Harlem musicians and performers in Montmartre, See William A. Shack's *Harlem in Montmartre: A Paris Jazz Story between the Great Wars* (Berkeley: University of California Press, 2001). In his text, Shack makes several references to Florence Jones.

45. Hughes, *The Big Sea*, 172.

46. Ibid., 172.

47. Ibid., 175.

48. Hughes, *The Big Sea*, 176

49. Even Bola de Nieve, who is discussed at length in my introduction, made an appearance at Chez Florence in 1951. Leonardo Depestre's "Bola de Nieve, con su sonrisa y su canción," in *Cuátro músicos de una villa* (La Habana: Editorial Letras Cubanas, 1990), 89.

50. For more on how I describe this as part of the "studies protocols" of jazz studies, see chapter 1. For a concise and brief history that takes into account the gendering of this phenomenon in criticism, see Nichole T. Rustin and Sherrie Tucker's "Introduction" to *Big Ears: Listening for Gender in Jazz Studies* (Durham, NC: Duke University Press, 2008), 1–30.

51. Geoffrey Jacques, "CuBop! Afro-Cuban Music and Mid-Twentieth-Century American Culture," in *Between Race and Empire: African-Americans and Cubans before the Cuban Revolution*, ed. Lisa Brock and Digna Castañeda Fuertes (Philadelphia: Temple University Press, 1998), 253.

52. George Lipsitz, "Song of the Unsung: The Darby Hicks History of Jazz," in *Uptown Conversation: The New Jazz Studies*, ed. Robert G. O'Meally, Brent Hayes Edwards, and Farah Jasmine Griffin (New York: Columbia University Press, 2004), 14.

53. Again, Langston Hughes documents that Jones occupied and developed the Chez Florence after departing Le Grand Duc for their mistreatment of a fellow worker. Hughes quotes Jones as exclaiming, "Can't nobody hit a woman in any place where I work" before her departure. Chez Florence was founded, among other reasons, as a place where that kind of violence was not tolerated.

54. Jody Blake, *Le Tumulte Noir: Modernist Art and Popular Entertainment in Jazz-Age Paris, 1900–1930* (University Park: Pennsylvania State University Press, 1999), 119.

55. On the turf of the Parisian metropolis, Graciela's performance stands up to André Breton's reverberating axiom that decreed "Silence as Golden" ten years prior—unbearable and uncontainable noises coming from an outside.

56. On a side note: Graciela, who was never married and is childless, has undoubtedly been asked to explain her "escuela rara" in a variety of forms. In one concrete example, the oral history interviewer Rene López seems to peck at this question at about hour three in the session asking her if she was ever married or had any children. Without missing a beat, Graciela immediately retorts that she has "lots of nieces and nephews."

57. Many thanks to José Esteban Muñoz for helping me work out this particular formulation.

58. Such viejo marketability would reach late century heights with the release of Ry Cooder's production *Buena Vista Social Club*.

59. The Cuban presence in Paris, especially before and between the wars, begs for continued scholarship of all kinds. Lydia Cabrera, Alejo Carpentier, the infamous tanguera dancer Gloria Ideal, Severo Sarduy, and countless others have all made an imprint in France. A catalogue of the musicians that specifically passed and played through Paris is a much larger project in vital need of realization.

60. Recent scholarship continues to emerge that undermines the myth of domestic stasis assumed of women of the African diaspora. For an examination of women as active participants in the Black Internationalism (specifically its print culture) of the 1920s, see Brent Hayes Edwards, "Feminism and *L'Internationalisme Noir*" in *The Practice of Diaspora*.

61. My evocation of "maroon encampments" is intended as a return to Moten and Harvey's formulation of the undercommons. But it also is an attempt to take up the important work of scholars such as Carolyn Cooper. In her book, *Noises in the Blood*, Cooper defines marronage as, "that tradition of resistance science that

establishes an alternative psychic space both within and beyond the boundaries of the enslaving plantation." Carolyn Cooper, *Noises in the Blood: Orality, Gender, and the "Vulgar" Body of Jamaican Popular Culture* (Durham, NC: Duke University Press, 1995), 4.

62. Caren Kaplan, Norma Alarcón, and Minoo Moallem, introduction to *Between Woman and Nation: Nationalisms, Transnational Feminisms, and the State*, ed. by Caren Kaplan, Norma Alarcón, and Minoo Moallem (Durham, NC: Duke University Press, 1999), 13.

63. I would like to call attention to Raquel Z. Rivera's *New York Ricans in the Hip Hop Zone* (New York: Palgrave Macmillan, 2003) as a contemporary example of scholarship that looks at the relationship between blackness and *latinidad*.

64. Graciela Pérez, interview by author, February 5, 2007, at her home in NYC.

65. Orovio, *Cuban Music from A to Z*, trans. Ricardo Bardo Portilla and Lucy Davies (Durham, NC: Duke University Press, 2004), 129.

66. Radamés Giro, *Diccionario enciclopédico de la música Cubana*, Tomo 1 (Havana: Editorial Letras Cubanas, 2007), s.v. "Bauzá Cárdenas, Mario," 100–101. Some of Bauzá's most covered songs include "Cubop City," "Tanga," and (with René Hernández and Bobby Woodlen) "Mambo Inn."

67. From Díaz Ayala's encyclopedia entry for "Machito": "La agrupación seinició con tres saxos y dos trompetas, piano, contrabajo, bongó, tumbadora y timbales, a la que luego se anexaron dos trombones, una trompeta y dos saxos -generalmente músicos de Jazz-. Ese mismo año grabaron para el sello Decca su primer éxito *Sopa de pichón*. En julio de 1942 la orquesta respaldó a Miguelito Valdés en 26 grabaciones para Decca y en 1943 la banda prácticamente se desintegró al ser llamados a las filas del ejército norteamericano varios integrantes, entre estos el propio Machito a quien Bauzá remplazó con Marcelino Guerra y Polito Galíndez y sumó a Graciela, hermana de Machito." Cristóbal Díaz Ayala, *The Encyclopedic Discography of Cuban Music 1925–1960 Online*, s.v. "Machito," accessed June 16, 2011, http://latinpop.fiu.edu/composersabbr.html.

68. For a sense of the mambo environment on the Borscht Belt, see John Kun's article, "Bagels, Bongos, and Yiddishe Mambos, or The Other History of Jews in America," *Shofar: An Interdisciplinary Journal of Jewish Studies* 23, no. 4 (Summer 2005): 50–68.

69. This version of "El Cerebro" is from Machito and His Afro-Cubans and an album titled "Guampampiro." Tumbao Cuban Classics TCD-089 (1997). The liner notes say that these recordings were done in New York from 1945–1947. No specific dates given for each song.

70. Graciela Pérez, interview by author, February 5, 2007, at her home in NYC.

71. Ibid.

72. Possibly, the first studio recording per Díaz Ayala's encyclopedic entry, "195 _ Perfect 78 Sí, sí, no, no RBS 55019/20" The recording is featured on the album Machito and His Orchestra *Si, Si, No, No* in 1956 (Tico Records, reissued on Sonido Inc.).

73. Symphony Sid was the DJ name of Sid Torin, born in the Lower East Side but raised in Brooklyn. I'm grateful to Graciela and her then assistant Mappy Torres for providing me with copies of these performances. They were the first two tracks featured on her homemade compilation, "Graciela: Happy New Year 2007."

74. For more on women's sexuality and the blues, see Angela Davis's influential *Blues Legacies and Black Feminism: Gertrude "Ma" Rainey, Bessie Smith, and Billie Holiday* (New York: Vintage, 1999). Although they might be considered rough contemporaries, Graciela is of the generation following Rita Montaner. The material they both covered can and should be thought about as enriching the differences possible in performance. See and hear, for example, their separate recordings of the song "Ay, Jose." Montaner filmed a version of the song for one of the classic films of the Mexican golden age of cinema, Emilio Fernández's 1950 "Victimas Del Pecado." Graciela performed the song as part of her repertoire for some time, but made a studio recording of it on her first solo venture, the album "Esta Es Graciela with Machito."

75. Eric Porter, *What Is This Thing Called Jazz? African American Musicians as Artists* (Berkeley: University of California Press, 2002), 79.

76. I have written on Summer's performance in my "Can You Feel the Beat? Freestyle's Systems of Living, Loving and Recording," *Social Text 102* 28, no. 1 (2010): 107–24.

77. George Hutchinson, "Introduction" from *In Search of Nella Larson: A Biography of the Color Line* (Cambridge and London: Belknap Press of Harvard University Press, 2006), 10. Thanks to Shane Vogel for sharing this important text with me.

78. Jamer Hunt, "The Mirrored Stage: Reflections on the Presence of Slyvia [Bataille] Lacan" in *The Ends of Performance*, eds. Peggy Phelan and Jill Lane (New York and London: New York University Press, 1998), 236–37.

79. Farah Jasmine Griffin, *If You Can't Be Free, Be a Mystery: In Search of Billie Holiday* (New York: The Free Press, 2001), 156–57.

80. Interview with the author, February 2007.

81. Perhaps it was retained from a primer by the nineteenth-century Spanish composer Hilarión Eslava, a figure musicians have long turned to for rules although he was considered musically adulterated in his time.

82. "Contigo en la distancia" was written by César Portillo de la Luz.

CHAPTER 3

1. From the documentary *The Palladium: Where Mambo Was King*, directed by Kevin Kaufman (Kaufman Films, 2002), VHS.

2. I am greatly indebted to Harryette Mullen's article for this text. In Harryette Mullen, "African Signs and Spirit Writing," *Callaloo* 19, no. 3 (1996): 681. Original in Timothy Maliqalim Simone, *About Face: Race in Postmodern America* (Brooklyn: Autonomedia, 1989).

3. I am also indebted to Jon Cruz's influential and beautiful discussion about the knowledge produced around African American song, particularly the confounding place of "noise" for interpretation. In his *Culture in the Margins*, Cruz writes,

Basically, noise is sound out of order. It is sound that lacks—and even defies organization. As such it cannot be grasped because the schemas with which it is to be comprehended lack the categories for processing it along lines of order. Noise simply evades. It eludes culturally normative categories of cognition because it does not fit them; it is rejected sound that spills out of, or flows over, the preferred channels along which known, accepted, and regulated sounds occur.

Jon Cruz, *Culture in the Margins: The Black Spiritual and the Rise of American Cultural Interpretation* (Princeton: Princeton University Press, 1999), 47–48.

4. Taken from a 1985 interview with Merry Mac Masters, "Dámaso Pérez Prado, el pueblo quiere mambo," in *Recurdos del son* (México: Periodismo Cultural, 1995), 126.

5. By the performative life of the grunt, I mean what it produces along the lines of the Derridian trace—the substances that remain in the wake of its apparent signification.

6. J. L. Austin, *How to Do Things with Words*, 2nd ed. (Cambridge: Harvard University Press, 1975). Although I nevertheless evoke it, Pérez Prado's grunt occupies a tenuous position within the Austinian formulation of the "performative." The performative utterance is "the issuing of the utterance is the performing of an action-it is not normally though of as just saying something" (7). The grunt would most likely make the first cut under the section titled "Preliminary Isolation of the Performative"; its linguistic "masquerade" with meaning might qualify the grunt as "a type of nonsense."

7. Notable Cuban musicological texts that have included Pérez Prado in their scope are Natalio Galán's *Cuba y sus sones*, Alejo Carpentier's somewhat dismissive comments in *Ese músico que llevo dentro*, an entry in Helio Orovio's *Cuban Music from A to Z*, and Leonardo Acosta's foundational *Cubano Be, Cubano Bop*. Outside of Cuba, there are a good amount of performance and record reviews by such crit-

ics as Robert Farris Thompson, John Storm Roberts in *The Latin Tinge*, and liner notes by Watson Wylie and Peter Grendysa. Several current texts have provided a few contextual blips of Pérez Prado's effects in their pages, including Ned Sublette's comprehensive hardcover *Cuba and Its Music*, Jory Farr's *Rites of Rhythm*, and Maya Roy's *Cuban Music*.

8. "El Mambo," *Newsweek*, September 4, 1950, 76.

9. Gustavo Pérez Firmat, *Life on the Hyphen: The Cuban-American Way* (Austin: University of Texas Press, 1994).

10. Leonardo Acosta, "Reajustes, aclaraciones y criterios sobre Dámaso Pérez Prado," in *El mambo*, ed. Radamés Giro (La Habana: Editorial Letras Cubanas, 1993), 61.

11. Gustavo Pérez Firmat, *Life on the Hyphen*, 91.

12. Fernando Ortiz, *Cuban Counterpoint*, trans. Harriet de Onís (Durham, NC: Duke University Press, 1995), xxix.

13. Erena Hernández, "Conversación con Pérez Prado," in *La música en persona* (La Habana: Editorial Letras Cubanas, 1986), 13. Reprinted in Radamés Giro, ed. *El mambo* (La Habana: Editorial Letras Cubanas, 1993), 43.

14. Erena Hernández, "Conversación con Pérez Prado," in *El mambo*, ed. Radamés Giro (La Habana: Editorial Letras Cubanas, 1993), 44.

15. Taken from a 1985 interview with Merry Mac Masters, "Dámaso Pérez Prado, el pueblo quiere mambo," in *Recurdos del son* (México: Periodismo Cultural, 1995), 120. It is amusing to see his curt replies to Masters who, throughout the interview, reveals how little homework she has done. Paulina Álvarez (1912–1965) was one of the most important women in Cuban popular music. She was an accomplished singer who began forming her own orchestras in 1938. See Radamés Giro's entry on her in the *Diccionario enciclopédico de la música Cubana*, Tomo 1. La Habana: Letras Cubanas, 2007.

16. Radamés Giro, *Diccionario enciclopédico de la música Cubana*, Tomo 3, 223.

17. Ana M. López, "Tears and Desire: Women and Melodrama in the 'Old' Mexican Cinema," in *Mediating Two Worlds: Cinematic Encounters in the Americas*, ed. John King, Ana M. López, and Manuel Alvarado (London: British Film Institute, 1993), 148.

18. Peter Grendysa, liner notes for "Pérez Prado and His Orchestra," *Mondo mambo!*, Rhino Records R2 71889/DRCI-1241.

19. Union logistics could cause long delays for performers. In 1951, for example, *DownBeat* magazine reported that Prado was prevented from playing with Local 802 musicians in New York; an expedited union card, "would be unfair to other leaders, and that the six-month waiting period would be necessary." "Prado Denied Job With Band Here; Needs AFM Card," *DownBeat* 18, no. 10, May 18, 1951.

20. Ned Sublette, *Cuba and Its Music* (Chicago: Chicago Review Press, 2004), 554.

21. I cannot and do not want to ignore other Cuban notables who were part of Mambo's formative air, including Orestes López, Beny Moré, Israel "Cachao" López, and Bebo Valdés.

22. "El Mambo," *Newsweek*, September 4, 1950, 76. In the December 28, 1951, issue of *Downbeat*, he offers the following on Stan Kenton, "It is my hope that the people will catch up to Kenton. . . . The Americans learn the dances so fast it amazes me . . . It proves they have a strong musical sense. Then why don't they understand the music of Stan Kenton? I cannot figure it out." Don Freeman, "Prado Has Touch That Sets Fire to Band, Says SideMan," *DownBeat*, December 28, 1951, 19.

23. Pérez Firmat, *Life on the Hyphen*, 87.

24. Ibid., 196, fn. 18.

25. Such a minimizing narration is also used to described Xavier Cugat. "Mambomania," *Newsweek*, August 15, 1954, 54.

26. Sublette, *Cuba and Its Music*, 579–80. Also see "Prado One-Nighter Sets L. A. On Ear," *Down Beat*, September 21, 1951, and "Swingin' the Golden Gate," *Down Beat*, October 5, 1951.

27. Leonardo Acosta, *Cubano Be, Cubano Bop,* trans. Daniel S. Whitesell (Washington and London: Smithsonian Books, 2003), 87–88.

28. The liner notes on this record deserve a brief mention as they reveal a provocative diversity of receptive practices. Jose Ferrer prepares the listener to this Prado-Clooney mash-up with the following: "But if, unaccountably, you are surprised by its easy excitement, devoid of stunts and freak effects, if you are puzzled by the comfortable blend of two apparently disparate talents, that's *your* problem."

29. In the textual realm, there currently exists a plethora of musical-travel narratives to Cuba, including Andrei Codrescu's *Ay Cuba!: A Socio-Erotic Journey* (1999), Jory Farr's *Rites of Rhythm* (2003), and Philip Sweeney's *The Rough Guide to Cuban Music* (2001). Allegories involving prostitutes, santería rituals, or metaphors using heat, all initiate these texts. In terms of recordings, there are too many compilations to mention here. Their casings seem to uniformly feature faux cigar box covers, American cars from the 1950s, a sweaty mojito cocktail, a light-skinned Cuban woman, or a dark skinned old Cuban man. These images are generally washed with sepia, at times interrupted by a splash of pastel. Of course, the *Buena Vista Social Club* created an enormous market for a handful of musicians. A Cuban representative is featured in the earth-friendly music series *Putumayo Presents*. A ubiquity of Cuban essentials or greatest-hits-type albums—typically of artists who were famous before 1959—are available for the novice collector. A few additional titles are *Cuban Patio, Stuck in Time, Cuba Si: Pure Cuban Flavor, Cuba: I Am*

Time, Diggin' in the Crates for Afro-Cuban Funk (which features a Puerto Rican flag on the cover). Anthologies that showcase Cuba with other Latino/a musicians, such as *Latin: The Essential Album* and *Salsa Clasica: A Taste of Classic Latin Flavors* are also available.

30. Ronaldo M. Radano and Philip V. Bohlman, "Music and Race, Their Past, Their Presence," Introduction from *Music and the Racial Imagination* (Chicago: University of Chicago Press, 2000), 6.

31. Ibid.

32. In addition to Giro's volume, which I will engage soon, there have been many narrations of mambo's history that I cite throughout these endnotes.

33. Wai Chee Dimock, "Genre as World System: Epic and Novel on Four Continents" in *Narrative* 14, no. 1 (January 2006): 85–101, quote on 86.

34. The "Special Period" refers to the difficult period in Cuba after the dissolution of the Soviet Union. The euphemism was coined by Fidel Castro to call upon the population to make (and be patient with) the sacrifices and shortages to come on the island as a result of losing their primary trading partner. This was one of the hungriest periods in Cuban history.

35. Radamés Giro, "Todo lo que usted quiso saber sobre el mambo," in *Mambo* ed. Radamés Giro (Editorial Letras Cubanas: La Habana, 1993), 5.

36. Literature on the subject abounds, even in mainstream US periodicals. See Ralph J. Gleason, "Latin Leaders Explain Origin of the Mambo," *DownBeat*, January 25, 1952. Also see the letter to the editor written by none other than Robert Farris Thompson to *Life Magazine* in response to their story, "Uncle Sambo, Mad for Mambo." In his letter, Thompson attempts to set the record straight by decentering Pérez Prado as mambo's sole inventor and instead describes mambo's multiple schools. *Life Magazine* 37, no. 25, December 20, 1954.

37. Giro, "Todo lo que usted quiso saber sobre el mambo," 6. The original citation comes from Helio Orovio's "Arsenio Rodríguez y el son Cubano," *Revolución y cultura* (la Habana), no. 7, July 1985.

38. The word "mambo" has many meanings and interpretations. Musicologist Odilio Urfé reminds that mambo has Haitian origins. In vodoun, a priestess is called mambo. Odilio Urfé, "La verdad sobre el mambo," in *Mambo*, ed. Radamés Giro (Editorial Letras Cubanas: La Habana, 1993), 31. Also see María Teresa Linares *La música y el pueblo* (La Habana: Editorial Pueblo y Educación, 1974), 159–68.

39. Hernández ibid.

40. Valdés was born in Cuba in 1918 and is considered one of Cuba's most important pianists, composers, and arrangers. He has been living in Sweden since 1963. As he pushed into his ninth decade, he experienced a bit of a career renaissance. The album *Lágrimas Negras* (and accompanying tour) he performed with the Spanish

flamenco singer Diego el Cigala was globally successful. He is also the father of Chucho Valdés whom I discuss in chapter 4.

41. Acosta, "Reajustes, aclaraciones y criterios sobre Dámaso Pérez Prado," 62.

42. Robert Farris Thompson has done much work to emphasize mambo's Africanness. See his *Flash of the Spirit: African and Afro-American Art and Philosophy* (New York: Random House, 1983).

43. Elena Pérez Sanjurjo, *Historia de la música Cubana* (Miami: La Moderna Poesía, 1986), 354.

44. Masters, "Dámaso Pérez Prado," 121. Mexico City is a crucial site of the mambo given the large numbers of practitioners who left Cuba and were able to popularize it there. Even the Cuban musical icon of all icons, Beny Moré, first found his audience in Mexico. Perhaps this is why he resorts to the Mexican slang word "chapparrito" (shorty) when launching Pérez Prado's nickname in "Locas por el mambo."

45. See Vernon Boggs, "The Palladium Ballroom and Other Venues," in *Salsiology: Afro-Cuban Music and the Evolution of Salsa in New York City* (New York: Greenwood Press, 1992), 127–31. See also Josh Kun, "Bagels, Bongos and Yiddishe Mambos, or the Other History of Jews in America," *Shofar: An Interdisciplinary Journal of Jewish Studies* 23, no. 4 (Summer 2005): 50–68.

46. See Danielle Goldman's work on mambo dancing in places such as the Palladium in her *I Want To Be Ready: Improvised Dance as a Practice of Freedom* (Ann Arbor: University of Michigan Press, 2010), 28–54.

47. See Raúl A. Fernández's *Latin Jazz: The Perfect Combination/La combinación perfecta*. Throughout his book Fernández takes refreshing care to mention the important developments of Latino/a musics on the West Coast, especially musicians such as Cal Tjader, Eddie Cano, Stan Kenton, and Paul López.

48. "Mambomania," *Newsweek*, August 15, 1954.

49. John Storm Roberts, *The Latin Tinge: The Impact of Latin American Music on the United States* (New York: Oxford University Press, 1999), 127.

50. "El Mambo," *Newsweek*, September 4, 1950, 76. Thanks to Patty Ahn for pointing me to this cover image.

51. *Life Magazine*, December 20, 1954. Accessed June 22, 2010 via http://books.google.com/books?id=WlMEAAAAMBAJ&pg=PA14&lpg=PA14&dq=uncle+sambo+mad+for+mambo+life+magazine&source=bl&ots=JdreCw5oUF&sig=buEj8oolom2odm13VFZ-2Mr3XiY&hl=en&ei=SkMWTPmoCMH71wfF54DTDA&sa=X&oi=book_result&ct=result&resnum=1&ved=oCBIQ6AEwAA#v=onepage&q=uncle%20sambo%20mad%20for%20mambo%20life%20magazine&f=false.

52. Gustavo Pérez Firmat has this to say about the defiant genre,

There's always been a certain petulance to the mambo, a kind of music that does not know its place. The name connotes excess, outrageousness, lack of decorum. A mambo mouth is a loud mouth, someone with a loose tongue, someone who doesn't abide by the rules of propriety. The mambo is nothing if not uncouth, improper, its musical improprieties sometimes even bordering on the *improperio*, the vulgar or offensive outburst. (81)

As provocative as Pérez Firmat's description is, the grunt, like virtually all performances of vulgar or offensive outbursts, often knows its time if not its proper place. After all, the musician serves as the focal and aural point in Pérez Firmat's chapter titled, "A Brief History of Mambo Time." Pérez Prado's grunt actually keeps the music in time as it is performed, much like a metronome or a conductor's arm keeps the tempo. What's more, it marks his labor as a conductor into the recording itself. Throughout Prado's discography, however, it is apparent that the grunt does not always come in at every marked measure or down beat. Here we have to imagine his conductive interplay with the band in the real-time of the recording. What did the bandleader want to produce by using the grunt at any given time? Pérez Prado marked the time (via the audible grunt) when he wanted to.

53. Acosta, *Cubano Be, Cubano Bop*, 66.

54. Pérez Firmat, *Life on the Hyphen*, 85.

55. Carpentier, *Music in Cuba*, trans. Alan West-Dúran (Minneapolis: University of Minnesota Press, 2001), 231. Also see Yvonne Daniel, "Cuban Dance: An Orchard of Carribean Creativity," in *Caribbean Dance from Abakuá to Zouk: How Movement Shapes Identity*, ed. Susanna Sloat (Gainesville: University Press of Florida, 2002), 23–55.

56. *Twist Goes Latin, Perez Prado*, Recorded at NYC's Webster Hall, produced by Herman Diaz Jr., engineered by Ray Hall, RCA LPM/LSP-2524, 1962.

57. *Las novias de Perez Prado*, Orfeon LP 12–630. The production of this album took place between Los Angeles and Naucalpan de Juárez, Edo. de Mexico.

58. In private conversations and interviews for example, Alfredo Rodríguez, Graciela, and La Lupe leave behind many disturbing and bitter reservations about the operations and legacies of Fania Records.

59. Richard Gehr, "World Beat: Perez Prado" *Spin Magazine* 9, no. 7 (October 1993): 106–7.

60. I briefly discuss the Cuban tradition of nicknaming via Sarduy in the Introduction. Sarduy came to pinpoint this tendency in the Cuban character after a conversation with Spanish writer Juan Goytisolo. Sarduy writes, "In a conversation, Juan Goytisolo pointed out to me the importance of diminutives in Cuban language. How curious, he said, that a country which always creates for itself such

a tremendous image of its wars would name one of its own wars the *Guerra Chiquita* (little war)." Severo Sarduy, *Written on a Body*, trans. Carol Maier (New York: Lumen Books, 1989), 64–65. For a description of choteo, see note 40 in chapter 3.

61. Watson Wylie, sleeve notes for *Pérez Prado and His Orchestra*, RCA Victor LPM 1883/ J2PP-502.

62. See Raquel Z. Rivera, *New York Ricans from the Hip Hop Zone* (New York: Palgrave Macmillan, 2003).

63. Piri Thomas, *Down These Mean Streets*, 3rd ed. (New York: Vintage Books, 1997), 109.

64. Danielle Goldman, *I Want to Be Ready: Improvised Dance as a Practice of Freedom* (Ann Arbor: University of Michigan Press, 2010), 5.

65. Pérez Firmat, *Life on the Hyphen*, 88.

66. Thomas, *Down These Mean Streets*, 86.

67. Where does the phonic material go? I liken its movement to maroonage, a practice that Carolyn Cooper describes as, "that tradition of resistance science that establishes an alternative psychic space both within and beyond the boundaries of the enslaving plantation." Carolyn Cooper, *Noises in the Blood: Orality, Gender, and the "Vulgar" Body of Jamaican Popular Culture* (Durham, NC: Duke University Press, 1995), 4.

68. "Mambo Show Has Biggest Number in Cast," *Norfolk New Journal and Guide*, October 23, 1954, D25. This is not to be confused with an earlier "Mambo U.S.A." tour (1951) that showcased Pérez Prado and his orchestra.

69. "Joe Loco Heads Company of 40 in 'Mambo USA' at Music Hall," *Clevland Call and Post*, November 6, 1954, 7B.

70. There is something here that rings of a reverse formulation of Althusserian hailing, the playful and undoubtedly pleasurable "chiming in" interpellated the state, consciously or not. Here I refer to the French Marxist Louis Althusser's ideology of interpellation. For Althusser, ideology is a central component to social relations in society, and from which there is no outside. The mechanisms of ideology interpellate its citizens as individual subjects. Althusser's primary example is when an individual subject answers to a police officer's call, "Hey, you there!" Another important example that informed much of Judith Butler's early work was the way in which gender would be constituted from birth, that is, "It's a girl." See Louis Althusser, "Ideology and Ideological State Apparatuses," in *Lenin and Philosophy and Other Essays*, trans. Ben Brewster (New York: Monthly Review Press, 1971). I first understood this formulation by way of Fred Moten.

71. Nathaniel Mackey, "Cante Moro," in *Sound States: Innovative Poetics and Acoustical Technologies*, ed. Adalaide Morris (Chapel Hill: University of North Carolina Press, 1997), 200.

72. *The American Heritage Dictionary*, 3rd ed., s.v. "cultivate."

73. Mackey, "Cante Moro," 203.

74. Jack Kerouac, *On the Road*, Penguin Books ed. (New York: Penguin Books, 2003), 286.

75. Ibid., 288.

76. Ibid., 286.

77. Ibid., 289.

78. Achy Obejas, *Memory Mambo* (Pittsburgh: Cleis Press, 1996), 9.

79. Grendysa, liner notes.

80. Obejas, *Memory Mambo*, 191.

81. Ibid., 75.

82. Ibid., 194.

83. Roland Barthes, "The Grain of the Voice," in *Image, Music, Text*, trans. Stephen Heath (New York: Hill and Wang, 1977), 179.

84. Author unknown, liner notes for Pérez Prado and Shorty Rogers, *Voodoo Suite/Exotic Suite of the Americas*, Bear Family Records BCD 15463.

85. Don Michael Randel, ed. *The Harvard Dictionary of Music*, 4th ed. (Cambridge: Harvard University Press, 2003), 848. The *Norton/Grove Concise Encyclopedia of Music* defines a "suite" as, "an ordered set of instrumental pieces meant to be performed in a single sitting."

CHAPTER 4

1. See "impression," n. *Oxford English Dictionary*; 2nd ed., 1989; online version March 2011. http://www.oed.com:80/Entry/92725; accessed June 13, 2011. Earlier version first published in *New English Dictionary*, 1899.

2. See Ariana Hernández-Reguant's important and informative, "Cuba" entry in the *Encyclopedia of Radio*, ed. Christopher H. Sterling (New York: Fitzroy Dearborn, 2003), 428–32.

3. Ibid., 428–32.

4. Dave Tompkins, *How to Wreck a Nice Beach: The Vocoder from World War II to Hip-Hop/The Machine Speaks* (Brooklyn: Melville House, 2010), 153–54.

5. See the Cuban post-revolutionary music imprints held at Princeton University's Firestone Library.

6. For a detailed overview of the shifts in recording and publishing during the early years of the Cuban Revolution, see Robin Moore's resourceful *Music and Revolution: Cultural Change in Socialist Cuba*. See also Vincenzo Perna's excellent *Timba: The Sound of the Cuban Crisis* (Burlington: Ashgate, 1995), 19–32; see also Sue Steward, *¡Música!: The Rhythm of Latin America: Salsa, Rumba, Merengue, and More* (San Francisco: Chronicle Books, 1999), 78. For a comprehensive look

at the effects on musicians, especially live performance and venues, see the Adriana Orejuela Martínez's incredible *El son no se fue de Cuba: Claves para una historia (1959–1973)* (La Habana: Editorial Letras Cubanas, 2006).

7. Hernandez-Reguant, *Encyclopedia of Radio*, 428–32.

8. Moore, *Music and Revolution*, 74. This observation originally appeared in Cristóbal Díaz Ayala's *Música Cubana del areíto a la nueva trova* (Miami: Ediciones Universal, 1981), 286.

9. For an concise (and singular) overview of the history of Panart, and its founder Ramon Sabat, see Judy Cantor's "When Cuba Sang," *Miami New Times*, December, 26, 1996; http://www.miaminewtimes.com/1996-12-26/news/when-cuba-sang/: Accessed September 9, 2011.

10. The sleeve notes promise remote contact: "Para que los cubanos mantengamos vivo en el corazón el amor al suelo patrio, nada mejor que recordar las melodías que mejor cantaron sus bellas tradiciones y sus alegrías." Panart records, LP 3092, 1962. Panart Recording, 276 Park Avenue South, New York 10, NY.

11. The original Spanish version reads: "cantos de rebeldía y esperanza que, en otra época de opresión, tristeza y amargura, guiaron a otra generación de cubanos, a la conquista de la Libertad."

12. See Cristóbal Díaz Ayala, "El son no se fue de Cuba," *Latin Beat Magazine*, May 2005. The article is a review of Orejuela Martinez's book, which I will refer to throughout this chapter.

13. See his e-mail exchanges with Adriana Orejuela Martínez printed in her, *El son no se fue de Cuba*, 38–39. Orejuela rightly observes that the history of the vitrola in Cuba is one of the most underinvestigated, and important, issues in the diffusion of Cuban popular music (38). Robin Moore also discusses the issue in *Music and Revolution*, 61. See also Cristóbal Díaz Ayala, *Música Cubana del areyto al rap Cubano*, 4th ed. (Miami: Ediciones Universal, 2003).

14. By "everynightlife" I refer to the title of Celeste Fraser Delgado and José Esteban Muñoz's influential collection of essays about music and dance in the Americas. This phrase helps me to shift the terms of the quotidian to include its vibrant after hours. Celeste Fraser Delgado and José Esteban Muñoz, eds. *Everynightlife: Culture and Dance in Latin/o America* (Durham, NC: Duke University Press, 1997).

15. The scandal is revisited by Orejuela Martínez, *El son no se fue de Cuba*, 59–63. For primary materials on the scandal, see "La farandula pasa" *Bohemia*, Año 51: 8, 22 de Febrero de 1959, 154; "Centro de cafés de la Habana y el conflicto de las victrolas," *Revolución*, 17 de Febrero de 1959, 5; and "Por ruidosas y negocios suspendieron las victrolas," *Revolución*, 18 de Febrero de 1959, 2.

16. "La farandula pasa," *Bohemia*, Año 51, no. 8, 22 de Febrero de 1959, 154.

17. Moore, *Music and Social Change*, 61.

18. Some of Cuba's greatest women singers, including Olga Guillot, Blanca Rosa Gil, and Celia Cruz left early and as a result and were unfairly pegged with accusations that they represented the "bad" excesses of Cuban society before the revolution. It is stunning to discover how much they have been rubbed out of Cuban popular musical history on the island.

19. Perna, *Timba: The Sound of the Cuban Crisis*, 26–27

20. Of the transition for some performers, Acosta adds,

The most notable tendency in the first years of the victorious revolution is the consolidation of styles, songwriters, and performers who had excelled in the previous decade, but who would now 'arrive,' as the barriers impending their definitive success were broken. A typical example is the feeling movement, whose primary exponents finally acquire unobstructed access to all media—records, television, and cinema—and many became singing stars in Cuba.

Acosta, *Cubano Be, Cubano Bop: One Hundred Years of Jazz in Cuba*, trans. Daniel S. Whitesell (Washington and London: Smithsonian Books, 2003), 173.

21. Perna, *Timba*, 27; Steward, *¡Música!*, 79.

22. Moore, *Music and Social Change*, 70.

23. In his *Music and Revolution*, Robin Moore takes painstaking care to offer an appendix on post-revolutionary publications on music (after 1960). Many if not most of these publications are difficult to come by outside of Cuba. However, Moore's work offers an ethical and necessary acknowledgment of this fact. I urge every scholar to use this excellent resource. See especially 265–74. Some critics that I would especially like to mention of are Zoila Lapique Becali, Argeliers León, Leo Brouwer, María del Carmen Mestas, María Teresa Linares, and Mayra Martínez.

24. This has to do with EGREM's liberalization of musical outlets during the special period. For a discussion of these policy shifts see Perna, *Timba*. For analysis on how such shifts impacted the everyday lives of Cubans, see Ariana Hernández-Reguant, "Radio Taíno and the Cuban Quest for Identi . . . qué?" in Doris Sommer, ed., *Cultural Agency in the Americas* (Durham, NC: Duke University Press, 2006). For observations about Cuban music's contemporary relationship to the "World Music" market, see Deborah Pacini Hernandez, "Dancing with the Enemy: Cuban Popular Music, Race, Authenticity, and the World-Music Landscape," *Latin American Perspectives* 3, no. 25 (May 1998): 110–25.

25. See my description of the *BVSC* in the introduction of the book.

26. I'm grateful to Raúl A. Fernández for introducing me to this important text.

27. Michael Chanan remarks on the frequency of musical documentaries from the 1960s and onward. See his overview in "Imperfect Cinema and the Seventies" from *Cuban Cinema* (Mineapolis: University of Minnesota Press, 2004), 319–24.

28. Bill Nichols, *Introduction to Documentary* (Bloomington and Indianapolis: Indiana University Press, 2001), 21.

29. Ana María Dopico, "Picturing Havana: History, Vision, and the Scramble for Cuba," *Nepantla: Views from South* 3: 3 (2002), Durham, NC: Duke University Press, 451–93.

30. "Phonoplay: Recasting Film Music" in *Beyond the Soundtrack: Representing Music in Cinema*, eds. Daniel Goldmark, Lawrence Kramer, and Richard Leppert (Berkeley and Los Angeles: University of California Press, 2007), 6. For another key text on the relationship between film and sound studies, see Jay Beck and Tony Grajeda, eds., *Lowering the Boom: Critical Studies in Film Sound* (Urbana: University of Illinois Press, 2008).

31. The innovative work of Luis Fresquet in particular shows the symbiotic relationship between sound and visual.

32. Ana M. López, "Memorias of a Home: Mapping the Revolution (and the Making of Exiles?), *Revista Canadiense de estudios Hispánicos* 20, no. 1, Mundos Contemporáneos en el Cine Español e Hispanoamericano (Otoño 1995), 6. López defines "Greater Cuba" as "a 'Cuba' that exceeds national boundaries and that includes the many individuals and communities outside the national territory that identify as Cuban and contribute to the production of a 'Cuban' cultural discourse," 15 fn3.

33. For more on Ana M. López's term "Greater Cuba," see my introduction.

34. In addition to Chanan's *Cuban Cinema*, for key ideas debated during this moment in Latin American film history see Julio García Espinosa, "For an Imperfect Cinema," trans. Julianne Burton *Jump Cut*, no. 20 (1979): 24–26; Elizabeth Sutherland, "Cinema of Revolution: 90 Miles from Home," *Film Quarterly* 15, no. 2, Special Humphrey Jennings Issue (Winter 1961–1962): 42–49; Ana M. López, "Early Cinema and Modernity in Latin America," *Cinema Journal* 40, no. 1 (2000): 48–78; John Shaw, *Magical Reels: A History of Cinema in Latin America* (New York: Verso, 2000); Fernando Solanas, et al., "Round Table Discussion: Latin American Cinema," *Framework* 11 (Fall 1979): 10–15; Fernando Solanas and Octavio Getino, "Towards a Third Cinema," *Afterimage* 3 (Summer 1971): 16–30, reprinted in *Cineaste* 4, no. 3 (Winter 1971): 1–10; Glauber Rocha, "Cabezas Cortadas," *Afterimage* no. 3 (Summer 1971): 68–77; Glauber Rocha, "The History of Cinema Novo," *Framework* no. 12 (Summer 1980): 18–27; Robert Stam, *Tropical Multiculturalism: A Comparative History of Race in Brazilian Cinema and Culture* (Durham, NC: Duke University Press, 1997); Chon Noriega, ed., *Visible Nations: Latin American Cinema and Video* (Minneapolis: University of Minnesota Press, 2000); Ann Marie Stock, ed., *Framing Latin American Cinema: Contemporary Critical Perspectives* (Minneapolis: University of Minnesota Press, 1997).

35. *Cine Cubano* 4, no. 22 (Augusto 1964): 24–26,. Daysi Granados is an im-

portant actress in classic Cuban films such as *Memorias del subdesarrollo, retrato de Teresa,* and *Cecilia.*

36. José Quiroga, *Cuban Palimpsests* (Minneapolis: University of Minnesota Press, 2005), 93.

37. The ICAIC was founded in 1959 by Alfredo Guevara, a colleague of Fidel Castro from the University of Havana. Michael Chanan describes the ICAIC as, "a novel kind of public entity: an autonomous institute, not unlike what in Britain is called a quango (quasi-autonomous nonovermental organization), but empowered to take over any part of the country's film industry that might be nationalized," *Cuban Cinema,* 17.

38. *Soy Cuba* is one of the most (and only) widely available films from the era. It is currently disseminated to global audiences due to Francis Ford Coppola and Martin Scorsese's sponsorship for rerelease.

39. This was also the year that Cuba suffered the loss of the great performer Rita Montaner. For a brief discussion of Montaner's illustrious career, see my first chapter.

40. The song was written by Pedro Felipe Figueredo, a soldier in Cuba's first independence war in 1867, who was later executed by the Spaniards the following year.

41. I am eternally grateful for the commitment to these musicians and their documentation shaped by París, editor Nelson Rodríguez, the director of photography Tucho Rodríguez, sound work by Eugenio Vesa and Germinal Hernández, and camera operation by Lopito and Luis Marzoa, which I first experienced almost forty years later at Lincoln Center in New York City. Though their generous work made a crucial education possible, I nevertheless decenter them in my analysis of the film. Instead, I focus on a few of the documentary's other undercredited names and their undercredited performances submerged in the larger history of Cuban film and music—those who often elude formal record keeping.

42. José Quiroga, *Cuban Palimpsests* (Minneapolis: University of Minnesota Press, 2005), 95.

43. This image is thought to be one of the most reproduced photographs in history.

44. Chanan, *Cuban Cinema,* 17.

45. Davitt Moroney, " 'Das wohltemperierte clavier' — The Correctly-Tempered Keyboard," liner notes to *Johann Sebastian Bach: Das wohltemperierte clavier, Teil 1 & 2 by Kenneth Gilbert.* Archiv Produktion 1984, Polydor International GmbH, Hamburg BWV 846–893.

46. This formal play, as Walter Piston clarifies, the "contrapuntal element in music" is "the interplay of agreement and disagreement between the various factors of the musical texture." Walter Piston, *Counterpoint* (New York: W. W. Norton 1947), 9.

47. Helio Orovio, *Cuban Music from A to Z*, trans. Ricardo Bardo Portilla and Lucy Davies (Durham, NC: Duke University Press, 2004), 216–17.

48. Radamés Giro, *Diccionario enciclopédico de la música en Cuba* Tomo IV. Entry: "Odilio Urfé" (La Habana: Editoral Letras Cubanas, 2007), 226.

49. Throughout this chapter, I evoke the "classical" and "popular"—and the discourses that accompany them—alongside other binaries that create problematic racial, ethnic, geographical and temporal orders such as the high/low, western/non-western, mind/body, etc.

50. Moroney describes Bach as "the great magpie himself"; see liner notes for *Johann Sebastian Bach*.

51. Quoted in Raúl A. Férnandez, "The Aesthetics of *Sabor*," in *From Afro-Cuban Rhythms to Latin Jazz* (Berkeley: University of California Press, 2006), 57.

52. This line opens Urfé's short essay. He continues,

Today, hastily writing these lines about the famous *habanero*, I do so with the impulsive aim of making a modest yet sincere contribution to bringing alive in imagination the work that musicians like Brindis de Salas, [Ignacio] Cervantes, [Manuel] Saumell, [Alejandro] Garcia Caturla and other no less singular figures have handed down to us, showing a clearly marked way to historical greatness and dedication.

Odilio Urfé, "Claudio José Domingo Brindis de Salas (1852–1911)," in *AfroCuba: An Anthology of Cuban Writings on Race, Politics, and Culture* (Melbourne: Ocean Press, 1993), 64–66. Published in association with the Center for Cuban Studies. The essay was originally published in *Pentagrama* 1, no. 4 (July 1956).

53. The "Ladder Conspiracy" is so named because the perpetrators would tie a ladder to both the hands and feet of its victims. For more on the conspiracy (and the events that led up to it) see Aline Helg's *Our Rightful Share: The Afro-Cuban Struggle for Equality 1886–1912* (Chapel Hill: University of North Carolina Press, 1995).

54. See Alejo Carpentier, "Blacks in Cuba" in *Music in Cuba*, trans. Alan West-Dúran (Minneapolis: University of Minnesota Press, 2001), 153–65.

55. Of Salas's repertoire, Carpentier writes, "he preferred the 'brilliant fantasy' spiked with spectacularly difficult passage to Bach or Handel." Carpentier, "Blacks in Cuba," 162–63.

56. The danzón genre is one in which he elsewhere attributes to his father, José Urfé and his song "El bombín de Barreto." Orovio, *Cuban Music from A to Z*, 66.

57. Raúl A. Férnandez, telephone interview, December 14, 2005.

58. Emilio Grenet, *Popular Cuban Music: 80 Revised and Corrected Compositions*, trans. R. Phillips. (Havana: Ucar García y Compañía, 1939), xxx. Also see

Jill Lane's important work on the danzón in her *Blackface Cuba 1840–1895*. (Philadelphia: University of Pennsylvania Press), 2005.

59. Many thanks to Raúl García and Ela Troyano for reaching out to París for the identification of the location.

60. From the video *Son sabroson: Antesala de la salsa*, directed and produced by Hugo Barroso. Videocassette, date unknown. HBM Productions.

61. In calling to question the sacrifices required of Cuban youth year after year, I am reminded of the bold and beautiful work of Yoani Sánchez and her blog *Generación Y*. Sánchez's work often has an undercurrent (and a righteous critique) of how the "we" affects the Cuban everyday. See http://www.desdecuba.com/generationy/. For analysis on how the "we" circulates in recent debates in Performance studies, see Elin Diamond's essay, "The Violence of 'We': Politicizing Identification" in *Critical Theory and Performance*, eds. Janelle G. Reinelt and Joseph R. Roach (Ann Arbor: University of Michigan Press, 2007), 403–12.

62. See note 35.

63. Here I am referencing Fidel Castro's famous speech "Palabras a los intellectuales" (Letter to the Intellectuals) in June of 1961. In this speech, Castro proclaimed the axiom that would determine the place of artists and intellectuals in the new society: "Within the Revolution everything, against the Revolution nothing."

64. Christopher Small, *Musicking: The Meanings of Performing and Listening* (Middletown: Wesleyan University Press, 1998), 9.

65. The gentleman in the photo is of the cinematographer Julio Valdés. My gratitude to Ana M. López and Dolores Calviño for their help identifying him.

66. This quote is taken from one of Cuba's most important and prolific film theorists, Juan Antonio García Borreo. Borrero's blog *Cine Cubano, la pupila insomne* is an excellent resource for locating his and other's writings and observations about Cuban cinema, especially from the island. http://cinecubanolapupilainsomne. wordpress.com/2007/03/18/sara-Gómez-1/. Accessed June 14, 2011. Also, as Michael Chanan points out, "Gómez clearly had a remarkable way of gaining the trust of her subjects, and drawing out of them stories and reflections that go far beyond most other documentaries." Chanan, *Cuban Cinema*, 342.

67. For an excellent, thoughtful, and concise overview of the arc of her film career, see Chanan, *Cuban Cinema*, 340–52.

68. Raúl A. Férnandez, *From Afro-Cuban Rhythms to Latin Jazz* (Berkeley: University of California Press, 2006), 45.

69. From *La revista Cuba*, Año 3, no. 2 (1964): 58–67.

70. As I stated in the introduction, Alejo Carpentier felt that his fieldwork on the history of Cuban music prepared him to write the later novels. In Gómez's case, *Y . . . tenemos sabor* was preparation for her great film *De cierta manera*.

71. Zayas was born in 1908 and died in 1988. Giro, *Enciclopédico*, "Alberto Zayas," 303. Also see Maria del Carmen Mestas, *Pasión de rumbero* (Barcelona: Puvill Libros; La Habana: Pablo de la Torrente, 1998). As a young man, Zayas had accompanied Fernando Ortiz as one of his main informants, to lecture on the sacred groups that populated Cuba. Though from the outset, it should be made clear that Zayas's work has historically played with the sacred and secular forms. For example, in an interesting encounter with the American anthropologist Harold Courlander in 1944, Zayas was described as an, "eager young man, a little on the plump side, well mannered, and very conscious of matters pertaining to cults. He comes from Matanzas Province, where Lucumi and Abakwa are particularly strong, and feels quite proud to be one of Fernando Ortiz's informants. He always smokes a cigar, which with his weight gives a definite impression of prosperity, even though the opposite is clearly the case." Harold Courlander, "Abakwa Meeting in Guanabacoa" *The Journal of Negro History* 29, no. 4 (October, 1944): 461. Courlander was a folklorist, musicologist, and ethnographer who studied many Afro-Caribbean cultures, especially those found in Haiti. He later authored *Cult Music of Cuba* (1951). He additionally conducted studies of Hopi, African American, and Ethiopian expressive cultural forms such as folk tales and musical instruments. He was most famously known as the author of the novel *The African*, the subject of a lawsuit he brought against Alex Haley. In 1978 Courlander successfully proved in court that substantial portions of *The African* made uncredited appearance in Haley's *Roots*. It is also worth noting that Courlander amassed an impressive archive of recorded materials from his research site, and as general editor of the "Ethnic Folkways Library," issued many of these recordings on the Folkways label. During this encounter, Zayas brought Courlander to his home in Guanabacoa where he showed him some objects from his own collection. Like many an anthropological play by play with any informant Courlander's account of Zayas's performance is described in both withholding and "ferocious" terms.

72. Chanan, *Cuban Cinema*, 341.

73. See Arnold Whittall's "arrangement" entry in *The Oxford Companion to Music*, Edited by Alison Latham (New York: Oxford University Press, 2002); *Oxford Reference Online*. Accessed November 26, 2010. http://www.oxfordreference .com/views/ENTRY.html?subview=Main&entry=t114.e410.

74. Peter Szendy, *Listen: A History of Our Ears,* trans. Charlotte Mandell (New York: Fordham University Press, 2008), 35–36.

75. See the epigraph that head's Szendy's chapter "Writing Our Listenings: Arrangement, Translation, Criticism." Szendy quotes the *Encyclopédie de la musique* (París: Fasquelle, 1958), "the erudite high style of what Bach wrote should be called *arrangement*, while *adaptation* (since this word has a more common flavor than the

other) should be used for the misappropriation of property practiced by so many philistines." Szendy, *Listen*, 35.

76. Giro, *Encyclopedia*. "Chucho Valdés," 236. Valdés states, "un amigo me insistió a oír más jazz, a conocer el trabajo de sus mejores pianistas. Opinaba que no improvisaba lo suficiente y yo sentí como una deficiencia. Compré mi primer disco de jazz, del tecladista Dave Brubeck. Me impactó y entré en un mundo nuevo para mí. A partir de Brubeck, estudié a fondo el piano del jazz."

77. Acosta, *Cubano Be, Cubano Bop*, 176.

78. José Esteban Muñoz *Cruising Utopia: The Then and There of Queer Futurity* (New York: NYU Press, 2009), 9. This quote refers to Warhol's Coke drawing Warhol and the O'Hara poem that inaugurate this stunning book.

CHAPTER 5

1. There has been a recent boom of materials on "Operation Pedro Pan" in print and other forms. See Victor Andres Triay, *Fleeing Castro: Operation Pedro Pan and the Cuban Children's Program* (Gainsville: University of Florida Press, 1998); María de los Angeles Torres, *The Lost Apple: Operation Pedro Pan, Cuban Children in the U.S., and the Promise of a Better Future* (Boston: Beacon Press, 2003); Yvonne M. Conde, *Operation Pedro Pan: The Untold Exodus of 14,048 Cuban Children* (New York: Routledge, 1999). In memoir form, see Román de la Campa, *Cuba on My Mind: Journeys to a Severed Nation* (New York: Verso, 2000); and Carlos Eire's experiential diptych *Waiting for Snow in Havana: Confessions of a Cuban Boy* (New York; London: Free Press, 2003) and *Learning to Die in Miami: Confessions of a Refugee Boy* (London: Free Press, 2010). CNBC recently aired a made-for-cable documentary narrated by Meredith Viera titled *Escape from Havana: An American Story*.

2. For a solid overview of this history, see María Cristina García, *Havana USA: Cuban Exiles and Cuban Americans in South Florida, 1959–1994* (Berkeley: University of California Press, 1996). For other key works that attempt to wade into these difficult thickets see Joan Didion, *Miami* (New York: Simon & Schuster, 1987); and David Reiff, *The Exile: Cuba in the Heart of Miami* (New York: Simon & Schuster, 1993).

3. By Cuba, once again, I don't only mean the island itself, but also its abroad strokes. I want to disrupt those unidirectional flows that often determine the acá and allá (here and there), for Cuba has not now nor ever been capable of being mere emitter or receiver. See my note on Ana M. López's "Greater Cuba" in the introduction and chapter 4.

4. Why Cuban American studies, unlike Latina/o studies, has not been subject to more metareflexive work about the field as a whole begs for further theorization.

Important exceptions include Damián J. Fernández and Madeline Cámara Betancourt, eds., *Cuba, the Elusive Nation* (Austin: University of Texas Press, 2000) and Ricardo Ortiz's "Introduction: Diaspora and Disappearance," in *Cultural Erotics in Cuban America* (Minneapolis: University of Minnesota Press, 2007). For a concise overview of the teleological and generational trends on and off the island, see Damien J. Fernández, "Politics and Romance on the Scholarship of Cuban Politics" *Latin American Research Review* 39, no. 2 (2004): 164–77. Although Fernández discusses texts about Cuban politics, his observations are interesting to weigh alongside studies of literature and culture.

5. One article that deals explicitly with the shift in demographics is Mario A. González-Corzo, "The Cuban Population in the United States since 2000: Concentration, Growth, and Socioeconomic Characteristics," *The Cuban Affairs Journal* 2, no. 3. Published by the Institute for Cuban and Cuban American Studies at the University of Miami (http://www.cubanaffairsjournal.org/).

6. Although González-Corzo's article is among the exceptions, peruse other recent entries to the online journal *The Cuban Affairs Journal*.

7. There have been important models for facilitating multiple forms and forums. Listed here are a few key readings. For literary collections that stage conversations between Cubans on and off the island, see Ruth Behar, ed., *Bridges to Cuba/Puentes a Cuba* (Ann Arbor: University of Michigan Press, 1995); Ruth Behar and Lucía M. Suárez, eds., *The Portable Island: Cubans at Home in the World* (New York: Palgrave Macmillan, 2008); Peter Bush, ed., *The Voice of the Turtle: An Anthology of Cuban Stories* (London: Quartet Books, 1997); and Cristina García, ed., ¡*Cubanísimo! The Vintage Book of Contemporary Cuban Literatures* (New York: Vintage, 2002). Scholarly collaborations include John Beverly, ed., Special Issue "From Cuba," *Boundary 2: An International Journal of Literature and Culture* 29, no. 3 (Fall 2002); Peter Manuel, ed., *Essays on Cuban Music: North American and Cuban Perspectives* (Lanham, MD: University Press of America, 1991); Ariana Hernández-Reguant, ed., *Cuba in the Special Period: Culture and Ideology in the 1990s* (New York: Palgrave Macmillan, 2009). See also Lisa Brock and Digna Castaneda-Fuertes, eds., *Between Race and Empire: African Americans and Cubans before the Cuban Revolution* (Philadelphia: Temple University Press, 1998). Although this collection is set in the revolutionary era, it gathers scholars on the island and off. For conversations that have been curated through visual arts exhibitions and catalogs, see Andrea O'Reilly Herrera, *Cuban Artists Across the Diaspora: Setting the Tent Against the House* (Austin: University of Texas Press, 2011). I also note musical collaborations later in the chapter.

8. An incredibly rich body of scholarship has attempted to grapple with the greater lament of the Cuban political situation. Many of these critics are woven

throughout *Listening in Detail.* A few contemporary key works include José Esteban Muñoz, "Notes on the Negotiation of Cubanidad and Exilic Memory in Carmelita Tropicana's *Milk of Amnesia," The Drama Review: The Journal of Performance Studies* 39, no. 3 (1995): 76–82), Cambridge: MIT Press; José Esteban Muñoz, *Disidentifications: Queers of Color and the Performance of Politics* (Minneapolis: University of Minnesota Press, 1999); José Quiroga, *Cuban Palimpsests* (Minneapolis: University of Minnesota Press, 2005); Ricardo Oritz, *Cultural Erotics in Cuban America* (Minneapolis: University of Minnesota Press, 2007); Antonio Viego, *Dead Subjects: Toward a Politics of Loss in Latino Studies* (Durham, NC: Duke University Press, 2007).

9. Raymond Williams defines "structures of feeling" this way:

The term is difficult, but "feeling" is chosen to emphasize a distinction from more formal concepts of "world-view" or "ideology". It is not only that we must go beyond formally held and systematic beliefs, though of course we have always to include them. It is that we are concerned with meanings and values as they are actively lived and felt, and the relations between these and formal or systematic beliefs are in practice variable (including historically variable), over a range from formal assent with private dissent to the more nuanced interaction between selected and interpreted beliefs and aced and justified experiences. An alternative definition would be structures of experience: in one sense the better and wider word, but with the difficulty that one of its senses has that past tense which is the most important obstacle to recognition of the area of social experience which is being defined. We are talking about characteristic elements of impulse, restraint, and tone: specifically affective elements of consciousness and relationships: not feeling against thought, but thought as felt and feeling as thought: practical consciousness of a present kind, in a living and inter-relating continuity. We are then defining these elements as a "structure": as a set, with specific internal relations, at once interlocking and in tension.

From Raymond Williams, *Marxism and Literature* (Oxford: Oxford University Press, 1977), 132.

10. I first evoked this term in a paper titled "What I Brought Back Here" that I presented at the annual meeting of the American Studies Association in Albuquerque 2008. I extend thanks and gratitude to the supportive scholars in attendance.

11. Long the domain of historians, "the cold war" has been made to perform much of the periodizing labor of the second half of the twentieth century. Ann Douglass has pointed out that although it is mostly historians who have used it as a periodizing device, it is cultural critics who "have the most to learn." She elaborates: "I do not mean that we should officially adopt yet another name for the second

half of the twentieth century, but rather that exploring this term might help us to understand better the period we are naming, and more important, living in." Ann Douglas, "Periodizing the American Century: Modernism, Postmodernism, and Postcolonialism in the Cold War Context," *Modernism/Modernity* 5, no. 3 (1998): 73–74 (especially 71–98). Here Douglas compellingly suggests more than adopting the cold war in order to organize the tumultuous specifics of the era. I would argue that organizing them does not, cannot make them any more manageable. By keeping the "cold war" in the present tense (the period we are "living in") Douglas shows its active impact in the here and now, especially on cultural production and individual psyches. Although there has been much investment in decreeing its end with the collapse of the Soviet Union in 1989, one need only think of Cuba, Viet Nam, and North and South Korea in current event form to realize the cold war is far from over. What Douglas suggests, in other words, is how to move past the cold war as merely a periodizing device and into its experiential conditioning. Referencing the upsurge of US surveillance, psychological and sociological profiling of individuals and communities during the 1940s and 50s, Douglas argues, "The cold war administration had decided the personal was the political long before postmodernists made the discovery" (82).

12. Jodi Kim, *Ends of Empire: Asian American Critique and the Cold War* (Minneapolis: University of Minnesota Press, 2010), 4. In her book, Kim is committed to moving the cold war beyond its traditional uses and misuses. The cold war for Kim is not merely a point of reference. By moving her sites through its maelstrom, she hopes to "refram[e] the Cold War by approaching it not solely as a historical epoch or event, but as itself a knowledge project or epistemology, which is always also a pedagogy, and asking how it continues to generate and teach 'new' knowledge by making sense of the world through the Manichaean logics and grammars of good and evil. . . . It is a reading practice through which the United States comes to construct and know itself and its Others" (8–9). Here Kim reveals some of the mechanics as to how the cold war project continues to reproduce itself. Its "logics and grammars" have left intractable imprints on contemporary US history for more than half a century, and their direct legacies are felt through the new enemies made to now drive US political discourses. Such a pedagogical project has both uncontrolled and controlled residues that are impossible to shake or deny. As Alex's song and album so exquisitely reveal, I would add that such a reading practice has additionally structured how the Other comes to know itself.

13. See Emilio Estefan, *The Rhythm of Success: How an Immigrant Produced His Own American Dream* (New York: Celebra, 2010).

14. What I cannot get to in this chapter—and that I deeply acknowledge here—are the forms that those affiliations have long taken in the homelands them-

selves. With the hope and the certainty that the work is being performed by others, these pages will stay with the potential of those affiliations as lived in the United States.

15. In US comparative ethnic studies in particular, the populations put alongside one another are often predictable: they are brought together in scholarship to examine conflicts over resources, via collaboration and tensions in shared neighborhoods, and to clumsily celebrate political solidarities.

16. When the comparative is used to analyze a population within the United States with one located in an outside country, the results can be pernicious, intentional or not. Micol Seigel's observations are especially useful in this regard. See Micol Seigel, "Beyond Compare: Comparative Method after the Transnational Turn," *Radical History Review Issue* 91 (Winter 2005): 62–90. As she has argued, "For U.S. audiences, the suggestion of legibility at home and confusion abroad stands as the cornerstone of a contemporary Orientalism, the handmaiden to American exceptionalism." It is not enough, she suggests, to point to an outside as an orienting foil that paradoxically works to uphold false US racial binaries of black/white, native and alien. Discourses on the racial spectrum or fuzzy heterogeneity of Brasil and Cuba in particular are used to redraw the rigid lines used to study race the United States. Accompanied (and summarily excused) by repeated assertions that race cannot be analyzed solely in a US context, the other, non-US side of transnational comparatives are left a carnivalesque and undifferentiated mass without politics or history. Seigel argues that transnational work requires sustained attention to the ways that the comparative is in itself an object of analysis, and of the inability of shorthand to consider the lived realities of racialization in other places outside of the United States. Seigel proposes, "Perhaps it is time to call a moratorium on comparative study," (65); to which I respond with a guttural here here. Seigel's analysis is indelible when thinking of approaches to the populations affected by the obscuring sign of the cold war, particularly when postcolonial insights are exchanged from within the official boundaries of the United States.

17. Vijay Prashad, "Ethnic Studies Inside Out," *Journal of Asian American Studies* 9, no. 2 (2006): 171–72. I am also very much in concert with Micol Seigel who observes, "Comparison requires the observer to name two or more units whose similarities and differences she or he will then describe. This setup discourages attention to exchange between the two, the very exchange postcolonial insight understands as the stuff of subject formation. . . . Comparisons obscure the workings of power." Micol Seigel, "Beyond Compare: Comparative Method after the Transnational Turn," *Radical History Review Issue* 91 (Winter 2005): 65.

18. I refer here to the "California Dreaming" symposium put together by Chris-

tine Bacareza Balance (UC Irvine) and Lucy Burns (UCLA) at UC Irvine on June 4, 2010. Balance and Burns gathered a group of brilliant and motley scholars across the University of California system to discuss their new work. Here is their mission statement:

"California Dreaming" is a UC working group that approaches California Studies through artistic processes and the circulation of art objects to understand the place of California in the artistic imaginary. We use as our focal point Asian American artists who claim a base in California to theorize arts' mobility and migration. In this opening panel, three illustrious scholars will share their respective research and offer new transnational and interdisciplinary methods for writing about the arts in a changing world.

19. Patty Ahn and Van Troung—as scholars and as people—have been enormously influential and encouraging to bringing cold war kids to these pages.

20. I'd like to also point out that Min's work has been featured at the Havana Biennial.

21. Antonio Viego, *Dead Subjects: Towards a Politics of Loss in Latino Studies* (Durham, NC: Duke University Press, 2007), 4.

22. For sociological perspectives and demographic studies on the transformation of Miami into a Latin American metropolis, see Alejandro Portes and Alex Stepick's *City on the Edge: The Transformation of Miami* (Berkeley: University of California Press, 1993); Kevin E. McHugh, Ines M. Miyares, and Emily H. Skop, "The Magnetism of Miami: Segmented Paths in Cuban Migration," *The Geographical Review* 87, no. 4 (October 1997): 504–19; and Sheila L. Croucher, *Imagining Miami: Ethnic Politics in a Postmodern World* (Charlottesville: University Press of Virginia, 1997).

23. Roberto González Echevarria, "Exiled by Ike, Saved By America," *New York Times*, January 6, 2011.

24. Even though times have changed, as late as 2003 the virtuoso Cuban pianist Gonzalo Rubalcaba was on the receiving end of death threats for his scheduled Miami appearance at the Knight Center.

25. Journalistic coverage of the concert and the events that led up to it was extensive. See Mike Clary, "Cuban Salsa Stars Missing the Beat in Miami Politics," *Los Angeles Times*, May 12, 1998, 5; Judy Cantor, "Hurricane Van Van," *Miami New Times*, September 23, 1999; Tyler Bridges, "Cuban Band Issue Splits Miami by Age, Poll Finds," *The Miami Herald*, September 13, 1999; Ariel Hidalgo, "Debate al ritmo de los Van Van," *El Nuevo Herald*, September 28, 1999, 15A; Manny Garcia, Jordan Levin, and Peter Whorliskey, "The Band Plays on as Protest Fills to Deter Van Van's Fans," *The Miami Herald*, October 10, 1999; Brett Sokol, "Another Round of

Los Van Van Insanity," *Miami New Times*, October 7–13, 1999. Websites devoted to Latin music also provided extensive coverage; see Jacira Castro, "Review of Los Van Van," from salsapower.com (October 10, 1999), www.salsapower.com/concerts /losvanvan/htm.

26. See Raymond A. Mohl, "Race and Space in the Modern City: Interstate 95 and the Black Community in Miami," in *Urban Policy in Twentieth-Century America*, ed. Arnold R. Hirsch and Raymond A. Mohl (New Brunswick: Rutgers University Press, 1993), 100–58. For an indispensable history of the area, and of black Miami in general, see Marvin Dunn's extraordinary *Black Miami in the Twentieth Century* (Gainesville: University Press of Florida, 1997).

27. *Van Van Live at Miami Arena*. DVD, ca. 2003 Havana Caliente, Miami. Distributed by Universal Music Latino. 60584–9.

28. "The Band Plays on as Protest Fails to Deter Van Van's Fans," Manny Garcia, Jordan Levin, and Peter Whoriskey, *Miami Herald*, October 10, 1999.

29. Ibid.

30. I want to take a brief detour to consider another spectacle and to pay homage to the Vietnamese American Arts and Letters Association (VAALA) and a cultural event it sponsored that was unwittingly forced into the combustible mix of cold war politics. Founded in 1991, VAALA has been prolific and tireless in its production and sponsorship of community-based cultural events, from book signings and art exhibitions, to the "Children's Moon Festival Art Contest" and "Vietnamese International Film Festival," to year-round music and art classes. The collective is a vital artery for the exploration of Vietnamese culture and diasporic experience as well as an association that advocates for communication, dialogue, and diversity within the Vietnamese community. See their website and mission statement at http:// www.vaala.org/history-mission.php. Accessed January 13, 2011. In January 2009 in Santa Ana, California, VAALA sponsored "F.O.B. II: Art Speaks/ Nghệ Thuật Lên Tiếng," an exhibition of more than fifty Vietnamese interdisciplinary artists based in the United States, Viet Nam, and other places across the globe. Curated by Lan Duong and Tram Le, they hoped that the event would encourage a place to, "come together to examine the broader issue of our community's identity and what we are allowed to say through art in the space of the national and international," (from the website's press release, January 13, 2011). The curators imagined a space for conversation often not permitted in mainstream Vietnamese American politics, namely, those that desire to engage with who and what was left behind, to address intercommunity hostility toward other points of view, and to investigate the roles that the United States and Viet Nam play in the intersections between the domestic and the diaspora. The show opened to great success. The day after the show opened, the *LA Weekly* published an article to publicize the event. It included one half of

a diptych created by artist Brian Doan titled, "Thuc Duc, Viet Nam 2008/Avon." The image featured a young woman wearing a tank top with the communist flag sitting next to a small bust of Ho Chi Minh, a cellphone, and some books staring thoughtfully out of the left frame. No matter that the work, according to his artist statement, "reflects upon the dilemma of change that has been the result of a turbulent century, leaving a nation split apart with its people spread around the globe. Many are still trapped, depressed, hurt, and full of hatred." VAALA Center, *F.O.B. II: Art Speaks/ Nghệ Thuật Lên Tiếng F.O.B. II*, exhibition catalog, 27. Regardless of the fact that the image was taken out of context, it was Doan's inclusion of communist symbols in the work that initiated a firestorm on behalf of those looking for a reason to fight. Many from the Vietnamese American communities in LA and Orange County showed up to the gallery, wrote angry letters, and left angry messages for VAALA and its curators.

On January 12, VAALA and the cocurators organized a public town hall meeting for those who wished to talk about the show and the events surrounding it. It was even advertised in the newspaper. When they arrived, they were subject to bodily harm, yelling, and intimidating violence and were forced to leave the space. Accused of being communists, whores, and most of all traitors—they had to leave for fear of being harmed. See *The Orange County Register*, January 17, 2009. http ://www2.ocregister.com/articles/vietnamese-exhibit-santa-2284370-communist -want. Accessed January 13, 2011. According to VAALA's timeline, assemblyman Van Tran then sent a letter asking the curators to take down Doan's picture. To this and the many calls they were receiving, VAALA offered this bold bullet point in response:

· **We wanted to tell the community that we understood their pain.**

They ended up shutting down the exhibit a day early and cancelled a series of panels and performances scheduled in conjunction with the exhibit. They could not guarantee the artists' safety. And finally, even after they closed, the exhibition was submitted to horrific acts of vandalism. Doan's and Steven Toly's works were defaced with red spray paint and spit. A pair of red panties with a pantyliner attached to it was taped to Doan's picture. If this timeline is exhausting to read, imagine what experiencing the events from the inside must have felt like. There are so many late nights, phone conversations, what pop singer Maxwell sung as "fistfulls of tears" and sadness hidden by the timeline. Rather than reiterate the familiarity of this kind of violence, I would rather honor the courage demonstrated by the curators and VAALA and their behind-the-scenes heartaches.

31. See note 29. As curator Lan Duong reflects in her heartbreaking post-show manifesto,

I also advocate that we reconceptualize the concept of familial relations within the community. This model of the community-as-family must be rejected because it presumes that there are no boundaries amongst our own. It allows for those who have access to power to slander anyone at will. It presumes that we need to be filial when we should all be more respectful of the multiple histories that we represent and the manifold stories that we have yet to tell. This model also discounts the traumas that take place behind closed doors, like sexual trauma, domestic abuse, living in poverty, and problems with racism. This model only accounts for a collective trauma based on generational experience and assumes that the space of the family and community are always safe. The traumas that do occur within the private space are not spoken of; instead, the public space serves as a forum for the iteration of nationalistic memories, ones often dominated by the voices of men. It is this form of nationalism within the community that breeds dirty politics and disallows any other dirty laundry to be aired. Now some of our "brothers and sisters" and "elders" demand that we issue an apology for the exhibit. I refuse this familial model and I refuse to apologize.

Lan Duong, "In the Aftermath of War and the Closing of *F.O.B.II: Art Speaks*" at *http://www.vaala.org/FOBII-commentary-board.php. Accessed December 28, 2010.* Refusing the familial model and refusing to apologize need not be received as an act of disobedience, but as an important act of separation necessary to the health of future generations.

32. See http://offbroadway.broadwayworld.com/article/Harlem_Stage_Presents _HABANAHARLEM_20010101#ixzz1BgaL2H1k

33. See my discussion of *BVSC* in the introduction.

34. Victoria Burnett, "In Havana, Jam Sessions with a Master Trumpeter," *New York Times,* October 10, 2010; http://www.nytimes.com/2010/10/11/arts/music /11jazz.html. Accessed October 12, 2010.

35. Achy Obejas, "Cuba's Real Revolution," posted September 23, 2009. http ://www.theroot.com/views/cubas-real-revolution?page=0,0. Accessed January 21, 2011.

36. In reference to its mirrored walls, Pérez Firmat once hilariously referred to Versailles as the "Cuban panopticon: you can lunch, but you can't hide." Pérez Firmat, *Life on the Hyphen* (Austin: University of Texas Press, 1994), 134–35.

37. For more on Síntesis and their incorporation of Yoruba religious music into Cuban popular sound, see Robin Moore, "Revolution and Religion: Yoruba Sacred Music in Socialist Cuba," in *The Yoruba Diaspora in the Atlantic World*, ed. Toyin Falola and Matt D. Childs (Bloomington: Indiana University Press, 2005), 278–79.

38. Radamés Giro, "Alfonso, X" in *Diccionario enciclopédico de la música en Cuba*, Tomo 1 (La Habana: Editorial Letras Cubanas, 2007), 38.

39. From an interview with X Alfonso on the website Havana-Cultura (http ://www.havana-cultura.com/html/en/cuban-music/x-alfonso/afro-cuban-music .html). Accessed February 17, 2011.

40. For a clip of the performance, see http://www.youtube.com/watch?v=vxYf 3Gj6fwc.

Bibliography

Acosta, Leonardo. *Cubano Be, Cubano Bop: One Hundred Years of Jazz in Cuba.* Translated by Daniel S. Whitesell. Washington and London: Smithsonian Books, 2003.

———. "Reajustes, aclaraciones y criterios sobre dámaso Pérez Prado." In *El Mambo.* Edited by Radamés Giro La Habana: Editorial Letras Cubanas, 1993.

———, Daniel Whitesell, and Raúl Fernández. "On Generic Complexes and Other Topics in Cuban Popular Music." *Journal of Popular Music Studies,* 17, no. 3 (December 2005): 246.

Adorno, Theodor W. *Minima Moralia: Reflections from Damaged Life.* Translated by E. F. Jephcott. London: Verso, 1996.

———. "Music, Language, and Composition." In *Essays on Music.* Edited by Richard Leppert. Translated by Susan H. Gillespie. Berkeley and Los Angeles: University of California Press, 2002.

———. "On Tradition." *Telos,* no. 94 (December 1992): 75.

———. "The Form of the Phonograph Record." In *Essays on Music.* Edited by Richard Leppert. Translated by Susan H. Gillespie. Berkeley and Los Angeles: University of California Press, 2002.

———. "The Problem of Musical Analysis." In *Essays on Music.* Edited by Richard Leppert. Translated by Susan H. Gillespie. Berkeley: University of California Press, 2002.

Aguilar, Luis E. "Cuba, c. 1860–c.1930." In *Cuba: A Short History.* Edited by Leslie Bethell. Cambridge: Cambridge University Press, 1993.

Ake, David. *Jazz Matters: Sound, Place, and Time Since Bebop.* Berkeley: University of California Press, 2010.

Alexander, Elizabeth. "The Black Poet as Canon-Maker: Langston Hughes and the Road to *New Negro Poets: USA.*" In *The Black Interior.* St. Paul: Graywolf Press, 2004.

Althusser, Louis. "Ideology and Ideological State Apparatuses." In *Lenin and Philosophy and Other Essays*. Translated by Ben Brewster. New York: Monthly Review Press, 1971.

Anderson, Benedict. *Imagined Communities: Reflections on the Origin and Spread of Nationalism*. London: Verso, 1991.

Aparicio, Frances R. "La Lupe, La India, and Celia: Toward a Feminist Genealogy of Salsa Music." In *Situating Salsa: Global Markets and Local Meaning in Latin Popular Music*. Edited by Lise Waxer. New York: Routledge, 2002.

———. *Listening to Salsa: Gender, Latin Popular Music, and Puerto Rican Cultures*. Hanover, NH: University Press of New England, 1998.

Arnedo, Miguel. "'Afrocubanista' Poetry and Afro-Cuban Performance." *The Modern Language Review* 96, no. 4 (October, 2001): 990–1005.

———. *Writing Rumba: The Afrocubanist Movement in Poetry*. Charlottesville: University of Virginia Press, 2006.

Auslander, Philip. "Performance Analysis and Popular Music: A Manifesto." *Contemporary Theatre Review* 14, no. 1 (2004): 1–13.

Austin, J. L. *How to Do Things With Words*. 2nd ed. Cambridge: Harvard University Press, 1975.

Baral, Robert. *Revue: The Great Broadway Period*. rev. ed. New York: Fleet Press, 1970.

Barret, Lindon. "The Gaze of Langston Hughes: Subjectivity, Homoeroticism, and the Feminine in *The Big Sea*." *The Yale Journal of Criticism* 12, no. 2 (1999): 383–97.

Barthes, Roland. *Camera Lucida: Reflections of Photography*. Translated by Richard Howard. New York: Hill and Wang, 1982.

———. "The Grain of the Voice." In *Image, Music, Text*. Translated by Stephen Heath. New York: Hill and Wang, 1977.

———. "Twenty Key Words for Roland Barthes." In *The Grain of the Voice: Interviews 1962—1980*. Translated by Linda Coverdale. Berkeley: University of California Press, 1985.

Beals, Carleton. *The Crime of Cuba*. Philadelphia: Lippincott, 1933.

Bechet, Sidney. *Treat It Gentle: An Autobiography*. Cambridge: Da Capo Press, 2002.

Beck, Jay, and Tony Grajeda, eds. *Lowering the Boom: Critical Studies in Film Sound*. Urbana: University of Illinois Press, 2008.

Behar, Ruth, ed. *Bridges to Cuba/Puentes a Cuba*. Ann Arbor: University of Michigan Press, 1995.

———, and Lucía M. Suárez, eds. *The Portable Island: Cubans at Home in the World*. New York: Palgrave Macmillan, 2008.

Benedict, Barbara M. *Making the Modern Reader: Cultural Mediation in Early Modern Literary Anthologies*. Princeton: Princeton University Press, 1996.

Benjamin, Walter. *Illuminations: Essays and Reflections*. New York: Knopf Doubleday.

———. *The Arcades Project*. Edited by Howard Eiland. Translated by Kevin Mc-Gloughlin. Cambridge: Belknap Press of Harvard University Press, 2002.

Bethell, Leslie, ed. *Cuba: A Short History*. Cambridge: Cambridge University Press, 1993.

Beverly, John, ed. Special issue. "From Cuba." *Boundary 2: An International Journal of Literature and Culture* 29, no. 3 (Fall 2002): 000–000.

Bial, Henry, ed. *The Performance Studies Reader*, 2nd ed. London: Routledge, 2007.

Blake, Jody. *Le Tumulte Noir: Modernist Art and Popular Entertainment in Jazz-Age Paris, 1900–1930*. University Park: Pennsylvania State University Press, 1999.

Boggs, Vernan. *Salsiology: Afro-Cuban Music and the Evolution of Salsa in New York City*. New York: Greenwood Press, 1992.

Brennan, Timothy. "Introduction to the English Edition." In *Music in Cuba*. Edited by Alejo Carpentier. Translated by Alan West-Durán. Minneapolis: University of Minnesota Press, 2001.

———. *Secular Devotion: Afro-Latin Music and Imperial Jazz*. London and New York: Verso, 2008.

Brock, Lisa and Digna Castaneda Fuertes, eds. *Between Race and Empire: African-Americans and Cubans before the Cuban Revolution*. Philadelphia: Temple University Press, 1998.

Brooks, Tim. "W. C. Handy." In *Lost Sounds: Blacks and the Birth of the Recording Industry 1890–1919*. Urbana and Chicago: University of Illinois Press, 2004.

Broughton, Simon. *The Rough Guide to World Music: 100 Essential CDs*. London: Rough Guides, 2000.

Broyles-González, Yolanda. "Background and Analysis." In *Lydia Mendoza's Life in Music/La historia de Lydia Mendoza*. New York: Oxford University Press, 2001.

Buckle, Richard. *Katherine Dunham: Her Dancers, Singers, Musicians*. London: Ballet Publications, 1949.

Bush, Peter, ed. *The Voice of the Turtle: An Anthology of Cuban Stories*. London: Quartet Books, 1997.

Cabeza de Vaca, Álvar Núñez, *The Narrative of Cabeza de Vaca*. Edited and translated by Rolena Adorno and Patrick Charles Pautz. Lincoln: University of Nebraska Press, 2003.

Cabrera Infante, Guillermo. "Una historia inaudita." Introduction to *Cuba y sus sones* by Natalio Galán, XI. Valencia: Pre-Textos, 1997.

Cabrera, Lydia. *Reglas de Congo: Palo Monte Mayombe*, 2nd ed. Miami: Ediciones Universal, 2005.

Carpentier, Alejo. "Blacks in Cuba." In *Music in Cuba*. Translated by Alan West-Dúran. Minneapolis: University of Minnesota Press, 2001.

———. *El músico que llevo dentro*. Madrid: Alianza Editorial, 2007.

———. *La música en Cuba*. México: Fondo de Cultura Económica, 1946.

Castro, Alicia, Ingrid Kummels and Manfred Schäfer. *Queens of Havana: The Amazing Adventures of Anacaona, Cuba's Legendary All-Girl Dance Band*. Translated by Steven T. Murray. New York: Grove Press, 2007.

Cesaire, Aime. *A Tempest*. Translated by Richard Miller. New York: Theater Communications Group, 1992.

Chanan, Michael. "Imperfect Cinema and the Seventies." In *Cuban Cinema*. Minneapolis: University of Minnesota Press, 2004.

———. *Repeated Takes: A Short History of Recording and Its Effects on Music*. New York: Verso, 1995.

Child, John. *The Guinness Encyclopedia of Popular Music*. Edited by Colin Larkin. Middlesex, England: Guinness Publishing, 1992.

Clark, Vèvè A. "Katherine Dunham's Tropical Revue." *Black American Literature Forum* 16, no. 4, Black Theatre Issue (Winter 1982): 147–52.

Codrescu, Andrei. *Ay Cuba!: A Socio-Erotic Journey*. New York: Picador, 2001.

Columbus, Christopher. *The Journal: Account of the First Voyage and Discovery of the Indies*. Introduction and notes by Paolo Emilio Taviani and Consuelo Varela. Translated by Marc A. Beckwith and Luciano F. Farina. Roma: Instituto Poligrafico e Zecca Dello Stato, Libreria Dello Stato, 1992.

Conde, Yvonne M. *Operation Pedro Pan: The Untold Exodus of 14,048 Cuban Children*. New York: Routledge, 1999.

Cooper, Carolyn. *Noises in the Blood: Orality, Gender, and the"Vulgar" Body of Jamaican Popular Culture*. Durham, NC: Duke University Press, 1995.

Courlander, Harold. "Abakwa Meeting in Guanabacoa." *The Journal of Negro History* 29, no. 4 (October 1944): 461.

Croucher, Sheila L. *Imagining Miami: Ethnic Politics in a Postmodern World* Charlottesville: University Press of Virginia, 1997.

Cruz, Jon. *Culture in the Margins: The Black Spiritual and the Rise of American Cultural Interpretation*. Princeton: Princeton University Press, 1999.

Daniel, Yvonne. "Cuban Dance: An Orchard of Caribbean Creativity." In *Caribbean Dance from Abakuá to Zouk: How Movement Shapes Identity*. Edited by Susanna Sloat. Gainesville: University Press of Florida, 2002.

Danticat, Edwidge. "We Are Ugly, But We Are Here." *The Caribbean Writer* 10 (1996): 137–41.

Davis, Angela. *Blues Legacies and Black Feminism: Gertrude "Ma" Rainey, Bessie Smith, and Billie Holiday.* New York: Vintage, 1999.

de la Campa, Román. *Cuba on My Mind: Journeys to a Severed Nation.* New York: Verso, 2000.

———. *Latin Americanisms.* Minneapolis: University of Minnesota Press, 1999.

De las Casas, Bartolomé. *A Short Account of the Destruction of the Indies.* Translated and edited by Nigel Griffin. London: Penguin Books, 1992.

de los Angeles Torres, María. *The Lost Apple: Operation Pedro Pan, Cuban Children in the U.S., and the Promise of a Better Future.* Boston: Beacon Press, 2003.

Delgado, Celeste Fraser, and José Esteban Muñoz, eds. *Everynightlife: Culture and Dance in Latin/o America.* Durham, NC: Duke University Press, 1997.

Depestre, Leonardo. "Bola de Nieve, con su sonrisa y su canción." In *Cuatro músicos de una villa.* La Habana: Editoriales Letras Cubanas, 1990.

Derrida, Jacques. *A Derrida Reader: Between the Blinds.* Edited by Peggy Kamuf. New York: Columbia University Press, 1991.

DeVeaux, Scott and Gary Giddin. *Jazz: Essential Listening.* New York: W. W. Norton, 2011.

Diamond, Elin. "The Violence of 'We': Politicizing Identification." In *Critical Theory and Performance.* Edited by Janelle G. Reinelt and Joseph R. Roach. Ann Arbor: University of Michigan Press, 2007.

Díaz Ayala, Cristóbal. *Música cubana del areíto a la nueva trova.* Miami: Ediciones Universal, 1981.

———. *Música Cubana del areyto al rap Cubano,* 4th ed. Miami: Ediciones Universal, 2003.

Didion, Joan. *Miami.* New York: Simon and Schuster, 1987.

Dimock, Wai Chee. "Genre as World System: Epic and Novel on Four Continents." *Narrative* 14, no. 1 (January 2006): 85–101.

Doggett, Scott and David Stanley. *Lonely Planet Havana,* 1st ed. Victoria, Australia: Lonely Planet Publications, 2001.

Dopico, Ana María. "Picturing Havana: History, Vision, and the Scramble for Cuba." *Nepantla: Views from South* 3, no. 3 (2002): 451–93.

Douglas, Ann. "Periodizing the American Century: Modernism, Postmodernism, and Postcolonialism in the Cold War Context." *Modernism/Modernity* 5, no. 3 (1998): 71–98.

Dunn, Marvin. *Black Miami in the Twentieth Century.* Gainesville: University Press of Florida, 1997.

Early, Gerald. *My Soul's High Song: The Collective Writings of Countee Cullen, Voice of the Harlem Renaissance.* New York: Doubleday, 1991.

Echevarría, Roberto González, "Where the Singers Come From: Fragments." Translated by Vera M. Kutzinski. *New England Review and Bread Loaf Quarterly* 8 (Summer 1985): 569.

Edwards, Brent Hayes. *The Practice of Diaspora: Literature, Translation, and the Rise of Black Internationalism.* Cambridge: Harvard University Press, 2003.

Edwards, Nadi. "Diaspora, Difference, and Black Internationalisms." *Small Axe* 9, no. 17 (March 2005): 120–28.

Eire, Carlos. *Learning to Die in Miami: Confessions of a Refugee Boy.* New York: Free Press, 2010.

———. *Waiting for Snow in Havana: Confessions of a Cuban Boy.* New York: Free Press, 2003.

Erenberg, Lewis A. *Steppin' Out: New York Nightlife and the Transformation of American Culture.* Chicago: University of Chicago Press, 1981.

Evans, Nicolas M. *Writing Jazz: Race, Nationalism, and Modern Culture in the 1920s.* New York and London: Garland, 2000.

Farr, Jory. *Rites of Rhythm: The Music of Cuba.* New York: Regan Books, 2003.

Feather, Leonard, and Ira Gitler, "Perez, Manuel (Emanuel aka Emile)" and "Dailey, Albert Preston." In *The Biographical Encyclopedia of Jazz.* Oxford and New York: Oxford University Press, 1999.

Ferguson, Roderick A. *Aberrations in Black: Toward a Queer of Color Critique.* Minnesota: University of Minnesota Press, 2004.

Fernandes, Sujatha. *Cuba Represent! Cuban Arts, State Power, and the Making of New Revolutionary Cultures.* Durham, NC: Duke University Press, 2006.

Fernández, Damián J. "Politics and Romance on the Scholarship of Cuban Politics." *Latin American Research Review* 39, no. 2 (2004): 164–77.

———, and Madeline Cámara Betancourt, eds. *Cuba, the Elusive Nation.* Austin: University of Texas Press, 2000.

Fernández, Raúl A. *From Afro-Cuban Rhythms to Latin Jazz.* Berkeley: University of California Press, 2006.

———. *Latin Jazz: The Perfect Combination/La combinación perfecta.* San Francisco: Chronicle Books, 2002.

Ferrer, Ada. *Insurgent Cuba: Race, Nation, and Revolution, 1868–1898.* Chapel Hill: University of North Carolina Press, 1999.

Figueredo, D. H. *The Complete Idiot's Guide to Latino History and Culture.* Royersford: Alpha, 2002.

Fiol-Matta, Licia. *A Queer Mother for the Nation: The State and Gabriela Mistral.* Minneapolis: University of Minnesota Press, 2002.

Foner, Phillip S. *A History of Cuba and Its Relations with the United States*, 1st ed. New York: International Publishers, 1962.

Fornés, María Irene, and Robb Creese. "I Write These Messages That Come." *The Drama Review* 21, no. 4, Playwrights and Playwriting Issue (December 1977): 25–40.

Foucault, Michel. *Discipline and Punish: The Birth of a Prison*. London: Vintage, 1995.

Galán, Natalio. *Cuba y sus sones*. Valencia: Pre-Textos, 1997.

Gallagher, Catherine and Stephen Greenblatt. *Practicing New Historicism*. Chicago: University of Chicago Press, 2000.

García Espinosa, Julio. "For an Imperfect Cinema." Translated by Julianne Burton. *Jump Cut: A Review of Contemporary Media*, no. 20 (1979): 24–26.

García, Cristina, ed. *¡Cubanísimo! The Vintage Book of Contemporary Cuban Literatures*. New York: Vintage, 2002.

García, María Cristina. *Havana USA: Cuban Exiles and Cuban Americans in South Florida, 1959–1994*. Berkeley: University of California Press, 1996.

Gilroy, Paul. *The Black Atlantic: Modernity and Double Consciousness*. Cambridge: Harvard University Press, 1993.

Gioia, Ted. *The History of Jazz*, 2nd ed. New York: Oxford University Press, 2011.

Giro, Radamés. *Diccionario enciclopédico de la música en Cuba*. Tomos I-IV. La Habana: Letras Cubanas, 2007.

———. "Todo Lo Que Usted Quiso Saber Sobre El Mambo" In *Mambo*. Edited by Radamés Giro. Editorial Letras Cubanas: La Habana, 1993.

Glasser, Ruth. *My Music Is My Flag: Puerto Rican Musicians and Their New York Communities, 1917–1940*. Berkeley: University of California Press, 1995.

Glissant, Edouard. "Introductions." In *Caribbean Discourse: Selected Essays*. Translated by J. Michael Dash. Charlottesville: University Press of Virginia, 1999.

Goehr, Lydia. *The Quest for Voice: Music, Politics, and the Limits of Philosophy*. Berkeley: University of California Press, 1998.

———. *Elective Affinities: Musical Essays on the History of Aesthetic Theory*. New York: Columbia University Press, 2008.

Goffman, Erving. *The Presentation of Self in Everyday Life*. Garden City, NY: Doubleday, 1959.

Goldman, Danielle. *I Want to Be Ready: Improvised Dance as a Practice of Freedom*. Ann Arbor: University of Michigan Press, 2010.

Goldmark, Daniel, Lawrence Kramer, and Richard Leppert, eds. "Phonoplay: Recasting Film Music." In *Beyond the Soundtrack: Representing Music in Cinema*. Berkeley and Los Angeles: University of California Press, 2007.

González Echevarría, Roberto. "Where the Singers Come From: Fragments." Translated by Vera M. Kutzinski. *New England Review and Bread Loaf Quarterly* 8 (Summer 1985): 569.

González-Corzo, Mario A. "The Cuban Population in the United States since 2000: Concentration, Growth, and Socioeconomic Characteristics." *The Cuban Affairs Journal* 2, no. 3. Published by the Institute for Cuban and Cuban American Studies at the University of Miami. http://www.cubanaffairsjournal.org/.

Grenet, Emilio. *Popular Cuban Music: 80 Revised and Corrected Compositions.* Translated by R. Phillips. Havana: Úcar, García y Compañia, 1939.

Griffin, Farah Jasmine. *If You Can't Be Free, Be a Mystery: In Search of Billie Holiday.* New York: The Free Press, 2001.

Gunther Kodat, Catherine. "Conversing with Ourselves: Canon, Freedom, Jazz." *American Quarterly* 55, no. 1 (2003): 1–28.

Haney, Patrick J. and Walt Vanderbush. *The Cuban Embargo: The Domestic Politics of an American Foreign Policy.* Pittsburgh: University of Pittsburgh Press, 2005.

Hartman, Saidiya. *Lose Your Mother.* New York: Farrar, Straus, and Giroux, 2007.

Hayes Edwards, Brent. *The Practice of Diaspora: Literature, Translation, and the Rise of Black Internationalism.* Cambridge: Harvard University Press, 2003.

Hegel, G. W. F. *Aesthetics: Lectures on Fine Art.* Translated by T. M. Knox. Oxford: Oxford University Press, 1975.

Helg, Aline. *Our Rightful Share: The Afro-Cuban Struggle for Equality 1886–1912.* Chapel Hill: University of North Carolina Press, 1995.

Helio Orovio, *Cuban Music from A to Z.* Durham, NC: Duke University Press, 2004.

Hernández, Erena. "Conversación con Pérez Prado," in *La música en persona.* La Habana: Editorial Letras Cubanas, 1986.

Hernández-Reguant, Ariana. "Radio Taíno and the Cuban Quest for Identi . . . qué?" In *Cultural Agency in the Americas.* Edited by Doris Sommer. Durham, NC: Duke University Press, 2006.

———, ed. *Cuba in the Special Period: Culture and Ideology in the 1990s.* New York: Palgrave Macmillan, 2009.

———. "Cuba" entry in the *Encyclopedia of Radio* Edited by Christopher H. Sterling. New York: Fitzroy Dearborn, 2003.

Hernández, Erena. "Conversación con Pérez Prado." In *La música en persona.* La Habana: Editorial Letras Cubanas, 1986. Reprinted in Radamés Giro, ed. *El Mambo.* La Habana: Editorial Letras Cubanas, 1993.

M. C. Howatson and Ian Chilvers, eds. *The Concise Oxford Companion to Classical Literature.* Oxford: Oxford University Press, 1996.

Hughes, Langston. *The Big Sea,* 2nd ed. New York: Hill and Wang, 1993.

Hunt, Jamer. "The Mirrored Stage: Reflections on the Presence of Slyvia [Bataille] Lacan." In *The Ends of Performance.* Edited by Peggy Phelan and Jill Lane. New York and London: New York University Press, 1998.

Hutchinson, George. "Introduction." In *In Search of Nella Larson: A Biography of the Color Line.* Cambridge and London: Belknap Press of Harvard University Press, 2006.

Iyer, Vijay. "Exploding the Narrative in Jazz Improvisation." In *Uptown Conversation: The New Jazz Studies.* Edited by Robert G. O'Meally, Brent Hayes Edwards, and Farah Jasmine Griffin. New York: Columbia University Press, 2004.

Jacques, Geoffrey. "CuBop! Afro-Cuban Music and Mid-Twentieth-Century American Culture." In *Between Race and Empire: African-Americans and Cubans before the Cuban Revolution.* Edited by Lisa Brock and Digna Castañeda Fuertes. Philadelphia: Temple University Press, 1998.

Jaén, Didier T. "Introduction." In *The Cosmic Race/La raza cósmica.* By José Vasconcelos. Baltimore: Johns Hopkins University Press, 1997.

Johnson, James Weldon, ed. "Preface." In *The Book of American Negro Poetry,* rev. ed. New York: Harcourt, Brace & World, 1931.

Kaplan, Caren, Norma Alarcón, and Minoo Moallem. "Introduction." In *Between Woman and Nation: Nationalisms, Transnational Feminisms, and the State.* Durham, NC: Duke University Press, 1999.

Kerouac, Jack. *On the Road.* New York: Penguin Books, 2003.

Kim, Jodi. *Ends of Empire: Asian American Critique and the Cold War.* Minneapolis: University of Minnesota Press, 2010.

Kinnamon, Kenneth. "Anthologies of African American Literature from 1845–1994." *Callaloo* 20, no. 2 (1997): 461–81.

Kittler, Friedrich A. *Gramaphone, Film, Typewriter.* Translated by Geoffrey Winthrop-Young and Michael Wutz. Stanford: Stanford University Press, 1999.

Kodat, Catherine Gunther, "Conversing with Ourselves: Canon, Freedom, Jazz" *American Quarterly* 55, no. 1 (2003): 1–28.

Kun, Josh. "Bagels, Bongos, and Yiddishe Mambos, or The Other History of Jews in America." *Shofar: An Interdisciplinary Journal of Jewish Studies* 23, no. 4 (Summer 2005): 50–68.

———. *Audiotopia: Music, Race, and America.* Berkeley: University of California Press, 2005.

Kutzinski, Vera M. *Sugar's Secrets: Race and the Erotics of Cuban Nationalism.* Charlottesville: University Press of Virginia, 1993.

Lane, Jill. *Blackface Cuba, 1840–1895*. Philadelphia: University of Pennylvania Press, 2005.

Lapidus, Benjamin L. *Origins of Cuban Music and Dance: Changüí*. Lanham, MD: Scarecrow, 2008.

Lash, John S. "The Anthologist and the Negro Author." *Phylon* 8, no. 1 (1940–1956; 1st Quarter, 1947): 71.

Lawrence, Tim. *Love Saves the Day: A History of American Dance Music Culture, 1970–1979*. Durham, NC: Duke University Press, 2003.

Leppert, Richard. "Introduction" to Theodor W. Adorno *Essays on Music*. Translated by Susan H. Gillespie. Berkeley: University of California Press, 2002.

Leymarie, Isabelle. *Cuban Fire: The Story of Salsa and Latin Jazz*. London: Continuum, 2002.

Linares, María Teresa. *La música y el pueblo*. La Habana: Editorial Pueblo y Educación, 1974.

Lipsitz, George. "Song of the Unsung: The Darby Hicks History of Jazz." In *Uptown Conversation: The New Jazz Studies*. Edited by Robert G. O'Meally, Brent Hayes Edwards, and Farah Jasmine Griffin. New York: Columbia University Press, 2004.

López, Ana M. "Early Cinema and Modernity in Latin America." *Cinema Journal* 40, no. 1 (2000): 48–78.

———. "Memorias of a Home: Mapping the Revolution (and the Making of Exiles?)." *Revista Canadiense de estudios Hispánicos* 20, no. 1 (Otoño 1995): 6. Mundos Contemporáneos en el cine Español e Hispanoamericano.

———. "Tears and Desire: Women and Melodrama in the 'Old' Mexican Cinema." In *Mediating Two Worlds: Cinematic Encounters in the Americas*. Edited by John King, Ana M. López, and Manuel Alvarado. London: British Film Institute, 1993.

Louis A. Pérez Jr. "Cuba, c.1930–1959." In *Cuba: A Short History*. Edited by Leslie Bethell. Cambridge: Cambridge University Press, 1993.

Mackey, Nathaniel. "Cante Moro." In *Sound States: Innovative Poetics and Acoustical Technologies*. Edited by Adalaide Morris. Chapel Hill: University of North Carolina Press, 1997.

Mañach, Jorge. *Indagación del choteo*. Miami: Ediciones Universal, 1991.

Mancing, Howard. "A Consensus Canon of Hispanic Poetry." *Hispania* 69, no.1 (March 1986): 53–81.

Manuel, Peter, ed. *Essays on Cuban Music: North American and Cuban Perspectives*. Lanham, MD: University Press of America, 1991.

Martínez-Echazábal, Lourdes. "Mestizaje and the Discourse of National/

Cultural Identity in Latin America, 1845–1959." *Latin American Perspectives* 25, no. 3 (1998): 21–42.

Martínez, Adriana Orejuela. *El son no se fue de Cuba: claves para una historia 1959–1973*. La Habana: Editorial Letras Cubanas, 2006.

Martínez-Malo, Aldo. *Rita, la única*. La Habana: Editora Abril, 1988.

Mason, Jr. Theodore O. "The African-American Anthology: Mapping the Territory, Taking the National Census, Building the Museum." *American Literary History* 10, no. 1 (1998): 185–98.

McAuslan, Fiona. *The Rough Guide to Cuba*, 1st ed. London: Rough Guides, 2000.

McHugh, Kevin E., Ines M. Miyares, and Emily H. Skop. "The Magnetism of Miami: Segmented Paths in Cuban Migration." *The Geographical Review* 87 (October 1997): 504–19.

Mestas, María del Carmen. *Pasión de rumbero*. Barcelona: Puvill Libros; La Habana: Pablo de la Torriente, 1998.

Mohl, Raymond A. "Race and Space in the Modern City: Interstate 95 and the Black Community in Miami." In *Urban Policy in Twentieth-Century America*. Edited by Arnold R. Hirsch and Raymond A. Mohl. New Brunswick: Rutgers University Press, 1993.

Moore, Robin D. *Music and Revolution: Cultural Change in Socialist Cuba*. Berkeley: University of California Press, 2006.

———. "Revolution and Religion: Yoruba Sacred Music in Socialist Cuba." In *The Yoruba Diaspora in the Atlantic World*. Edited by Toyin Falola and Matt D. Childs. Bloomington: Indiana University Press, 2005.

———. *Nationalizing Blackness: Afrocubanismo and Artistic Revolution in Havana*. Pittsburg: University of Pittsburg Press, 1997.

Moraga, Cherrie. *Heroes and Saints and Other Plays: Giving Up the Ghost, Shadow of a Man, Heroes and Saints*. Albuquerque: West End Press, 1994.

Morales, Ed. *The Latin Beat: The Rhythms and Roots of Latin Music, from Bossa Nova to Salsa and Beyond*. Cambridge, MA: Da Capo Press, 2003.

Moreno, Jairo. "Bauzá-Gillespie-Latin/Jazz: Difference, Modernity, and the Black Caribbean." *The South Atlantic Quarterly* 103, no. 1 (2004): 81–99.

Morris, Adalaide, ed. *Sound States: Innovative Poetics and Acoustical Technologies*. Chapel Hill: University of North Carolina Press, 1997.

Moten, Fred and Stefano Harney. "The University and the Undercommons: Seven Theses." *Social Text 79* 22, no. 2 (Summer 2004): 101–2.

———. "'Words Don't Go There': An Interview with Fred Moten." With Charles Henry Rowell. In *B Jenkins*. Durham, NC: Duke University Press, 2010.

———. *In the Break: The Aesthetics of the Black Radical Tradition*. Minneapolis: University of Minnesota Press, 2003.

Mullen, Edward. "The Emergence of Afro-Hispanic Poetry: Some Notes on Canon Formation." *Hispanic Review* 56, no. 4 (Autumn 1988): 435–53.

Mullen, Harryette. "African Signs and Spirit Writing." *Callaloo* 19, no. 3 (1996): 681. Original in Timothy Maliqalim Simone, *About Face: Race in Postmodern America*. Brooklyn: Autonomedia, 1989.

Muñoz, José Esteban. "Notes on the Negotiation of Cubanidad and Exilic Memory in Carmelita Tropicana's *Milk of Amnesia*." *The Drama Review: The Journal of Performance Studies* 39, no. 3 (1995): 76–82. Cambridge: MIT Press.

———. "Performing Greater Cuba: Tania Bruguera and The Burden of Guilt." In *Women and Performance: A Journal of Feminist Theory*. New York University: Department of Performance Studies, 2000.

———. *Cruising Utopia: The Then and There of Queer Futurity*. New York: NYU Press, 2009.

———. *Disidentifications: Queers of Color and the Performance of Politics*. Minneapolis: University of Minnesota Press, 1999.

Negus, Keith. *Music Genres and Corporate Cultures*. New York: Routledge, 1999.

Nichols, Bill. *Introduction to Documentary*. Bloomington: Indiana University Press, 2001.

Noriega, Chon, ed. *Visible Nations: Latin American Cinema and Video*. Minneapolis: University of Minnesota Press, 2000.

———, and Ana M. López. "Greater Cuba." In *The Ethnic Eye: Latino Media Arts*. Minneapolis: University of Minnesota Press, 1996.

O'Reilly Herrera, Andrea. *Cuban Artists Across the Diaspora: Setting the Tent Against the House*. Austin: University of Texas Press, 2011.

Obejas, Achy. *Memory Mambo*. Pittsburgh: Cleis Press, 1996.

Oritz, Ricardo. *Cultural Erotics in Cuban America*. Minneapolis: University of Minnesota Press, 2007.

Orovio, Helio. *Cuban Music from A to Z*. Translated by Ricardo Bardo Portilla and Lucy Davies. Durham, NC: Duke University Press, 2004.

Ortiz Ricardo. "Introduction: Diaspora and Disappearance." In *Cultural Erotics in Cuban America*. Minneapolis: University of Minnesota Press, 2007.

Ortiz, Fernando. *Cuban Counterpoint*. Translated by Harriet de Onís. Durham, NC: Duke University Press, 1995.

———. *Los instrumentos de la música afrocubana: el quinto, el llamador, tambores de rumba, el taburete, tambores de las comparsas carabalíes*. La Habana: Letras Cubanas, 1995.

Pacini Hernandez, Deborah. "Dancing with the Enemy: Cuban Popular Music, Race, Authenticity, and the World-Music Landscape." *Latin American Perspectives* 25, no. 3 (May, 1998): 110–25.

Paquette, Robert L. *Sugar Is Made with Blood: The Conspiracy of la Escalera and the Conflict between Empires over Slavery in Cuba*. Middletown: Wesleyan University Press, 1990.

Paredes, Américo. *With His Pistol in His Hand: A Border Ballad and Its Hero*. Austin: University of Texas Press, 1958.

Pattee, Richard. "Notes" sections from *The Journal of Negro History*, under the title "Cuban Negro Studies" 23, no. 1 (January, 1938): 118–19. For the original version in Spanish, see the collectively authored "Los estatutos de la sociedad de estudios Afrocubanos." *Estudios Afrocubanos* 1 (1937).

Pavis, Patrice. *Dictionary of the Theatre: Terms, Concepts, and Analysis*. Translated by Christine Shantz. Toronto and Buffalo: University of Toronto Press, 1998.

Perdomo, Willie. "Nuyorican School of Poetry." In *Where a Nickel Costs a Dime*. New York: W. W. Norton, 1996.

Pérez Firmat, Gustavo. "Riddles of the Sphincter." In *Literature and Liminality: Festive Readings in the Hispanic Tradition*. Durham, NC: Duke University Press, 1986.

———. *Life on the Hyphen: The Cuban-American Way*. Austin: University of Texas Press, 1994.

Pérez Jr., Louis A. "Cuba, c.1930–1959," in *Cuba: A Short History*. Edited by Leslie Bethell. Cambridge: Cambridge University Press, 1993.

———. *Cuba: Between Reform and Revolution*, 4th ed. New York: Oxford University Press, 2011.

———. *Cuba in the American Imagination: Metaphor and the Imperial Ethos*. Chapel Hill: University of North Carolina Press, 2008.

Pérez Sanjurjo, Elena. *Historia de la música Cubana*. Miami: La Moderna Poesía, 1986.

Perna, Vincenza. *Timba: The Sound of the Cuban Crisis*. Burlington, VT: Ashgate, 1995.

Piston, Walter. *Counterpoint*. New York: W. W. Norton, 1947.

Porter, Eric. *What Is This Thing Called Jazz? African American Musicians as Artists*. Berkeley: University of California Press, 2002.

Portes, Alejandro and Alex Stepick. *City on the Edge: The Transformation of Miami*. Berkeley: University of California Press, 1993.

Prashad, Vijay. "Ethnic Studies Inside Out." *Journal of Asian American Studies* 9, no. 2 (2006): 171–72.

Price, Leah. *The Anthology and the Rise of the Novel*. Cambridge: Cambridge University Press, 2000.

Quiroga, José. *Cuban Palimpsests*. Minneapolis: University of Minnesota Press, 2005.

Radano, Ronald and Philip V. Bohlman, eds. *Music and the Racial Imagination*. Chicago: University of Chicago Press, 2000.

Randel, Don Michael ed. *The Harvard Dictionary of Music*, 4th ed. Cambridge and London: Harvard University Press, 2003.

Reich, Howard, ed. *Let Freedom Swing: Collected Writings on Jazz, Blues, and Gospel*. Evanston, IL: Northwestern University Press, 2010.

Reiff, David. *The Exile: Cuba in the Heart of Miami*. New York: Simon & Schuster, 1993.

Reinelt, Janelle G. and Joseph R. Roach, eds. *Critical Theory and Performance*, rev. and enlarged ed. Ann Arbor: University of Michigan Press, 2007.

Rich Kaplowitz, Donna. *Anatomy of a Failed Embargo: U.S. Sanctions Against Cuba*. Boulder, CO: Lynne Rienner Publishers, 1998.

Rivera, Raquel Z. *New York Ricans from the Hip Hop Zone*. New York: Palgrave Macmillan, 2003.

Roach, Joseph. *Cities of the Dead: Circum-Atlantic Performance*. New York: Columbia University Press, 1996.

Robato Mañach, Jorge. *Indagacion del choteo*. Spanish edition. Barcelona: Linkgua, 2011.

Roberts, John Storm. *The Latin Tinge: The Impact of Latin American Music on the United States*. New York: Oxford University Press, 1979.

Robinson, Marc. *The Other American Drama*. Cambridge and New York: Cambridge University Press, 1994.

Rocha, Glauber. "Cabezas Cortadas." *Afterimage*, no. 3 (Summer 1971): 68–77.

———. "The History of Cinema Novo." *Framework*, no. 12 (Summer 1980): 18–27.

Robert Stam. *Tropical Multiculturalism: A Comparative History of Race in Brazilian Cinema and Culture*. Durham, NC: Duke University Press, 1997.

Roosevelt, Theodore. "The Platt Amendment." In *The Cuba Reader: History, Culture, Politics*. Edited by Aviva Chomsky, Barry Carr, and Pamela Smorkaloff. Durham, NC: Duke University Press, 2003.

Roy, Maya. *Cuban Music: From Son and Rumba to the Buena Vista Social Club and Timba Cubana*. Princeton, NJ: Markus Wiener, 2002.

Rustin, Nichole T. and Sherrie Tucker. *Big Ears: Listening for Gender in Jazz Studies*. Durham, NC: Duke University Press, 2008.

Sarduy, Severo. *Christ on the Rue Jacob*. Translated by Susanne Jill Levine and Carol Maier. San Francisco: Mercury House, 1995.

———. *Written on a Body*. Translated by Carol Maier. New York: Lumen Books, 1989.

Schechner, Richard. *Between Theater and Anthropology*. Philadelphia: University of Pennsylvania Press, 1985.

———. *Performance Studies: An Introduction*, 2nd ed. New York: Routledge, 2006.

Schons, Dorothy. "Negro Poetry in the Americas." *Hispania* 25, no. 3 (October 1942): 309–19.

Schor, Naomi. *Reading in Detail: Aesthetics and the Feminine*. New York: Routledge, 2007.

Schoultz, Lars. "Benevolent Domination: The Ideology of U.S. Policy toward Cuba." *Cuban Studies* 41 (2010): 1–19.

Schwab, Peter. *Cuba: Confronting the U.S. Embargo*. New York: St. Martin's Press, 1999.

Seigel, Micol. "Beyond Compare: Comparative Method after the Transnational Turn." *Radical History Review Issue* 91 (Winter 2005).

Shack, William A. *Harlem in Montmartre: A Paris Jazz Story between the Great Wars*. Berkeley: University of California Press, 2001.

Shaw, John. *Magical Reels: A History of Cinema in Latin America*. New York: Verso, 2000.

Skidmore, Thomas E. and Peter H. Smith. "Cuba: Late Colony, First Socialist State." In *Modern Latin America*, 4th ed. New York: Oxford University Press, 1997.

Small, Christopher. *Musicking: The Meanings of Performing and Listening*. Middletown: Wesleyan University Press, 1998.

Smith, Pamela J. "Caribbean Influences on Early New Orleans Music." Masters thesis. Tulane University, 1986.

Solanas, Fernando and Octavio Getino. "Towards a Third Cinema." *Afterimage* no. 3, (Summer 1971): 16–30. Reprinted in *Cineaste* 4, no. 3 (Winter 1971): 1–10.

———, et al., "Round Table Discussion: Latin American Cinema." *Framework* no. 11 (Fall 1979): 10–15.

Spillers, Hortense. "Peter's Pans: Eating in the Diaspora." In *Black, White and In Color: Essays on American Literature and Culture*. Chicago: University of Chicago Press, 2003.

Spivak, Gayatri. *Death of a Discipline*. New York: Columbia University Press, 2003.

Sterne, Jonathan. *The Audible Past: Cultural Origins of Sound Reproduction*. Durham, NC: Duke University Press, 2003.

Steward, Sue with a preface by Willie Colón. *Musica!: The Rhythm of Latin America: Salsa, Rumba, Merengue, and More*. San Francisco: Chronicle Books, 1999.

Stock, Ann Marie, ed. *Framing Latin American Cinema: Contemporary Critical Perspectives*. Minneapolis: University of Minnesota Press, 1997.

Sublette, Ned. *Cuba and Its Music: From the First Drums to the Mambo*. Chicago: Chicago Review Press, 2004.

———. *The World That Made New Orleans: From Spanish Silver to Congo Square*. Chicago: Lawrence Hill Books, 2008.

Sutherland, Elizabeth. "Cinema of Revolution: 90 Miles from Home." *Film Quarterly* 15, no. 2 Special Humphrey Jennings Issue (Winter 1961–1962): 42–49.

Szendy, Peter. *Listen: A History of Our Ears*. Translated by Charlotte Mandell. New York: Fordham University Press, 2008.

Tavares, George. "The Record Industry in Latin America." *Journal of the Audio Engineering Society* 25, no. 10/11 (October/November 1977): 795–99.

Taylor, Diana. The *Archive and Repertoire: Performing Cultural Memory in the Americas*. Durham, NC: Duke University Press, 2003.

Thomas, Hugh. *Cuba: In Pursuit of Freedom*. New York: Da Capo Press, 1998.

Thomas, Piri. *Down These Mean Streets*, 3rd ed. New York: Vintage Books, 1997.

Thompson, Robert Farris. *Flash of the Spirit: African and Afro-American Art and Philosophy*. New York: Random House, 1983.

Tompkins, Dave. *How to Wreck a Nice Beach: The Vocoder from World War II to Hip-Hop/The Machine Speaks*. Brooklyn: Melville House, 2010.

Triay, Victor Andres. *Fleeing Castro: Operation Pedro Pan and the Cuban Children's Program*. Gainsville: University of Florida Press, 1998.

Turner, Victor. *The Anthropology of Performance*. New York: PAJ Publications, 1988.

Úrfe, Odilio. "Claudio José Domingo Brindis de Salas (1852–1911)." In *AfroCuba: An Anthology of Cuban Writings on Race, Politics, and Culture*. Melbourne: Ocean Press, 1993. Published in association with the Center for Cuban Studies. The essay was originally published in *Pentagrama* 1, no. 4 (July 1956).

——— "La verdad sobre el mambo," in *Mambo* ed. Radamés Giro. Editorial Letras Cubanas: La Habana, 1993.

Vazquez, Alexandra. "Can You Feel the Beat? Freestyle's Systems of Living, Loving and Recording." *Social Text* 28, 1, no. 102 (Spring 2010): 107–24.

———. "Toward an Ethics of Knowing Nothing." In *Pop When the World Falls Apart*. Edited by Eric Weisbard. Durham, NC: Duke University Press, 2012.

Viego, Antonio. *Dead Subjects: Toward a Politics of Loss in Latino Studies*. Durham, NC: Duke University Press, 2007.

Vogel, Shane. "The Scene of Harlem Cabaret: 1926 and After." In *The Scene of Harlem Cabaret: Race, Sexuality, Performance*. Chicago: University of Chicago Press, 2009.

Wald, Gayle F. *Shout, Sister, Shout!: The Untold Story of Rock-and-Roll Trail-blazer Sister Rosetta Tharpe.* Boston: Beacon Press, 2007.

Washburne, Christopher. "Latin Jazz: The Other Jazz." *Current Musicology,* nos. 71–73 (Spring 2001–Spring 2002): 420.

———. "The Clave of Jazz: A Caribbean Contribution to the Rhythmic Foundation of an African-American Music." *Black Music Research Journal* 17, no. 1 (1997): 59–80.

———. *Sounding Salsa: Performing Latin Music in New York City.* Philadelphia: Temple University Press, 2008.

Whyton, Tony. *Jazz Icons: Heroes, Myths and the Jazz Tradition.* Cambridge: Cambridge University Press, 2010.

Williams, Raymond. *Keywords: A Vocabulary of Culture and Society,* rev. ed. New York: Oxford University Press, 1983.

———. *Marxism and Literature.* Oxford: Oxford University Press, 1977.

Wood, Michael. "A Passage to England." *New York Review of Books* 57, no. 4 (March 11, 2010): 8–10.

Index

habanera, 53, 60
Haitian Revolution, 85
Handy, W. C., 53; "St. Louis Blues,"
251n24
Harney, Stefano, 93, 272n61
Harris, Wilson, 224
Hartman, Saidiya, 70, 259n68
Havana, Cuba: New Orleans's inter-
action with, 32, 50–55; Plaza de la
Revolución, 230
Havana-Madrid Club (New York),
100, *100*, 108, 121, 145, 265n106
Hawkins, Coleman, 83
Hearst, William Randolph, 174
Held, Anna, 260n70
Helg, Aline, 33, 305n53
Henderson, Fletcher, 118
Hentoff, Nat, 258n59
Hermanas Martí, Las, 268n19
Hermanos Alvarez, Las, 268n19
Hernández, Erena, 135, 143–144
Hernández, Gregorio "El Goyo," 77,
80, 81–82, 84, 87, 88, 263n91
Hernández Reguant, Ariana, 282n2
Herskovits, Melville, 71
Holiday, Billie, 122, 125; "Strange
Fruit," 259n68
Horatio and Lana, 154
Hubbard, Freddy, 49
Hughes, Langston, 26, 54, 63, 86,
272n53; *The Big Sea*, 110–111, 271n43
Hunt, Jamer, 125
Hutchinson, George, 125

ICAIC, 178, 181, 286n37
Ideal, Gloria, 272n59
incidental music, concept of, 242n44
Indias del Caribe, Las, 268n19
inklings, concept of, 247n73

interdisciplinary studies, 56
International Casino of New York
(Paris), 271n41
Irakere, 176
Iyer, Vijay, 19, 66–67, 74–75

Jackson Michael, 232
Jacques, Geoffrey, 111–112
jazz: anthologization of, 63–66;
Cuban-African American collaborations, 20, 48–50, 117–118, 249–
250n11; in Cuba post-Revolution,
199–200; early, 52–54; in Paris,
111–112; reissues of recordings, 258n57
Jazz Latino Plaza Festival (Havana), 52
Jazz Review, The, 258n59
Jazz Studies: anthologies and, 64–66;
institutionalization of, 63–64,
249–250n11, 257–258n57,
258nn59–60; neglect of Latin jazz
in, 64–65, 249–250n11; neglect of
women in, 64, 65
"Jeepers Creepers" (Warren and Mer-
cer), 31
Joe Loco Quintet, 154
Johnson, Ben, 74
Johnson, James Weldon: *The Book of
American Negro Poetry*, 57, 59–63,
256n46, 257n52; on pitfalls of can-
onization, 65
Jolson, Al, 69, 71
Jones, Florence Embry, 86, 108–117
Jones, Gayl, 64
Jones, Quincy, 131
Journal of Cold War Studies, The, 210
Juanes, 230, *233*
Justiz, Pedro ("Peruchín"), 31, 78, 80
Justiz Marquez, Pedro ("Peruchín Jr."),
78

Moore, Kevin, 39
Moore, Robin, 171, 284n23
Moraga, Cherríe, 259n68
Moré, Beny, 131, 178–179, 182, 183–184,
277n21, 280n44
Moreno, Jairo, 54
Moroney, Davitt, 182
Morrison, Toni, 54
Morton, Jelly Roll, 53
Moten, Fred, 21, 35, 93, 272n61
Mullen, Edward, 58, 255n43
Muñequitos de Matanzas, Los, 35
Musician's Union of Cuba, 170
musicking, concept of, 190, 236n9
Myrdal, Gunner, 257n55

NARAB (North American Regional
Broadcasting Agreement), 167
Nash, John: "The Anthologist and the
Negro Author," 59–60
National Institute for Folkloric Re-
search, 183
New Orleans, Louisiana: Congo
Square, 52; Havana's interaction
with, 32, 50–55; Spanish/Cuban
period in, 51–52
"New Orleans Blues" (Morton), 53
New York, New York: clubs in, 70,
100, *100*, 108, 117–126,
264–265n106; mambo in, 144–145;
Musicians' Union, 137, 276n19; re-
vues in, 69, 70, 71, 73
Nichols, Bill, 173
nicknames, Cuban use of, 149–150, 159
Nosotros, la música (París documentary), 22, 166, 173–190, 201; Bach
prelude in, 182–183, 190, 264n98;
larger meaning of "we" in, 189–190;

musicians in, 180; plan of, 177–182;
Silvio and Ada dancing in, 186–190,
188; title, 177; tribute to Moré,
178–179; Urfé in, 182–186, 190
novias de Perez Prado, Las (Pérez
Prado), 148

Obejas, Achy, 159–162, 230
Ochoa, Eliades, 237n11
O'Farrill, Arturo, 50
Oliver, Joe "King," 52
O'Meally, Robert G., 64, 66–67,
258n60
"One o'Clock Leap," 20
Onward Brass Band, 52
"Operation Peter Pan," 203
Orejuela Martínez, Adriana, 171–172,
283n13, 283n15
Orovio, Helio, 142–143, 248n78,
251n21, 263n92, 267n15
Orquesta Anacaona, 98–103, *100, 112*;
1938 tour, 107–117; founding and
name, 98–99; genre fluency, 99;
Graciela and, 101–103, 107–117, 121;
historical neglect of, 99–100; lon-
gevity, 101; male guest performers,
100; membership, 100–101; queer-
ness of, 114; research on, 266n14
Orquesta Casino de la Playa, 136
Orquesta Ensueño, 268n19
Orquesta Estrellas Cubanas, 195
Orquesta Maravilla de Florida,
264n101
Orquesta Orbe, 268n19
Orquesta Ritmo Oriental, 39–40
Orquesta Riverside, 31
Orquesta Social, 268n19
Ortiz, Fernando, 135, 194, 289n71

Palace du Paris (Paris), 69, 72

Palladium! (documentary), 154

Palladium Ballroom (New York), 118, 145, 154

Pan African Culture Festival (Algiers, 1969), 183

Panart label, 168–169

Paredes, Américo, 37–38

Paris, France: after-hours clubs, 112–113; Cuban music and émigrés in, 69, 73, 86–87, 100, 108–117, 271n41, 271n49, 272n59; revues in, 69, 72–73; surrealist movement, 113

París, Rogelio, 22, 166, 173–190, 201

Parker, Charlie, 118

Park Plaza (New York), 118

"Patricia" (Pérez Prado), 138

Pattman, Dave, 79

Pavis, Patrice, 242n44

"Paz Sin Fronteras" event, 230–234, *233*

Peer-Southern publishing group, 137

Peraza, Armando, 262n84

Perdomo, Willie, 34

Pérez, Amaury, 230

Pérez, Graciela, 86, 93–130, *129*; advice for young musicians, 117; Americanness and, 105–106; bass playing technique, 108–109, 113–114; career range, 94–95; "Contigo en la distancia" performance, 130; death of, 129; early career, 101–103; on Fania Records, 280n58; interview for National Museum of American History, 103–107, 112, 114–117; "Mi cerebro" performance, 118–126; mobility of, 138; narrative technique, 116–117; New York apartment, 127;

Orquesta Anacaona and, 101–103, 107–117; performance techniques in conversation, 125–130; personal life, 272n56; shamelessness of, 103, 122–124; "Sí, Sí, No, No" performances, 122–124; Vera and, 20, 102; voice quality, 104–105, 120–121; writing a biography of, 124–126

Pérez, Louis, 97

Pérez, Louis, Jr., 31–33, 245n63

Pérez, Manuel, 52, 251n21

Pérez Firmat, Gustavo: "A Brief History of Mambo Time," 134–135, 152, 279–280n52; on the one-and-a-half generation, 207; on Versailles Restaurant, 298n36.

Pérez Prado, Dámaso, 131–164; "Chattanooga de Mambo," 157; classical training of, 135–136, 137; difficulties in music industry, 137, 276n19; *Dilo (Ugh!)* album, 149–151, *150;* drawing of, 149, *150;* early career, 135–136; as "El Rey del Mambo," 131, 134; *Exotic Suite of the Americas,* 162–164, *163,* 277n28; grunt of, 19, 131–134, 139–140, 141, 146, 148–164, 165, 275nn5–6; with La Charanga de Senén Suárez, 136; mambo and, 143–144, 278n36; "Mambo Jambo," 158; "Mambo No. 8," 146, 157; in Mexico City, 136, 144, 280n44; music portrayed in Obejas's *Memory Mambo,* 159–162; popularity but underappreciation of, 138–139; portrayed in Kerouac's *On the Road,* 156–159, 162; in United States, 136–141.

Pérez Sanjurjo, Elena, 144

CPSIA information can be obtained
at www.ICGtesting.com
Printed in the USA
LVHW010538130821
695224LV00017B/2016